P9-CRZ-239

Chinese Link

中 文 天 地

Zhōng   Wén   Tiān   Dì

Elementary Chinese

吳素美   于月明   張燕輝   田維忠

Sue-mei Wu   Yueming Yu   Yanhui Zhang   Weizhong Tian

Carnegie Mellon University

PEARSON
Prentice Hall

woRLd Languages

Upper Saddle River, New Jersey 07458

Library of Congress Cataloging-in-Publication Data

Chinese link : Zhong wen tian di : elementary Chinese / Sue-mei Wu … [et al]—Traditional
    character version.
        p. cm.
    ISBN 0-13-193033-8 (alk. paper)
    1. Chinese language—Textbooks for foreign speakers—English. I. Title: Elementary
Chinese. II. Wu, Sue-mei, 1968–

PL1129.E5C418 2006
495.1′82421—dc22

2005050939

Acquisitions Editor: Rachel McCoy
Publishing Coordinator: Claudia Fernandes
Executive Director of Market Development: Kristine Suárez
Director of Editorial Development: Julia Caballero
Production Supervision: Nancy Stevenson
Project Manager: Margaret Chan, Graphicraft
Assistant Director of Production: Mary Rottino
Supplements Editor: Meriel Martínez Moctezuma
Media Editor: Samantha Alducin
Media Production Manager: Roberto Fernandez
Prepress and Manufacturing Buyer: Brian Mackey
Prepress and Manufacturing Manager: Nick Sklitsis
Interior and Cover Design: Wanda España/Wee Design Group
Director, Image Resource Center: Melinda Reo
Interior Image Specialist: Beth Boyd Brenzel
Manager, Rights & Permissions IRC: Zina Arabia
Senior Marketing Manager: Jacquelyn Zautner
Marketing Assistant: William J. Bliss
Publisher: Phil Miller
Cover image: Jerry Darvin

This book was set in 12/15 Sabon by Graphicraft Ltd., Hong Kong, and was printed
and bound by Courier – Westford. The cover was printed by Phoenix Color Corp.

© 2006 by Pearson Education, Inc.
Upper Saddle River, NJ 07458

Printed in the United States of America
10 9 8 7 6 5 4

ISBN 0-13-193033-8

Pearson Education Ltd.
Pearson Education Singapore Pte. Ltd.
Pearson Education Canada, Ltd.
Pearson Education — Japan
Pearson Education Australia Pty. Limited
Pearson Education North Asia Ltd.
Pearson Educación de México, S.A. de C.V.
Pearson Education Malaysia Pte. Ltd.

目錄 CONTENTS

Preface		前言	xiii
Map of China		中國地圖	xx
Introduction to Chinese		中文簡介	xxi
Pinyin Foundation		拼音基礎	F-1
Pinyin Table		拼音表	F-12
Pinyin Exercises		拼音練習	F-13
The Chinese Writing System		漢字入門	F-26
Classroom Expressions		課堂用語	F-33
Classroom Expressions and Exercises		課堂用語練習	F-36
Abbreviations of Parts of Speech		詞類簡稱	F-37

Lesson 1	Hello!	第一課 你好!	1
Lesson 2	What's Your Surname?	第二課 您貴姓?	13
	Review Lessons 1–2	復習 第一課至第二課	28
Lesson 3	Which Country Are You From?	第三課 你是哪國人?	29
Lesson 4	What Do You Study?	第四課 你學什麼?	43
	Review Lessons 3–4	復習 第三課至第四課	60
Lesson 5	This Is My Friend	第五課 這是我朋友	63
Lesson 6	My Family	第六課 我的家	77
Lesson 7	Where Do You Live?	第七課 你住哪兒?	95
	Review Lessons 5–7	復習 第五課至第七課	110
Lesson 8	Do You Know Him?	第八課 你認識不認識他?	111
Lesson 9	He Is Making a Phone Call	第九課 他正在打電話	125
	Review Lessons 8–9	復習 第八課至第九課	143
Lesson 10	I Get Up at 7:30 Every Day	第十課 我每天七點半起床	145
	Review Lessons 1–10	復習 第一課至第十課	167
Lesson 11	Do You Want Black Tea or Green Tea?	第十一課 你要紅茶還是綠茶?	169

Lesson 12   May I Borrow Your Car?   第十二課 我可以借你的
車嗎?   187

    Review   Lessons 11–12   復習 第十一課至第十二課   202

Lesson 13   I Want to Buy a Shirt   第十三課 我想買一件襯衫   203

Lesson 14   I Am 20 This Year   第十四課 我今年二十歲   227
    Review   Lessons 13–14   復習 第十三課至第十四課   242

Lesson 15   The Library Is in Front of the Dorm   第十五課 圖書館在宿舍前邊   243

Lesson 16   She Plays Basketball Very Well   第十六課 她打籃球打得很好   259
    Review   Lessons 15–16   復習 第十五課至第十六課   275

Lesson 17   Spring Is Coming Soon   第十七課 春天就要來了   277

Lesson 18   We Are Going to Take a Train Trip   第十八課 我們要坐火車去旅行   293
    Review   Lessons 17–18   復習 第十七課至第十八課   312

Lesson 19   I Caught a Cold   第十九課 我感冒了   313

Lesson 20   I've Brought Xiao Xie Over . . .   第二十課 我把小謝帶來了...   331
    Review   Lessons 19–20   復習 第十九課至第二十課   354

Lesson 21   What Will You Do During the Summer Vacation?   第二十一課 暑假你要做什麼?   355

Lesson 22   I Have Arrived in Shanghai   第二十二課 我到上海了   371
    Review   Lessons 21–22   復習 第二十一課至第二十二課   392

Vocabulary List   生詞表   395
Traditional/Simplified Character Table   繁簡體字對照表   402
Language in Use (Traditional/Simplified Characters) (Lessons 1–22)   課文(繁簡體字) (第一課至第二十二課)   405
English Translation of Language in Use   課文英文翻譯   426
Pinyin Index   拼音索引   435
English Index   英文索引   458
Characters in The Character Book   寫字簿的生字   481

範圍和順序 Scope and Sequence

Foundation

Introduction to Chinese *p. xxi*
Pinyin Foundation and Exercises *p. F-1*
The Chinese Writing System *p. F-26*
Classroom Expressions and Exercises *p. F-33*
Abbreviations of Parts of Speech *p. F-37*

Lessons & Topics	Objectives & Communications	Grammar	Culture Link
1 Hello! 你好! *p. 1*	■ Conduct simple greetings in Chinese ■ Ask simple yes/no questions ■ Answer simple yes/no questions ■ Discuss other people	1. Chinese Sentences 2. The Pronouns 我, 你 and 他 3. The Interrogative Particle 嗎 4. The Modal Particle 呢 5. 是 Sentences 6. The Adverb 也	**Culture Notes:** Basic Chinese Greetings 問候語 **Fun With Chinese:** Motto: 學而時習之。 **Let's Go:** Sign: Service Stand 服務台
2 What's Your Surname? 您貴姓? *p. 13*	■ Exchange names ■ Get to know each other ■ Find out who someone else is	1. 您 2. 您貴姓 3. The Interrogative Pronouns 什麼，誰 4. The Particle 的	**Culture Notes:** Chinese Names 中文姓名 **Fun With Chinese:** Idiom: 同名同姓 **Let's Go:** ID Card 身份證
3 Which Country Are You From? 你是哪國人? *p. 29*	■ Find out someone's nationality ■ Ask which language they speak ■ Talk about each others' nationalities and languages	1. 哪(哪國人) Which Nationality? 2. 國名和國人 Country Names and People 3. 說 and 語言 4. 一點兒 5. Conjunction 和	**Culture Notes:** Chinese Concept of "Native Town" 中國人的家鄉觀念 **Fun With Chinese:** Idiom: 說來話長 **Let's Go:** On-line Language Tutoring Center 網上語言家教中心

Lessons & Topics	Objectives & Communications	Grammar	Culture Link
4 What Do You Study? 你學什麼? *p. 43*	■ Ask what something is ■ Explain what something is ■ Ask about majors in school ■ Talk about courses	1. Demonstrative Pronouns 這, 那 2. 量詞 (Measure Word/Classifier) (1): 本 3. Adverb 很 4. Suffix 們 (我們, 你們, 他們) 5. Grammar Summary 語法小結	**Culture Notes:** The Chinese Educational System 中國的教育制度 **Fun With Chinese:** Proverb: 書中自有黃金屋，書中自有顏如玉。 **Let's Go:** After-school Learning Center 補習班
5 This Is My Friend 這是我朋友 *p. 63*	■ Introduce people ■ Make small talk ■ Find out what someone owns	1. 有 Sentences (沒有) 2. Question Word 幾 3. Adverb 都 4. 都 With 不 5. 都 With 也 6. Location of Adverbs 也都常很 (Summary of 也都常很)	**Culture Notes:** Chinese Forms of Address 中國的稱謂文化 **Fun With Chinese:** Motto: 有朋自遠方來，不亦樂乎? **Let's Go:** Marriage and Friendship Social Center 婚友聯誼中心
6 My Family 我的家 *p. 77*	■ Introduce yourself ■ Talk about your family	1. 是...的 Construction 2. 在 3. 量詞 (2) 個, 輛, 隻, 本. Questions: 幾個, 幾輛, 幾隻, 幾本	**Culture Notes:** Chinese Families 中國家庭 **Fun With Chinese:** Idiom: 愛屋及烏 **Let's Go:** Propaganda Posters 宣傳標語

Lessons & Topics	Objectives & Communications	Grammar	Culture Link
7 Where Do You Live? 你住哪兒？ *p. 95*	■ Ask someone's address ■ Tell them your address ■ Describe a place ■ Ask/give phone numbers	1. 住 2. 住址的寫法 Word Order for Addresses 3. Topic-Comment Sentences 4. 多少 and 幾	**Culture Notes:** Traditional Chinese Houses — Si He Yuan 中國傳統住房— 四合院 **Fun With Chinese:** Motto: 遠親不如近鄰。 **Let's Go:** Handle with Care 小心輕放
8 Do You Know Him? 你認識不認識他？ *p. 111*	■ More yes and no questions ■ Make and respond to a plan	1. Affirmative-Negative Questions ("A 不 A" Pattern) 2. Tag Question	**Culture Notes:** Business Cards in China 中國的名片文化 **Fun With Chinese:** Idiom: 一見鍾情 **Let's Go:** Important Figures on Currency 鈔票上的大人物
9 He Is Making a Phone Call 他正在打電話 *p. 125*	■ Make a phone call ■ Handle various phone situations ■ Ask what someone is doing ■ Explain what you are doing	1. The Progressive Aspect of an Action 在/正在 2. Summary: Ways of Asking Questions	**Culture Notes:** Cell Phones in China 手機在中國 **Fun With Chinese:** Slang: 不管三七二十一 **Let's Go:** Telephone Card 電話卡

Lessons & Topics	Objectives & Communications	Grammar	Culture Link
10 I Get Up at 7:30 Every Day 我每天七點半起床 *p. 145*	■ Give times and dates in Chinese ■ Describe your daily schedule ■ Write letters in Chinese	1. How to Tell the Time 2. Adverbs 就 and 才 3. Grammar Summary 語法小結	**Culture Notes:** University Life in China 中國的大學生活 **Fun With Chinese:** Slang: 開夜車 **Let's Go:** TV Programming Schedule 電視節目時間表
11 Do You Want Black Tea or Green Tea? 你要紅茶還是綠茶? *p. 169*	■ Order food at a restaurant ■ Present/choose from alternatives ■ Ask what someone wants ■ Tell someone what you want	1. 還是 2. 量詞 (Measure Words/Classifiers) (3)	**Culture Notes:** Chinese Food 中國菜系介紹 **Fun With Chinese:** Slang: 飯後百步走，活到九十九。 **Let's Go:** Chinese Snacks 小吃
12 May I Borrow Your Car? 我可以借你的車嗎? *p. 187*	■ Make a request ■ Express wishes, obligations, capabilities, possibilities, or permissions	1. Optative Verbs (能願動詞)：要，想，應該，得，能，可以，會 2. 從 ... 去(到) ... 3. 多 VP (學習，練習)	**Culture Notes:** China's Auto Industry 中國的汽車工業 **Fun With Chinese:** Slang: 有借有還，再借不難。 **Let's Go:** Parking Sign and Car for Sale 停車標誌和汽車出售

Lessons & Topics	Objectives & Communications	Grammar	Culture Link
13 I Want to Buy a Shirt 我想買一件襯衫 *p. 203*	■ Go shopping ■ Talk about clothing, colors, and prices ■ Provide opinions	1. Conjunction 或者 2. 量詞 (Measure Words/Classifiers) (4): 件，條，張 3. Duplication of Verbs	**Culture Notes:** Chinese Traditional Dress 中國的傳統服飾 **Fun With Chinese:** Slang: 情人眼裡出西施。 **Let's Go:** Shopping: Bill, Receipt, and Invoice 購物：錢幣，收據和發票
14 I Am 20 This Year 我今年二十歲 *p. 227*	■ Say the days of the week ■ Extend/accept an invitation ■ Talk about people's birthdays	1. Days of the Week 2. Expressing Dates, Year, Month, and Days of the Week 3. Preposition 為	**Culture Notes:** Chinese Zodiac 十二生肖 **Fun With Chinese:** Slang: 女大十八變。 **Let's Go:** Common Phrases for Congratulations and Best Wishes 慶祝賀詞
15 The Library Is in Front of the Dorm 圖書館在宿舍前邊 *p. 243*	■ Show people around ■ Ask where something is located ■ Explain where something is located	1. Position Words 2. Sentences Expressing Location and Existence with 在，有, and 是	**Culture Notes:** The Chinese Art of Placement 風水 **Fun With Chinese:** Slang: 有緣千里來相會，無緣對面不相識。 **Let's Go:** Scenic Spots in Beijing 北京觀光景點

Lessons & Topics	Objectives & Communications	Grammar	Culture Link
16 She Plays Basketball Very Well 她打籃球打得很好 *p. 259*	■ Describe how an action is performed ■ Talk about hobbies and exercises	1. Degree of Complement Sentences	**Culture Notes:** Chinese Sport 中國體育 **Fun With Chinese:** Slang: 臨時抱佛腳 **Let's Go:** Announcements and Notifications 公佈告示
17 Spring Is Coming Soon 春天就要來了 *p. 277*	■ Talk about the four seasons ■ Describe the weather ■ Express that something will happen in the near future	1. 就/快要... 了 2. 最 3. Adj. + 極了	**Culture Notes:** The Three Main Chinese Festivals 中國的主要節慶 **Fun With Chinese:** Slang: 熱鍋上的螞蟻 **Let's Go:** Weather Forecast 天氣預報
18 We Are Going to Take a Train Trip 我們要坐火車去旅行 *p. 293*	■ Describe means of transportation ■ Talk about travel plans	1. 離 2. 先......(再)......然後...... 3. 坐, 騎 and 開	**Culture Notes:** Traffic Signs and Rules in China 中國的交通標誌與規則 **Fun With Chinese:** Proverb: 讀萬卷書，行萬里路。 **Let's Go:** Train and Airplane Tickets 火車和飛機票

Lessons & Topics	Objectives & Communications	Grammar	Culture Link
19 I Caught a Cold 我感冒了 *p. 313*	■ Describe the symptoms of an illness ■ Describe something that has happened	1. The Aspect Particle 了 2. 的, 得, and 地	**Culture Notes:** Traditional Chinese Medicine and Pharmacology 中醫中藥 **Fun With Chinese:** Proverb: 良藥苦口，忠言逆耳。 **Let's Go:** Watermelon Frost Throat Lozenges 西瓜霜潤喉片
20 I've Brought Xiao Xie Over . . . 我把小謝帶來了... *p. 331*	■ Rent an apartment ■ Indicate the direction of a movement ■ Describe an event and its cause	1. Directional Complement 趨向補語 (DC) 2. 把 Sentences 3. 把 Sentences and the Directional Complement 4. 把 Construction	**Culture Notes:** Housing Reform in China 中國的住房改革 **Fun With Chinese:** Proverb: 秀才不出門，能知天下事。 **Let's Go:** Houses for Rent and Houses for Sale 出租和出售房子
21 What Will You Do During the Summer Vacation? 暑假你要做什麼? *p. 355*	■ Talk about plans ■ Express blessings and wishes	1. 一面......一面...... 2. 語法總復習 (1): Summary of the Aspects of Verbs	**Culture Notes:** Travel in China 中國的旅遊業 **Fun With Chinese:** Slang: 活到老，學到老。 **Let's Go:** Receipt for Transcript Printing 申請成績單的發票

Lessons & Topics	Objectives & Communications	Grammar	Culture Link
22 I Have Arrived in Shanghai 我到上海了 *p. 371*	■ Exchange e-mails ■ Describe your current situation	1. 比如 2. Summary of Measure Words in Chinese 3. Summary of Conjunctions in Chinese	**Culture Notes:** Peking Opera; Chinese Calligraphy 京劇; 書法 **Fun With Chinese:** Idiom: 心想事成 **Let's Go:** Slogan 標語

Appendices

Vocabulary List 生詞表 *p. 395*

Traditional/Simplified Character Table 繁簡體字對照表 *p. 402*

Language in Use (Traditional/Simplified Characters) (Lessons 1–22) 課文(繁簡體字) (第一課至第二十二課) *p. 405*

English Translation of Language in Use 課文英文翻譯 *p. 426*

Indices:

Pinyin Index 拼音索引 *p. 435*

English Index 英文索引 *p. 458*

Characters in The Character Book 寫字簿的生字 *p. 481*

Recognizing that the world is becoming increasingly interlinked and globalized, the goal of the **CHINESE LINK: Zhongwen Tiandi 中文天地** (Elementary Chinese) project has been to integrate the "5Cs" principles of the National Standards for Foreign Language Education — Communication, Cultures, Comparisons, Connections, and Communities — throughout the program in order to provide a new approach for the teaching and learning of Chinese language in the 21st century. The program aims to help beginners develop their communicative competence in the four basic skills of listening, speaking, reading, and writing, while gaining competence in Chinese culture, exercising their ability to compare aspects of different cultures, making connections to their daily life, and building links among communities.

A language curriculum should be attractive to both students and instructors, therefore the authors provide a practical, learner-centered, and enjoyable language and culture learning experience for beginning students of Chinese, as well as an efficient and comprehensive teaching resource for instructors.

Proficiency in a language involves knowing both the structural forms of the language and their appropriate use in different cultural contexts. Care has been taken to introduce and explain grammar points clearly and systematically, yet not in a fashion that would be overwhelming to beginners. In keeping with the communicative focus of the text, grammar points are related to communicative, task-oriented content.

Each version of the text (Traditional and Simplified) presents both traditional and simplified versions of Chinese characters, since it is likely that students will encounter both forms. Similarly, care has been taken to present both Taiwan and Mainland China usage where they differ, and to incorporate new vocabulary items, such as "Internet," "cell phone," and "VCD." Culture notes at the end of each lesson are designed to catch the interest of the beginning learner and to explain important features of Chinese culture. Photographs and drawings are provided to make the text vivid and eye-catching, and to provide visual cues to aid in communicative exercises and activities.

Features of CHINESE LINK: Zhongwen Tiandi 中文天地 (Elementary Chinese)

- A clear and organized **Scope and Sequence** of the textbook is presented that provides an overview of the entire textbook, listing each lesson and its objectives, as well as the contents of the lesson's subsections. The **Scope and Sequence** lists the contents of four major sub-sections of each lesson: Grammar, Culture Notes, Fun with Chinese, and Let's Go!

- The 5Cs (**National Standards**) are blended consistently throughout the content and exercises in the program.

- The **Foundation** unit introduces important background information on Chinese language, useful classroom expressions, and a complete introduction to Pinyin and pronunciation.

- From the beginning of the text, we help students build from words and phrases to sentences and cohesive passages and then to application in **communicative tasks**.

- The textbook contains many **drawings** and **authentic photographs**, and utilizes a clear, attractive layout.

- **Grammar** points are introduced systematically and with a writing style that attempts to avoid excessive linguistic jargon. Grammar points include many examples.

- **Pronunciation and Pinyin** exercises are consistently emphasized throughout the entire text.

- **Both Traditional and Simplified character forms** are listed for every **vocabulary** item. When students see the two forms side by side it helps them to make an association between the two.

- **In-class exercises** are included in the main text as handy teaching aids and guidelines for instructors.

- Each lesson consists of **four types of exercises**: Pinyin, character, grammar, and communicative tasks. The exercises progress from drills and practice to content-based communicative tasks.

- Differences in usage between **Mainland China and Taiwan** are consistently identified.

- Interesting **cultural notes** are included in each lesson and supplemented with authentic photographs from Mainland China, Taiwan, and Hong Kong.

Organization of the Textbook

The textbook is divided into three main parts: **Foundation, core lessons**, and **Appendices**. The flexible design of the text allows instructors to use it in varying ways, depending on the number of contact hours per week and whether a school is on the semester or quarter system. Sample syllabi are available in the Instructor's Resource Manual.

Foundation:

The **Foundation** module provides fundamental knowledge about Chinese and learning Chinese that is useful for beginning students. It contains linguistic as well as cultural background material. Following are the major sections of the **Foundation** unit:

- **Introduction to Chinese:** This section briefly introduces some characteristics of Chinese language such as tones, the importance of word order, pictographic characters and its history and development.

- **Pinyin Foundation and Exercises:** Pinyin is the most widely used phonetic transliteration system to be introduced as a tool for representing the sounds of Chinese. This section introduces the Pinyin system as well as the structural components of Chinese syllables: initials, finals, and tones. There are many Pinyin exercises. Tongue twisters are introduced to show different aspects of rhythm and rhyme and the sounds of Chinese.

- **The Chinese Writing System:** This section discusses the formation of Chinese characters. It introduces the common components, radicals, and the structure of Chinese characters. Exercises are included.

- **Classroom Expressions and Exercises:** This section introduces the most useful and common phrases encountered in the Chinese classroom. Introducing these phrases early helps the instructors to limit use of English in the classroom. It also allows students to learn some phrases that they can make use of right away.

■ **Abbreviations of Parts of Speech:** This section lists the abbreviations used later in the grammar notes and vocabulary sections.

Core Lessons:

The content of the 22 lessons is selected to meet the practical needs and interests of students. The focus of the content begins with individual, family, and school activities, then gradually expands to include wider social occasions and societal contact. Great care has been taken to clearly and systematically present and practice the core vocabulary and grammatical expressions of elementary Chinese.

The major sections of each lesson are described below:

■ **Core Vocabulary:** Core vocabulary terms, which appear in the **Language Link** section, are introduced here. For each vocabulary item, traditional and simplified character forms are presented along with Pinyin pronunciation, grammatical function, and English meaning. This section also points out differences between Mainland China and Taiwan usage.

■ **Language Link:** This section contains situations that incorporate the lesson's core vocabulary and grammar points. It is accompanied by an art program that adds context and makes the lesson more interesting. **Language Link** serves as a model of the correct usage of the vocabulary and grammar points introduced in the lesson. Notes are provided to further explain the text. For most of the lessons, **Language Link** includes dialogues; for some selections it includes essays, diaries, e-mail, and letters. The length of **Language Link** is carefully controlled, and gradually increases to provide pedagogical sufficiency and challenge.

■ **Grammar:** Core grammar points from **Language Link** are explained in this section. We adopt the pedagogical grammar approach to better fit with the communicative approach to language learning. Grammar explanations are supplemented with examples that use vocabulary items previously covered in the textbook. We have tried to avoid linguistics jargon, with the exception of such commonly used terms as *syntax, sentence, clause, subject, predicate, object, modifier*, etc. For review and consolidation, the communicative exercises of each lesson are designed to elicit the use of grammatical structures introduced in the lesson.

■ **Supplementary Practice:** Each lesson has a **Supplementary Practice** section with themes, vocabulary, and grammar similar to those found in **Language Link**. This allows students to practice immediately what they have learned from their study of the main text. Care has been taken to use a different format from that found in **Language Link**. For example, if **Language Link** contains a dialogue, **Supplementary Practice** will include a prose format, and vice versa. The pedagogical purpose is to help students learn to use vocabulary and grammar structures in varying forms of communication.

■ **Activities:** This section is designed primarily for classroom use. Listening, character, grammar, and communicative exercises are included throughout the text. Care has been taken to provide balance between structural drills and real-life communicative tasks. The exercises integrate with the grammar points to provide a systematic extension of usage skills from vocabulary-item level to sentence level and on to discourse-level narration and description. Since these exercises are for class meeting time, they are designed to be dynamic and interactive. Most involve interaction between instructor and students, student and student, or group and group. Communicative activities are based on situations designed to elicit the grammar points and vocabulary students have learned in the lesson and in prior lessons. Visual aids are provided to help set the context for the communicative activities. Our goal in providing classroom exercises is to help save instructor time, which makes the text convenient and efficient for instructors to use.

- **Culture Link:** This section contains three components:
  - **Culture Notes:** The topics of the **Culture Notes** are carefully chosen to relate to those of the core lessons. It is hoped that the **Culture Notes** will help students to better understand Chinese societies, as well as how language reflects culture. Authentic photos are provided to create a vivid and interesting learning experience. The discussion questions are designed to encourage students to discuss and compare cultural differences by helping them to be aware of the features of their own culture and to be more understanding and tolerant toward other cultures.

  - **Fun with Chinese:** This section introduces a common slang expression, an idiom, or a motto that either utilizes new vocabulary presented in the lesson or is closely related to the theme of the lesson. Drawings are included to help make this section more fun and eye-catching. Discussion questions are provided to offer another fun way to relate the common Chinese expressions to the theme of the lesson.

  - **Let's Go!:** This section gives students an opportunity to interact with Chinese in an authentic context. It assists the students to connect themselves to authentic Chinese societies and communities. This section promotes students' motivation and helps them develop survival skills for life in authentic Chinese societies.

Appendices: The appendices serve as a learning resource for both students and instructors. It can also be used for review exercises in class or for self-study. The Appendices include the following:

- Vocabulary List
- Traditional/Simplified Character Table
- Chinese Transcriptions of **Language in Use**
- English Transcriptions of **Language in Use**: These can be used for translation or interpretation practice, for self-study or in-class review.
- Index (Pinyin and English)
- Characters in The Character Book

Other Program Components

Workbook: Homework and Character Book

The **Homework** portion contains a homework assignment for each lesson in the main textbook. A typical assignment is 3–4 pages, including space for students to write their responses. Homework activities are divided among listening, character recognition and writing, grammar exercises, and communicative tasks.

The **Character** portion provides the Chinese characters for the core vocabulary in every lesson. It shows the following for each character:

1. Character with its stroke order indicated by numbers
2. Traditional form of the character
3. Simplified form of the character
4. Pinyin pronunciation, grammatical usage, and sample sentences or phrases
5. Stroke order illustrated by writing the character progressively
6. Radical of the character with its Pinyin pronunciation and meaning
7. Ghosted images for students to trace over
8. Dotted graph lines to aid students' practice

Blank boxes are also included for students to practice writing the character. As a handy reference, three types of indices are provided in the Character Book: (1) By number of strokes; (2) By Lesson number; (3) Alphabetic by Pinyin.

Instructor's Resource Manual

The **Instructor's Resource Manual** provides sample syllabi, daily schedules, the answer key for in-class and homework exercises, and sample test questions.

Audio Materials

The audio files for all the lesson texts, vocabulary, listening exercises, tongue twisters, and poems in the textbook, as well as the listening exercises in the **Homework Portion of the Workbook** are provided on audio CDs.

Companion Website, <www.prenhall.com/chineselink>

This open-access Web site will provide useful tools that will allow students to further their learning of the Chinese language and culture.

致謝 ACKNOWLEDGMENTS

While we have a sense of accomplishment for completing this project, we are also keenly aware and appreciative of the support and encouragement we have received from the many individuals who contributed. We would like to express our gratitude to everyone who offered us support, suggestions, and encouragement.

We would like to thank Mark Haney for his assistance with English proofreading of the manuscript during many different stages of its preparation. We also owe our thanks to Denny Chen for his delicate skills in tracing the stroke order of most of the Chinese characters in the character book. With Mark and Denny's devotion and patience, the **Chinese Link** project moved along smoothly and well.

We sincerely appreciate the illustrators for our manuscript and the custom copy, Chi-chen Wu, Chung-ning Lu, and Yi-ju Chen. Their wonderful line art with Chinese flavor helped the manuscript to be more vivid and pleasing. Their line art also provided good models for this project.

Thanks to our loving families in Taiwan and Mainland China and the sincere friends who served as our photographers and photo providers: Vincent Sha, Mark Shope, Wenze Hu, Su-ying Wu, Tsan-lung Wu, Su-yueh Wu, Yi-ching Liu, and Mark Haney. Their artistic and authentic photos bring our project to a professional level.

We would like to express our gratitude to the Elementary Chinese instructors and students at Carnegie Mellon University and St. Vincent College in 2003–2004 and 2004–2005 who took the time to assist us with comments and suggestions during the course of our revision of the manuscript. Thanks also go to our colleagues in the Department of Modern Languages at CMU for their consistent encouragement. Special thanks to our department head, Professor Richard Tucker, for his warm support, and to Dean Gary Quinlivan of St. Vincent College for his enthusiasm and promotion of Chinese Link.

We would like to give our sincerest thanks to the folks at Prentice Hall for bringing their talent and professional publishing experience to this project. Many thanks go to Rachel McCoy, Acquisitions Editor, for her enthusiasm, sincere dedication, and professional guidance. Many thanks also go to Nancy Stevenson, Senior Production Editor, and Mary Rottino, Assistant Director of Production, for their patient and detailed instructions and guidelines about production procedures. We would also like to thank Meriel Martínez Moctezuma, Supplements Editor, for carefully overseeing the production of the Instructor's Resource Manual, Workbook, and Audio program. Thanks to Claudia Fernandes, Publishing Coordinator, for handling the mail and details in a timely fashion. Thanks to Phil Miller for his faith and commitment to this project, and to Wanda España, Weedesign, whose creativity resulted in a wonderful design for this project.

Many thanks to Margaret Chan, Project Manager, and her Graphicraft team members. Their prompt communication and hard work helped this project to reach the production stage.

We would like to conclude by thanking our families, without whose love and support this project would not have been possible. Many thanks to our husbands, Mark, Denny, Dejun, and Jinghong, for enduring our long hours. Special thanks to our children, Carrie, Marion, Sara, and Ryan, for giving up a lot of time with their moms so that this project could be completed.

We extend our sincere thanks and appreciation to the colleagues who reviewed the manuscript and provided valuable input. Their detailed comments and insightful suggestions helped us to further refine our manuscript.

Gary Quinlivan, Saint Vincent College, PA
Xiaohong Wen, University of Houston, TX
Wenze Hu, Harvard University, MA
Weijia Huang, Brown University, RI
Mingjung Chen, De Anza College, CA
Dana Scott Bourgerie, Brigham Young University, UT
Zheng-sheng Zhang, San Diego State University, CA
Jun Yang, University of Chicago, IL
Jean Yu, The Hotchkiss School, CT

Sue-mei Wu
Yueming Yu
Yanhui Zhang
Weizhong Tian

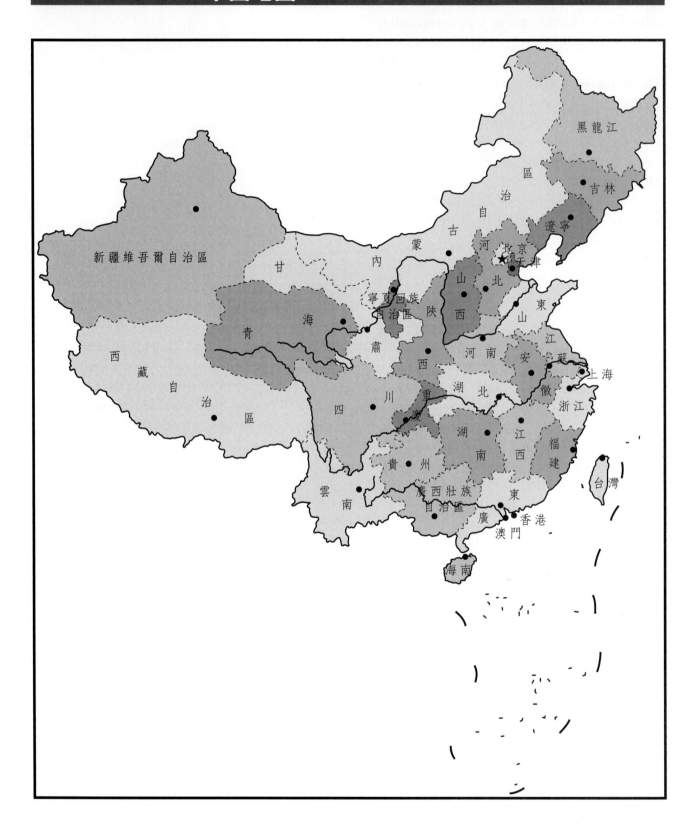

Chinese is a language spoken by about a quarter of the world's population. It is also one of the six working languages of the United Nations. It is called 漢語 [Hànyǔ] (Hanyu) in Chinese because it is spoken by the Han people, the largest ethnic group in China.

A member of the Sino-Tibetan language family, Chinese differs from other languages in many respects. Following are a few of its distinctive characteristics:

- It has no inflection of words to indicate person, gender, number, tense, or mood. The meaning of a sentence relies heavily on the context and word order.

- It is a tonal language. There are many Chinese words whose meanings are differentiated solely by which of the four tones is assigned to them.

- It comprises a large number of dialects, which share the same written form but can be mutually unintelligible when spoken. The Chinese dialects are generally categorized into eight groups: Mandarin (Northern), Northern Min (Northern Fujian), Southern Min (Southern Fujian, Taiwan), Xiang (Hunan), Gan (Jiangxi), Wu (Jiangsu and Zhejiang), Hakka (Guangdong, Guangxi), and Yue (Guangdong).

- The written form of the language consists of roughly square-shaped characters, each of which are formed by a number of strokes. The number of Chinese characters keeps growing. Scholars believe that 3,000 years ago there were around 4,500 characters in use. More recently the Kangxi Dictionary, compiled in 1710, lists about 48,000 characters. A dictionary published in 1994 lists around 86,000 characters! But don't let the sheer number of characters scare you away from studying Chinese. According to a list of commonly used Chinese characters published by China's Education Commission, only 3,500 characters are commonly used in daily life. It is generally acknowledged that a well-educated Chinese person has mastered 6,000 to 7,000 characters.

- Radicals often provide clues to the meaning of the character. The radical is also important for ordering and grouping characters. For example, dictionaries often have characters grouped by radical, and then by the number of strokes required to write the character. According to Chinese linguists, there are approximately 1,500 radicals in total, but most modern Chinese dictionaries only include 214.

About 400 years ago, a unified system of pronunciation for Chinese began to be established, which would be intelligible to everybody in the country. These efforts continued up until the beginning of the 20th century. As a result, *Guoyu* (the National Language) developed and became the language for all official communication. *Guoyu* takes Beijing Dialect as the standard for pronunciation and is based on dialects used in the northern part of the country. It also incorporates some language features of other dialects.

After the People's Republic of China was founded in 1949, some changes in the pronunciation of *Guoyu* were made and its name was changed to *Putonghua*, which means "Common Language." *Putonghua* has been the official language in Mainland China ever since, while *Guoyu* is still being used in Taiwan. In Singapore, Chinese is referred to locally as *Huawen*. In the West, "Mandarin Chinese" is the common term for Chinese.

Phonetic Transliteration Systems

In the last few centuries there have been efforts to develop a method of representing the Chinese language using the Latin alphabet. The most widely used system is called the *Pinyin* system. It was developed in Mainland China in the 1950s and officially adopted in 1979. *Pinyin*, which literally means "spell the sounds," is used to help people learn the pronunciation of characters or to look up words in dictionaries. The "Pinyin Foundation" section of this textbook gives you a more detailed introduction to this phonetic system.

Characters

Legend says that Chinese characters were created by Cang Jie, an official recorder of the Yellow Emperor, over 5,000 years ago. But the earliest use of a fully developed form of Chinese characters can be traced back to around 3,300 years ago in the Shang Dynasty. These writings, called the "Oracle Bone Scripts," consist of characters carved on ox bones or tortoise shells. Scholars believe that Chinese characters originally were pictographs that represented objects in the real world. Recent archeological discoveries also show that character-like pictographs existed as far back as 7,000 years ago. Xu Shen (58–147), a well-known linguist of the Eastern Han Dynasty (25–220 A.D.), analyzed the existing characters, examined their shapes, pronunciations and meanings, traced their roots, and finally compiled the first ever Chinese dictionary in history — *Shuo Wen Jie Zi* 《說文解字》— in which he collected over 9,000 characters categorized under 540 radicals. He concluded that Chinese characters were basically formed in six forms, called *Liu Shu* (the six writings):

- *Xiang xing* (Pictographs to represent real objects): e.g., 木、月、女,
- *Zhi shi* (Pictographs with an indicative sign; indirect symbols): e.g., 上、下、本,
- *Hui yi* (Meeting of ideas; compound characters): e.g., 明、休、好,
- *Xing sheng* (Picture and sound; semantic-phonetic combinations): e.g., 想、清、爸,
- *Zhuanzhu* (Transferable meaning; transformed characters): e.g., 考、老,
- *Jiajie* (Borrowed or loaned characters): e.g., 莫、其.

Shuo Wen Jie Zi is not only the first dictionary in Chinese history, it is also a scholarly masterpiece with great theoretical and practical value. Xu Shen's analysis of "Liu Shu" has been followed by scholars in China and other East Asian countries as well.

The section "The Chinese Writing System" provides a more detailed introduction on the rules for writing Chinese characters.

Simplification of Characters

Because of a belief that the complexity of Chinese characters constituted an obstacle to raising the nation's literacy level, and also to learning of the language by non-Chinese, efforts to simplify the characters began in the 19th century. In the 1950s, a simplified system of characters was promulgated in Mainland China. This system eliminated 1,053 variant characters and reduced the number of strokes for many other characters. The "Complete List of Simplified Characters" published in May 1964 listed 2,236 simplified characters. This system of simplified characters has become the major writing system used in Mainland China and Singapore. The traditional forms are still the standard way of writing in Taiwan and many overseas Chinese communities.

China has a history of several thousand years. In spite of periods of unity and disunity, China has remained intact as a country and is one of the only ancient civilizations that still exists today. It is believed that the Chinese writing system has played a crucial role by serving as an important binding factor in the cohesiveness of the country.

I.

The Pinyin system is a tool used by native Chinese speakers in Mainland China to learn the sounds of Chinese, or to look up unknown characters in dictionaries. It uses the 26 letters of the Latin alphabet to represent the sounds of Chinese. Many of the letters are pronounced in a similar way to their English pronunciation, but not all of them. Some are, in fact, pronounced quite differently from what an English speaker might expect. In this section, for many of the Chinese sounds we have pointed out similar sounds in English for students to use as a reference point. However, it is very important to imitate your instructors and recordings of native speakers so that you learn standard Mandarin pronunciation.

II. Structure of Chinese Syllables

A Chinese syllable consists of three elements: initial, final, and tone.

TONE		
INITIAL	FINAL	
(Consonant)	(y/w) Vowel (Ending) (i u ü medial) (a e o i u ü) (n ng)	

For example,

	Character	Meaning	Pinyin	Initial	Final			Type of final
1.	八	eight	bā	**b**	**a** (vowel)			simple final (a simple vowel)
2.	好	good	hǎo	**h**	**a** (vowel)	**o** (vowel)		compound final (a compound vowel)
3.	班	class	bān	**b**	**a** (vowel)	**n** (ending)		a nasal final
4.	忙	busy	máng	**m**	**a** (vowel)	**ng** (ending)		a nasal final
5.	也	also	yě	**y**	**e** (vowel)			final (with -y)
6.	我	I, me	wǒ	**w**	**o** (vowel)			final (with -w)
7.	亮	bright	liàng	**l**	**i** (medial)	**a** (vowel)	**ng** (ending)	a nasal final (with medial -i)
8.	國	country	guó	**g**	**u** (medial)	**o** (vowel)		double final (with medial -u)
9.	略	brief	lüè	**l**	**ü** (medial)	**e** (vowel)		double final (with medial -u (ü sound))

Notes:

1. There are four basic tones, which are indicated by marks placed over a vowel.
   For example, **bā bá bǎ bà**

2. In modern Chinese, there are 21 initials and 38 finals altogether. In a Chinese syllable, the vowel has to be present. Other components such as an initial or ending are optional.

3. The initial, if present, is always a consonant.

4. The final always contains a vowel. The final may be a simple final (a simple vowel, e.g., **bā**); a compound final (a compound vowel, e.g., **hǎo**; note that the tone mark is placed over the first vowel), or a nasal final, e.g., **bān** (vowel followed by a nasal consonant).

5. When -i-, -u-, and -ü- are not preceded by any initials, their Pinyin presentations are **y**, **w**, and **y**, respectively, e.g., **yě**, **wǒ**, and **yǔ**. If they are preceded by an initial, they are presented as **i**, **u**, and **ü** (as medial element, not the main vowel), e.g., **liàng**, **guó**, and **lüè**.

   There are three medials: **i**, **u**, and **ü**. They serve as transitional sounds, not as main vowels. For example, in **liàng**, **guó**, and **lüè**, **i**, **u**, and **ü** are the medial elements. **à**, **ó**, and **è** are the main vowels. Note that the tone marks are placed over the main vowels rather than over the medials.

III. Tones and Tone Marks

Chinese is a tonal language. This means different levels of pitch and the contour of its pronunciation are capable of differentiating meanings. There are four basic tones: the first tone, the second tone, the third tone, and the fourth tone.

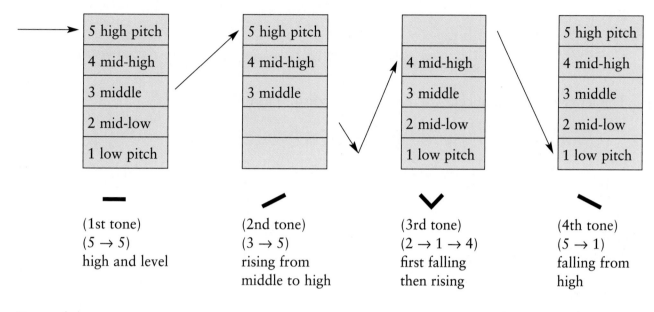

	(1st tone)	(2nd tone)	(3rd tone)	(4th tone)
	(5 → 5)	(3 → 5)	(2 → 1 → 4)	(5 → 1)
	high and level	rising from middle to high	first falling then rising	falling from high

Examples:

1.

PINYIN	bā	bá	bǎ	bà
CHARACTER	八	拔	靶	爸
MEANING	eight	to pull out	target	dad

2.

PINYIN	mā	má	mǎ	mà
CHARACTER	媽	麻	馬	罵
MEANING	mom	hemp	horse	to scold

3.

PINYIN	bō	bó	bǒ	bò
CHARACTER	波	伯	跛	擘
MEANING	wave	uncle	lame	thumb

4.

PINYIN	dā	dá	dǎ	dà
CHARACTER	搭	答	打	大
MEANING	to build up	to answer	to hit	big

IV. Vowels/Simple Finals

a   o   e   i   u   ü

- The letter **a** is pronounced like the "a" in English "father."

PRACTICE
(repeat after your teacher):   ba   ma   pa

- The letter **o** is pronounced like the "o" in English "more."

PRACTICE
(repeat after your teacher):   bo   po   mo

- The letter **e** sounds very similar to the "u" in English "b**u**d."

PRACTICE
(repeat after your teacher):   de   ke   ne

- The letter **i** is pronounced like the "ee" in English "bee."
  (except after the initials: z c s, zh ch sh r, details later).

PRACTICE
(repeat after your teacher):   mi   pi   li

- The letter **u** is pronounced like the "ue" in "**tru**e" or "oe" in "sh**oe**" in English.

PRACTICE
(repeat after your teacher):   gu   ku   lu

- The letter **ü** is pronounced like the [u] in French "tu." This sound is produced by first preparing to pronounce a long [i] sound, then holding that mouth position and rounding your lips as if to pronounce [**u**].

PRACTICE
(repeat after your teacher):   ju   qu   xu

V. Initials

There are 21 initials. They can be categorized into six groups (labials, velars, palatals, alveolars, dental sibilants, and retroflex) as illustrated below:

	Unaspirated	Aspirated[8]	Nasal	Fricative[9]	Voiced[10]
1. Labial[1]	b	p	m	f	
2. Alveolar[2]	d	t	n		l
3. Velar[3]	g	k		h	
4. Palatal[4]	j	q		x	
5. Dental[5] sibilant[6]	z	c		s	
6. Retroflex[7]	zh	ch		sh	r

Notes:

1. Labial: (speech sound) made using one or both lips.
2. Alveolar: (speech sound) made by putting the end of the tongue at the top of the mouth just behind the upper front teeth.
3. Velar: (speech sound) made with the back of the tongue against or near the soft part of the top of the mouth.
4. Palatal: (speech sound) made by putting the tongue against or near the hard palate. (Palate: the top inside part of the mouth)
5. Dental: (speech sound) made by putting the end of the tongue against the upper front teeth.
6. Sibilant: (speech sound) made by forcing air through a constricted passage.
7. Retroflex: (speech sound) made with the tip of the tongue curled upwards and backwards.
8. Aspirated: (speech sound) made with audible breath accompanying the articulation of the sound.
9. Fricative: (speech sound) made by impeding the flow of air through a narrow channel at the place of articulation.
10. Voiced: (speech sound) made when the vocal cords vibrate.

The following two groups are pronounced like their English counterparts.

1. Labials: b　p　m　f

PRACTICE
ba bi bo bu　　pa pi po pu　　ma mi mo mu me　　fa fo fu

2. Alveolars: d　t　n　l

PRACTICE
da de du　　ta ti te tu　　na ni ne nu　　la li le lu

Note: To practice what has been presented above, please see Pinyin Exercises, In-class Practice I.

3. Velars: g k h

The letter **g** sounds similar to the "g" in "**g**o."
The letter **k** sounds similar to the "k" in "**k**ing."
The letter **h** sounds similar to the "h" in "**h**appy."

Note that **g**, **k**, and **h** are never followed by the [i] sound.

PRACTICE
ge gu   ka ke ku   ha he hu

The sounds in groups 4, 5, and 6 below are some of the most challenging for learners of Chinese. Please note that the English counterpart sounds are listed here only as a rough approximation of the Chinese sounds. To pronounce these sounds correctly, it is very important to imitate your instructors and the recordings.

4. Palatals: j q x

The letter **j** sounds somewhat like the "g" in English "**g**esture" or the "j" in "**j**eep."
The letter **q** is formed like j above, but j is unaspirated, while q is aspirated. It sounds like "ch" in English "**ch**eap."
The letter **x** sounds somewhat like "sh" in English "**sh**eep."
Note that **j**, **q**, and **x** are never followed by the [u] sound.

PRACTICE
ji   qi   xi

5. Dental sibilants: z c s

The letter **z** sounds like "ds" in English "la**ds**."
The letter **c** is formed in the same way as "z" above but is aspirated while "z" is unaspirated. It sounds like "ts" in English "ca**ts**."
The letter **s** is very similar to "s" in English "**s**on."

PRACTICE
za ze zu zi   ca ce cu ci   sa se su si

Note that with zi, ci, and si, the vowel [i] acquires a special sound quality. It is pronounced as [ɿ] (blade-alveolar vowel), a continuation of a [z] sound. The tongue is kept still. Be aware that it must not be pronounced like the simple final [i] (as in "bi," "pi," "mi," and "di").

6. Retroflexes: zh ch sh r

This group is pronounced by curling the tip of the tongue to touch the front of the hard palate, leaving a narrow opening between the tongue and roof of the mouth to allow some air to flow through.

zh sounds like "g" in English "**g**erm."
ch sounds like "ch" in English "**ch**urch."
sh sounds like "sh" in English "**sh**irt."
r is pronounced like the "r" sound in English "plea**sure**," "trea**sure**," and "lei**sure**."

PRACTICE
zha zhe zhu zhi　　cha che chu chi
sha she shu shi　　re ru ri

Note that as with the [i] sound in "zi," "ci," and "si" above, in "zhi," "chi," "shi," and "ri" the vowel [i] also acquires a special sound quality. It is pronounced as [ʃ] (blade-palatal vowel), a continuation of a [zh] sound.

Summary: the pronunciation of -i sound

- pronounced as [i] in **bi pi mi di ti**
- pronounced as [ʔ] (blade-alveolar vowel) in **zi ci si**
- pronounced as [ʃ] (blade-palatal vowel) in **zhi chi shi and ri**

Note: To practice what has been presented in points 3 to 6 (gkh; jqx; zcs; zh; ch; sh; r), please see Pinyin Exercises, In-class Practice II.

VI. Compound Finals

Compound finals comprise a main vowel and a secondary vowel. There are four types as illustrated below.

1. main vowel + secondary vowel　　**ai　ei　ao　ou**
2. medial i + main vowel　　**ia　iao　ie　iu (iou)**#
3. medial u + main vowel　　**ua　uo　uai　ui (uei)**##
4. medial ü + main vowel　　**üe/yue**###

Note: #Please see IX. Special Pinyin Rules for details (#rule 3; ##rule 2; ###rule 1: ü → y).

In group (1), the first vowel is the main vowel (and the tone mark is placed over it). It is stressed, and is the longer of the two vowel sounds. The following vowel is soft and brief. For example, "ai" is pronounced beginning with the [a] sound then gliding into the direction of the [i] sound. Groups (2), (3), and (4) are compound finals that begin with medials (transitional sounds) followed by main vowels.

PRACTICE
bai　pei　mao　dou　　jia jiao jie jiu
zhua zhuo shuai rui

Note: To practice VI Compound Finals, please see Pinyin Exercises, In-class Practice III.

VII. Nasal Finals

Finals ending with "**n**" are called front nasals, and finals ending with "**ng**" [ŋ] are called back nasals.

1. Front nasals (+ n):

vowel + n	**an**	**en**
medial i + main vowel + n	**ian**	**in**
medial u + main vowel + n	**uan**	**un (uen)**#
medial ü + main vowel + n	**üan**	**ün (üen)**##

Note: Please see IX. Special Pinyin Rules for details (#rule 4; ##rule 1).

To produce the front nasal final, first form the final vowel sound. Then, without stopping the air flow, form the ending "n." The [n] sound is pronounced similarly to "n" in the English "i**n**" and "noo**n**."

PRACTICE

ban	pan	man	fan		gen	ken	hen
jian	qian	xian			jin	qin	xin
gun	kun	hun	wen (uen)#		huan	guan	kuan ([u] sound)
jun	qun	xun	([ü] sound)##		juan	quan	xuan ([ü] sound)

Notes: # Please see IX. Special Pinyin Rules for details (#rule 1).
Note that "j q x" can be followed by the [i] and [ü] sounds, but never by the [u] sound. So the umlaut (two dots) is omitted over the [ü] sound (##rule 5).

2. Back nasals (+ ng)

vowel + ng [ŋ]	**ang**	**eng**	**ong**
medial i + main vowel + ng	**iang**	**ing**	**iong**
	(yang)#	(ying)#	(yong)#
medial u + main vowel + ng	**uang**	**ueng**	
	(wang)##	(weng)##	

Note: #Please see IX. Special Pinyin Rules for details (#rule 1; ##rule 1).

To produce a back nasal final, form the final vowel sound. Then, without stopping the air flow, follow it with the nasal "ng."

PRACTICE

bang	pang			deng	neng	feng		dong	long	kong
jiang	qiang	xiang	yang	jing	qing	xing	ying	jiong	qiong	xiong
wang	weng									

Note: To practice Nasal Finals, please see Pinyin Exercises, In-class Practice IV.

VIII. Summary of Finals

Simple finals	a o e i u ü
Compound finals	ai　ei　ao　ou ia　iao　ie　iu (iou) ua　uo　uai　ui (uei) üe/yue
Nasal finals	an　en　ang　eng　ong ian　in　iang　ing　iong uan　un (uen)　uang　ueng üan　ün (üen)

IX. Special Pinyin Rules

1. i u ü without initial consonant.

   i → y　　　e.g.,　ya　ye　yao　yan　yong　you　yi　yin　ying
   u → w　　　e.g.,　wa　wo　wai　wang　wu　wei　wen
   ü → y　　　e.g.,　yu　yue　yuan　yun

2. When the final "uei" has an initial, it is written as "ui."

   uei → ui　　e.g.,　dui　tui　gui　kui　hui

3. When the final "iou" has an initial, it is written as "iu."

   iou → iu　　e.g.,　liu　niu　jiu　qiu　xiu

4. When the final "uen" has an initial, it is written as "un" e.g., sun.

   uen → un　　e.g.,　zun　cun　sun　zhun　chun　shun

5. The initials **j q x** are only followed by -i and -ü. They are never followed by -u. Therefore, when j q x are followed by the ü sound, the umlaut (two dots) above the u is omitted.

   　　　　e.g.,　ju　qu　xu　　juan　quan　xuan　　jun　qun　xun

6. Initials **z c s** and **zh ch sh r** are only followed by -i and -u. They are never followed by the -ü sound.

7. When the initials are l and n, the two dots on the ü sound have to be present in order to differentiate it from the u sound.

   　　　e.g.,　lǜ　綠　"green"　　lù　路　"road"
   　　　　　　nǚ　女　"female"　　nǔ　努　"diligent"

8. Neutral tone: Some syllables are unstressed; this is known as the neutral tone. There is no need to place a tone mark over neutral tone syllables.

PRACTICE	
bàba 爸爸 (Dad)	māma 媽媽 (Mom)
gēge 哥哥 (older brother)	jiějie 姐姐 (older sister)

9. Retroflex final -er: In Mandarin Chinese, sometimes we can see a final [er] attached to another final to form a retroflex final. There are some special rules for the spelling as illustrated below. These rules are listed here only as a reference. Note that the final [er] sound occurs more frequently in northern China.

■ When -er attaches to another final:

   a. In general, add only -r:

huār	花兒	(flower)	(huā + ér → huār)
hàomǎr	號碼兒	(number)	(hàomǎ + ér → hàomǎr)
zhèr	這兒	(here)	(zhè + ér → zhèr)
yíxiàr	一下兒	(one time)	(yíxià + ér → yíxiàr)

   b. with -ai -ei -an -en, drop the last letter and add -r:

nánhár	男孩兒	(boy)	(nánhái + ér → nánhár)
yíkuàr	一塊兒	(together)	(yíkuài + ér → yíkuàr)
wár	玩兒	(play)	(wán + ér → wár)
yìdiǎr	一點兒	(a little)	(yìdiǎn + ér → yìdiǎr)
shùgēr	樹根兒	(root)	(shùgēn + ér → shùgēr)

   c. with **zhi chi shi ri**, drop -i and add -er.

shùzhēr	樹枝兒	(branch)	(shùzhī + ér → shùzhēr)
shèr	事兒	(matter)	(shì + ér → shèr)

   d. with -in, drop -n and add -er

xìer	信兒	(message)	(xìn + ér → xìer)

   e. with -ng endings, drop -ng and add only -r.

dàshēr	大聲兒	(louder)	(dàshēng + ér → dàshēr)
bǎndèr	板凳兒	(stool)	(bǎndèng + ér → bǎndèr)

10. When two syllables come together to form a word and the second syllable begins with a vowel, they are sometimes separated with an apostrophe " ' ":

xī ān	西安 (a city in China)	→ xī'ān
xiāng ài	相愛 (love each other)	→ xiāng'ài

Without an apostrophe, [xī'ān] 西安 and [xiāng'ài] 相愛 may be misread as [xiān] 先 (first) and [xiān gài] 先蓋 (to build first).

X. Special Tone Rules

1. Tone change for 3rd tone:

   - 3rd tone is pronounced as a full 3rd tone when it occurs alone.

     e.g.,　nǐ 你 (you)　　　　hǎo 好 (good)　　　hěn 很 (very)　　　hǎo 好 (good)
     　　　yǔ 語 (language)　fǎ 法 (rule)　　　biǎo 表 (surface)　yǎn 演 (perform)

   - When two 3rd tones co-occur, the first 3rd tone will be pronounced as the 2nd tone, but with its tone mark unchanged.

     3 + 3 → 2 + 3

     e.g.,　nǐhǎo 你好 (hello)　　　　　　(pronounced as níhǎo)
     　　　hěnhǎo 很好 (very good)　　　(pronounced as hénhǎo)
     　　　yǔfǎ 語法 (grammar)　　　　　(pronounced as yúfǎ)
     　　　biǎoyǎn 表演 (perform)　　　　(pronounced as biáoyǎn)

   - Half 3rd tone[#]: 3rd tone + the 1st, 2nd, 4th tone or most neutral tones.

     nǐtīng 你聽 (you listen)　　nǐshuō 你說 (you speak)　　nǐlái 你來 (you come)
     nǐkàn 你看 (you see)　　　　hěnmáng 很忙 (very busy)　jiějie 姐姐 (older sister)

     Note: [#]Half 3rd tone: The rising part of the tone is curtailed. This results in a half-finished 3rd tone.

2. Conditional tone change for " 一 ":

   - When " 一 " stands alone, it is pronounced as 1st tone [**yī**].
   - When " 一 " + the 1st, 2nd, or 3rd tones, it is pronounced as the 4th tone [**yì**].

     yì + 1st tone　　yìtiān　　一天 (one day)
     yì + 2nd tone　　yìtóng　　一同 (together)
     yì + 3rd tone　　yìqǐ　　　一起 (together)

   - When " 一 " + the 4th tone, it is pronounced as the 2nd tone [**yí**].

     yímiàn 一面 (at the same time)　　　yíjiàn 一件 (one piece of <e.g., clothing>)

3. Conditional tone change for " 不 ":

   - When " 不 " stands alone, or is followed by a 1st, 2nd, or 3rd tone, it is pronounced as the 4th tone [**bù**].

     bùmáng 不忙 (not busy)　　bùhǎo 不好 (not good)

   - When " 不 " + the 4th tone, it is pronounced as the 2nd tone [**bú**].

     búshì 不是 (is not)　　búduì 不對 (incorrect)　　búkàn 不看 (not see)

     Notes: 1. To practice IX. Special Pinyin Rules and X. Special Tonal Rules, please see Pinyin Exercises, In-class Practice V.
     　　　　2. To review the Pinyin Foundation, please see Pinyin Exercises, In-class Practice VI.

拼音表　PINYIN TABLE

Initials/Finals		-	b	p	m	f	d	t	n	l	g	k	h	j	q	x	zh	ch	sh	r	z	c	s
1	a	a	ba	pa	ma	fa	da	ta	na	la	ga	ka	ha				zha	cha	sha		za	ca	sa
2	o	o	bo	po	mo	fo																	
3	e	e			me		de	te	ne	le	ge	ke	he				zhe	che	she	re	ze	ce	se
4	ê																						
5	ai	ai	bai	pai	mai		dai	tai	nai	lai	gai	kai	hai				zhai	chai	shai		zai	cai	sai
6	ei	ei	bei	pei	mei	fei	dei		nei	lei	gei	kei	hei				zhei				zei		
7	ao	ao	bao	pao	mao		dao	tao	nao	lao	gao	kao	hao				zhao	chao	shao	rao	zao	cao	sao
8	ou	ou			mou	fou	dou	tou	nou	lou	gou	kou	hou				zhou	chou	shou	rou	zou	cou	sou
9	an	an	ban	pan	man	fan	dan	tan	nan	lan	gan	kan	han				zhan	chan	shan	ran	zan	can	san
10	en	en	ben	pen	men	fen			nen		gen	ken	hen				zhen	chen	shen	ren	zen	cen	sen
11	ang	ang	bang	pang	mang	fang	dang	tang	nang	lang	gang	kang	hang				zhang	chang	shang	rang	zang	cang	sang
12	eng	eng	beng	peng	meng	feng	deng	teng	neng	leng	geng	keng	heng				zheng	cheng	sheng	reng	zeng	ceng	seng
13	ong	ong					dong	tong	nong	long	gong	kong	hong				zhong	chong		rong	zong	cong	song
14	er	er																						
15	i	yi	bi	pi	mi		di	ti	ni	li				ji	qi	xi							
16	-i																	zhi	chi	shi	ri	zi	ci	si
17	ia	ya												jia	qia	xia							
18	iao	yao	biao	piao	miao		diao	tiao	niao	liao				jiao	qiao	xiao							
19	ie	ye	bie	pie	mie		die	tie	nie	lie				jie	qie	xie							
20	iu (iou)	you			miu		diu		niu	liu				jiu	qiu	xiu							
21	ian	yan	bian	pian	mian		dian	tian	nian	lian				jian	qian	xian							
22	in	yin	bin	pin	min				nin	lin				jin	qin	xin							
23	iang	yang							niang	liang				jiang	qiang	xiang							
24	ing	ying	bing	ping	ming		ding	ting	ning	ling				jing	qing	xing							
25	iong	yong												jiong	qiong	xiong							
26	u	wu	bu	pu	mu	fu	du	tu	nu	lu	gu	ku	hu				zhu	chu	shu	ru	zu	cu	su
27	ua	wa									gua	kua	hua				zhua	chua	shua				
28	uo	wo					duo	tuo	nuo	luo	guo	kuo	huo				zhuo	chuo	shuo	ruo	zuo	cuo	suo
29	uai	wai									guai	kuai	huai				zhuai	chuai	shuai				
30	ui (uei)	wei					dui	tui			gui	kui	hui				zhui	chui	shui	rui	zui	cui	sui
31	uan	wan					duan	tuan	nuan	luan	guan	kuan	huan				zhuan	chuan	shuan	ruan	zuan	cuan	suan
32	un (uen)	wen					dun	tun		lun	gun	kun	hun				zhun	chun	shun	run	zun	cun	sun
33	uang	wang									guang	kuang	huang				zhuang	chuang	shuang				
34	ueng	weng																					
35	ü	yu							nü	lü				ju	qu	xu							
36	üe	yue							nüe	lüe				jue	que	xue							
37	üan	yuan												juan	quan	xuan							
38	ün(üen)	yun												jun	qun	xun							

In-class Practice I

Simple finals: a o e i u ü　　*Labial initials: b p m f*　　*Alveolar initials: d t n l*

> **USEFUL CLASSROOM EXPRESSIONS:**
>
> | 請你再說一遍 。 | Qǐng nǐ zài shuō yí biàn. | Please say it again. |
> |---|---|---|
> | 對(了)。 | Duì(le). | Correct. |
> | 不對 。 | Bú duì. | Incorrect. |
> | 第幾聲? | Dì jǐ shēng? | Which tone? |
> | 第一聲 | dì yī shēng | the first tone |
> | 第二聲 | dì èr shēng | the second tone |
> | 第三聲 | dì sān shēng | the third tone |
> | 第四聲 | dì sì shēng | the fourth tone |
> | 輕聲 | qīng shēng | neutral tone |

F-1　Repeat after the instructor:

1. bā　bá　bǎ　bà
2. mī　mí　mǐ　mì
3. dē　dé　dě　dè
4. nū　nú　nǔ　nù
5. pō　pó　pǒ　pò
6. fā　fá　fǎ　fà
7. tī　tí　tǐ　tì
8. lǖ　lǘ　lǚ　lǜ

F-2　In each group, circle the syllable your instructor pronounces:

1. mū　mú　mǔ　mù
2. mō　mó　mǒ　mò
3. lī　lí　lǐ　lì
4. lǖ　lǘ　lǚ　lǜ
5. tū　tú　tǔ　tù
6. dū　dú　dǔ　dù
7. nā　ná　nǎ　nà
8. pō　pó　pǒ　pò

F-3　Read aloud the following syllables:

1. pá　bá
2. bó　pó
3. mǔ　nǔ
4. lù　nù
5. lú　lǘ
6. dī　tī
7. lǚ　nǚ
8. tā　tē
9. mō　mū

F-4   Read aloud the following words or phrases:

1.	lùdì	land	陸地	11.	bìmá	castor oil plant	蓖麻
2.	báhé	tug-of-war	拔河	12.	mǎlù	road, street	馬路
3.	pífū	skin	皮膚	13.	dútè	unique	獨特
4.	tèlì	special case	特例	14.	púfú	crawl	匍匐
5.	lǚbó	aluminum foil	鋁箔	15.	fābù	issue, release	發佈
6.	mùmǎ	wooden horse	木馬	16.	mābù	rag	抹布
7.	bófù	uncle	伯父	17.	tūpò	break through	突破
8.	dìtú	map	地圖	18.	dībà	dam	堤壩
9.	lǐfà	haircut	理髮	19.	làbǐ	crayon	蠟筆
10.	tǐlì	physical strength	體力	20.	fùmǔ	parents	父母

F-5   In each pair, circle the one your instructor pronounces:

1. lǔ   nǔ   3. lù   nù   5. dū   dē
2. mā   mō   4. mò   mù   6. tā   tē

F-6   Fun with Pinyin

Read the following ràokǒulìng (tongue twister):

bóbo	伯伯	uncle
bàba	爸爸	dad
mǎ	馬	horse
pá	爬	to climb
dǎ	打	to hit, play
tǔpō	土坡	muddy slope
lùbō	綠波	green water

Bóbo de mǎ,	伯伯的馬，	Uncle's horse,
Bàba de é.	爸爸的鵝。	Father's goose.
Mǎ pá tǔpō,	馬爬土坡，	The horse is climbing a muddy slope,
É dǎ lùbō.	鵝打綠波。	The goose is playing in the green water.

In-class Practice II

Velar initials: g k h　　　　*Palatal initials: j q x*
Dental sibilant initials: z c s　　*Retroflex initials: zh ch sh r*

USEFUL CLASSROOM EXPRESSIONS:

請你再說一遍 。	Qǐng nǐ zài shuō yí biàn.	Please say it again.
對(了) 。	Duì(le).	Correct.
不對 。	Bú duì.	Incorrect.
第幾聲?	Dì jǐ shēng?	Which tone?
第一聲	dì yī shēng	the first tone
第二聲	dì èr shēng	the second tone
第三聲	dì sān shēng	the third tone
第四聲	dì sì shēng	the fourth tone
輕聲	qīng shēng	neutral tone

F-7　Repeat after the instructor:

1. shā　shá　shǎ　shà
2. chū　chú　chǔ　chù
3. sū　sú　sǔ　sù
4. jī　jí　jǐ　jì
5. xī　xí　xǐ　xì

6. zū　zú　zǔ　zù
7. zhē　zhé　zhě　zhè
8. rū　rú　rǔ　rù
9. qī　qí　qǐ　qì
10. cū　cú　cǔ　cù

F-8　Read the following words or phrases. Pay attention to the initials "j, q, x" and "z, c, s."

1.	qìxī	breath	氣息	11.	zájì	acrobatics	雜技
2.	xīqǔ	absorb	吸取	12.	zǐxì	attentively	仔細
3.	qìjù	utensil	器具	13.	cíqì	porcelain	瓷器
4.	jīxù	savings	積蓄	14.	cíxù	word order	詞序
5.	qícì	secondly	其次	15.	zìjù	written pledge	字據
6.	jīqì	machine	機器	16.	cūsú	vulgar	粗俗
7.	qízǐ	chess piece	棋子	17.	jìcè	stratagem	計策
8.	zìjǐ	oneself	自己	18.	qǐsù	sue	起訴
9.	sījī	driver	司機	19.	xìjù	drama	戲劇
10.	xíjī	raid	襲擊	20.	zìsī	selfish	自私

F-9   Read the following words or phrases. Pay attention to the initials "j, q, x" and "zh, ch, sh, r."

1.	chúxī	New Year's Eve	除夕		11.	zhàqǔ	extort	榨取
2.	rèqì	heat	熱氣		12.	zhījǐ	intimate	知己
3.	xīshì	Western style	西式		13.	zhìxù	order	秩序
4.	xùshì	narrate	敘事		14.	zhúzì	word for word	逐字
5.	qìzhì	temperament	氣質		15.	zhǔxí	chairman	主席
6.	qūshǐ	spur on	驅使		16.	chājù	gap	差距
7.	qízhì	flag	旗幟		17.	chíxù	continue	持續
8.	jīzhì	quick-witted	機智		18.	shíjī	opportunity	時機
9.	jīchǔ	foundation	基礎		19.	shìqì	morality	士氣
10.	jùchǐ	sawtooth	鋸齒		20.	rúqī	on schedule	如期

F-10   Read the following words or phrases. Pay attention to the initials "z, c, s" and "zh, ch, sh, r."

1.	zǔzhī	organize	組織		11.	chúshī	chef	廚師
2.	sīshì	personal affairs	私事		12.	shìsú	secular	世俗
3.	zīzhù	subsidize	資助		13.	shùzì	figure	數字
4.	zhízé	duty	職責		14.	chūrù	discrepancy	出入
5.	qìchē	car	汽車		15.	rúcǐ	in this way	如此
6.	chìzì	deficit	赤字		16.	rǔzhī	milk	乳汁
7.	zhīchí	support	支持		17.	shízǐ	cobble	石子
8.	zhùcí	congratulatory speech	祝詞		18.	shízì	learn to read	識字
9.	shísù	board and lodging	食宿		19.	chìrè	blazing	熾熱
10.	shǐcè	annals	史冊		20.	chūcì	the first time	初次

F-11 In each pair, circle the one your instructor pronounces:

1. rì　shì   4. shī　sī   7. zhà　chà   10. cā　zā
2. xī　sī   5. qì　xì   8. shú　chú   11. zǔ　sǔ
3. zhè　zè   6. xì　shì   9. jǐ　xǐ   12. cè　chè

F-12 Listen to the instructor pronounce each syllable, then fill in the initials:

Part I:

1. ____ē   4. ____í   7. ____à
2. ____ī   5. ____ù   8. ____ú
3. ____è   6. ____ì   9. ____ǐ

Part II:

10. ____è   13. ____ù   16. ____ā
11. ____ù   14. ____á   17. ____ì
12. ____é   15. ____ě   18. ____ǔ

F-13 Fun with Pinyin

Read the following ràokǒulìng (tongue twister):

shí shīzi	石獅子	stone lion
shī shīzi	濕獅子	wet lion
sǐ shīzi	死獅子	dead lion
sī shīzi	絲獅子	silk lion
chī shīzi	吃獅子	eat lion
cí shīzi	瓷獅子	porcelain lion

Sì zhī shí shīzi,	四隻石獅子，	Four stone lions,
Shí zhī zhǐ shīzi.	十隻紙獅子。	Ten paper lions.
Zhǐ shīzi bù kě chī,	紙獅子不可吃，	Paper lions cannot be eaten,
Shí shīzi bù kě sī.	石獅子不可撕。	Stone lions cannot be torn.

In-class Practice III

Compound finals: ai ei ao ou   ia iao ie iu   ua uo uai ui üe

---

USEFUL CLASSROOM EXPRESSIONS:

請你再說一遍。	Qǐng nǐ zài shuō yí biàn.	Please say it again.
對(了)。	Duì(le).	Correct.
不對。	Bú duì.	Incorrect.
第幾聲?	Dì jǐ shēng?	Which tone?
第一聲	dì yī shēng	the first tone
第二聲	dì èr shēng	the second tone
第三聲	dì sān shēng	the third tone
第四聲	dì sì shēng	the fourth tone
輕聲	qīng shēng	neutral tone

F-14 Repeat after the instructor:

1. juē   jué   juě   juè
2. jiā   jiá   jiǎ   jià
3. tuī   tuí   tuǐ   tuì
4. zhōu   zhóu   zhǒu   zhòu
5. fēi   féi   fěi   fèi
6. qiāo   qiáo   qiǎo   qiào
7. xiē   xié   xiě   xiè
8. niū   niú   niǔ   niù
9. zāo   záo   zǎo   zào
10. duō   duó   duǒ   duò

F-15 Listen to the instructor pronounce each syllable, then add the correct tone mark:

1. bie   4. hua   7. mao   10. zhua   13. shuo
2. shuai   5. biao   8. tou   11. nuo   14. lüe
3. zhou   6. liu   9. cui   12. ren   15. pei

F-16 Read aloud the following syllables:

1. huó   hóu   4. bǎo   biǎo   7. luó   lóu   10. shāo   xiāo
2. diū   duī   5. jué   xué   8. chāo qiāo   11. lín   liú
3. rào   ròu   6. lüè   nüè   9. chóu zhóu   12. xuē   xiū

F-17 Read aloud the following words or phrases:

1.	báicài	Chinese cabbage	白菜	11.	nǎilào	cheese	奶酪
2.	cáixué	scholarship	才學	12.	páiliè	put in order	排列
3.	còuqiǎo	luckily	湊巧	13.	quèqiè	exact	確切
4.	dàotuì	go backwards	倒退	14.	róudào	judo	柔道
5.	fēikuài	very fast	飛快	15.	sǎomiáo	scan	掃描
6.	gàobié	bid farewell to	告別	16.	shōuhuò	harvest	收穫
7.	huàxué	chemistry	化學	17.	táoshuì	evade a tax	逃稅
8.	jiézòu	rhythm	節奏	18.	tuóniǎo	ostrich	駝鳥
9.	liúxué	study abroad	留學	19.	wèilái	future	未來
10.	měimiào	wonderful	美妙	20.	zuòjiā	writer	作家

F-18 In each pair, circle the one your instructor pronounces:

1. jué　xué		3. huó　hóu		5. guò　gòu		7. jiǔ　xiǔ
2. lüè　nüè		4. xuē　xiū		6. shāo　xiāo		8. rào　ròu

F-19 Fun with Pinyin

Read the following ràokǒulìng (tongue twister):

huīmāo	灰貓	gray cat
huāniǎo	花鳥	spotted bird
táopǎo	逃跑	to run away

Huīmāo zhuī huāniǎo	**灰貓追花鳥**
Huīmāo tiào, huāniǎo jiào,	灰貓跳，花鳥叫，
Huīmāo tiào qǐ zhuā huāniǎo.	灰貓跳起抓花鳥。
Huāniǎo pà huīmāo,	花鳥怕灰貓，
Bátuǐ jiù táopǎo.	拔腿就逃跑。

The Gray Cat Chases the Spotted Bird

The gray cat leaps, the spotted bird cries,
The gray cat leaps up to catch the spotted bird.
The spotted bird is afraid of the gray cat,
It flies away quickly.

In-class Practice IV

Nasal finals: *an en*   *ian in*   *uan un*   *ang eng ong*   *iang ing iong*   *uang*

USEFUL CLASSROOM EXPRESSIONS:		
請你再說一遍。	Qǐng nǐ zài shuō yí biàn.	Please say it again.
對(了)。	Duì(le).	Correct.
不對。	Bú duì.	Incorrect.
第幾聲?	Dì jǐ shēng?	Which tone?
第一聲	dì yī shēng	the first tone
第二聲	dì èr shēng	the second tone
第三聲	dì sān shēng	the third tone
第四聲	dì sì shēng	the fourth tone
輕聲	qīng shēng	neutral tone

F-20 Repeat after the instructor:

1. liān   lián   liǎn   liàn
2. guān   guán   guǎn   guàn
3. kūn   kún   kǔn   kùn
4. mēng   méng   měng   mèng

5. tōng   tóng   tǒng   tòng
6. qiāng   qiáng   qiǎng   qiàng
7. xīng   xíng   xǐng   xìng
8. jiōng   jióng   jiǒng   jiòng

F-21 Listen to the instructor pronounce each syllable, and then add the correct tone mark:

1. mian
2. ling
3. zhun
4. hen
5. zhuang
6. qiang
7. lun
8. rong

F-22 Read aloud the following syllables:

1. jūn   qūn
2. cóng   chóng
3. huán   huáng
4. zhàn   zhèn
5. juān   jūn
6. tūn   tuān
7. xūn   sūn
8. xiàng   xuàn
9. qiáng   qióng
10. zhāng   jiāng
11. rǎn   zhǎn
12. kěn   kǔn

F-23 Read aloud the following words or phrases:

1.	ānjìng	quiet	安靜	11.	miànfěn	flour	麵粉
2.	bàngwǎn	at dusk	傍晚	12.	niánqīng	young	年輕
3.	Chángchéng	the Great Wall	長城	13.	píngjūn	average	平均
4.	diànyǐng	movie	電影	14.	qiānzhèng	visa	簽證
5.	fāngbiàn	convenient	方便	15.	ruǎnjiàn	software	軟件
6.	guāngxiàn	ray	光線	16.	sēnlín	forest	森林
7.	hǎnjiàn	rare	罕見	17.	tiānrán	natural	天然
8.	jǐnzhāng	nervous	緊張	18.	xiāngcūn	village	鄉村
9.	kěndìng	affirm	肯定	19.	zhèngcháng	normal	正常
10.	línggǎn	inspiration	靈感	20.	huánjìng	environment	環境

F-24 In each pair, circle the one your instructor pronounces:

1. zhèn	shè	5. xūn	sūn	9. jūn	qūn	13. háng	huáng
2. zhàn	zhèn	6. qiáng	qióng	10. kàn	kèn	14. rēng	zhēng
3. lín	líng	7. tūn	tuān	11. xiàng	xuàn	15. shāo	shōu
4. juān	jūn	8. huán	huáng	12. zhāng	jiāng	16. shùn	shèn

F-25 Listen to the instructor pronounce each syllable, then fill in the blank with the correct final:

1. k _____   5. x _____   9. r _____
2. h _____   6. zh _____   10. z _____
3. j _____   7. ch _____   11. c _____
4. q _____   8. sh _____   12. s _____

F-26 Fun with Pinyin:

Read the following ràokǒulìng (tongue twister):

dēngshān:	登山	to climb a mountain
Xiǎosān:	小三	Little San (name of a person)
sān lǐ sān:	三里三	three miles plus three feet
sān jiàn shān:	三件衫	three shirts

Dēngshān	登山	**Climb the Mountain**
Xiǎosān qù dēngshān,	小三去登山，	Little San went to climb a mountain,
Pǎo le sān lǐ sān.	跑了三里三。	He ran for three miles plus three feet.
Chū le yì shēn hàn,	出了一身汗，	He was sweaty all over,
Shī le sān jiàn shān.	濕了三件衫。	Three of his shirts were wet.

In-class Practice V

Special Pinyin and tonal rules

F-27 Listen to the instructor pronounce each syllable, then fill in the blank with the correct tone and final:

1. y ____   5. m ____   9. j ____   13. l ____
2. y ____   6. n ____   10. q ____   14. n ____
3. h ____   7. s ____   11. zh ____   15. b ____
4. zh ____   8. ch ____   12. ch ____   16. y ____

F-28 Tone change for the 3rd tone. Read aloud the following words or phrases:

Part I: 3rd + 3rd → 2nd + 3rd

1.	jǔzhǐ	manner	舉止	6.	nǎohǎi	mind	腦海
2.	fǎmǎ	weight used on a balance	砝碼	7.	měihǎo	fine	美好
3.	liǎojiě	understand	了解	8.	suǒyǒu	all	所有
4.	shǒubiǎo	watch	手錶	9.	chǎnpǐn	product	產品
5.	shuǐguǒ	fruit	水果	10.	wǎnzhuǎn	tactful	婉轉

Part II: Half 3rd tone

1.	hěn máng	very busy	很忙	7.	Fǎguó	France	法國
2.	wǒ de	my, mine	我的	8.	lǎoshī	teacher	老師
3.	wǒ shì	I am	我是	9.	kǎoshì	test	考試
4.	Qǐng wèn	May I ask . . . ?	請問	10.	Qǐng gēn wǒ shuō.	Please repeat after me.	請跟我說。
5.	Nǎ guó rén?	What nationality?	哪國人	11.	Dǒng le ma?	Do you understand?	懂了嗎?
6.	Měiguó	US	美國	12.	Dì jǐ shēng?	Which tone?	第幾聲?

F-29 Repeat after the instructor. Mark the tones of "yi" (一) and "bu" (不) in accordance with the "yi-bu" tonal rules:

1.	yí	gè	one	一個	11.	bù	xíng
2.	yì	bǎi	hundred	一百	12.	bù	néng
3.	yì	qiān	thousand	一千	13.	bù	xiǎng
4.	yí	wàn	ten thousand	一萬	14.	bù	duō
5.	yí	zhào	trillion	一兆	15.	bù	shǎo
6.	yì	yuán	dollar	一元	16.	bú	dà
7.	yí	kuài	dollar	一塊	17.	bù	xiǎo
8.	yì	jiǎo	ten cents	一角	18.	bú	pà
9.	yì	máo	ten cents	一毛	19.	bú	liào
10.	yì	fēn	cent	一分	20.	bù	zǎo

11. bù xíng cannot 不行
12. bù néng not be able 不能
13. bù xiǎng don't want 不想
14. bù duō not many 不多
15. bù shǎo not few 不少
16. bú dà not big 不大
17. bù xiǎo not small 不小
18. bú pà not afraid 不怕
19. bú liào not expected 不料
20. bù zǎo not early 不早

21. yí lùpíng'ān have a safe trip 一路平安
22. yì gǔzuòqì get something done in one vigorous effort 一鼓作氣
23. yì hūbǎiyìng be ready to go into action in their hundreds 一呼百應
24. yì míngjīngrén amaze the world with a single brilliant feat 一鳴驚人
25. yì fānfēngshùn have a good innings 一帆風順
26. bù gōngzìpò collapse of itself 不攻自破
27. bú jìnzétuì not to advance is to go back 不進則退
28. bù tóngfánxiǎng out of the common run 不同凡響
29. bù xiāngshàngxià be equally matched 不相上下
30. bú dòngshēngsè stay calm and collected 不動聲色

F-30 Fun with Pinyin

Read the following ràokǒulìng (tongue twister):

gǔ:　鼓　drum
hǔ:　虎　tiger
bù:　布　cloth
bǔ:　補　patch

Gǔ hé hǔ	**鼓和虎**	**Drum and Tiger**
Yì zhī xiǎo huāgǔ,	一隻小花鼓，	A little colored drum,
Gǔ lǐ huà zhī hǔ.	鼓裏畫隻虎。	On the drum a tiger is drawn.
Hǔ pá gǔ pò bù lái bǔ,	虎爬鼓破布來補，	Tiger climbs, drum breaks, a cloth patch is applied,
Bùzhī shì bù bǔ gǔ?	不知是布補鼓？	Is the drum being patched?
Háishì bù bǔ hǔ?	還是布補虎？	Or the tiger being patched?

In-class Practice VI

Comprehensive Pinyin Review

F-31 Read aloud the following Pinyin:

1.	yǔ yǒu	5.	jūn zhēn	9.	wō ōu
2.	xià xiào	6.	xiōng jiōng	10.	lián liáng
3.	niè lèi	7.	jié zéi	11.	lǔ liǔ
4.	zuō cuō	8.	dàng dèng	12.	lǔ nǔ

F-32 Read and compare the following words or phrases:

1. míngshēng — reputation — 名聲
   míngshèng — scenic spot — 名勝

   4. shǔsè — light of early dawn — 曙色
   sùshè — dormitory — 宿舍

2. tiáojiě — mediate — 調解
   tiáojié — adjust — 調節

   5. chājù — disparity — 差距
   chájù — tea set — 茶具

3. shíqī — period — 時期
   shíqì — stoneware — 石器

   6. zhīshi — knowledge — 知識
   zhìshǐ — result in — 致使

F-33 In each pair, circle the one your instructor pronounces:

1.	lǔ nǔ	4.	lián liáng	7.	xià xiào
2.	bīn bīng	5.	xiōng jiōng	8.	jié zéi
3.	dàng dèng	6.	lǔ liǔ	9.	jūn zhēn

F-34 Listen to the instructor pronounce the following classroom expressions, and then write them out in Pinyin:

1. 大家好。_____

2. 上課。_____

3. 中文怎麼說? _____

4. 沒有問題。_____

5. 第四聲 _____

6. 請打開書。_____

F-35 Fun with Pinyin

Read the following ràokǒulìng (tongue twister):

xī:	錫	tin
qī:	漆	paint
xījiàng:	錫匠	tinsmith
qījiàng:	漆匠	lacquerer

Xījiàng hé qījiàng	**錫匠和漆匠**
Xījiàng mài xī, qījiàng mài qī,	錫匠賣錫，漆匠賣漆，
Xījiàng shuō qījiàng tōu le tāde xī,	錫匠說漆匠偷了他的錫，
Qījiàng shuō xījiàng tōu le tāde qī,	漆匠說錫匠偷了他的漆，
Bùzhī shì xījiàng tōu le qījiàng de qī,	不知是錫匠偷了漆匠的漆，
Háishì qījiàng tōu le xījiàng de xī.	還是漆匠偷了錫匠的錫。

Tinsmith and Lacquerer

Tinsmith sells tins; lacquerer sells paint,
The tinsmith charges the lacquerer with stealing his tins,
The lacquerer charges the tinsmith with stealing his paints,
Who knows whether the tinsmith has stolen the lacquerer's paints,
Or the lacquerer has stolen the tinsmith's tins.

Chinese characters can be thought of as square-shaped "signs" which fit into blocks that are independent of each other. Generally speaking, a character may consist of one, two, or three parts, each standing for an independent semantic unit. In general, the arrangement of these semantic units in Chinese characters falls into the following patterns:

1. One-semantic-unit characters:

   e.g., 女，山

2. Two-semantic-unit characters:

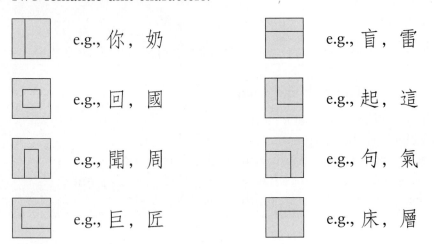

   e.g., 你，奶　　　　e.g., 盲，雷

   e.g., 回，國　　　　e.g., 起，這

   e.g., 聞，周　　　　e.g., 句，氣

   e.g., 巨，匠　　　　e.g., 床，層

   e.g., 凶

3. Three-semantic-unit characters:

   e.g., 謝　　　　e.g., 意

   e.g., 想　　　　e.g., 筷

   e.g., 語　　　　e.g., 部

Radicals

Radicals are pictographs which represent objects in the real world. Some of them can stand alone as independent, one-semantic-unit characters. Examples include 人 (person), 口 (mouth), and 雨 (rain). Radicals may also be combined with other components to form a new character for which the radical serves as a clue to its meaning. Examples include 吹 (to blow) and 妹 (younger sister). Some radicals cannot be used as independent characters but only serve as a part of another character. Their function is to provide a semantic clue to the character, such as 宀 in 家 (home), 艹 in 菜 (vegetable), and 辶 in 逛 (to stroll). According to most dictionaries, there are 214 commonly used radicals in Chinese. Look at the following archaic examples of radicals:

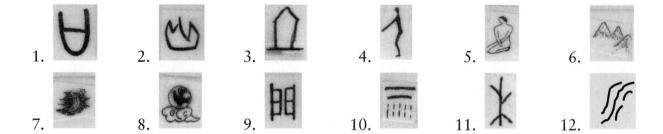

1.　　　2.　　　3.　　　4.　　　5.　　　6.

7.　　　8.　　　9.　　　10.　　　11.　　　12.

Below are their modern forms. Can you use the archaic forms as clues to figure out the meaning of the modern forms?

人 rén	口 kǒu	山 shān	水 shuǐ	日 rì	月 yuè
(　　)	(　　)	(　　)	(　　)	(　　)	(　　)
土 tǔ	木 mù	雨 yǔ	火 huǒ	女 nǚ	門 mén
(　　)	(　　)	(　　)	(　　)	(　　)	(　　)

Each of these characters, when combined with other components to form a new character, provides a clue to the meaning of that character. For example, 吃 [chī] (to eat) is formed by the radical 口 (mouth) and a phonetic clue 乞 [qǐ]. Characters with the radical 口 generally have meanings related to the mouth, such as 喝 [hē] (to drink), 唱 [chàng] (to sing) and 吸 [xī] (to suck). Here are some more examples:

心 xīn (heart)	耳 ěr (ear)	目 mù (eye)	手 shǒu (hand)	魚 yú (fish)	馬 mǎ (horse)
車 chē (vehicle)	門 mén (door)	刀 dāo (knife)	足 zú (foot)	金 jīn (metal)	玉 yù (jade)

練習一   Practice (1)

Circle the radicals in the following characters:

姐	鱷	晴	悲	駕	輪	劈	枝	聰	期
jiě	è	qíng	bēi	jià	lún	pī	zhī	cōng	qī
sister	crocodile	sunny	grief	to drive	wheel	cleave	branch	clever	period

Some of these characters also take a slightly different form when used as radicals. They often have a specific name commonly used by Chinese when referring to them as radicals. The following are those most frequently used:

人	rén – person	→	亻	*dān lìrén* – single standing person e.g., 你 (nǐ – you) 他 (tā – he)
手	shǒu – hand	→	扌	*tíshǒu* – lift hand e.g., 打 (dǎ – to strike) 拉 (lā – to pull)
水	shuǐ – water	→	氵	*sān diǎn shuǐ* – three dot water e.g., 江 (jiāng – river) 海 (hǎi – sea)
	bīng – ice	→	冫	*liǎng diǎn shuǐ* – two dot water e.g., 冷 (lěng – cold) 冰 (bīng – ice)
心	xīn – heart	→	忄	*shùxīn* – vertical heart e.g., 忙 (máng – busy) 情 (qíng – feelings)
火	huǒ – fire	→	灬	*sì diǎn huǒ* – four dot fire e.g., 煮 (zhǔ – to boil) 蒸 (zhēng – to steam)
刀	dāo – knife	→	刂	*lìdāo* – standing knife e.g., 到 (dào – to arrive) 利 (lì – sharp)
邑	yì – town	→	阝	*yòu ěr dāo* – right ear knife e.g., 都 (dōu – all) 那 (nà – that)
阜	fǔ – dam	→	阝	*zuǒ ěr dāo* – left ear knife e.g., 陡 (dǒu – steep) 陸 (lù – land)
犬	quǎn – dog	→	犭	*fǎn quǎn* – reversed dog e.g., 狗 (gǒu – dog) 狐 (hú – fox)

練習二　Practice (2)

F-36 Circle the radicals in the following characters:

凍	伯	怪	摔	信	踢	拔	煎	海	割
dòng	bó	guài	shuāi	xìn	tī	bá	jiān	hǎi	gē
freeze	uncle	strange	tumble	believe	kick	pull	fry	sea	cut

F-37 Match the following radicals with their original characters:

( )　　　( )　　　( )　　　( )　　　( )　　　( )

火　　　水　　　心　　　刀　　　手　　　人

a. 扌　　b. 刂　　c. 灬　　d. 亻　　e. 氵　　f. 忄

There are some radicals which are actually only part of the original characters, such as:

絲	sī – silk	→	糸(糹)	*jiǎosī (mì)* – tangled silk e.g., 紙 (zhǐ – paper)　　　綢 (chóu – silk)
草	cǎo – grass	→	艹	*cǎo zì tóu* – top of grass character e.g., 花 (huā – flowers)　　　菜 (cài – vegetable)

The following characters show very little change when used as radicals. For example,

金	jīn – gold	→	釒	e.g., 鐘 (zhōng – clock)　　　錢 (qián – money)
食	shí – food/eat	→	飠	e.g., 飯 (fàn – rice)　　　餓 (è – hungry)
衣	yī – clothes	→	衤	e.g., 裙 (qún – skirt)　　　褲 (kù – pants)
示	shì – display/reveal	→	礻	e.g., 禮 (lǐ – ritual)　　　視 (shì – to view)
玉	yù – jade	→	王	e.g., 珍 (zhēn – treasure)　　　珠 (zhū – pearl)
竹	zhú – bamboo	→	⺮	e.g., 籃 (lán – basket)　　　筆 (bǐ – pen)
火	huǒ – fire	→	火	e.g., 炸 (zhà – to fry)　　　爆 (bào – to explode)
足	zú – foot	→	𧾷	e.g., 跑 (pǎo – to run)　　　跳 (tiào – to jump)

A few radicals do not have corresponding characters and can only be used as a component of a character to provide the semantic clue to the character:

宀	mián	*bǎo gài tóu*, precious cover head, which is used to imply "roof" e.g., 家 (jiā – home)　　　室 (shì – room)
辶	chuò	*zǒuzhī*, walking zhi, used to imply walking or running e.g., 道 (dào – path/way)　　　逃 (táo – to run/escape)

練習三   Practice (3)

Circle the radicals in the following characters:

緞	逛	珍	笛	釘	衫	飽	燒	神	寓
duàn	guàng	zhēn	dí	dīng	shān	bǎo	shāo	shén	yù
satin	stroll	treasure	flute	nail	jacket	full	burn	god	apartment

Strokes

The basic elements of Chinese characters are strokes. In order to know how to write Chinese characters, one must know how to write each stroke. Knowledge of strokes will not only lay the foundation for character writing, but is essential for looking up a word in a Chinese dictionary.

There are a total of 31 different kinds of strokes used in Chinese writing. Among these are eight basic strokes that are most commonly used. These eight strokes are illustrated as follows:

1. 橫 héng (Horizontal stroke)		2. 豎 shù (Vertical stroke)		3. 撇 piě (Left-slanted stroke)		4. 捺 nà (Right-slanted stroke)	
一	王	丨	中	丿	大	乀	文
5. 點 diǎn (Dot)		**6. 提 tí (Up-lift stroke)**		**7. 鉤 gōu (Hook)**		**8. 折 zhé (Bend stroke)**	
丶	游	╱	泳	亅	小	㇇	姐

In writing Chinese characters, the correct stroke order should be followed so that the characters look "right" to native Chinese. The following principles should be observed in the order of strokes:

Top first, then bottom:

　　e.g.，　交　⟶　亠　六　交

Left first, then right:

　　e.g.，　很　⟶　彳　很

Horizontal first, then vertical:

　　e.g.，　十　⟶　一　十

Left-slanted first, then right-slanted:

　　e.g.，　父　⟶　八　⺈　父

Center first, then both sides:

　　e.g.，　小　⟶　亅　小　小

Outside first, then inside:

　　e.g.，　同　⟶　冂　同

Enter first, and then close the door:

　　e.g.，　國　⟶　冂　國　國

練習四　Practice (4)

F-38 For each of the following characters, write out the first stroke:

交 ＿＿＿　　月 ＿＿＿　　水 ＿＿＿　　去 ＿＿＿　　中 ＿＿＿

不 ＿＿＿　　他 ＿＿＿　　洪 ＿＿＿　　吃 ＿＿＿　　代 ＿＿＿

F-39 Write the following characters progressively, following the correct stroke order:

再 ＿＿＿＿＿＿＿＿＿＿＿＿＿＿＿＿＿＿＿＿＿＿＿＿＿＿＿＿＿

但 ＿＿＿＿＿＿＿＿＿＿＿＿＿＿＿＿＿＿＿＿＿＿＿＿＿＿＿＿＿

因 ＿＿＿＿＿＿＿＿＿＿＿＿＿＿＿＿＿＿＿＿＿＿＿＿＿＿＿＿＿

京 ＿＿＿＿＿＿＿＿＿＿＿＿＿＿＿＿＿＿＿＿＿＿＿＿＿＿＿＿＿

看 ＿＿＿＿＿＿＿＿＿＿＿＿＿＿＿＿＿＿＿＿＿＿＿＿＿＿＿＿＿

In writing Chinese characters, the following principles guide the directions of the strokes:

a. Start the horizontal strokes from the left and move to the right.
b. Start the vertical strokes from the top and move downwards.
c. Left-slanted strokes start from the upper right and go towards the lower left.
d. Right-slanted strokes move from top left to bottom right.

Here are some examples:

The shape of Chinese character strokes follows strict rules. A tiny change in the shape may change the meaning of the whole character. For example, 貝 [bèi] means "shell" and 見 [jiàn] means "to see." The top parts of the two characters are the same, but the bottom parts are different. Though the difference is not very conspicuous, it needs to be taken seriously. Otherwise, misunderstanding may result.

Writing Chinese characters may be difficult but it is also great fun. Character writing can be an art as well. If you put some effort into it, practice, and learn the cultural implications of characters, you may find writing Chinese an enjoyable and rewarding experience.

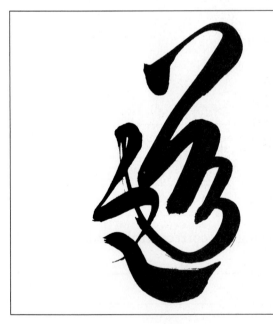

道可道，非常道。
Dào kě dào, fēi cháng dào.

The path that can be articulated is not the eternal path.

老子：道德經
Laozi: Dao De Jing

課 堂 用 語
Kè táng yòng yǔ

Chinese characters	Pinyin	Meaning
1. 同學們好。	Tóngxuémen hǎo.	Hello, students.
2. 你們好。	Nǐmen hǎo.	Hello, everyone.
3. 大家好。	Dàjiā hǎo.	Hello, everybody.
4. 老師好。	Lǎoshī hǎo.	Hello, teacher.
5. 你好。	Nǐ hǎo.	Hello.
6. 上課。	Shàng kè.	Class begins.
7. 下課。	Xià kè.	Class is dismissed.
8. 請跟我說。	Qǐng gēn wǒ shuō.	Please repeat after me.
9. 對(了)。	Duì (le).	Correct.
10. 不對。	Bú duì.	Incorrect.
11. 很好。	Hěn hǎo.	Very good.
12. 謝謝。	Xièxie.	Thank you.
13. 不客氣。	Bú kèqi.	You are welcome.
14. 再見。	Zài jiàn.	Goodbye.
15. 請你再說一遍。	Qǐng nǐ zài shuō yíbiàn.	Please say it again.
16. 中文怎麼說?	Zhōngwén zěnme shuō?	How do you say ____ in Chinese?
17. 英文怎麼說?	Yīngwén zěnme shuō?	How do you say ____ in English?
18. 請打開書。	Qǐng dǎkāi shū.	Please open your book.
19. 請看第__頁。	Qǐng kàn dì __ yè.	Please take a look at page __.
20. 請看第__題。	Qǐng kàn dì __ tí.	Please take a look at question __.
21. 請念課文。	Qǐng niàn kèwén.	Please read the text.
22. 請跟我念。	Qǐng gēn wǒ niàn.	Please read after me.
23. 請你念。	Qǐng nǐ niàn.	You read, please.
24. 請你寫。	Qǐng nǐ xiě.	You write, please.
25. 懂了嗎?	Dǒng le ma?	Do you understand?
26. 懂了。	Dǒng le.	Understand.
27. 不懂。	Bù dǒng.	Don't understand.
28. 有問題嗎?	Yǒu wèntí ma?	Any questions?
29. 我有問題。	Wǒ yǒu wèntí.	I have questions.
30. 沒有問題。	Méi yǒu wèntí.	No questions.

Chinese characters	Pinyin	Meaning
31. 練習練習	Liànxi liànxi.	Practice a bit.
32. 表演	biǎoyǎn	Perform
33. 作業	zuòyè	Homework
34. 生詞	shēngcí	Vocabulary
35. 考試	kǎoshì	Test
36. 生詞考試	shēngcí kǎoshì	Character quiz
37. 第一聲	dì yī shēng	The first tone
38. 第二聲	dì èr shēng	The second tone
39. 第三聲	dì sān shēng	The third tone
40. 第四聲	dì sì shēng	The fourth tone
41. 輕聲	qīng shēng	Neutral tone
42. 第幾聲?	Dì jǐ shēng?	Which tone?

43.

一	二	三	四	五	六	七	八	九	十
yī	èr	sān	sì	wǔ	liù	qī	bā	jiǔ	shí
one	two	three	four	five	six	seven	eight	nine	ten

課堂用語練習 CLASSROOM EXPRESSIONS AND EXERCISES

Form groups of two to three students and practice the following situations:

Items 1–14

F-40 The teacher enters the classroom, greets the students, and starts the class. Try to use the following phrases: tóng xué men hǎo, nǐ hǎo, shàng kè, qǐng gēn wǒ shuō, duì (le), hěn hǎo, zài jiàn.

F-41 Students introduce themselves in turn to the class (greeting, their names, where they are from . . . etc.)

Example: Nǐmen hǎo. Wǒ shì ____. Wǒ cóng ____ lái. . . . Hǎo. Xièxie. Zàijiàn.
Hello, everyone, I am ___. I am from _____. . . . OK, thank you. Bye-bye.

Items 15–27

F-42 On campus you run into one of your Chinese classmates. Greet and introduce yourselves to each other in Chinese. (Include greeting, names, where you come from, very good, bye . . . etc.)

Items 28–42

F-43 In the library, you run into one of your Chinese classmates. Greet and introduce yourselves in Chinese, and then practice Pinyin and the four tones. (Remember to give your partners some feedback!)

F-44 Before class, you are waiting outside the classroom with your Chinese classmates. You would like to take the chance to get to know them better (and you might want to review yesterday's lessons).

F-45 On campus, you run into your Chinese teacher. Greet your teacher, and then ask some questions about Pinyin and tones, and how to say something in English or Chinese.

F-46 You have some Chinese friends and would like to ask them some questions. (For example, ask how to say the following words in Chinese or English: textbooks, Chinese, friends — some examples can be from Classroom Expressions items.)

F-47 You are the Chinese teacher teaching Pinyin practice, Lesson 1, Lesson 2, and Classroom Expressions.

詞類簡稱　ABBREVIATIONS OF PARTS OF SPEECH

Adj.	= adjective	形容詞	[xíngróngcí]	e.g.,	好 [hǎo] (good) 美 [měi] (beautiful)
Adv.	= adverb	副詞	[fùcí]	e.g.,	很 [hěn] (very) 也 [yě] (also)
Aux.	= auxiliary verb	助動詞	[zhùdòngcí]		
Conj.	= conjunction	連詞	[liáncí]	e.g.,	可是 [kěshì] (but)
Int.	= interjection	嘆詞	[tàncí]	e.g.,	啊 [a] (Ah?)
M.W.	= measure word (or classifier)	量詞	[liàngcí]	e.g.,	一本 [běn] 書 (a book)
N.	= noun	名詞	[míngcí]	e.g.,	老師 [lǎoshī] (teacher) 書 [shū] (book)
Num.	= numeral	數詞	[shùcí]	e.g.,	二 [èr] (two) 十 [shí] (ten)
Part.	= particle	助詞	[zhùcí]	e.g.,	嗎 [ma] (turn a sentence into a question)
Prep.	= preposition	介詞	[jiècí]	e.g.,	在 [zài] (in; at) 從 [cóng] (from)
Pron.	= pronoun	代詞	[dàicí]	e.g.,	你 [nǐ] (you) 他 [tā] (he)
V.	= verb	動詞	[dòngcí]	e.g.,	學 [xué] (to study) 說 [shuō] (to speak) 跑 [pǎo] (to run)
V.O.	= verb + object	動賓	[dòng bīn]	e.g.,	說中文 [shuō Zhōngwén] (to speak Chinese)
V.C.	= verb + complement	動補	[dòng bǔ]	e.g.,	搬過來 [bān guò lái] (to move over) 打破 [dǎ pò] (to hit-broken)

你好!
Hello!

- Conduct simple greetings in Chinese
- Ask simple yes/no questions
- Answer simple yes/no questions
- Discuss other people

Greetings are common in many different situations.

Shaking hands is a common gesture of greeting among Chinese people.

Chinese people use both hands when making a toast.

生詞   VOCABULARY

核心詞   Core Vocabulary

	TRADITIONAL	SIMPLIFIED	PINYIN		
1.	你	你	nǐ	Pron.	you
2.	好	好	hǎo	Adj.	good, well
3.	是	是	shì	V.	to be, (affirmative answer) yes
4.	學生 學	学生 学	xuésheng xué	N. V.	student to study, to learn
5.	嗎	吗	ma	Part.	(used at the end of a declarative sentence to transform it into a question)
6.	我	我	wǒ	Pron.	I, me
7.	呢	呢	ne	Part.	(used at the end of an interrogative sentence)
8.	也	也	yě	Adv.	also
9.	他	他	tā	Pron.	he, him
10.	不	不	bù	Adv.	(used to form a negative) not, no
11.	老師	老师	lǎoshī	N.	teacher

語文知識   LANGUAGE LINK

The Sentence Patterns provide models that will help you with the Language in Use section. In both sections, pay attention to the grammar points, vocabulary, and expressions.

句型   Sentence Patterns

A: 你好!
Nǐhǎo!

B: 你好!
Nǐhǎo!

A: 你是學生嗎?
Nǐ shì xuésheng ma?

B: 我是學生。你呢?
Wǒ shì xuésheng. Nǐ ne?

A: 他也是學生嗎?
Tā yě shì xuésheng ma?

B: 不，他不是學生。
Bù, tā bú shì xuésheng.

課文　Language in Use: 你好! Nǐhǎo!

MARY: 你好!
Nǐhǎo!

JOHN: 你好!
Nǐhǎo!

MARY: 你是學生嗎?
Nǐ shì xuésheng ma?

JOHN: 我是學生。你呢?
Wǒ shì xuésheng. Nǐ ne?

MARY: 我也是學生。
Wǒ yě shì xuésheng.

JOHN: 他呢? 他是學生嗎?
Tā ne? Tā shì xuésheng ma?

MARY: 他不是學生。他是老師。
Tā bú shì xuésheng. Tā shì lǎoshī.

注釋 LANGUAGE NOTES

你好

你好 means "Hello!" It is a common greeting that may be used for "Good morning," "Good afternoon," or "Good evening."

Note: Tone change in 你好:
When two 3rd tones co-occur, the first 3rd tone is pronounced as a 2nd tone.

3rd tone + 3rd tone → 2nd tone + 3rd tone
你好 nǐhǎo   → pronounced as [níhǎo]

Tone Change of 不 in 不是

Note: When 不 is followed by the 4th tone, it is pronounced as a 2nd tone as illustrated below:

不 + 4th tone → 不 is pronounced as a 2nd tone
不是 bù shì → pronounced as [bú shì]

語法 GRAMMAR

Chinese Sentences

Chinese sentences usually consist of a subject and a predicate. For example,

Subject	Predicate
你	好

你好 ("Hello!" or "How are you?") is a common expression of greeting. 好 is an adjective. In Chinese, adjectives are stative verbs that can function independently as a predicate.

The Pronouns 我, 你 and 他

我, 你, and 他 are used as the 1st person, 2nd person, and 3rd person pronouns, respectively. Note that Chinese pronouns do not change case like English pronouns. For example, the pronoun 我 is used for both "I" and "me."

The Interrogative Particle　嗎

The most common way to turn a sentence into a question is to place the particle 嗎 at the end of the sentence.

你是老師 。　　　　你是老師嗎?
You are a teacher.　　Are you a teacher?

他是學生 。　　　　他是學生嗎?
He is a student.　　　Is he a student?

The Modal Particle　呢

The particle 呢 is used after a noun, pronoun, or noun phrase to turn the sentence into a question that could be translated as "How about N?" 呢 is used when a topic or some piece of information is established or shared in the preceding statements. For example,

A: 你是學生嗎?　　　Are you a student?
B: 我是學生 。你呢?　I am a student. How about you?
A: 我也是學生 。　　　I am also a student.

是　Sentences

是 is a linking verb. It functions almost as an equal sign between nouns, pronouns, or nouns and pronouns. For example,

我是學生 。他是老師 。　　　　I am a student. He is a teacher.
(between a pronoun and a noun)

老師是中國人 [Zhōngguórén] 。　　The teacher is Chinese.
(between two nouns)

To negate the 是 sentence, simply place the adverb 不 before 是. To turn the 是 sentence into a question, we may simply add the interrogative particle 嗎 to the end of the sentence. The 是 sentences can be illustrated as follows:

Interrogative form:　A是B嗎?　e.g. 他是學生嗎?　Is he a student?
Affirmative form:　　A是B　　e.g. 他是學生 。　He is a student.
Negative form:　　　A不是B　e.g. 他不是學生 。He is not a student.

The Adverb　也

也 is an adverb placed before a verb. It is often translated as "also" or "too." Note that 也 cannot be placed at the beginning or end of a sentence as "also" or "too" can in English. For example, the English sentence, "I am a student and a teacher too" would be expressed as "我是學生，也是老師" in Chinese.

補充課文 ⊶⊶⊶ SUPPLEMENTARY PRACTICE

This selection will help you test your comprehension of the grammar and vocabulary you have learned in this lesson. Be prepared to answer questions about the meaning of the passage.

你好! 我不是學生，我是老師。他也不是學生，他是教授。你呢? 你是學生嗎? 你是教授嗎?

Note: 教授 [jiàoshòu]: professor

練習   ACTIVITIES

I. Listening Exercises

1-1   In each pair, circle the one your instructor pronounces:

1. tā/dā	2. lǎo/nǎo	3. bō/pō	4. wǔ/nǔ	5. hé/lé
6. shì/xì	7. mà/nà	8. néng/léng	9. xué/jué	10. tǎo/dǎo

1-2   In each pair, circle the one your instructor pronounces:

1. bú/bó	2. láo/lái	3. nā/nē	4. mà/mù	5. shì/shè
6. xī/xū	7. yuè/yè	8. wǒ/wǔ	9. nǐ/ně	10. hà/hé

1-3   Listen to the instructor pronounce the following words, and then add the tone marks:

1. hao	2. laoshi	3. ni	4. ta	5. bu
6. ye	7. xuesheng	8. shi	9. wo	10. ne

1-4   Read the following poem, paying special attention to the tones and the rhythm:

Jìng Yè Sī (Lǐ Bó/Lǐ Bái)	靜夜思 (李白)	Thoughts on a Tranquil Night (Li, Bo/Li, Bai)
Chuáng qián míng yuè guāng,	床前明月光，	In front of my bed, bright moonlight,
Yí shì dì shàng shuāng?	疑是地上霜。	Can it be frost on the ground?
Jǔ tóu wàng míng yuè,	舉頭望明月，	Lifting my head, I gaze upon the bright moon,
Dī tóu sī gù xiāng.	低頭思故鄉。	Lowering my head, I think of my hometown.

Note: 李白 Lǐ Bái is pronounced as Lǐ Bó in Classical Chinese.

II. Character Exercises

1-5　Read the following words and sentences:

學生	老師
他是學生。	我是老師。
他不是學生。	我不是老師。
他也不是學生。	我也不是老師。

Now try to use the following characters to make words, phrases, and then sentences:

1. 你　　2. 好　　3. 是　　4. 嗎　　5. 我　　6. 呢

7. 也　　8. 他　　9. 不　　10. 生　　11. 學　　12. 師

1-6　Match the following characters with the English expressions:

老師	student
你好	and you
不	also
你呢	teacher
也	hello
學生	not

1-7　Create flashcards.

To help learn new characters, and also as an aid for future review, students are strongly encouraged to create flashcards for each lesson's vocabulary items. See the following example for a suggested format:

FRONT

學生
xuésheng

我是學生
I am a student.

BACK

(N.) student

III. Grammar Exercises

1-8 Put the word given in the brackets in the appropriate place:

1. 你　學生　　。　　　　　　(是)
2. 不　是　老師　。　　　　　(我)
3. 他　不　是　學生　。　　　(也)
4. 你　不　是　老師　?　　　　(嗎)

1-9 Fill in the blanks with either 也, 不, or 是 to complete the dialogue:

A: 請問 [qǐng wèn] (may I ask)，你 ＿＿ 學生嗎?

B: 我 ＿＿ 學生。你 ＿＿ ＿＿ 學生嗎?

A: 不，我 ＿＿ ＿＿ 學生，我 ＿＿ 老師。他 ＿＿ ＿＿ 老師。

B: 老師好!

A: 你好!

1-10 Fill in the blanks with "嗎" or "呢":

A: 你好! 你是學生 ＿＿ ?

B: 是，你 ＿＿ ? 你也是學生 ＿＿ ?

A: 不，我不是學生。我是老師。

B: 他也是老師 ＿＿ ?

A: 不，他是學生。

IV. Communicative Activities

1-11 Picture talk: With the help of the clues provided, give an introduction for each of the following pictures (say as much as you can).

I
Lǐ Xiǎowén
(student)

You
Wú Hànzhōng
(teacher)

He
Wáng Xuéwén
(student)

She
Dīng Wényīng
(professor)

1-12 Find a partner, choose a role from the pictures above, and create a dialogue.

1-13 Suppose you are at a welcoming party for new students. Try to introduce yourself to a new student and start a conversation. Remember, your professor is also at the party.

文化知識 ⟨∞∞⟩ **Culture Link**

文化點滴 CULTURE NOTES

問候語 [Wèn hòu yǔ]
Basic Chinese Greetings

Chinese greetings can be classified into two types: (1) exchanged greetings and (2) question-and-answer greetings.

(1) Exchanged greetings:

Both parties say the same words or phrases almost at the same time. The most common ones are "你好！" "早！" and "嗨！"

Exchanged greetings	Features
你好 [Nǐ hǎo!] (Hello!)	• Usually used for the first meeting. • Often used by receptionists when taking an incoming phone call or greeting visitors.
早 [Zǎo!] (Morning!)	• Used in the early and late morning.
嗨 [Hāi!] (Hi!)	• Taken from English "Hi!"

(2) Question-and-answer greetings:

Like the English "How are you?" and its answer, "Fine," these simple questions and answers are often fixed expressions. They should not be taken literally as questions and answers. The common greetings are "你好嗎？" "怎麼樣？" and "你吃了嗎？"

9

Question	Common answer		Feature
你好嗎？ [Nǐ hǎo ma?] 好嗎？ [Hǎo ma?] *How are you?*	很好 [Hěn hǎo] 還好 [Hái hǎo] 不錯 [Bú cuò]	*Fine.* *All right.* *Not bad.*	• Frequently used when you haven't seen someone for a while.
怎麼樣？ [Zěn me yàng?] *What's up?* *What's new?*	很好 [Hěn hǎo] 還好 [Hái hǎo] 不錯 [Bú cuò]	*Fine.* *All right.* *Not bad.*	• Can also be taken as an invitation to start a conversation.
(你)吃了嗎？ [(Nǐ) chī le ma?] *Have you eaten yet?*	吃了 [Chī le] 還沒 [Hái méi]	*I have.* *I haven't yet.*	• Used close to meal times. • Not really asking whether you have eaten or not.

Another interesting aspect of Chinese greetings is that they often consist of stating the obvious, as in the following examples:

When running into an acquaintance while grocery shopping, a Chinese person might say:

A: 買菜啊？　　[Mǎi cài a?]　　(So you're) grocery shopping, eh?
B: 嗯，買菜。　[En, mǎi cài.]　Yes, (I'm) grocery shopping.

Other examples might include:

看電視啊？　[Kàn diàn shì a?]　(So you're) watching TV, eh?
做功課啊？　[Zuò gōng kè a?]　(So you're) doing homework, eh?

Shaking hands is a common Chinese gesture of greeting or introduction.

During an election, candidates show up everywhere to greet, campaign, and ask for votes. Several candidates visited this wedding banquet (in Taiwan).

Questions:

1. When you come to Chinese class, which greeting do you use to your classmates? How about to your teacher? How about when you run into your Chinese friends in a Chinese restaurant?

2. Can you provide any similar greetings in English or other languages?

趣味中文　FUN WITH CHINESE

> 學而時習之。
> to learn/study and review it from time to time

xué	ér	shí	xí	zhī
學	而	時	習	之
learn/study	and	often	review	it

This famous saying of Confucius encourages his disciples to study.

Question:

Are there any similar sayings in English or other languages to encourage students to study?

行動吧!　LET'S GO!

服務台　Service Stand

This is 吳大中's first time traveling in China, Taiwan, and Hong Kong. He has had several chances to greet people with 你好. He has also sought out the sign below several times, beginning with when he needed to ask for information at the airport.

Useful words and expressions:

服務(服务) [fúwù]: service
服務台(服务台) [fúwùtái]: information counter
台 [tái]: stand, counter

第二課
LESSON

2

您貴姓？
What's Your Surname?

- Exchange names
- Get to know each other
- Find out who someone else is

Exchanging names is a common way to start getting to know one another.

Upon first meeting someone in a business setting, it is common to exchange business cards, which usually include one's full name and title.

生詞　VOCABULARY

核心詞　Core Vocabulary

TRADITIONAL	SIMPLIFIED	PINYIN		
1. 您	您	nín	Pron.	(polite) you
2. 貴	贵	guì	Adj.	noble, honored, expensive
3. 姓	姓	xìng	N. V.	surname, family name to be surnamed
4. 請問 請 問	请问 请 问	qǐng wèn qǐng wèn	V.	may I ask (polite) please to ask
5. 的	的	de	Part.	(a structural particle)
6. 英文	英文	Yīngwén	N.	English (language)
7. 名字	名字	míngzi	N.	name
8. 中文	中文	Zhōngwén	N.	Chinese (language)
9. 叫	叫	jiào	V.	to call
10. 什麼	什么	shénme	Pron.	what
11. 她	她	tā	Pron.	she, her
12. 誰	谁	shéi/shuí (shéi also pronounced as shuí in some regions)	Pron.	who, whom
13. 同學	同学	tóngxué	N.	classmate

專名　Proper Nouns

TRADITIONAL	SIMPLIFIED	PINYIN		
1. 李文中	李文中	Lǐ Wénzhōng	N.	(name) Wenzhong Li
2. 吳小美	吴小美	Wú Xiǎoměi	N.	(name) Xiaomei Wu
3. 于英	于英	Yú Yīng	N.	(name) Ying Yu

補充詞　Supplementary Vocabulary

	TRADITIONAL	SIMPLIFIED	PINYIN		
1.	漢語	汉语	Hànyǔ	N.	Chinese (language)
2.	英語	英语	Yīngyǔ	N.	English (language)

語文知識　LANGUAGE LINK

The Sentence Patterns provide models that will help you with the Language in Use section. In both sections, pay attention to the grammar points, vocabulary, and expressions.

句型　Sentence Patterns

A: 請問您貴姓?
Qǐng wèn nín guì xìng?

B: 我姓李。
Wǒ xìng Lǐ.

A: 你叫什麼名字?
Nǐ jiào shénme míngzi?

B: 我叫吳小美。
Wǒ jiào Wú Xiǎoměi.

A: 她是誰?
Tā shì shéi?

B: 她是于英。
Tā shì Yú Yīng.

課文   Language in Use: 您貴姓? Nín guì xìng?

MARY: 你好！請問您貴姓？
Nǐhǎo! Qǐng wèn nín guì xìng?

JOHN: 我姓李，我的英文名字是John Lee，中文名字是
Wǒ xìng Lǐ, wǒ de Yīngwén míngzi shì John Lee, Zhōngwén míngzi shì

李文中。你呢？請問你叫什麼名字？
Lǐ Wénzhōng. Nǐ ne? Qǐng wèn nǐ jiào shénme míngzi?

MARY: 我叫Mary。我的英文名字是Mary Wood，
Wǒ jiào Mary. Wǒ de Yīngwén míngzi shì Mary Wood,

中文名字是吳小美。
Zhōngwén míngzi shì Wú Xiǎoměi.

JOHN: 她呢？她是誰？
Tā ne? Tā shì shéi?

MARY: 她是我的同學于英。
Tā shì wǒ de tóngxué Yú Yīng.

注釋　LANGUAGE NOTES

The Verb　叫；請問

The verb 叫 ("to call" or "to be called") is used to ask one's full name or given name. "請問" means "May I ask . . ." "請 . . ." is an expression of polite request.

Remember to add "請問" (May I ask . . .) to be polite when asking someone's name in Chinese.

For example,

請問，你叫什麼名字？　May I have your name, please?

Chinese Names　姓名

A person's name in Chinese has two parts: the surname 姓 and the given name 名. The word order of a Chinese name is different from that of an English name. In a Chinese name, the surname comes before the given name. For example, in the Chinese names 吳小美, 李文中, and 于英, 吳, 李, and 于 are the surnames. 小美, 文中, and 英 are the given names. Chinese given names are commonly one or two syllables. In all but a few cases, Chinese surnames are one syllable.

Surname　　　　　Given name
吳　　　　　　　小美
李　　　　　　　文中
于　　　　　　　英

語法　GRAMMAR

您

您 is the polite form of the pronoun for the second person singular 你. It is normally used to address one's elders or those with a higher social status. For example,

<u>Situation:</u>　A student and a teacher
Student:　李老師，您好!　　How are you, Teacher Li?
Teacher:　你好。　　　　　How are you?

For the sake of politeness or courtesy it is also used to address someone of similar age or social status, but only at the first meeting.

<u>Situation:</u>　A and B are about the same age, and this is their first meeting
A: 您好!　　　　　　　Hi! *or* How are you?
B: 您好!　　　　　　　Hi! *or* How are you?

您貴姓

您貴姓 is a polite way of asking someone's surname. The person who is asked the question "您貴姓?" commonly replies with his/her surname or his/her full name. Note that one should never use 貴姓 in the reply when somebody asks your surname.

For example,

| A: | 請問，您貴姓? | May I ask your surname? |
| B: | 我姓李。 | My surname is Li. |

| A: | 請問，您貴姓? | May I ask your surname? |
| B: | 我姓李。我叫李文中。 | My surname is Li, and my full name is Wenzhong Li. |

The Interrogative Pronouns   什麼，誰

As an interrogative pronoun, 什麼 can be used alone to ask "what?" Its most common usage, however, is to be placed before a general noun when requesting more specific information. For example, the Chinese sentence "你叫什麼名字? " can be thought of as "You are called *what* name?" and translated as "What's your name?" The word order in Chinese "who, what, where, which, when, how" questions is usually different from that in English. Chinese does not place the question word at the beginning of the sentence. In Chinese, the question word occurs where the expected answer would be. That is, the question and the answer have a similar word order as illustrated below.

| 你叫什麼名字? | What's your name? |
| 我叫小美。 | I am called 小美. |

誰 (who, whom) is an interrogative pronoun. As mentioned above, the Chinese word order of a question formed with an interrogative word is the same word order as would be used in the answer. Thus we see question-and-answer combinations like the following:

| Question: | 他們是誰? | Who are those people? |
| Answer: | 他們是我的同學。 | They are my classmates. |

The position of 誰 in the question is the same as the position of 我的同學 in the answer.

Again, remember that this contrasts with the English word order. Another thing to remember is that there is no need to put 嗎 at the end of the sentence to mark it as a question, since the interrogative word already fulfills this function.

The Particle   的

In Chinese word order, a modifier typically precedes the word or phrase it modifies. The possessive construction is formed by placing the particle 的 after a noun to form the possessor. It is similar to the "'s" of English indicating the genitive association.

For example,

我的	名字	my name
modifier	modified	

教師的	名字	teacher's name
modifier	modified	

老師的	學生	teacher's students
modifier	modified	

補充課文 ○━○━○ SUPPLEMENTARY PRACTICE

This selection will help you test your comprehension of the grammar and vocabulary you have learned in this lesson. Be prepared to answer questions about the meaning of the passage.

大家好！我來自我介紹一下。我姓吳，我叫吳小美，我的英文名字是Mary Wood。你呢？請問您貴姓？你叫什麼名字？她呢？她是誰？你不知道，對不對？沒關係，我來告訴你吧。她是我的同學，她叫于英。

Notes: 大家 [dàjiā]: everybody
　　　來 [lái]: come (placed in front of a verb, indicates the intention of doing something)
　　　自我介紹 [zìwǒjièshào]: self-introduction
　　　一下 [yíxià]: a little bit
　　　知道 [zhīdào]: to know
　　　告訴 [gàosu]: to tell

練習 ACTIVITIES

I. Listening Exercises

2-1　In each pair, circle the one your instructor pronounces:

　　1. nín/lín　　2. wén/mén　　3. xǐng/qǐng　　4. zì/zhì　　5. níng/míng
　　6. qiào/jiào　7. tǒng/dǒng　8. miǎo/xiǎo　9. yìng/xìng　10. shénme/zénme

2-2　In each pair, circle the one your instructor pronounces:

　　1. guǐ/gěi　　2. yīng/yīn　　3. shén/shéi　　4. wài/wèi　　5. mén/mín
　　6. jiào/jiù　　7. zì/cì　　　8. xǐng/xiǎo　9. tóng/tíng　10. mèi/miàn

2-3   Listen to the instructor pronounce the following words, then add the tone marks:

1. mingzi   2. tongxue   3. qing   4. Yingwen   5. shenme
6. nin shi   7. shei   8. guixing   9. Zhongwen   10. jiao

2-4   Form groups of three to four members. Take turns reading the following tongue twister out loud, as quickly as you can. Each group will select one member to represent the group in a class competition.

sìshí: 四十   forty

shísì: 十四   fourteen

shì: 是   is, are

Sìshí shì sìshí.	四十是四十。	Forty is forty.
Shísì shì shísì.	十四是十四。	Fourteen is fourteen.
Sìshí búshì shísì.	四十不是十四。	Forty is not fourteen.
Shísì yě búshì sìshí.	十四也不是四十。	Fourteen is not forty, either.

II. Character Exercises

2-5   Read the following words, phrases, and sentences:

名字	姓
什麼名字	貴姓
你叫什麼名字?	您貴姓?
你的老師叫什麼名字?	請問您貴姓?
你的中文老師叫什麼名字?	請問您的老師貴姓?

Now try to use the following characters to make words, phrases, and then sentences:

1. 您   2. 姓   3. 請   4. 問   5. 的   6. 英
7. 文   8. 中   9. 叫   10. 她   11. 誰   12. 同

2-6   Write the Chinese characters for the following words:

1. name _____ _____   2. please _____   3. who _____

4. ask _____   5. surname _____   6. English _____ _____

7. to call _____   8. what _____ _____

2-7　Create flashcards.

To help learn new characters, and also as an aid for future review, students are strongly encouraged to create flashcards for each lesson's vocabulary items. See the following example for a suggested format:

FRONT　　　　　　　　　　　　　　　　BACK

名字
míngzi

我的名字是吳小美。
My name is Xiaomei Wu.

(N.) name

III. Grammar Exercises

2-8　Substitution exercises: Create sentences following the examples given:

1. <u>她</u>是誰?
   <u>她</u>是<u>小美</u>。

你	李文中
小美	我的同學
于英	我的老師

2. <u>你</u>叫什麼名字?
   我叫<u>李文中</u>。

他	吳小同
你的同學	于學文

3. 請問,<u>你的</u>名字是什麼?
   <u>我的</u>名字是<u>李文中</u>。

她的	于文英
你的老師的	李師美
他的同學的	吳同文
你的中文老師的	文漢中

2-9 Form pairs. Following the example given, ask and answer as many questions as you can on each of the following sentences:

For example,   我的同學叫小美。
　　　　　　　　　你的同學叫小美嗎?
　　　　　　　　　誰叫小美?
　　　　　　　　　誰的同學叫小美?
　　　　　　　　　你的同學叫什麼名字?
　　　　　　　　　你的同學的名字是什麼?

Hint: 誰，什麼，什麼名字，誰的，貴姓。

1. 她是李小英。
2. 我姓吳。
3. 我的老師的名字是于文中。
4. 我的同學姓文，他的中文名字是文同生。

IV. Communicative Activities

2-10 Form groups of three. Each group should have a piece of paper. Go around the classroom and get acquainted with as many people as you can. First introduce yourself, then find out what other students' names are. Write them down in Pinyin on the paper. Based on the information you have collected, design a roster of your classmates for later use.

For example,

	xìng 姓 surname	míngzi 名字 name
1.	Wáng	Xiǎoměi
2.	. . .	. . .
3.	. . .	. . .
4.	Wú	Wénzhōng

2-11 Introductions:

Write your name on the blackboard. Add the Pinyin and the English translation for each character in your name. Then introduce yourself to the class.

Useful expressions:

大家 [dàjiā] (everyone) 好　　　　　　　　你們 [nǐmen] ([pl.] you) 好
我姓......　　　　　　　　　　　　　　　我叫......
我的英文名字是......，中文名字是......
我是學生，不是老師。
他/她是我的同學。他/她的英文名字是......，中文名字是......

文化知識 ⊖⊖⊖ Culture Link

文化點滴　CULTURE NOTES

中文姓名 [Zhōngwén xìngmíng]
Chinese Names

Chinese names have two parts: a 姓 [xìng] (surname) and a 名 [míng] (given name). In a Chinese name, the surname precedes the given name.

In general, the surname is inherited from the father. Chinese surnames are usually referred to as the 百家姓 [bǎi jiā xìng] (hundreds of family surnames), which is the name of a famous listing of Chinese surnames. Most Chinese surnames are monosyllabic, such as 趙 [Zhào], 錢 [Qián], 孫 [Sūn], 李 [Lǐ], which happen to be the first four surnames on the 百家姓 list. A few surnames are disyllabic (having two syllables), the most common being 歐陽 [Ōuyáng] and 司馬 [Sīmǎ].

A child's given name is significant and meaningful. It is generally chosen by the parents and usually has one or two characters.

Naming a child generally involves two important considerations. First, the given names that the parents choose usually reflect the parents' hopes for their child. Parents always hope to have a virtuous child who becomes successful and achieves great things. For boys, honor, success, strength, bravery, and brilliance are common themes in names. Girls' names are usually related to beauty, purity, and elegance.

Siblings sometimes have similar or identical elements in their given names. The shared elements can be either the first or the second character of a two-character given name, as illustrated below:

美 [měi] beautiful, fine 　　the first character is shared	傑 [jié] heroic, outstanding 　　the second character is shared
美玲 [Měilíng] 　　beautiful, cute, and bright	志傑 [Zhìjié] 　　ambitious and outstanding
美玉 [Měiyù] 　　beautiful, fine, and delicate	俊傑 [Jùnjié] 　　handsome and outstanding
美秀 [Měixiù] 　　beautiful and brilliant	豪傑 [Háojié] 　　talented and outstanding

23

In order to help the child have a prosperous and lucky future, parents, especially those in Taiwan, usually also consult with a fortuneteller. The fortuneteller will match the name with the child's birthday and provide advice.

Common one-syllable Chinese surnames:

Zhào	Qián	Sūn	Lǐ		Féng	Chén	Chǔ	Wèi		Zhū	Qín	Yóu	Xǔ
趙	錢	孫	李		馮	陳	褚	衛		朱	秦	尤	許
Kǒng	Cáo	Yán	Huà		Qī	Xiè	Zōu	Yù		Shào	Sū	Pān	Gě
孔	曹	嚴	華		戚	謝	鄒	喻		邵	蘇	潘	葛
Zhōu	Wú	Zhèng	Wáng		Jiǎng	Shěn	Hán	Yáng		Xuē	Lǚ	Shī	Zhāng
周	吳	鄭	王		蔣	沈	韓	楊		薛	呂	施	張
Jīn	Wèi	Táo	Jiāng		Léi	Hè	Dòu	Zhāng		Rén	Fàn	Péng	Láng
金	魏	陶	姜		雷	賀	竇	章		任	范	彭	郎
Yú	Tián	Yáo	Lín		Dīng	Yú	Fāng	Huáng		Hé	Gāo	Xià	Kē
于	田	姚	林		丁	余	方	黃		何	高	夏	柯
Bāo	Xú	Liáng	Zhōng		Hú	Hóng	Cuī	Liú		Qiáo	Liǔ	Gān	Dèng
包	徐	梁	鍾		胡	洪	崔	劉		喬	柳	甘	鄧
Máo	Jiāng	Zhān	Zhuāng		Gǒng	Niú	Zēng	Yóu		Bì	Wū	Guō	Móu
毛	江	詹	莊		鞏	牛	曾	游		畢	巫	郭	牟
Xiè	Dài	Dǒng	Láo		Qiū	Mò	Jiǎ	Miáo		Shǐ	Tāng	Mèng	Táng
謝	戴	董	勞		邱	莫	賈	苗		史	湯	孟	唐

Common two-syllable Chinese surnames:

Sīmǎ	Ōuyáng	Xiàhóu	Zhūgě	Huángfǔ
司馬	歐陽	夏侯	諸葛	皇甫
Dōngfāng	Lìnghú	Duānmù	Shàngguān	Gōngsūn
東方	令狐	端木	上官	公孫

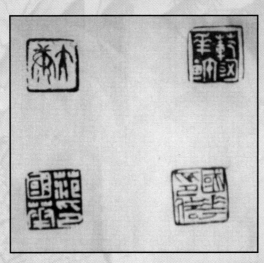

**Jade, wood, and stone are common materials used for carving chops.
Various calligraphic styles can be chosen to add artistic effects.**

A frequently heard sentence in everyday Chinese life is, "Please sign your name and put your chop on it." Chops are also known as seals; they are specially carved stamps that the Chinese use almost as a signature. A chop is still required to legalize a contract, pick up registered mail, withdraw money from the bank, acknowledge receipt of official documents, etc.

Questions:

1. What are the similarities and differences between naming in Chinese and English (or other languages)? (e.g., How is a child's name given? Are there any special considerations?)

2. Do you have any stories to share (e.g., the story of your name; Chinese people you know who share some elements in their names)?

趣味中文　FUN WITH CHINESE

> 同名同姓
> having the same given name and surname

tóng	míng	tóng	xìng
同	名	同	姓
same	name	same	surname

China has one of the largest populations in the world. There are around 1.3 billion people in Mainland China. As a result, it is very common to have the same given name and surname as someone else.

Question:

Have you ever encountered a "同名同姓" situation? What would you do if you did?

行動吧！ LET'S GO!

身份證 ID Card

美英 is helping her Chinese friend translate his identity card for a lawyer. Can you help?

Useful words and expressions:

身份證(身份证) [shēnfèn zhèng]: identity card

性別 [xìngbié]: sex

男 [nán]: male

女 [nǚ]: female

民族 [mínzú]: ethnicity

漢(汉) [hàn]: Han (ethnic group)

出生 [chūshēng]: to be born

年 [nián]: year

月 [yuè]: month

日 [rì]: date

住址 [zhùzhǐ]: address

北京市 [Běijīng shì]: Beijing (Beijing City)

中山路 [Zhōngshān lù]: Zhongshan Road

公安局 [gōng'ān jú]: police bureau

號(号) [hào]: number

編號(编号) [biānhào]: ID number

簽發(签发) [qiānfā]: to be issued

有效期限 [yǒuxiào qīxiàn]: valid date

姓名：王大中

性別：男　　　民族：漢

出生：1970年8月19日

住址：北京市中山路10號

北京市公安局 2002年6月26日 簽發 有效期限10年
編號：111111197008191111

Your translation: _____

_____

_____

Questions:

1. 他叫什麼名字？　_____
2. 他是從哪兒來的？_____

復習   Review

Read Aloud

Read the following sentences aloud. Pay attention to pronunciation and tones.

1. A: 他是學生。
   B: 他不是學生。

2. A: 他也是學生。
   B: 他也是學生嗎?

3. A: 他是學生嗎?
   B: 他不是學生嗎?

4. A: 我是他的同學,你呢?
   B: 我不是他的同學,你呢?

Conversation

Find a partner and practice the following dialogues:

1. A: 你好! 請問,您貴姓?
   B: 我姓 ____ 。你呢?

2. A: 請問,你叫什麼名字?
   B: 我的英文名字是 _____ ,中文名字是 _____ 。

3. A: 請問,你的中文老師是誰?
   B: 我的中文老師是 ____ 老師。

Write Chinese

Write your Chinese name in both Pinyin and Chinese characters.

For example,   Wú   Xiǎoměi
                 吳   小 美

我 的 名 字 是: _____

Traditional and Simplified Characters

Read each character aloud. Write its traditional form. Then create a phrase and a sentence using the character.

For example,   学 → 學 → 學生 → 我是學生。

吗 (   )   师 (   )   贵 (   )   请 (   )   问 (   )   么 (   )   谁 (   )

第三課
LESSON

3

你是哪國人?
Which Country Are You From?

教學目標 OBJECTIVES

- Find out someone's nationality
- Ask which language they speak
- Talk about each others' nationalities and languages

China has visitors from all over the world.

Chinese like to make friends with people of all nationalities.

Shanghai attracts many foreign students interested in studying Chinese language and culture.

生詞 VOCABULARY

核心詞 Core Vocabulary

	TRADITIONAL	SIMPLIFIED	PINYIN		
1.	哪	哪	nǎ/něi (nǎ also pronounced as něi in some regions)	Pron.	which
2.	國	国	guó	N.	country
3.	人	人	rén	N.	person
4.	很	很	hěn	Adv.	very, quite
5.	對了	对了	duìle		by the way (a phrase used to start a new topic)
6.	法國	法国	Fǎguó Fàguó (pronunciation in Taiwan)	N.	France
7.	美國	美国	Měiguó	N.	United States
8.	英國	英国	Yīngguó	N.	Britain
9.	中國	中国	Zhōngguó	N.	China
10.	說	说	shuō	V.	to speak
11.	會	会	huì	Aux.	can, be able to
12.	一點兒兒	一点儿儿	yìdiǎr ér		a little (retroflex ending)
13.	法文	法文	Fǎwén	N.	French (language)
14.	和	和	hé hàn (pronunciation in Taiwan)	Conj.	and

補充詞 Supplementary Vocabulary

	TRADITIONAL	SIMPLIFIED	PINYIN		
1.	德國	德国	Déguó	N.	Germany
	德國人	德国人	Déguórén	N.	German (person)
	德語(德文)	德语(德文)	Déyǔ (Déwén)	N.	German (language)
2.	韓國	韩国	Hánguó	N.	Korea
	韓國人	韩国人	Hánguórén	N.	Korean (person)
	韓語(韓文)	韩语(韩文)	Hányǔ (Hánwén)	N.	Korean (language)
3.	加拿大	加拿大	Jiānádà	N.	Canada
	加拿大人	加拿大人	Jiānádàrén	N.	Canadian (person)
4.	泰國	泰国	Tàiguó	N.	Thailand
	泰國人	泰国人	Tàiguórén	N.	Thai (person)
	泰語(泰文)	泰语(泰文)	Tàiyǔ (Tàiwén)	N.	Thai (language)
5.	日本	日本	Rìběn	N.	Japan
	日本人	日本人	Rìběnrén	N.	Japanese (person)
	日語(日文)	日语(日文)	Rìyǔ (Rìwén)	N.	Japanese (language)
6.	西班牙	西班牙	Xībānyá	N.	Spain
	西班牙人	西班牙人	Xībānyárén	N.	Spanish (person)
	西班牙語 (西班牙文)	西班牙语 (西班牙文)	Xībānyáyǔ (Xībānyáwén)	N.	Spanish (language)

語文知識 LANGUAGE LINK

The Sentence Patterns provide models that will help you with the Language in Use section. In both sections, pay attention to the grammar points, vocabulary, and expressions.

句型 Sentence Patterns

A: 你是哪國人？
　Nǐ shì nǎ guó rén?

B: 我是法國人。
　Wǒ shì Fǎguórén.

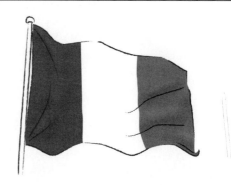

A: 你會說中文嗎?
Nǐ huì shuō Zhōngwén ma?

B: 我會說中文。
Wǒ huì shuō Zhōngwén.

課文   Language in Use: 你是哪國人? Nǐ shì nǎ guó rén?

李文中: 小美,你好嗎?
Xiǎoměi, nǐhǎo ma?

吳小美: 我很好。對了,文中,你是哪國人?
Wǒ hěnhǎo. Duìle, Wénzhōng, nǐ shì nǎ guó rén?

李文中: 我是法國人。你呢? 你是美國人嗎?
Wǒ shì Fǎguórén. Nǐ ne? Nǐ shì Měiguórén ma?

吳小美: 不是,我不是美國人,我是英國人。
Bú shì, wǒ bú shì Měiguórén, wǒ shì Yīngguórén.

李文中: 老師呢?
Lǎoshī ne?

吳小美: 他是中國人。他說中文。
Tā shì Zhōngguórén. Tā shuō Zhōngwén.

李文中: 你會說中文嗎?
Nǐ huì shuō Zhōngwén ma?

吳小美: 我會說一點兒中文,我也會說法文和英文。
Wǒ huì shuō yìdiǎr Zhōngwén, wǒ yě huì shuō Fǎwén hé Yīngwén.

注釋 LANGUAGE NOTES

你好嗎？ How Are You?

"你好嗎?" is a common greeting. The common reply is "我很好".

For example,

A: 你好嗎？
B: 我很好，你呢？

Adverb 很(他很好)

很 is an adverb meaning "very" that occurs before verbs or adjectives. (For more details on the adverb 很, please refer to Lesson 4.)

Note: 是 is not used to link a subject and an adjective in a descriptive sentence, such as the English sentence "He is good." That sentence would be expressed in Chinese as "他很好。"

對了

對了 is often used in informal conversation to start a new topic so that the transition won't sound too abrupt. It is similar to "by the way" in English.

For example,

A: 小美，你好嗎？　　　　　　　　　　　How are you, Xiaomei?
B: 我很好。對了，文中，你是哪國人？　　I am fine. By the way, Wenzhong, what's your nationality?

語法 GRAMMAR

哪(哪國人) Which Nationality?

哪 is a question word that means "which." "哪國人" is an interrogative phrase used to ask someone's nationality. For example,

他是哪國人？　　　What's his nationality?

國名和國人 Country Names and People

In Chinese, the character 國 means "country, nation." 國 is placed after a one-syllable character to form a country name. If there are two or more syllables, 國 is not used. See the following examples:

One syllable (with 國)

Country	Pinyin	Meaning
美 國	Měiguó	United States
德 國	Déguó	Germany
英 國	Yīngguó	Britain
泰 國	Tàiguó	Thailand
中 國	Zhōngguó	China
韓 國	Hánguó	Korea
法 國	Fǎguó	France

More than two syllables (without 國)

Country	Pinyin	Meaning
日 本	Rìběn	Japan
越 南	Yuènán	Vietnam
印 尼	Yìnní	Indonesia
印 度	Yìndù	India
伊 朗	Yīlǎng	Iran
伊 拉 克	Yīlākè	Iraq
西 班 牙	Xībānyá	Spain
墨 西 哥	Mòxīgē	Mexico
加 拿 大	Jiānádà	Canada
新 加 坡	Xīnjiāpō	Singapore
意 大 利	Yìdàlì	Italy
俄 羅 斯	Éluósī	Russia
馬 來 西 亞	Mǎláixīyà	Malaysia

To indicate a person from a certain country, simply add 人 after the country name.

People	Pinyin	Meaning
美 國 人	Měiguórén	American
德 國 人	Déguórén	German
英 國 人	Yīngguórén	British
泰 國 人	Tàiguórén	Thai
中 國 人	Zhōngguórén	Chinese
日 本 人	Rìběnrén	Japanese
法 國 人	Fǎguórén	French
越 南 人	Yuènánrén	Vietnamese
印 尼 人	Yìnnírén	Indonesian
印 度 人	Yìndùrén	Indian
伊 朗 人	Yīlǎngrén	Iranian
伊 拉 克 人	Yīlākèrén	Iraqi
西 班 牙 人	Xībānyárén	Spanish
墨 西 哥 人	Mòxīgērén	Mexican
加 拿 大 人	Jiānádàrén	Canadian
意 大 利 人	Yìdàlìrén	Italian
韓 國 人	Hánguórén	Korean
新 加 坡 人	Xīnjiāpōrén	Singaporean
馬 來 西 亞 人	Mǎláixīyàrén	Malaysian

Chinese people commonly add 人 after a place or city to indicate where they are from. For example,

我是北京人。	Wǒ shì Běijīngrén.	I am from Beijing.
他是台北人。	Tā shì Táiběirén.	He is from Taipei.
老師是上海人。	Lǎoshī shì Shànghǎirén.	The teacher is from Shanghai.
你是香港人。	Nǐ shì Xiānggǎngrén.	You are from Hong Kong.

說 and 語言

The character 說 means "to speak." "我會說中文" means "I can speak Chinese." In Taiwan and some other regions of China, 講 [jiǎng] is used in place of 說 (我會講中文). In most cases the word for a language is formed by adding 文 or 語 after the country name (without 國). For example,

英文 English	法文 French	德文 German	日文 Japanese
英語 English	法語 French	德語 German	日語 Japanese

Note: Chinese is expressed as either 中文 or 漢語.

The subtle difference between 文 and 語 is that 文 tends to refer to written language and literature, while 語 tends to refer to spoken language.

一點兒

一點兒 is a phrase used before a noun to indicate "a little."

Note: When 一 is followed by 1st, 2nd, and 3rd tone, it is pronounced as [yì]. Therefore "一點兒" should be pronounced as [yì diǎr].

一點兒 (a little) [yì diǎr] + Noun	
我會說一點兒中文。	I can speak a little Chinese.
我也會說一點兒法文。	I can also speak a little French.

Conjunction 和

和 is a common conjunction for nouns and pronouns. Note that it may be translated as English "and." However, it is not equivalent to the all-purpose English conjunction "and." (In English, the conjunction "and" can be used for nouns and pronouns, for verbs, and between sentences or clauses.) Following are some examples of the use of 和:

老師和學生都[dōu](all)很忙[máng](busy)。	Teacher and student are both busy.
我和我的室友都是中國人。	My roommates and I are all Chinese.
他們是丁明和方小文。	They are Ming Ding and Xiaowen Fang.

補充課文 ᴏᴏᴏ SUPPLEMENTARY PRACTICE

This selection will help you test your comprehension of the grammar and vocabulary you have learned in this lesson. Be prepared to answer questions about the meaning of the passage.

　　我是美國人,我會說英文和法文,我也會說一點兒中文。他是我的中文老師,我的老師很好。他是中國人,他說中文,他也說一點兒英文。對了,你呢? 請問,你是哪國人? 你會說什麼語言? 你會說中文嗎?

Note: 語言 [yǔyán]: language

練習 ACTIVITIES

I. Listening Exercises

3-1 In each pair, circle the one your instructor pronounces:

1. nǎguó	Fǎguó	2. liàn Zhōngwén	niàn Zhōngwén
3. suō	shuō	4. Tàiyǔ	Dǎiyǔ
5. Rìběn	Lǐběn	6. Déwēn	Éwén

3-2 In each pair, circle the one your instructor pronounces:

1. Měiguó	Měiguō	2. yìrén	yīrén
3. nàběn	nǎběn	4. Fāguó	Fǎguó
5. shuòshì	shuōshì	6. Hànyǔ	Hányǔ

3-3 Form groups of three to four. Read the following poem in your group, paying special attention to the rhythm.

Yóuzǐ Yín (Mèng Jiāo)	遊子吟 (孟郊)	Song of the Parting Son (Meng, Jiao)
Cí mǔ shǒuzhōng xiàn,	慈母手中線,	A loving mother with thread in her hands,
Yóuzǐ shēnshàng yī.	遊子身上衣。	For the parting son weaves the gown.
Línxíng mìmì féng,	臨行密密縫,	Before he leaves she stitches carefully,
Yì kǒng chíchí guī.	意恐遲遲歸。	Fearing his return will be long delayed.
Shéi yán cùn cǎo xīn,	誰言寸草心,	Who believes that the heart of young grass,
Bào dé sān chūn huī?	報得三春暉?	Can repay three springs of sunshine?

II. Character Exercises

3-4 Read the following words, phrases, and sentences:

人	說
國人	說中文
美國人	我會說中文。
我是美國人。	我不會說中文。
我不是美國人。	我會說中文，不會說日文。
我不是英國人，也不是美國人。	老師也會說中文，他也不會說日文。

Now try to use the following characters to make words, phrases, and then sentences:

1. 哪 2. 國 3. 很 4. 對 5. 法 6. 美
7. 會 8. 點 9. 兒 10. 和 11. 人 12. 說

3-5 Draw lines to match the traditional and simplified forms of the following characters:

點　說　誰　貴　學　師　國　嗎

说　国　吗　师　点　谁　学　贵

3-6 Stroke and radical exercises:

1. Write several characters you have learned which start with a horizontal stroke "一":

一: _____

2. Write several characters you have learned which start with a vertical stroke "丨":

丨: _____

3. Write several characters you have learned which start with a left-slanted stroke "丿":

丿: _____

3-7 Create flashcards.

To help learn new characters, and also as an aid for future review, students are strongly encouraged to create flashcards for each lesson's vocabulary items. See the following example for a suggested format:

FRONT　　　　　　　　　　BACK

美國
Měiguó

我是美國人。
I am American.

(N.) United States

III. Grammar Exercises

3-8   The following are the names of countries. Please tell the class how to refer to the nationality and the language for each of them:

Country	People	Language		Connect the right flag to the country
1. 中國	_____	_____	a.	
2. 日本	_____	_____	b.	
3. 英國	_____	_____	c.	
4. 美國	_____	_____	d.	
5. 加拿大	_____	_____	e.	
6. 法國	_____	_____	f.	
7. 德國	_____	_____	g.	

3-9   Substitution exercises:

1. A: 你是哪國人?
   B: 我是中國人。
   A: 你會說英文嗎?
   B: 我不會說英文,我會說中文。

英國人	法文	英文
美國人	日文	英文
日本人	中文	日文
法國人	德文	法文
德國人	西班牙文	德文
韓國人	法文	韓文

2. **A:** 你會說<u>中文</u>嗎？

　　B: 我會說<u>中文</u>，我也會說一點兒<u>英文</u>。

英文	法文
法文	德文
德文	日文
日文	西班牙文
西班牙文	韓文
韓文	中文

3-10 Fill in the blanks with appropriate words to complete the following sentences:

(Words: 叫, 會, 說, 是, 不, 也)

1. 我 ＿＿ 中國人。

2. 她 ＿＿ ＿＿ 英文，也 ＿＿ ＿＿ 一點兒法文。

3. 他 ＿＿ 李中，他 ＿＿ 美國人。

4. 我 ＿＿ 吳英。我 ＿＿ 法國人。我 ＿＿ 法語。

5. 小文 ＿＿ 英國人。他 ＿＿ ＿＿ 說日文，他 ＿＿ ＿＿ 英文。
   他 ＿＿ ＿＿ ＿＿ 一點兒中文。

IV. Communicative Activities

3-11 In the exercises for Lesson 2, you gathered information about your classmates and created a list of all the students in the class. Now you need to update the list with new information. First check the accuracy of the information you gathered last time by asking the following questions (among others — use whatever you find necessary). Then, update your list of information to add the country each is from and the language each speaks.

1. 我是……。

2. 請問，你是……嗎？

3. 請問，你叫……？

4. 你的中文名字……？

文化點滴　CULTURE NOTES

中國人的家鄉觀念
[Zhōngguórén de jiāxiāng guānniàn]
Chinese Concept of "Native Town"

One of the items you are usually required to fill out on forms in China is your 家鄉 [jiāxiāng] (native town/hometown). This term refers to the place from which your family originally came. While the English term "hometown" typically refers to where a person was born or grew up, this is not necessarily the case with the Chinese term. Given the increased mobility of modern society it is not unreasonable or even uncommon for Chinese to list as their hometown a place they have never seen in their lives.

Whether they grew up there or not, Chinese people often feel a sense of attachment to their family's hometown as well as a sense of affinity with others who share the same hometown. In fact, among overseas Chinese there are various townsman societies whose major goal is to help their fellow townsmen in difficulty. You will find 廣東同鄉會 [Guǎngdōng tóngxiānghuì] (the Guangdong Fellow Townsman Society), 寧波同鄉會 [Níngbō tóngxiānghuì] (the Ningbo Fellow Townsman Society), 福建同鄉會 [Fújiàn tóngxiānghuì] (the Fujian Fellow Townsman Society), and recently 溫州同鄉會 [Wēnzhōu tóngxiānghuì] (the Wenzhou Fellow Townsman Society).

"葉落歸根 [yè luò guī gēn]," which means "fallen leaves settle on their roots," is a phrase very much appreciated by Chinese. No matter where they are or how many generations separate them from it, many Chinese would like to visit their hometown at least once in their lifetime. This is evident when you consider that, after 40 years of separation between Mainland China and Taiwan, countless Taiwanese people still visit the Mainland.

In modern society, the feeling of attachment among Chinese to their hometown has become much weaker. People no longer have to rely on their townsmen for support and help. However, meeting someone from your hometown is still a pleasure, and traveling to one's hometown still remains a dream of many Chinese.

Traditionally, families have a small altar for remembering deities and ancestors, and for seeking their blessings and protection.

Questions:

1. Is there a similar saying in English (or other languages) that communicates the concept of "葉落歸根"? Do you have any related stories to share?

2. In what situations in your country do you need to indicate your "家鄉"?

趣味中文   FUN WITH CHINESE

> 說來話長。
> It's a long story.

shuō	lái	huà	cháng
說	來	話	長
speak	come	words	long

說來話長 is commonly used Chinese slang. It is usually used to refer to something that is very complicated.

Question:

Do you have any stories that are examples of "說來話長"? Would you like to share one with the class?

行動吧！ LET'S GO! ....

網上語言家教中心
On-line Language Tutoring Center

Mary is filling in her data at an online language tutoring center. Below is what she filled out.

Useful words and expressions:

個人(个人) [gèrén]: personal
資料(资料) [zīliào]: data, information
性別 [xìngbié]: sex
女 [nǚ]: female
男 [nán]: male
國籍(国籍) [guójí]: nationality
電話(电话) [diànhuà]: telephone
電子郵件(电子邮件) [diànzǐ yóujiàn]: e-mail address
能 [néng]: be able to
教 [jiāo]: to teach

Mary Lee 李文英的個人資料：

英文姓名：Mary Lee
中文姓名：李文英
性別：女
國籍：英國
電話：311-1122
電子郵件：marywenying@zhongwen.edu
能教的語言：英文，西班牙文，法文，德文

Questions:

1. Mary 的中文名字叫什麼？ _____

2. 她是哪國人？ _____

3. 她能教什麼語言？ _____

你學什麼?
What Do You Study?

- Ask what something is
- Explain what something is
- Ask about majors in school
- Talk about courses

A senior high school in Taiwan.

In a Taiwan school, you will see many girls wearing uniforms with long skirts.

Fudan University in Shanghai.

生詞 VOCABULARY

核心詞 Core Vocabulary

	TRADITIONAL	SIMPLIFIED	PINYIN		
1.	那	那	nà/nèi (nà also pronounced as nèi in some regions)	Pron.	that
2.	書	书	shū	N.	book
3.	這	这	zhè/zhèi (zhè also pronounced as zhèi in some regions)	Pron.	this
4.	本	本	běn	M.W.	(measure word for book)
5.	文學	文学	wénxué	N.	literature
6.	工程	工程	gōngchéng	N.	engineering
7.	難	难	nán	Adj.	difficult
8.	太	太	tài	Adv.	too
9.	可是	可是	kěshì	Conj.	but, yet, however
10.	功課	功课	gōngkè	N.	homework, assignment
11.	多	多	duō	Adj.	many, much
12.	我們 們	我们 们	wǒmen men	Pron.	we, us (used after a personal pronoun or a noun to show plural number)
13.	少	少	shǎo	Adj.	few, little

補充詞　Supplementary Vocabulary

	TRADITIONAL	SIMPLIFIED	PINYIN		
1.	系	系	xì	N.	department
2.	數學	数学	shùxué	N.	mathematics
3.	計算機 (電腦)#	计算机 (电脑)	jìsuànjī (diànnǎo)	N.	computer
4.	專業 (主修)##	专业 (主修)	zhuānyè (zhǔxiū)	N.	major
5.	輔修	辅修	fǔxiū	N.	minor
6.	容易	容易	róngyì	Adj.	easy
7.	忙	忙	máng	Adj.	busy
8.	累	累	lèi	Adj.	tired
9.	作業	作业	zuòyè	N.	homework, assignment
10.	考試	考试	kǎoshì	N.	exam
11.	有點兒	有点儿	yǒudiǎr	Adv.	a little
12.	還好	还好	hái hǎo		not bad, okay

Notes: # In Mainland China, a computer is called "計算機"; now it is also commonly called "電腦".
In Taiwan, it is called "電腦".
主修 is mainly used in Taiwan, while 專業 is used in Mainland China.

語文知識　LANGUAGE LINK

The Sentence Patterns provide models that will help you with the Language in Use section. In both sections, pay attention to the grammar points, vocabulary, and expressions.

句型   Sentence Patterns

A: 那是一本什麼書?
   Nà shì yìběn shénme shū?

B: 那是一本英文書。
   Nà shì yìběn Yīngwén shū.

A: 你學什麼?
   Nǐ xué shénme?

B: 我學英國文學, 你呢?
   Wǒ xué Yīngguó wénxué, nǐ ne?

A: 工程難嗎?
   Gōngchéng nán ma?

B: 不太難。
   Bú tài nán.

課文   Language in Use: 你學什麼? Nǐ xué shénme?

吳小美: 文中, 那是你的書嗎?
        Wénzhōng, nà shì nǐ de shū ma?

李文中: 那是我的書。
        Nà shì wǒ de shū.

吳小美: 那是一本什麼書?
        Nà shì yìběn shénme shū?

李文中: 那是一本英文書。
        Nà shì yìběn Yīngwén shū.

吳小美: 這本呢? 這是一本什麼書?
        Zhè běn ne? Zhè shì yìběn shénme shū?

李文中:　這是一本中文書。
Zhè shì yìběn Zhōngwén shū.

吳小美:　對了,你學什麼?
Duì le, nǐ xué shénme?

李文中:　我學英國文學,你呢?
Wǒ xué Yīngguó wénxué, nǐ ne?

吳小美:　我學工程。
Wǒ xué gōngchéng.

李文中:　工程難嗎?
Gōngchéng nán ma?

吳小美:　不太難。可是功課很多。
Bú tài nán. Kěshì gōngkè hěnduō.

李文中:　我們的功課也不少。
Wǒmen de gōngkè yě bùshǎo.

注釋　LANGUAGE NOTES

英國文學

英國文學 means "English literature." When referring to the literature of a certain country, in Chinese the country name is followed by the word for literature, 文學. For example,

中國文學	Chinese literature
美國文學	American literature
法國文學	French literature
德國文學	German literature
日本文學	Japanese literature

語法 GRAMMAR

Demonstrative Pronouns　這,那

這 ("this") and 那 ("that") are the most commonly used demonstrative pronouns in Chinese. They can be used with 是 to form 這是 ("this is"), 那是 ("that is").

那是什麼?	What is that?
這是我的中文書。	This is my Chinese book.

量詞　(Measure Word/Classifier) (1): 本

本 is a measure word (also called a classifier). One of the special characteristics of Chinese is that it makes extensive use of measure words. That is, when denoting the number of entities, the number alone cannot function as an attributive but must be combined with a measure word inserted between the number and the noun it modifies. For example,

Numeral	Measure word	Noun
一	本	書

English also makes limited use of measure words, such as "pieces" in "three pieces of cake." However, in Chinese, their use is much more pervasive. In Chinese, measure words must also be placed between demonstrative pronouns (這 and 那) and nouns.

• The measure word 本 is for bound items such as books and magazines.	兩本中文書 Two Chinese books.
	這本書是中文書。 This book is a Chinese book.
	那本書是英文書。 That book is an English book.
	那本 That one. (when referring to a book)

Adverb　很

很 is an adverb that occurs before the adjective it modifies. Note that 很 has two senses depending on whether it is stressed or not. When it is stressed, it means "very." For example,

我很忙。　I am very busy.　　　　　　工程很難。　Engineering is very difficult.

However, in most cases, 很 is not stressed. Its unstressed usage has to do with the reality that in Chinese the adjectives are inherently comparative. For example,

爸爸忙, 媽媽不忙。　　　　Father is busy. Mother is not busy.
他好, 我不好。　　　　　　He is doing fine. I am not doing well.

These two sentences imply comparison between father and mother, and he and I. But how can we simply say "Father is busy" or "He is doing fine"? The way we do this is to use 很 without stressing it: "爸爸很忙", "他很好". Therefore the sentence, "我很忙" could mean either "I am very busy" or simply "I am busy," depending on whether the 很 is stressed.

Suffix 們(我們，你們，他們)

們 is a plural suffix that is commonly placed after the singular pronouns, such as 我, 你, 他 to form their plural pronouns 我們, 你們, 他們. For example,

Singular	Plural
我 (I, me)	我們 (we, us)
你 (you, you)	你們 (you, you)
他 (he, him)	他們 (they, them)
她 (she, her)	她們 (they, them)

This suffix may also be placed after animate nouns to give an intimate feeling to the people named. Note that it is never added to inanimate nouns. For example,

老師們
朋友們

Grammar Summary 語法小結

Chinese words:
So far we have learned the following words:

personal pronouns	我　你　他　她　您
demonstrative pronouns	這　那
interrogative pronouns	什麼　誰　哪
nouns	老師　學生　名字　中文　英文　書
verbs	是　姓　說　學　叫
adverbs	也　很　太
adjectives	好　忙　累　多　少　難
particles	嗎　呢　的
negation	不
conjunctions	和　可是
optative verbs	會
measure word (classifier)	本

Chinese sentences:
Chinese sentences usually consist of a subject and a predicate. Chinese is a non-inflectional language. That means it does not change word endings to reflect person, gender, tense, number, or case. In place of word endings, word order (the arrangement of words) plays an important role in indicating these different grammatical relationships. In general, Chinese word order is:

Subject　+　Adverbial　+　Verb　+　Object
(Adverbial: e.g., prepositional phrase, auxiliary verb, adverb)

For example,

我說中文。   I speak Chinese.

我學工程。   I study engineering.

So far we have learned about the following types of sentences:

1. Sentences with an adjectival predicate. (The main element of the predicate is an adjective.)

Subject	Predicate (adjective)	
我	很好。	I am fine.
老師	很忙。	Teacher is busy.
工程	不難。	Engineering is not difficult.
他們	都很累。	They are all very tired.
中文書	不太多。	Chinese books are quite few.

2. 是 sentences. (The main element of the predicate is 是.)

Subject	Predicate	
我	是學生。	I am a student.
你	也是學生。	You are also a student.
他	不是老師。	He is not a teacher.

3. Sentences with a verbal predicate. (The main element of the predicate is a verb.)

Subject	Predicate	
我	會說中文。	I can speak Chinese.
我	學文學。	I study literature.
他	不叫李文中。	He is not named Wenzhong Li.

4. Interrogative sentences.

   a. 嗎 and 呢 sentences

你是老師。	You are a teacher.
你是老師嗎?	Are you a teacher?
A: 你是學生嗎?	Are you a student?
B: 是,我是學生,你呢?	Yes, I am a student. How about you?
A: 我也是學生。	I am also a student.

   b. Sentences with an interrogative pronoun. (Remember that the question word occurs where the expected answer would be.)

這是什麼書?	這是中文書。
他是誰?	他是李文中。
你是哪國人?	我是美國人。

補充課文 —o◇o— SUPPLEMENTARY PRACTICE

This selection will help you test your comprehension of the grammar and vocabulary you have learned in this lesson. Be prepared to answer questions about the meaning of the passage.

你們好! 我叫美英, 是大學生。我是二年級的學生, 我學中國文學。這是我的書, 這是一本中國文學書。中國文學不太難, 可是功課不少。你們呢? 你們學什麼? 是工程嗎? 那是你們的工程書嗎? 工程難嗎? 功課多嗎?

Notes: 大學生 [dàxuéshēng]: college student
二年級 [èrniánjí]: sophomore, second year

練習 ACTIVITIES

I. Listening Exercises

4-1 Listen to the instructor and fill in each blank with the correct Pinyin:

1. zhuān _____
2. kǎo _____
3. _____ yè
4. _____ kè
5. kuài _____
6. wén _____
7. gōng _____
8. _____ yì
9. bù _____

4-2 Listen to the instructor and mark the following words with the correct tones:

1. kecheng
2. shuxue
3. yinyue
4. duoshao
5. tai nan
6. keneng
7. wenxue shu
8. zhexie

4-3 Form groups of three to four. Take turns reading the following tongue twister out loud, as quickly as you can. Each group will select one member to represent the group in a class competition.

mā: 媽   mom

má: 麻   hemp

mǎ: 馬   horse

mà: 罵   to scold

Māma Mà Mǎ	媽媽罵馬	**Mom Scolded the Horse**
Māma zhòng má,	媽媽種麻,	Mom planted some hemp,
Wǒ qù fàng mǎ.	我去放馬。	I let the horse out.
Mǎ chīle má,	馬吃了麻,	The horse ate the hemp,
Māma mà mǎ.	媽媽罵馬。	Mom scolded the horse.

4-4 Listen to the instructor and write down the sentences in Pinyin:

1. _____

2. _____

3. _____

4. _____

II. Character Exercises

4-5 Read the following words, phrases, and sentences:

書	學
什麼書	文學
工程書	中國文學
誰的工程書	學中國文學
同學的工程書	誰學中國文學
我的同學的工程書	美國人學中國文學

Now try to use the following characters to make words, phrases, and then sentences:

1. 那   2. 這   3. 本   4. 工   5. 程   6. 難

7. 太   8. 可   9. 功   10. 課   11. 多   12. 們

4-6 Match the following English sentences with the Chinese equivalents:

He studies engineering.	功課很多。
This is my Chinese book.	那是一本英國文學書。
That is a book on English literature.	他學工程。
There is a lot of homework.	這是我的中文書。

III. Grammar Exercises

4-7 Substitution exercises:

1. 這是什麼？
   這是……。

   一本書
   小美的英文名字
   他的功課

2. 那是什麼？
   那是……。

   一本法文書
   他的中文名字
   我的美國文學功課

4-8 Select an expression from each group and create a valid Chinese sentence. Create as many sentences as you can.

法國　學生　很難
工程　書　　很好
中文　老師　很貴
美國　功課　很多

Note: 貴 [guì]: expensive

IV. Communicative Activities

4-9 Find a partner and ask each other questions to collect information to fill in the blanks in the form below. Then use the sentence patterns provided to introduce your partner to the class.

英文名字	中文姓	中文名字	哪國人	學生/老師	說......文	學......

Sentence patterns and expressions to be used in the introduction:

這是...... (那是......)   姓   叫   他/她是......   說   學

文化知識 ⟨⟨⟨ Culture Link

文化點滴　CULTURE NOTES

中國的教育制度 [Zhōngguó de jiàoyù zhìdù]
The Chinese Educational System

In 1978, Mainland China implemented a 九年義務教育制 [jiǔnián yìwù jiàoyù zhì] (nine-year compulsory schooling system). In Taiwan, also, children are required to have nine years of compulsory schooling. After nine years of study, they either go on to further study at a senior high school, attend a vocational school, or enter the work force. This is, however, not a free choice because students must pass a national entrance exam to get into a senior high school. Students who receive lower scores will either have to go to a vocational school or enter the work force. Upon graduation from senior high school, students must take the national entrance exam, called 高考 [gāo kǎo] in Mainland China and 大學聯考 [dàxué liánkǎo] in Taiwan to determine which colleges or universities they can get into, and even what majors they may pursue. The exam used to take place only in early July each year in both Mainland China and Taiwan, but it has been moved to early June in the Mainland. In addition, it is now offered once in the winter in both places. It is one of the biggest events in the entire country, and students usually begin concentrated preparation for the exam a year or more beforehand.

Before the mid-1990s, most schools in Mainland China were government-run and basically tuition was free. Today, free tuition is a thing of the past. Since the late 1980s, more and more private schools funded by big businesses or wealthy individuals have appeared. There are also "aristocratic schools" — usually private boarding schools run by big businesses that charge very high tuition and claim to provide the highest quality of education. Only a small number of people can afford to send their children to these schools.

University students in Mainland China used to be assigned a job by the university upon graduation, but they did not have too many choices. This situation has also changed. As in many other countries, students need to find a job on their own. More and more students are pursuing graduate studies to become more competitive in the job market.

With the rapid changes in China's society, it can be anticipated that more extensive and substantial changes will take place in the field of education in China in the next decade.

趣味中文   FUN WITH CHINESE

書中自有黃金屋，書中自有顏如玉。
Inside the books themselves, there are gold houses and beauties.

shū	zhōng	zì	yǒu	huángjīn	wū
書	中	自	有	黃金	屋
book	inside	itself	have	gold	house

shū	zhōng	zì	yǒu	yán	rú	yù
書	中	自	有	顏	如	玉
book	inside	itself	have	face	as if	jade

顏如玉 refers to beauties. This expression indicates that whoever studies hard will achieve good results, such as a gold house (getting rich) and a beautiful wife. In old China, there was a civil service examination system called 科舉制度 [kē jǔ zhì dù]. Local and district competitions had to be passed in order to get to the final examination, the imperial examination 殿試 [diàn shì]. As a result, it was considered normal to spend several years preparing to pass the various local exams and become a candidate for the final imperial examination. The candidate who scored highest was called 狀元 [zhuàngyuán], and was usually granted an audience with the emperor and awarded a high official status. This person usually achieved both fame and wealth, and married a princess or daughter of a high official.

Question:

Form groups of two to three, then tell a story that is an example of
"書中自有黃金屋，書中自有顏如玉。"

行動吧! LET'S GO!

補習班　After-school Learning Center

于小英 is a college student majoring in English. She teaches English at two after-school learning centers to earn some extra money. Look at the signs for the two centers (below) and then answer the questions.

Useful words and expressions:

補習班(补习班) [bǔxíbān]:
　　after-school learning center

中心 [zhōngxīn]: center

理化 [lǐhuà]: physics and chemistry

安親班(安亲班) [ān qīn bān]:
　　after-school childcare center

鋼琴(钢琴) [gāngqín]: piano

家教 [jiājiào]: private tutor

數學(数学) [shùxué]:
　　mathematics

幼兒(幼儿) [yòu'ér]: child

音樂(音乐) [yīnyuè]:
　　music

招牌 [zhāopái]: shop sign

Center A

Center B

1. What subjects does Center A provide?

2. What subjects does Center B provide?

3. 大文 is a junior high school student. To help him perform better on the college entrance exam, he would like to attend after-school learning centers to improve his mathematics and English. Which shop signs below would 大文 be interested in?

　a. 大天英數補習班　　　b. 大天電腦中心
　c. 大天理化家教　　　　d. 大天幼兒安親班

4. 美美 was a music major at college. She runs a piano tutoring center. Let's help her create a shop sign.

復習　Review

Conversation

Find a partner and practice the following dialogues:

1. 請問，你是哪國人?
   我是 _____ (e.g. 美國人)。我不是中國人，也不是英國人。

2. 你會說中文嗎?
   我會說中文。我也會說 _____ (e.g. 法文) 和英文。
   我不會說 _____ (e.g. 日文)。

3. 請問，你是法國人嗎?
   我不是 _____，我是 _____ 。
   你的中文老師是中國人嗎?

4. 這是一本什麼書?
   這是一本 _____ (e.g. 工程書，中國文學書)。

5. 那是誰的書?
   那是 _____ (e.g. 我的同學的書)，是 _____ (e.g. 我的同學的中國文學書)。

6. 我是美國人，我學中文。你的同學學什麼?
   他學 _____ (e.g. 工程)。
   他的功課 _____ (e.g. 很多，很難)。

   Note: 難 [nán]: difficult

Fill in the Blanks

You are at the consulate applying for a visa to visit China. You are asked to write down your Chinese name and your citizenship in Chinese characters.

姓名 [xìngmíng] Name: _____

國籍 [guójí] Nationality: _____

Write Chinese

Read the sentences, then practice writing the underlined characters. Pay attention to stroke order.

Lesson 3: 請問，你是<u>哪國人</u>? 我是法國人，<u>我會說一點兒</u>中文<u>和</u>英文。

_____

_____

Lesson 4: <u>那本書</u>是工程書。<u>這</u>本書很<u>難</u>，可是，<u>我們</u>的功課不太多。

_____

_____

Traditional and Simplified Characters

Read each character aloud. Write its traditional form. Then make a phrase and a sentence using the character.

For example,　学 → 學 → 學生 → 我是學生。

国（　）　说（　）　点（　）　儿（　）　书（　）　这（　）　难（　）
课（　）　们（　）

這是我朋友
This Is My Friend

- Introduce people
- Make small talk
- Find out what someone owns

Friends play important roles in our lives. Chinese enjoy hanging out, going out to eat, hiking, and traveling with their friends.

Friends get together to chat, order take-out, and have some tea and wine. Dig in and have fun!

生詞 VOCABULARY

核心詞 Core Vocabulary

	TRADITIONAL	SIMPLIFIED	PINYIN		
1.	朋友	朋友	péngyou	N.	friend
2.	來	来	lái	V.	to come; (used before a verb to indicate that one is about to do something)
3.	介紹	介绍	jièshào	V. N.	to introduce introduction
4.	一下	一下	yíxià		(used after a verb to indicate a brief action)
5.	室友	室友	shìyǒu	N.	roommate
6.	有	有	yǒu	V.	to have
7.	幾	几	jǐ		how many
8.	兩	两	liǎng	Num.	two
9.	個	个	gè	M.W.	(the most commonly used measure word for people, buildings, characters, etc.)
10.	他們	他们	tāmen	Pron.	they, them
11.	都	都	dōu	Adv.	all, both
12.	常	常	cháng	Adv.	often, frequently
13.	跟	跟	gēn	Prep.	with

專名 Proper Nouns

	TRADITIONAL	SIMPLIFIED	PINYIN		
1.	王紅	王红	Wáng Hóng	N.	(name) Hong Wang
2.	丁明	丁明	Dīng Míng	N.	(name) Ming Ding
3.	方小文	方小文	Fāng Xiǎowén	N.	(name) Xiaowen Fang

補充詞　Supplementary Vocabulary

	TRADITIONAL	SIMPLIFIED	PINYIN		
1.	沒有	没有	méiyǒu	V.	to not have, to be without
2.	女朋友	女朋友	nǚpéngyou	N.	girlfriend
3.	男朋友	男朋友	nánpéngyou	N.	boyfriend
4.	認識	认识	rènshi	V.	to know

語文知識　LANGUAGE LINK

The Sentence Patterns provide models that will help you with the Language in Use section. In both sections, pay attention to the grammar points, vocabulary, and expressions.

句型　Sentence Patterns

A: 這是我室友，王紅。
Zhèshì wǒ shìyǒu, Wáng Hóng.

這是我朋友，文中。
Zhèshì wǒ péngyou, Wénzhōng.

B: 你好!
Nǐhǎo!

C: 你好!
Nǐhǎo!

A: 你有室友嗎?
Nǐ yǒu shìyǒu ma?

B: 有，我有室友。我有
Yǒu, wǒ yǒu shìyǒu. Wǒ yǒu

兩個室友。
liǎngge shìyǒu.

課文 Language in Use: 這是我朋友 Zhè shì wǒ péngyou

吳小美： 文中，來！我來介紹一下。這是我室友，王紅。
Wénzhōng, lái! Wǒ lái jièshào yíxià. Zhèshì wǒ shìyǒu, Wáng Hóng.

這是我朋友，文中。
Zhèshì wǒ péngyou, Wénzhōng.

李文中： 你好！
Nǐhǎo!

王紅： 你好！你有室友嗎？
Nǐhǎo! Nǐ yǒu shìyǒu ma?

李文中： 有，我有室友。
Yǒu, wǒ yǒu shìyǒu.

王紅： 你有幾個室友？
Nǐ yǒu jǐge shìyǒu?

李文中： 我有兩個室友。
Wǒ yǒu liǎngge shìyǒu.

王紅： 他們都是誰？
Tāmen dōu shì shéi?

李文中： 他們是丁明和方小文。他們都是中國人。
Tāmen shì Dīng Míng hé Fāng Xiǎowén. Tāmen dōu shì Zhōngguórén.

我常跟他們說中文。
Wǒ cháng gēn tāmen shuō Zhōngwén.

注釋　LANGUAGE NOTES

我來介紹一下

我來介紹一下 is a common expression used for introducing people. It means "Let me introduce you." 介紹 is a verb meaning "to introduce," 一下 is used after a verb to indicate a brief action. It is adopted here to make the tone softer and more informal to ease the task of introducing people to each other.

For example,

文中，來，我來介紹一下，這是我室友王紅。
Wenzhong, come! Let me introduce you. This is my roommate, Hong Wang.

室友

室友 means "roommate." In Mainland China, 同屋 [tóngwū] is also used.

跟

跟 "with" is a preposition that precedes an object to form a prepositional phrase, and it is often placed before the verb as an adverbial adjunct.

我常跟他說中文。　　I often speak Chinese with him.

The Measure Word (Classifier)　個

個 is a measure word used for people.

Numeral	+	Measure word	+	Noun	
一		個		人	one person
兩		個		室友	two roommates

語法　GRAMMAR

有　Sentences　(沒有)

有 means "have" or "there is (are)" in Chinese. Its negative form is 沒有 [méiyǒu]. Its interrogative is formed by putting 嗎 at the end of the sentence.

Interrogative form:	你有室友嗎?	Do you have roommates?
Affirmative form:	我有一個室友。	I have one roommate.
Negative form:	我沒有室友。	I don't have any roommates.

Question Word   幾

幾 is a question word used for asking "How many?" When asking about amounts under ten, 幾 is used. It is placed before the measure word. For example,

Question word	Measure word	Noun	English
幾	個	人	How many persons?
幾	本	書	How many books?

Adverb   都

都 is an adverb meaning "all." It occurs before a predicate. It refers to persons or things already mentioned in the sentence. For example,

他們都是中國人。	They are all Chinese.
我們都學工程。	They all study engineering.
老師和學生都說中文。	The teacher and students all speak Chinese.

都   With   不

都不 means "none"; 不都 means "not all (some do, some don't)."

我們都不是日本人。	None of us is Japanese.
我們不都是日本人。	Not all of us are Japanese.

都   With   也

也 always precedes 都 as 也都.

他們也都是中國人。	They are all also Chinese.
我們也都學工程。	They all also study engineering.

Location of Adverbs   也都常很   (Summary of   也都常很)

So far we have learned the adverbs 也, 都, 常, 很: "also," "all," "often," and "very." They all occur before verbs or adjectives to modify them. When more than one of these words occur together, there are certain word order rules to follow, as illustrated below:

1. 我們　　　　　常　　說中文。　　　We often speak Chinese.
   我們　　　都　常　　說中文。　　　We all often speak Chinese.
   我們　也　都　常　　說中文。　　　We all also often speak Chinese.

2. 我們　　　都　很　忙。　　　　We are all very busy.
   我們　也　　　很　忙。　　　　We are also very busy.
   我們　也　都　很　忙。　　　　We are all also very busy.

補充課文 ⚬⚬⚬ SUPPLEMENTARY PRACTICE

This selection will help you test your comprehension of the grammar and vocabulary you have learned in this lesson. Be prepared to answer questions about the meaning of the passage.

你們好！我來介紹一下我的室友。我有兩個室友，一個叫美美，一個叫文英，她們都是我的好朋友。美美是英國人，文英是法國人，我是美國人。

我們都學英國文學，也學中文，我們都會說英文和一點兒中文。

我們有很多中國朋友，他們都是留學生，我們常跟他們說中文，他們都很好，常常幫助我們練習中文。

你們呢？你們有室友嗎？有幾個？

Notes: 留學生 [liúxuéshēng]: international students
　　　 幫助 [bāngzhù]: to help
　　　 練習 [liànxí]: to practice

練習　ACTIVITIES

I. Listening Exercises

5-1　In each pair, circle the one the instructor pronounces:

1. shíyóu　shìyǒu
2. liǎnggè　liànggé
3. jiéshào　jièshào
4. zhèshí　zhèshì
5. dǒushì　dōushì
6. pēngyou　péngyou

5-2　Listen to the instructor and fill in the initials for each of the following:

1. ___ǒu ___ì
2. ___iè ___ào
3. ___éng ___ou
4. ___áng ___ái
5. ___ué ___èn
6. ___è ___iē
7. ___ǔ ___ǎ
8. ___iú ___ēn
9. ___iǎng ___ié

5-3   Read the following poem, paying special attention to the tones and rhythm:

Chūn Xiǎo (**Mèng Hàorán**)	**春曉** (孟浩然)	**Spring Morning** (Meng, Haoran)
Chūn mián bù jué xiǎo,	春眠不覺曉，	Morning comes unannounced to my spring slumber,
Chù chù wén tí niǎo.	處處聞啼鳥。	I hear birds calling all around.
Yè lái fēng yǔ shēng,	夜來風雨聲，	In the night came sounds of wind and showers,
Huā luò zhī duō shǎo.	花落知多少。	Many of the flowers must have fallen.

II. Character Exercises

5-4   Read the following words, phrases, and sentences:

這	有
這是	我有
這是王紅	我有室友
這是我朋友王紅	我有美國室友
這是我的中國朋友王紅	我有兩個美國室友
這是我們的中國朋友王紅	我有兩個很好的美國室友

Now try to use the following characters to make words, phrases, and then sentences:

1. 友   2. 來   3. 介   4. 紹   5. 下   6. 室
7. 幾   8. 兩   9. 個   10. 都   11. 常   12. 跟

5-5   Write out the Pinyin and the traditional form of each of the following characters and then create a phrase with the character:

	Pinyin	Traditional	Phrase
1. 绍			
2. 个			
3. 两			
4. 们			
5. 这			

III. Grammar Exercises

5-6 Substitution exercises:

1. 他們是誰？
   我來介紹一下。這是<u>吳小美</u>，
   那是<u>李文中</u>。

丁明	方文
我的同學	我的室友
我的文學老師	工程老師

2. 你有<u>課</u>嗎？
   我有<u>中文課</u>，沒有<u>法文課</u>。

書	中文書	英文書
室友	中國室友	日本室友
中文名字	英文名字	中文名字

3. 你有幾個<u>室友</u>？
   我有<u>兩個</u>室友。

本	工程書	三
個	中國朋友	很多

4. <u>小美</u>和<u>小文</u>都<u>不是學生</u>。

文明	李中	是老師
于英	吳學程	學文學
英文	法文	難

5-7 Based on the following pairs of sentences, write a new sentence using the clues provided in parentheses:

For example,　　他會說英文。他會說中文。(也)
　　　　　　　→ 他會說英文，也會說中文。

1. 丁文是小美的室友。方中也是小美的室友。(有)

   _____

2. 紅美會說中文。小文也會說中文。(們，都)

   _____

3. 這是我的室友大紅，她也學英文。(介紹)

   _____

4. 大中是我朋友。小美是我朋友。(和，都)

   _____

IV. Communicative Activities

5-8   Picture talk: Use your imagination to say as much as you can based on the pictures below. You must use (but not limit yourself to) the following words, expressions, and sentence patterns.

這是……。
那是……。
介紹一下
他們
有(沒有)
都
兩

_____

_____

_____

_____

_____

_____

_____

_____

_____

_____

_____

_____

_____

_____

文化知識 ∞ Culture Link

文化點滴　CULTURE NOTES

中國的稱謂文化
[Zhōngguó de chēngwèi wénhuà]
Chinese Forms of Address
The Art beneath Complexity

Addressing people in China is indeed complex. Even native Chinese occasionally become bewildered, especially when traveling to a new place or simply coming into contact with a new social circle.

In general, "先生 [xiānsheng]" (Mister) and "小姐 [xiǎojie]" (Miss) are regarded as the proper forms of address for initiating talk with an adult stranger in large cities. But "xiǎojie" (Miss) is suitable for young women only. "大姐/大嫂 [dàjiě/dàsǎo]" (Older Sister) and "伯母 [bómǔ]" (Aunt) should be used for addressing middle-aged or older women, respectively.

Professional titles are always preferred in business communications or governmental affairs. For example, if Mr. Zhang is a manager, it is polite to call him "張經理 [Zhāng jīnglǐ] (Manager Zhang)" rather than "張先生 [Zhāng xiānsheng] (Mr. Zhang)". But, if he is a vice-manager, instead of calling him "張副經理 [Zhāng fù jīnglǐ] (Vice-Manager Zhang)", which would make him feel his prestige is diminished, you should call him "張經理 [Zhāng jīnglǐ] (Manager Zhang)". The word "副 [fù] (vice)" should be dropped.

In social circles, individuals are addressed according to their age compared to the addresser. You should not address people much older than you by their full names. If you know the senior person well, the surname followed by "伯父/叔叔 [bófù/shūshu] (Uncle)" or "伯母/阿姨 [bómǔ/āyí] (Aunt)" is well accepted. If you are not familiar with the senior person, a simple address of "伯伯 [bóbo] (Uncle)" or "阿姨 [āyí] (Aunt)" is safe. People close to your age may be addressed by their full name, especially when it has only two Chinese characters. If you feel very familiar with the person, and the name has three Chinese characters, you may address them with only the given name. "小 [xiǎo] (little)" plus the surname is another

Eating, karaoke singing, and playing Majiang (打麻將 [dǎ májiàng]) are very common activities among Chinese acquaintances. These activities help them get to know each other better and expand their social circles. How to address people in an appropriate way is really a learned art!

popular way to address people when they are your age or younger. For example, if someone is named "張紅 [Zhāng Hóng]", you can call him "小張 [Xiǎo Zhāng]". When talking to children, they can simply be called "小朋友 [xiǎo péngyou] (little friend)" or their given names.

People are almost never offended when addressed with the pronoun "您 [nín] (the esteemed you)". This especially applies when you are seeking help from an adult stranger. But when a friend is addressed with "您 [nín]," there is usually a hint of distance, irony, or sneering.

Questions:

1. What are the similarities and differences between the means of addressing people in Chinese and English (or other languages)?

2. Form groups of two to three enact situation involving addressing people (e.g., visit your Chinese friend's parents; meet people at a Chinese company; meet your girl/boyfriend's relatives for the first time . . .).

趣味中文 FUN WITH CHINESE

有朋自遠方來，不亦樂乎？
Isn't it a delight to have friends coming from afar?

yǒu	péng	zì	yuǎnfāng	lái
有	朋	自	遠方	來
have	friend	from	a distant place	come

bú	yì	yuè	hū
不	亦	樂	乎
not	particle	happy	question particle

有朋自遠方來，不亦樂乎？

This is another famous saying of Confucius. "不亦......乎?"
is a rhetorical question meaning "isn't it . . . ?" in Classical Chinese.
It carries a tone of courtesy. "樂" is pronounced as [yuè] in
Classical Chinese, while it is pronounced as [lè] in modern Chinese.
The whole sentence means you are very happy when your friends
come to visit you, especially when they come from afar.

Question:

Form groups of two to three, then act out a "有朋自遠方來，
不亦樂乎?" situation.

行動吧！   LET'S GO!

婚友聯誼中心
Marriage and Friendship Social Center

Read the following newspaper advertisement and translate it into English.

Useful words and expressions:

聯誼(联谊) [liányì] (pronounced as [liányí] in Taiwan):
  social contact

中心 [zhōngxīn]: center

未婚 [wèihūn]: unmarried

先 [xiān]: first

認識(认识) [rènshi]: to know

再 [zài]: then, again

交往 [jiāowǎng]: to have friendly relations

手機(手机) [shǒujī]: cell phone

婚友聯誼中心

未婚男女介紹，先認識，再交往。

手機: 0800-555-5555

Translation: _____

_____

_____

6

我的家
My Family

- Introduce yourself
- Talk about your family

Three generations living together is still a common pattern in Chinese societies.

In Taiwan, where there is no one-child policy like Mainland China, a nuclear family commonly includes two or three children.

生詞 VOCABULARY

核心詞 Core Vocabulary

	TRADITIONAL	SIMPLIFIED	PINYIN		
1.	家	家	jiā	N.	home, family
2.	大家	大家	dàjiā	P.	all, everybody
3.	從	从	cóng	Prep.	from
4.	在	在	zài	V. Prep.	to be at, be in at, in
5.	一	一	yī	Num.	one
6.	四	四	sì	Num.	four
7.	爸爸	爸爸	bàba	N.	father
8.	媽媽	妈妈	māma	N.	mother
9.	姐姐	姐姐	jiějie	N.	elder sister
10.	工作	工作	gōngzuò	N. V.	job to work
11.	工程師	工程师	gōngchéngshī	N.	engineer
12.	男 男朋友	男 男朋友	nán nánpéngyou	N. N.	male boyfriend
13.	沒有	没有	méiyǒu	V.	to not have, to be without
14.	輛	辆	liàng	M.W.	(measure word for vehicles)
15.	車	车	chē	N.	car
16.	隻	只	zhī	M.W.	(measure word for certain animals, boats, or containers, or for one of a pair)
17.	狗	狗	gǒu	N.	dog
18.	愛	爱	ài	V.	to love

專名 Proper Nouns

TRADITIONAL	SIMPLIFIED	PINYIN		
1. 紐約	纽约	Niǔyuē	N.	New York

補充詞 Supplementary Vocabulary

	TRADITIONAL	SIMPLIFIED	PINYIN		
1.	自我介紹	自我介绍	zìwǒjièshào	N. V.	self-introduction, to introduce oneself
2.	自己	自己	zìjǐ	N.	oneself
3.	兄弟姐妹	兄弟姐妹	xiōngdìjiěmèi	N.	siblings
4.	哥哥	哥哥	gēge	N.	elder brother
5.	妹妹	妹妹	mèimei	N.	younger sister
6.	弟弟	弟弟	dìdi	N.	younger brother
7.	女 女朋友	女 女朋友	nǚ nǚpéngyou	N. N.	female girlfriend
8.	孩子	孩子	háizi	N.	child
9.	寵物	宠物	chǒngwù	N.	pet
10.	貓	猫	māo	N.	cat

親屬稱謂 [Qīnshǔ chēngwèi]   Addressing One's Relatives

	Relatives on the father's side		Relatives on the mother's side	
grandparents	爺爺 [yéye] 祖父 [zǔfù] grandfather	奶奶 [nǎinai] 祖母 [zǔmǔ] grandmother	外公 [wàigōng] 外祖父 [wàizǔfù] 老爺 [lǎoye] maternal grandfather	外婆 [wàipó] 外祖母 [wàizǔmǔ] 姥姥 [lǎolao] maternal grandmother
uncles	伯伯 [bóbo] father's elder brother 叔叔 [shūshu] father's younger brother	伯母 [bómǔ] wife of father's elder brother 嬸嬸 [shěnshen] wife of father's younger brother	舅舅 [jiùjiu] mother's brother	舅媽 [jiùmā] wife of mother's brother
aunts	姑姑 [gūgu] 姑媽 [gūmā] father's sister	姑父 [gūfù] 姑丈 [gūzhàng] husband of father's sister	阿姨 [āyí] 姨媽 [yímā] mother's sister	姨父 [yífù] 姨丈 [yízhàng] husband of mother's sister
cousins#	堂哥 [tánggē] 堂姐 [tángjiě] 堂弟 [tángdì] 堂妹 [tángmèi]	堂嫂 [tángsǎo] 堂姐夫 [tángjiěfu] 堂弟妹 [tángdìmèi] 堂妹夫 [tángmèifu]	表哥 [biǎogē] 表姐 [biǎojiě] 表弟 [biǎodì] 表妹 [biǎomèi]	表嫂 [biǎosǎo] 表姐夫 [biǎojiěfu] 表弟妹 [biǎodìmèi] 表妹夫 [biǎomèifu]
nephews	姪子 [zhízi] brother's son		外甥 [wàisheng] sister's son	
nieces	姪女 [zhínǚ] brother's daughter		外甥女 [wàishengnǚ] sister's daughter	

Note: #Children of your father's brothers are 堂 [táng] cousins
New word: 嫂 [sǎo] sister-in-law.

職業 [Zhíyè]　Occupations

TRADITIONAL	SIMPLIFIED	PINYIN		
1. 會計師	会计师	kuàijìshī	N.	accountant
2. 經紀人	经纪人	jīngjìrén	N.	agent
3. 建築師	建筑师	jiànzhùshī	N.	architect
4. 老闆	老板	lǎobǎn	N.	boss
5. 商人	商人	shāngrén	N.	businessman
6. 大學生	大学生	dàxuéshēng	N.	college student
7. 顧問	顾问	gùwèn	N.	consultant
8. 醫生	医生	yīshēng	N.	doctor
9. 經濟師	经济师	jīngjìshī	N.	economist
10. 教育工作者	教育工作者	jiàoyù gōngzuòzhě	N.	educator
11. 工程師	工程师	gōngchéngshī	N.	engineer
12. 官員	官员	guānyuán	N.	government official
13. 家庭主婦	家庭主妇	jiātíng zhǔfù	N.	housewife
14. 留學生	留学生	liúxuéshēng	N.	international students
15. 律師	律师	lùshī	N.	lawyer
16. 郵遞員 (郵差)	邮递员 (邮差)	yóudìyuán (yóuchāi)	N.	mailman
17. 經理	经理	jīnglǐ	N.	manager
18. 護士	护士	hùshi	N.	nurse
19. 飛行員	飞行员	fēixíngyuán	N.	pilot
20. 程序員 (程序設計師)	程序员 (程序设计师)	chéngxùyuán (chéngshì shèjìshī)	N.	computer programmer
21. 教授	教授	jiàoshòu	N.	professor

	TRADITIONAL	SIMPLIFIED	PINYIN		
22.	房地產顧問	房地产顾问	fángdìchǎn gùwèn	N.	real estate agent
23.	秘書	秘书	mìshū	N.	secretary
24.	推銷員	推销员	tuīxiāoyuán	N.	salesman
25.	職員	职员	zhíyuán	N.	staff
26.	老師	老师	lǎoshī	N.	teacher
27.	導遊	导游	dǎoyóu	N.	tourist guide

語文知識   LANGUAGE LINK

The Sentence Patterns provide models that will help you with the Language in Use section. In both sections, pay attention to the grammar points, vocabulary, and expressions.

句型   Sentence Patterns

A: 你家在<u>哪兒</u>?
Nǐ jiā zài nǎr?

B: 我家在紐約。
Wǒ jiā zài Niǔyuē.

Note: 哪兒 [nǎr]: where

A: 你是從紐約來的嗎?
Nǐ shì cóng Niǔyuē lái de ma?

B: 是,我是從紐約來的。
Shì, wǒ shì cóng Niǔyuē lái de.

A: 你家有幾個人？
　　Nǐ jiā yǒu jǐge rén?

B: 我家有四個人：爸爸、
　　Wǒ jiā yǒu sìge rén: bàba,

　　媽媽、姐姐和我。
　　māma, jiějie hé wǒ.

A: 你爸爸是<u>做</u>什麼的？
　　Nǐ bàba shì zuò shénme de?

B: 我爸爸是工程師。
　　Wǒ bàba shì gōngchéngshī.

Note: 做 [zuò]: to do

課文　Language in Use: 我的家 Wǒ de jiā

大家好！我叫吳小美，我是從紐約來的，我學工程。
Dàjiā hǎo! Wǒ jiào Wú Xiǎoměi. Wǒ shì cóng Niǔyuē lái de. Wǒ xué gōngchéng.

我來介紹一下我的家。我家在紐約，有四個人：爸爸、媽媽、姐姐
Wǒ lái jièshào yíxià wǒ de jiā. Wǒ jiā zài Niǔyuē, yǒu sìge rén: bàba, māma, jiějie

和我。爸爸是英國人，媽媽是美國人。他們都在紐約工作。
hé wǒ. Bàba shì Yīngguó rén, māma shì Měiguó rén. Tāmen dōu zài Niǔyuē gōngzuò.

爸爸是工程師，媽媽是老師，我和姐姐都是學生。姐姐有
Bàba shì gōngchéngshī, māma shì lǎoshī, wǒ hé jiějie dōu shì xuésheng. Jiějie yǒu

男朋友，我沒有。我們有兩輛車，
nánpéngyou, wǒ méiyǒu. Wǒmen yǒu liǎngliàng chē,

一隻狗。我的家很好。我很愛我的家。
yìzhī gǒu. Wǒ de jiā hěnhǎo. Wǒ hěn ài wǒ de jiā.

注釋 LANGUAGE NOTES

大家好

"大家好!" is a common greeting meaning "Hello, everyone!"

四個人和四口人

"四個人" means four people. 個 is the measure word (classifier). When talking about family members, it is very common to use 口 [kǒu] (mouth) as the measure word, indicating how many mouths (people) need to be fed in the family.

男朋友

"Boyfriend" in Chinese is 男朋友, while 男的朋友 means "male friend." This is parallel to 女朋友 and 女的朋友 which mean "girlfriend" and "female friend" respectively.

語法 GRAMMAR

是 ... 的 Construction

When an event has already taken place and we want to emphasize when, where, or how the event occurred, the "是...的" construction is used.

他是 在大學的時候 [shíhou] 學中文的。 (when he was in college)	It was when he was in college that he studied Chinese.	(focus on when)
他是 在北京 學中文的。 (in Beijing)	It was in Beijing where he studied Chinese.	(focus on where)
他是 跟李老師 學中文的。 (with Teacher Li)	It was with Teacher Li that he studied Chinese.	(focus on how)

The 是...的 construction may also be used without a time, place, or manner expression. In such cases, 是...的 does not imply a past event, but is used to emphasize the predicate that appears between 是 and 的. For example,

我是學英國文學的。   It is English literature that I study.

Note that "I study English literature" can be expressed as "我學英國文學" or "我是學英國文學的", but the latter is more emphatic.

在

在 can be a verb or a preposition meaning "be at, be in" and "at, in," respectively. It is placed before a noun to indicate location.

For example,

- 在 used as a verb meaning "be at, be in"
  他在家。　　　　　　He is at home.
  李老師在中國。　　　Teacher Li is in China.

- 在 used as a preposition meaning "at, in." 在 occurs before a place word (forming a prepositional phrase) to express where an action is carried out.

Subject	在	Place word	Verb	
我爸爸	在	紐約	工作。	My Dad works in New York.

When 在 is used as a preposition, the 在 phrase is placed before the verb phrase. Note that this word order is different from that of English.

量詞(2)個，輛，隻，本． Questions: 幾個，幾輛，幾隻，幾本

As we mentioned in previous lessons, Chinese is a language that makes extensive use of measure words.

The following are some guidelines for the use of Chinese measure words:

Measure word	Features	Examples	
個 个	• The most commonly used measure word • Used to denote the number of people, buildings, characters etc.	一個人 一個室友 兩個老師 四個漢字 [hànzì]	(one person) (one roommate) (two teachers) (four characters)
輛	• Used for vehicles	兩輛車	(two cars)
隻	• Used for animals	一隻狗	(one dog)
本	• Used for bound items such as books or magazines	兩本中文書	(two Chinese books)

幾個，幾輛，幾隻，幾本
When asking about amounts under ten, the question word 幾 is used.

For example,

你家有幾個人?	How many people are there in your family?
你有幾輛車?	How many cars do you have?
你媽媽有幾隻狗?	How many dogs does your mom have?
你姐姐有幾本書?	How many books does your older sister have?

補充課文 ⚭⚭ SUPPLEMENTARY PRACTICE

This selection will help you test your comprehension of the grammar and vocabulary you have learned in this lesson. Be prepared to answer questions about the meaning of the passage.

書友： 學文，來，我來介紹一下，這是我爸爸、媽媽和妹妹。爸爸、
　　　 媽媽、妹妹，這是我室友學文。

學文： 你們好!

爸爸，媽媽，妹妹： 你好!

爸爸： 來，請坐。請問，你是從哪兒來的? 你家在哪兒?

學文： 我是從中國來的，我家在北京。

媽媽： 你家都有哪些人?

學文： 我家有爸爸，媽媽和我。

妹妹： 我們有寵物，我們養了一隻狗，你呢? 你家有狗嗎?

學文： 我們家沒有狗，可是我們有貓。

書友： 你們養了幾隻貓?

學文： 我媽媽很愛貓，我們家養了三隻貓。

爸爸： 你爸爸，媽媽工作嗎? 他們都做什麼?

學文： 我爸爸工作，媽媽不工作。我爸爸是老師，媽媽是家庭主婦。

妹妹： 對了，你有女朋友嗎?

學文： 沒有，我沒有女朋友。你呢，你有男朋友嗎?

妹妹： 有，我有男朋友。

書友： 我妹妹的男朋友叫明明。他很愛車，他有四輛車。

學文： 妳男朋友好像很有錢!

Notes: 請坐 [qǐngzuò]: Please be seated.
　　　　 哪些 [nǎxiē]: What . . .
　　　　 養 [yǎng]: to raise
　　　　 了 [le]: an aspect particle indicating completion
　　　　 家庭主婦 [jiātíng zhǔfù]: housewife
　　　　 好像 [hǎoxiàng]: seems like
　　　　 有錢 [yǒuqián]: rich
　　　　 你 [nǐ]: you. In simplified characters, 你 is used for both the male and female "you." In traditional characters, 妳 is sometimes used for the female "you."

練習 ACTIVITIES

I. Pinyin Exercises

6-1 Read the following Pinyin words and pay special attention to any tone changes:

A. 3rd tonal change

1. wǒ jiā	2. Niǔyuē	3. lǎoshī	4. hěnduō
5. nǐ lái	6. Fǎguó	7. Měiguó	8. nǎ guó
9. hěnhǎo	10. Xiǎoměi	11. yě yǒu	12. hěnshǎo
13. qǐngwèn	14. jǐge	15. liǎngliàng	16. kǎoshì

B. "一" [yī] and "不" [bù] tonal change

17. yídìng	18. yìdiǎr	19. yíxiàr	20. yī èr sān sì
21. bù shuō	22. bú duì	23. bùhǎo	24. búcuò

6-2 Listen to the instructor read the paragraph and fill in the blanks with the correct Pinyin:

1. Wǒ shì _____ de.
2. Wǒ jiā _____.
3. Wǒ bàba _____ māma _____ shì _____.
4. Wǒ _____ yǒu nán péngyou, wǒ _____.
5. Wǒ _____ wǒde _____.

6-3 Form groups of three to four. Take turns reading the following tongue twister out loud, as quickly as you can. Each group will select one member to represent the group in a class competition.

rènmìng　任命　appointment
rénmíng　人名　name
cuò　錯　wrong

Rènmìng, Rénmíng	任命，人名	Appointments and Names
Rènmìng shì rènmìng,	任命是任命，	Appointments are appointments,
Rénmíng shì rénmíng.	人名是人名。	Names are names.
Rènmìng, rénmíng bùnéng cuò,	任命，人名不能錯，	Appointments and names should not be messed up,
Cuò le rénmíng rènmìng cuò.	錯了人名任命錯。	If they are, appointments will be names, and vice versa.

II. Character Exercises

6-4   Read the following words, phrases, and sentences:

家	車
我的家	我的車
這是我的家。	這是我的車。
我很愛我的家。	這是我哥哥的車。
姐姐也很愛我們的家。	這是我哥哥和我的車。
我們大家都很愛我們的家。	這也是我哥哥和我的車。

Now try to use the following characters to make words, phrases, and then sentences:

1. 大   2. 從   3. 在   4. 四   5. 爸   6. 媽

7. 作   8. 男   9. 沒   10. 輛   11. 隻   12. 愛

6-5   Write out the characters for the following Pinyin words:

1. bàba   ☐☐   2. māma   ☐☐

3. jiějie   ☐☐   4. dàjiā   ☐☐

5. gōngzuò   ☐☐   6. yíliàng chē   ☐☐☐

7. yìzhī gǒu   ☐☐☐   8. gōngchéngshī   ☐☐☐

6-6   Match the traditional forms of the following words with their simplified forms:

國	紹	兩	愛	隻	個	輛	師

(1)   (2)   (3)   (4)   (5)   (6)   (7)   (8)

爱   兩   国   辆   师   个   绍   只

III. Grammar Exercises

6-7 Substitution exercises:

1. 你是從哪兒來的?
   我是從<u>紐約</u>來的。

北京	[Běijīng]	Beijing
上海	[Shànghǎi]	Shanghai
香港	[Xiānggǎng]	Hong Kong
台北	[Táiběi]	Taipei
波士頓	[Bōshìdùn]	Boston

2. 你是在哪兒學中文的?
   我是在<u>紐約</u>學中文的。

中國		
北京大學		
加州	[Jiāzhōu]	California
華盛頓特區	[Huáshèngdùntèqū]	
		Washington, D.C.

3. 你是學什麼的?
   我是學<u>中國文學</u>的。

工程		
數學	[shùxué]	mathematics
英國文學		

4. 你爸爸是做什麼的?
   我爸爸是<u>工程師</u>。

英文老師		
醫生	[yīshēng]	doctor
律師	[lùshī]	lawyer
商人	[shāngrén]	businessman

5. 你在哪兒?
   我在<u>家</u>。

學校		
大學		
姐姐家		
宿舍	[sùshè]	dorm

6. 小美有幾<u>個</u>老師?
   小美有<u>兩個</u>老師。

四	本	中文書
一	隻	狗
兩	輛	車
一	個	姐姐
三	隻	貓

IV. Communicative Activities

6-8 Go around the classroom and talk to as many people as you can. Ask questions on the following topics, among others:

1. 他/她的名字
2. 他/她學什麼?
3. 他/她家在哪兒?
4. 他/她的家人

Note: 家人 [jiārén]: family members

6-9 Three or four students should give short introductions about themselves and their families. The rest should listen and prepare to ask questions about their introductions.

文化點滴　CULTURE NOTES

中國家庭 [Zhōngguó jiātíng]
Chinese Families

Traditional Chinese families were established on the theory of Confucianism, and large families have been valued in China for thousands of years. It was common for several generations to live together under one roof. Four generations living together was considered a sign of family prosperity and happiness. The man of the senior generation was the leader of the family and had the greatest authority in making decisions regarding all important issues, including the education, marriage, and careers of younger members of the family. It was assumed that younger generations would obey their elders, even if they did not see eye to eye, and would take care of them in their old age. Indeed, filial piety, the respect and care of elders in the family, was traditionally considered the most important of all qualities.

Today the situation has changed drastically because of the enforcement of the government's one-child-per-family policy and influences from other cultures. Chinese households now usually consist of the nuclear family, although it is still common for the elderly to live with their children. The only child often takes the role of family head and exercises great influence on family decisions. Filial piety is no longer emphasized, especially among the younger generation.

Families in China had been stable for thousands of years until very recently. This, to a large extent, was due to the traditional Chinese emphasis on family and the relationship between husband and wife. Marriages were based on responsibility more than love, and divorce was forbidden. Women could marry only once in their lifetime. Men were supposed to shoulder the responsibility of taking care of the family. A man who could not keep his family stable would face pressure from all directions. In modern China, until very recently, families remained stable because young men and women still attached great importance to marriage and would spend a long time getting to know each other before they finally got married. Frequently both husband and wife worked, which contributed to the equality between them.

91

Useful words and expressions:

宣傳(宣传) [xuānchuán]: propaganda
標語(标语) [biāoyǔ]: slogan
碧水 [bìshuǐ]: green water
藍天(蓝天) [lántiān]: blue sky
綠色(绿色) [lǜsè]: green
家園(家园) [jiāyuán]: home
做 [zuò]: to be
文明 [wénmíng]: civilized
市民 [shìmín]: city citizen
樹(树) [shù]: to establish
社會(社会) [shèhuì]: society
新風(新风) [xīnfēng]: new atmosphere

Questions:

1. How would you translate these two slogans?

2. Did you notice the parallel pattern of the two slogans?

7

你住哪兒？
Where Do You Live?

教學目標　OBJECTIVES

- Ask someone's address
- Tell them your address
- Describe a place
- Ask/give phone numbers

These mailboxes for an apartment complex are each clearly marked with an address.

Balconies are used for hanging laundry to dry. Note that many buildings have steel bars over windows to prevent thieves from entering.

生詞 VOCABULARY

核心詞 Core Vocabulary

	TRADITIONAL	SIMPLIFIED	PINYIN		
1.	住	住	zhù	V.	to live
2.	哪兒	哪儿	nǎr	Pron.	where
3.	宿舍	宿舍	sùshè	N.	dorm
4.	多少	多少	duōshǎo	Pron.	how many, how much
5.	號	号	hào	N.	number
6.	房間	房间	fángjiān	N.	room
7.	大	大	dà	Adj.	big
8.	電話	电话	diànhuà	N.	phone
9.	小	小	xiǎo	Adj.	small
10.	號碼	号码	hàomǎ	N.	number
11.	二	二	èr	Num.	two
12.	三	三	sān	Num.	three
13.	五	五	wǔ	Num.	five
14.	六	六	liù	Num.	six
15.	七	七	qī	Num.	seven
16.	八	八	bā	Num.	eight
17.	九	九	jiǔ	Num.	nine
18.	手機	手机	shǒujī	N.	cell phone
19.	校外	校外	xiàowài	N.	off campus

專名 Proper Nouns

TRADITIONAL	SIMPLIFIED	PINYIN		
1. 陳愛文	陈爱文	Chén Àiwén	N.	(name) Aiwen Chen
2. 張友朋	张友朋	Zhāng Yǒupéng	N.	(name) Youpeng Zhang

補充詞 Supplementary Vocabulary

TRADITIONAL	SIMPLIFIED	PINYIN		
1. 校內	校内	xiàonèi	N.	on campus
2. 公寓	公寓	gōngyù	N.	apartment
3. 房子	房子	fángzi	N.	house, room
4. 十	十	shí	Num.	ten
5. ○	○	líng	Num.	zero

Formal Way to Write Zero to Ten in Chinese

líng ○ 零	yī 一 壹	èr 二 貳	sān 三 叁	sì 四 肆	wǔ 五 伍	liù 六 陸	qī 七 柒	bā 八 捌	jiǔ 九 玖	shí 十 拾

Note: In some situations, "one" is also pronounced as [yāo] in Mainland China (e.g., phone numbers and room numbers).

語文知識 LANGUAGE LINK

The Sentence Patterns provide models that will help you with the Language in Use section. In both sections, pay attention to the grammar points, vocabulary, and expressions.

句型 **Sentence Patterns**

A: 你住在哪兒?
Nǐ zhù zài nǎr?

B: 我住宿舍。
Wǒ zhù sùshè.

A: 多少號?
Duōshǎo hào?

B: 三一四號。
Sān yī sì hào.

A: 你的房間大嗎?
Nǐde fángjiān dà ma?

B: 房間很小。
Fángjiān hěn xiǎo.

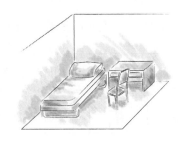

A: 你的電話號碼是多少?
Nǐde diànhuà hàomǎ shì duōshǎo?

B: (一四二)二六八九三七五。
(Yī sì èr) èr liù bā jiǔ sān qī wǔ.

課文　Language in Use: 你住哪兒？ Nǐ zhù nǎr?

陳愛文：　友朋，你住在哪兒?
　　　　　Yǒupéng, nǐ zhù zài nǎr?

張友朋：　我住宿舍。
　　　　　Wǒ zhù sùshè.

陳愛文：　多少號?
　　　　　Duōshǎo hào?

張友朋：　三一四號。
　　　　　Sān yī sì hào.

陳愛文：　你的房間大嗎? 有沒有電話?
　　　　　Nǐde fángjiān dà ma? Yǒuméiyǒu diànhuà?

張友朋：　房間很小。有電話。
　　　　　Fángjiān hěn xiǎo. Yǒu diànhuà.

陳愛文：　你的電話號碼是多少?
　　　　　Nǐde diànhuà hàomǎ shì duōshǎo?

張友朋：　(一四二)二六八九三七五。
　　　　　(Yī sì èr) èr liù bā jiǔ sān qī wǔ.

陳愛文：　你有手機嗎?
　　　　　Nǐ yǒu shǒujī ma?

張友朋：　有。號碼是 (一四二)五一二六八三七。
　　　　　Yǒu. Hàomǎ shì (yī sì èr) wǔ yī èr liù bā sān qī.

　　　　　你也住宿舍嗎?
　　　　　Nǐ yě zhù sùshè ma?

陳愛文：　不，我不住宿舍，我住校外。
　　　　　Bù, wǒ bú zhù sùshè, wǒ zhù xiàowài.

注釋 LANGUAGE NOTES

哪兒 and 哪裡

哪兒 means "where." It is common to use " 裡 [lǐ]" to replace 兒 as in 哪裡 [nǎlǐ] (where). It also applies to "here" as in 這兒 [zhèr] and 這裡 [zhèlǐ] and "there" as in 那兒 [nàr] and 那裡 [nàlǐ].

多少號

多少 is the question word for asking about a number. " 多少號?" means "Which number?"

有沒有

有 means "have," 沒有 means "don't have." 有沒有 is a question meaning "have or not have." It is equivalent to " 有...嗎?"

手機

手機 literally means "hand machine." It is used to refer to a "cellular phone." Chinese also refer to cell phones as 大哥大 [dàgēdà], and 行動電話 [xíngdòng diànhuà] (mobile phone) in Taiwan, and 移動電話 [yídòng diànhuà] in Mainland China.

語法 GRAMMAR

住

住 means "to live." Because the verb 住 typically is used to indicate a location, the locative preposition 在 ("at, in") sometimes is omitted. For example,

Where do you live?	你住在哪兒？	or	你住哪兒？
I live in room 314.	我住在三一四號。	or	我住三一四號。
I do not live in the dorm.	我不住在宿舍。	or	我不住宿舍。

住址的寫法 Word Order for Addresses

Chinese word order for addresses is from larger scope to smaller scope. It is opposite to that of English. See the contrast below,

#245 Baker Street
Pittsburgh, PA 15143
USA

美國賓州匹茲堡市
15143貝克街245號

or

美國賓州匹茲堡市
貝克街245號
郵政編碼: 15143

Notes: 賓州 [Bīnzhōu]: Pennsylvania State
州 [zhōu]: state
匹茲堡 [Pǐzībǎo]: Pittsburgh
市 [shì]: city
郵政編碼 [yóu zhèng biān mǎ]: zip code
郵遞區號 [yóu dì qū hào]: zip code, used in Taiwan
街 [jiē]: street

#2 Zhongshan Road
Beijing, 100083
China

中國北京市100083中山路2號

Notes: 北京市 [Běijīng shì]: Beijing City
市 [shì]: city
路 [lù]: road

Topic-Comment Sentences

The topic-comment sentence pattern is one in which a noun or phrase serves as a topic, and is followed by a clause commenting on the topic. Other examples we have learned so far are as follows:

Topic	Comment	English
你的房間	大嗎?	Is your room big?
我的房間	很大。	My room is big.
工程	難嗎?	Is engineering difficult?
工程	不太難。	Engineering is not too difficult.
功課	多嗎?	Is there a lot of homework?
功課	也不少。	There is also a lot of homework.

多少 and 幾

多少 and 幾 "how many, how much" are both used in asking about numbers. The differences between 多少 and 幾 are detailed below:

幾	多少
For fewer than 10 objects	For more than 10 objects
Must occur with a measure word	May occur with or without a measure word
For countable nouns only	For both countable and noncountable nouns

補充課文 ─○○○─ SUPPLEMENTARY PRACTICE

This selection will help you test your comprehension of the grammar and vocabulary you have learned in this lesson. Be prepared to answer questions about the meaning of the passage.

　　大家好! 這是我的宿舍。我的宿舍是四一三號, 房間很小, 有一個電話, 我的電話號碼是(一四二)九三二六五八七。我有三個室友, 他們都有手機。我們都很喜歡我們的宿舍。你呢? 你也住在宿舍嗎? 宿舍大嗎? 你有沒有手機? 號碼是多少? 他呢? 他是我們的新同學嗎? 他住宿舍還是校外?

Notes: 喜歡 [xǐhuān]: to like
　　　新 [xīn]: new
　　　還是 [háishì]: or

練習 ACTIVITIES

I. Pinyin Exercises

7-1　In each pair, circle the one your instructor pronounces:

1. xùshè　sùshè
2. duōshǎo　dōushǎo
3. diànhuà　diànhuā
4. hǎomā　hàomǎ
5. shǒujī　shǎojī
6. qiàowāi　xiàowài

7-2　Listen to the instructor read the sentences and fill in the blanks with the correct Pinyin:

1. Nǐ _____ nǎr?
2. Nǐde _____ dà ma?
3. Wǒ _____ diànhuà.
4. Nǐde diànhuà _____ shì _____ ?

7-3 Read the lyrics to the following Chinese folk song, paying special attention to the tones and rhythm:

Yí qù èr sān lǐ	一去二三里	**A Walk of Two or Three Miles**
Yí qù èr sān lǐ,	一去二三里，	I strolled for two or three miles,
Yān cūn sì wǔ jiā.	煙村四五家。	Saw four or five villages in the fog.
Tíng tái liù qī zuò,	亭台六七座，	Viewed six or seven pavilions,
Bā jiǔ shí zhī huā.	八九十枝花。	And enjoyed many flowers.

II. Character Exercises

7-4 Read the following words and phrases:

住	大
住(在)宿舍	很大
住(在)校外	太大
住(在)校內	不太大
住(在)公寓	不大
住(在) 朋友家	一點兒也不大

Now try to use the following characters to make words, phrases, and then sentences:

1. 宿　　2. 號　　3. 房　　4. 電　　5. 話　　6. 小
7. 碼　　8. 手　　9. 機　　10. 校　　11. 外　　12. 間

7-5 Match the English translations with the correct characters, and then read them aloud:

1.
four	九
five	八
six	四
seven	六
eight	五
nine	七

2.
good	容易
many	難
little	好
difficult	忙
easy	少
busy	多

III. Grammar Exercises

7-6　Substitution exercises:

1. 你住哪兒？
   我住在<u>宿舍</u>，<u>二一六</u>號。

校內
校外
公寓　　　　五二三

2. 你的電話號碼是多少？
   <u>是(124)268-9375</u>。

(192)886-7532
(148)623-5790
我沒有電話

3. 你的<u>房間</u><u>大</u>嗎？
   我的<u>房間</u>很<u>小</u>。

功課	難
學習	忙
中文書	多
學習 [xuéxí] study	

7-7　Read the following sentences, then ask questions on the underlined words:

1. 我住在<u>宿舍</u>。
2. 我住在<u>三五六</u>號。
3. 我的房間<u>不大</u>。
4. 你的功課很<u>多</u>。
5. 我哥哥有<u>手機</u>。
6. 我哥哥的手機號碼是<u>(一五五)二六七三九四八</u>。
7. 他有<u>四</u>個兄弟姐妹。
8. 他有<u>兩</u>個妹妹。
9. 她和她的室友都<u>很忙</u>。
10. 老師也是<u>中國人</u>。

IV. Communicative Activities

7-8　Classroom activities:

Form pairs. Exchange information about each other, including addresses and phone numbers, then act out for the class.

Hints: Words or phrases that can be used:

住在哪兒？　　有沒有電話？　　電話號碼是多少？
有室友嗎？　　有幾輛車？　　　功課多嗎？

文化點滴　CULTURE NOTES

中國傳統住房 [Zhōngguó chuántǒng zhùfáng] — 四合院 [sì hé yuàn]
Traditional Chinese Houses — Si He Yuan

China is a large country with very complicated natural conditions and weather that varies widely from region to region. With 56 different ethnic groups, there is a rich variety of customs and habits. This leads to very diverse styles and structures in the residential architecture of China. Si He Yuan, a housing compound enclosed on four sides, is the typical traditional housing in the northern part of China, especially in Beijing.

Si He Yuan is a rectangular compound with traditional one-story buildings built on four sides. They are connected by corridors with a yard in the center. The whole compound is enclosed except for the gate, which is usually located at the southeast corner. The rooms situated in the north of the compound facing the south are the largest and the brightest and, therefore, are typically occupied by the master of the family. Those on the east and the west are for the children. The kitchen and the bathroom are on either side of the master's suite.

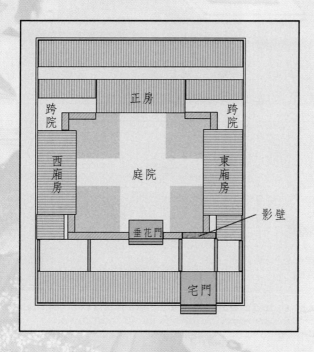

A Si He Yuan usually consists of two yards, one in the front and one in the back. The master's suite is located in the back yard (also called inner yard) while rooms in the front yard (also called outer yard) are used for guests or servants. Housemaids are placed in the far back north of the compound behind the master's suite. Those back rooms may also be used as storage rooms.

As you enter the main gate of a Si He Yuan, you will see before you a low wall with various decorations on it. This serves as a barrier to prevent outsiders from seeing the inner yard, something considered necessary for good Feng Shui 風水 [Fēng Shuǐ] (geomancy). In the middle of the inner yard is an open space that serves as a venue for all kinds of activities. There are usually trees and flowers there as well.

Today, as cities move towards modernization, many Si He Yuan have been replaced by high-rise apartment buildings. In order to preserve the tradition and the culture of Si He Yuan, the Chinese government has formulated laws to protect them so that future generations will still be able to see how their ancestors lived.

Questions:

1. What kind of houses do you see in the U.S.? What do you think are the most obvious differences between Western-style houses and traditional Chinese houses?

2. Have you heard about Feng Shui? Do you think it is important?

These are examples of Si He Yuan in Taiwan. The Si He Yuan is a rectangular compound with traditional one-story buildings on all four sides. In the middle is a yard with open space for all kinds of activities.

This Si He Yuan in Taiwan has been preserved as an important aspect of traditional Chinese culture. It is a big attraction for visitors.

Today, high-rise buildings are common in China. (Shanghai)

Fancy and luxurious apartment in Hong Kong.

This mansion is built on the corner of a rice paddy in Taiwan.

趣味中文   FUN WITH CHINESE

遠親不如近鄰。

Relatives who live in a distant place are not as helpful as neighbors.

yuǎn	qīn	bù	rú	jìn	lín
遠	親	不	如	近	鄰
distant	relatives	not	as if	close	neighbor

"遠親不如近鄰" is a common Chinese saying used to emphasize the importance of your neighbors or community. It indicates that if there is any help needed, your neighbors will usually be the ones to offer it.

Question:

Have you ever encountered a situation that proves "遠親不如近鄰" to be true? Would you like to share an example with the class?

行動吧!   LET'S GO!

小心輕放   **Handle with Care**

家文 is sending a Chinese tea set to her family. The post office staff helped her place a special sticker on the package. Take a look at the sticker. What is its message?

Useful words and expressions:

脆弱 [cuìruò]: fragile

郵件(邮件) [yóujiàn]: mail item

小心 [xiǎoxīn]: careful

輕放(轻放) [qīngfàng]: to handle gently

注意 [zhùyì]: watch out

事項(事项) [shìxiàng]: item

顧客(顾客) [gùkè]: customer

依 [yī]: according to

內裝物(内装物) [nèizhuāngwù]: contents

妥為封裝(妥为封装) [tuǒwéi fēngzhuāng]: to pack carefully

郵政(邮政) [yóuzhèng]: postal service

寄 [jì]: to send

東西(东西) [dōngxi]: things, stuff

貼(贴) [tiē]: to paste

Questions:

1. Translate the sticker on the right.

2. 你寄什麼東西要貼這個?

復習　**Review**

Conversation

Ask your partner the following questions. Then report the information you collect to the class.

1. 請問，你住在哪兒? 你住宿舍嗎? (什麼宿舍? 多少號? 你住校外嗎?)
2. 你有室友嗎? 他們是誰? 他們都是哪國人?
3. 你們的宿舍(房子)有電話嗎? 號碼是多少?
4. 你的房間大嗎?
5. 你有手機嗎? 號碼是多少? 你室友也有手機嗎?
6. 你有中國朋友嗎? 有幾個? 他們都是從哪兒來的?
7. 你呢? 你是從哪兒來的?
8. 你家有幾個人? 他們是誰? 他們都好嗎? 他們忙嗎?
9. 你們家有寵物 [chǒngwù] (pets) 嗎? (狗/貓)
10. 你家有幾個房間? 房間大嗎?
11. 你有車嗎? 什麼車? 你的功課多嗎? 難嗎? 你是在哪兒學中文的?
12. 你有車嗎? (什麼車?) 你爸爸呢? 你家有幾輛車?

Character Writing

Situation: You win a lottery while you are traveling in China! You need to confirm your birthday and address in order to claim it. Pay attention to stroke order.

Useful words:

年 [nián]: year　　　月 [yuè]: month　　　日 [rì]: day　　　生日 [shēngrì]: birthday

州 [zhōu]: state　　　街 [jiē]: street　　　路 [lù]: road　　　樓 [lóu]: floor

郵編 [yóubiān]: zip code

號 [hào]: number: 一 (1), 二 (2), 三 (3), 四 (4), 五 (5), 六 (6), 七 (7), 八 (8), 九 (9),
十 (10), 十一 (11), 十二 (12), 十五 (15), 二十 (20), 二十三 (23), 三十 (30)

中文名字: _____

生　　日: _____ 年 _____ 月 _____ 日

中文地址: _____

Traditional and Simplified Characters

Read each character aloud. Write its traditional form. Then create a phrase and a sentence using the character.

For example，　学 → 學 → 學生 → 我是學生。

号 (　)　　电 (　)　　机 (　)　　爱 (　)　　从 (　)　　来 (　)　　绍 (　)

妈 (　)　　间 (　)　　码 (　)

8

你認識不認識他?
Do You Know Him?

教學目標　OBJECTIVES

- More yes and no questions
- Make and respond to a plan

Do you know them?
(Yao Ming and Chairman Mao)

生詞 VOCABULARY

核心詞 Core Vocabulary

	TRADITIONAL	SIMPLIFIED	PINYIN		
1.	認識	认识	rènshi	V.	to know; to recognize
2.	去	去	qù	V.	to go
3.	上課	上课	shàngkè	V.O.	to attend class
4.	下課	下课	xiàkè	V.O.	to end class, class dismissed
5.	以後	以后	yǐhòu	N.	after, afterwards; later
6.	事兒	事儿	shèr	N.	matter, thing, business
7.	想	想	xiǎng	V.	to want
8.	回	回	huí	V.	to return
9.	一起	一起	yìqǐ	Adv.	together
10.	吃	吃	chī	V.	to eat
11.	飯	饭	fàn	N.	cooked rice, meal
12.	吃飯	吃饭	chīfàn	V.O.	to eat, have a meal
13.	菜	菜	cài	N.	dish
14.	今天	今天	jīntiān	N.	today
15.	下次	下次	xiàcì		next time
16.	怎麼樣	怎么样	zěnmeyàng	Pron.	(used as a predicative or complement) how
17.	行	行	xíng	V.	to be all right, okay
18.	再見	再见	zàijiàn		see you again; goodbye
	再	再	zài	Adv.	again
	見	见	jiàn	V.	to see

專名 Proper Nouns

	TRADITIONAL	SIMPLIFIED	PINYIN		
1.	韓國	韩国	Hánguó	N.	Korea
2.	日本	日本	Rìběn	N.	Japan

補充詞 Supplementary Vocabulary

	TRADITIONAL	SIMPLIFIED	PINYIN		
1.	名片	名片	míngpiàn	N.	name card
2.	休息	休息	xiūxi	V.	to rest
3.	早飯	早饭	zǎofàn	N.	breakfast
4.	午飯 (中飯)	午饭 (中饭)	wǔfàn (zhōngfàn)	N.	lunch
5.	晚飯	晚饭	wǎnfàn	N.	dinner
6.	宵夜	宵夜	xiāoyè	N.	midnight snack

語文知識 LANGUAGE LINK

The Sentence Patterns provide models that will help you with the Language in Use section. In both sections, pay attention to the grammar points, vocabulary, and expressions.

句型 Sentence Patterns

A: 你去哪兒？
Nǐ qù nǎr?

B: 我去上課。
Wǒ qù shàngkè.

A: 你有事兒嗎？
Nǐ yǒu shèr ma?

B: 我沒有事兒。
Wǒ méiyǒu shèr.

A: 你認識不認識他？
Nǐ rènshi bú rènshi tā?

B: 我認識他。
Wǒ rènshi tā.

A: 我們吃韓國菜，怎麼樣？
Wǒmen chī Hánguó cài, zěnmeyàng?

B: 行。
Xíng.

課文　Language in Use: 你認識不認識他？ Nǐ rènshi bú rènshi tā?

張友朋：　愛文，你去哪兒？
　　　　　Àiwén, nǐ qù nǎr?

陳愛文：　是你，友朋，我去上課。你呢？
　　　　　Shì nǐ, Yǒupéng, wǒ qù shàngkè. Nǐ ne?

張友朋：　我也去上課。下課以後你有事兒嗎？
　　　　　Wǒ yě qù shàngkè. Xiàkè yǐhòu nǐ yǒu shèr ma?

陳愛文：　我沒有事兒。我想回宿舍。有什麼事兒嗎？
　　　　　Wǒ méiyǒu shèr. Wǒ xiǎng huí sùshè. Yǒu shénme shèr ma?

張友朋：　你認識不認識我的朋友小文？
　　　　　Nǐ rènshi bú rènshi wǒ de péngyou Xiǎowén?

陳愛文：　我認識他。我們一起上英國文學課。
　　　　　Wǒ rènshi tā. Wǒmen yìqǐ shàng Yīngguó wénxué kè.

張友朋：　下課以後我跟他一起去吃飯。你去不去?
　　　　　Xiàkè yǐhòu wǒ gēn tā yìqǐ qù chīfàn. Nǐ qù bú qù?

陳愛文：　太好了！去哪兒吃飯?
　　　　　Tài hǎo le! Qù nǎr chī fàn?

張友朋：　你想不想吃韓國菜?
　　　　　Nǐ xiǎng bù xiǎng chī Hánguó cài?

陳愛文：　想。可是我也想吃日本菜。
　　　　　Xiǎng. Kěshì wǒ yě xiǎng chī Rìběn cài.

張友朋：　我們今天吃韓國菜，
　　　　　Wǒmen jīntiān chī Hánguó cài,

　　　　　下次吃日本菜，怎麼樣?
　　　　　xiàcì chī Rìběn cài, zěnmeyàng?

陳愛文：　行。下課以後再見。
　　　　　Xíng. Xiàkè yǐhòu zàijiàn.

張友朋：　再見。
　　　　　Zàijiàn.

注釋　LANGUAGE NOTES

事兒/事

事兒 means "matter, business." "我沒有事兒" means "I have no business to attend to" or "I am free." 兒 can be omitted, as in "我沒有事."

太好了！

"太好了！" is a phrase meaning "That's great!"

好，行

"好," "行" are both the expressions meaning "Good!" "Ok!" They are also used to indicate agreement with what others have just mentioned.

語法 GRAMMAR

Affirmative-Negative Questions ("A 不 A" Pattern)

The affirmative-negative question (also called "A 不 A" pattern) is a choice type of question. It requires a "yes" or "no" answer. It is formed by saying the positive and negative forms of a verb (or an adverb) together in the same sentence.

"A 不 A" pattern	
是不是	想不想
難不難	好不好
行不行	忙不忙
說不說	在不在
常不常	住不住
多不多	會不會
叫不叫	問不問
來不來	去不去
#認識不認識	有沒有

Note: #"你認識不認識他?" ("Do you know him?") Some Chinese would use "你認不認識他?"

Note (1): Affirmative-negative question for 有 is 有沒有.

Question ("A 不 A")	Reply "yes"	Reply "no"
你認識不認識他？	認識。(我認識他。)	不認識。(我不認識他。)
你想不想吃韓國菜？	想。(我想吃韓國菜。)	不想。(我不想吃韓國菜。)

Note (2): The "A 不 A" pattern functions in the same way as a question ending with 嗎. For example,

Question with 嗎	"A 不 A" pattern
你是中國人嗎？	你是不是中國人？
你認識他嗎？	你認識不認識他？

Note (3): In the "A 不 A" pattern, the object generally comes after the negative form of the predicate, but it may also be placed between the "A 不 A" form. For example,

你說不說中文？	Do you speak or not speak Chinese?
你說中文不說？	Do you speak Chinese or not?

Tag Question

The tag question is a short question that is attached to a statement. It is used for confirmation of the previous statement, or for making a suggestion. In Chinese, it is usually formed with "A 不 A" pattern or "是嗎," "好嗎," "行嗎," "對嗎" and "怎麼樣." For example,

你認識他，對不對？	You know him, right?
你想回宿舍，是不是？	You want to go back to the dorm, right?
你是學生，是嗎？	You are a student, right?
我們今天吃韓國菜，好嗎？	Let's go to eat Korean food today. How's that?
我們下次吃日本菜，行嗎？	Let's eat Japanese food next time, all right?
我們一起去上課，怎麼樣？	Let's go to attend class together. How does that sound?

補充課文 ⟞⟝ SUPPLEMENTARY PRACTICE

This selection will help you test your comprehension of the grammar and vocabulary you have learned in this lesson. Be prepared to answer questions about the meaning of the passage.

你們好！請問，你們認識不認識他？如果你們不認識他也沒關係，現在我來給你們介紹一下兒，他是我的室友。他叫學友，他是韓國人，他學英國文學。他會說韓語，英文和一點兒中文。我們常常一起上課，下課。下課以後我們常一起回宿舍。

我們是好室友，好同學，也是好朋友。我們也常常一起去吃飯。今天我們想去吃日本菜，下次吃中國菜。你們呢？下課以後你們有事兒嗎？你們想不想吃日本菜？跟我們一起去吃日本菜，怎麼樣？好，再見！

Notes: 如果 [rúguǒ]: if
沒關係 [méiguānxi]: it doesn't matter

練習 ACTIVITIES

I. Pinyin Exercises

8-1 In each of following pairs, circle the one your instructor pronounces:

1. rènxi	rènshi	2. shàngkè	sàngkè	3. xiākè	xiàkè
4. yǐhuò	yǐhòu	5. yíqǐ	yìqǐ	6. qīfàn	chīfàn
7. jīntiān	jiāntiān	8. sàcì	xiàcì	9. zhàizhàn	zàijiàn

8-2 Listen to the instructor and fill in the initial in the following Pinyin:

1. ___ù   2. ___iǎng   3. ___àng   4. ___ià
5. ___èr   6. ___ī   7. ___ài   8. ___íng
9. ___īn   10. ___ěn   11. ___ì   12. ___iàn

8-3 Form groups of three or four. Take turns reading the following tongue twister out loud, as quickly as you can. Each group will select one member to represent the group in a class competition.

Xiǎosì: 小四   Little Si (name of a person)
Xiǎoshí: 小十   Little Shi (name of a person)
lǎoshí: 老實   honest

Xiǎosì hé Xiǎoshí	**小四和小十**	**Little Si and Little Shi**
Xiǎosì shì lǎoshi rén,	小四是老實人，	Little Si is an honest man,
Xiǎoshí búshì lǎoshi rén.	小十不是老實人。	Little Shi is not an honest man.
Xiǎoshí qīfu Xiǎosì,	小十欺負小四，	Little Shi bullies Little Si,
Xiǎosì bèi Xiǎoshí qīfu.	小四被小十欺負。	Little Si is bullied by Little Shi.

II. Character Exercises

8-4 Read the following words and phrases:

課	去	一起
英文課	去宿舍	一起吃飯
中文課	去考試	一起去宿舍
上課	去中國	一起學中文
上日語課	去上課	一起上英國文學課
下課	去上工程課	跟朋友一起住

Now try to use the following characters to make words, phrases, and then sentences:

1. 認   2. 識   3. 以   4. 事   5. 想   6. 回
7. 今   8. 次   9. 樣   10. 再   11. 飯   12. 菜

8-5 Write the Chinese characters for the following words, using one character for each blank:

1. know ___ ___   2. go _____   3. attend class ___ ___

4. after ___ ___   5. want _____   6. have a meal ___ ___

7. return ___ ___   8. dish _____   9. goodbye _____

10. today ___ ___   11. how ___ ___   12. next time ___ ___

III. Grammar Exercises

8-6 Substitution exercises:

1. 你去哪兒？
   我去上課。

上數學課 [shùxué] mathematics
考試
宿舍
吃飯
跟我室友吃日本菜

2. 下課以後你有事兒嗎？
   有，我有事兒。我去上英文課。

有	有事兒	想跟朋友吃飯
有	有事兒	有一個考試
沒有	沒有事兒	

3. 你認識不認識我的朋友小文？
   我認識。

那個學生	認識
我的室友	不認識
他的哥哥	認識
[gēge] older brother	
我的中文老師	不認識

8-7 Ask questions on the underlined words, in three different ways:

I. A 不 A　　II. 嗎　　III. Tag questions

For example,　我學中文。
Questions:　你學不學中文？
　　　　　　你學中文嗎？
　　　　　　你學中文，對不對/是不是/對嗎/是嗎？

1. 下課以後我有事兒。
2. 我今天想吃日本菜。
3. 我跟小文一起上文學課。
4. 我的爸爸是工程師。
5. 我學法文。
6. 我的功課很多。

IV. Communicative Activities

8-8   Situational dialogue:

<u>Situation 1:</u>
Your high-school friend from another city is
visiting you. Please tell him/her some information
about the way you live and study right now.
Then ask your friend some similar questions.

Hints:
1. Topics to cover:
   - Greetings.
   - Chat about one of your common friends.
   - Ask about/describe where you live,
     your Chinese studies, courses, etc.

2. Words and expressions to use:

房間大不大？　　有沒有電話？　　忙不忙？　　功課多不多？
對嗎？　　　　　是嗎？　　　　　怎麼樣？

<u>Situation 2:</u>
Your roommate brings a new friend to your dorm.
Please introduce yourself to the new friend and
ask him/her some questions. Then discuss what
to do in the evening.

Hints:
1. Topics to cover:
   - Greetings.
   - Recommend a restaurant for dinner together.
   - Exchange addresses and phone numbers.

2. Words and expressions to use:

介紹一下　　住在哪兒　　下課以後有事兒嗎？
好嗎？　　　行嗎？　　　怎麼樣？

文化點滴　CULTURE NOTES

中國的名片文化
[Zhōngguó de míngpiàn wénhuà]
Business Cards in China
A Symbol of Social Position

Business cards in China, usually printed in both Chinese and English, not only show the owner's current position and responsibilities in a company or institution, but often list previous positions, roles of value, and even awards. Some business owners also like to use their name cards as advertisements to promote their business. With so much detail included, it is not uncommon to find Chinese business cards that are two-folded or even three-folded.

Often you might see on a business card someone's position as an adviser to a government institution, which indicates his/her strong connections with the government. However, top government officials do not usually present their business cards.

People are also becoming very particular about the decoration and selection of materials for their business cards. Many business cards have a colored background showing the city or the building where the card owner works. Some cards use special paper that cannot be torn easily by hand, and they are fireproof or waterproof. A few really wealthy people in China now have limited edition business cards made of pure gold. Those who are given gold business cards are usually guests of honor or trusted friends. In addition to its value as a precious gift, the card becomes a special pass for the recipient as well; if they need to see the card owner no one will prevent them from doing so.

Fancy card holders in leather used to be fashionable but these days gold-plated ones are preferred.

Questions:

1. How important are business cards in the U.S.?

2. How would you like your own business card to be designed?

Let's study the following Chinese business cards:

大中國科技有限公司
王美美
行銷部經理

地址：上海市南京路21號3樓	郵編：200030
電話：021-32168688	宅電：(021) 68811688
傳真：021-3213000	手機：13935356969
總機：021-3211111	直線：021-3211110
分機：021-3211112	
傳呼：128-223355	電郵：wangmeimei@dazhongguo_tech.com

真好吃快餐店

中餐西餐	便當外賣
電話：02-26886123	手機：(02) 922-886123

台北市忠孝東路三段25號

Useful words and expressions:

大中國(大中国) [Dàzhōngguó]: the great China
科技 [kējì]: technology
有限公司 [yǒuxiàn gōngsī]: limited-liability company
行銷部(行销部) [xíngxiāo bù]: marketing department
經理(经理) [jīnglǐ]: manager
樓(楼) [lóu]: floor
郵編(邮编) [yóubiān]: zip code
宅電(宅电) [zháidiàn]: home phone number
傳真(传真) [chuánzhēn]: fax
總機(总机) [zǒngjī]: switchboard
直線(直线) [zhíxiàn]: direct call
分機(分机) [fēnjī]: extension
傳呼(传呼) [chuánhū]: pager
快餐店 [kuàicāndiàn]: fast-food store
中餐 [zhōngcān]: Chinese food
西餐 [xīcān]: Western-style food
便當(便当) [biàndāng]: lunchbox
外賣(外卖) [wàimài]: deliver, take-out

趣味中文 FUN WITH CHINESE

一見鍾情
to fall in love at first sight

yí	jiàn	zhōng	qíng
一	見	鍾	情
one	see	concentrate	love

Question:

Can you think of any stories or movies which have an "一見鍾情" scene? Do you believe in "一見鍾情"? Why or why not? Would you like to experience this?

行動吧！ LET'S GO!

鈔票上的大人物
Important Figures on Currency

Below are samples of currency in 人民幣 [Rénmínbì] (人民币) (RMB) and 新台幣 [Xīntáibì] (NT) (新台币)

Useful words and expressions:

鈔票(钞票) [chāopiào]: bill
有名 [yǒumíng]: famous
歷史(历史) [lìshǐ]: history
人物 [rénwù]: people
毛澤東(毛泽东) [Máo Zédōng]: Mao Zedong
孫逸仙(孙逸仙) [Sūn Yìxiān]: Sun Yat-sen
國父(国父) [guófù]: national father
蔣介石(蒋介石) [Jiǎng Jièshí]: Chiang Kai-shek
地位 [dìwèi]: status
知道 [zhīdào]: to know of
近代史 [jìndài shǐ]: modern history

Questions:

1. 他們是誰，你知道嗎？你知道不知道他們？
2. 你知道他們在中國近代史上的地位嗎？

他正在打電話
He Is Making a Phone Call

- Make a phone call
- Handle various phone situations
- Ask what someone is doing
- Explain what you are doing

Cell phones are very common in China.

Public telephones in China and Taiwan are commonly used by inserting a prepaid phone card.

生詞 VOCABULARY

核心詞 Core Vocabulary

TRADITIONAL	SIMPLIFIED	PINYIN		
1. 正在	正在	zhèngzài	Adv.	(to indicate an action in progress) in the process of; in the course of
2. 打電話	打电话	dǎ diànhuà	V.O.	to make a phone call
3. 喂	喂	wèi (wéi)	Int.	(used in greeting or to attract attention) hello; hey
4. 等一下兒	等一下儿	děng yíxiàr		to wait for a moment; hang on (on the phone)
等	等	děng	V.	to wait
5. 知道	知道	zhīdào	V.	to know; to be aware of; to realize
6. 了	了	le	Part.	(indicates assumption)
7. 謝謝	谢谢	xièxie		thanks
8. 吧	吧	ba	Part.	(indicates assumption or suggestion)
9. 對	对	duì	Adj.	correct; right
10. 忙	忙	máng	Adj.	busy
11. 看	看	kàn	V.	to look at; to see; to watch
12. 電視	电视	diànshì	N.	television
13. 做	做	zuò	V.	to do
14. 上網	上网	shàngwǎng	V.O.	to be online
15. 我就是	我就是	wǒ jiù shì		(on the phone) this is he/she speaking
16. 位	位	wèi	M.W.	(polite form, measure word for people)
17. 留言(留話)	留言(留话)	liúyán (liúhuà)	V.O.	to leave a message

Note: 留言 is used in Mainland China, while 留話 is also used in Taiwan.

	TRADITIONAL	SIMPLIFIED	PINYIN		
18.	對不起	对不起	duìbuqǐ		sorry
19.	時候	时候	shíhou	N.	(the duration of) time; (a point in) time
20.	回來	回来	huílai	V.	to return
21.	晚上	晚上	wǎnshàng	N.	evening
22.	要	要	yào	V.	to want, desire
23.	給	给	gěi	Prep. V.	for, to to give

補充詞　Supplementary Vocabulary

	TRADITIONAL	SIMPLIFIED	PINYIN		
1.	佔線	占线	zhànxiàn	V.O.	to occupy a (phone) line, the line is busy
2.	打錯了	打错了	dǎcuòle		to dial a wrong number
3.	小說	小说	xiǎoshuō	N.	novel
4.	電影	电影	diànyǐng	N.	movie
5.	網絡 (網路)	网络 (网路)	wǎngluò (wǎnglù)	N.	Internet
6.	網吧 (網咖)	网吧 (网咖)	wǎngbā (wǎngkā)	N.	Internet cafe
7.	網站	网站	wǎngzhàn	N.	web site
8.	網頁	网页	wǎngyè	N.	web page
9.	聊天室	聊天室	liáotiānshì	N.	chat room
10.	電腦遊戲	电脑游戏	diànnǎoyóuxì	N.	computer game
11.	在線遊戲 (線上遊戲)	在线游戏 (线上游戏)	zàixiànyóuxì (xiànshàngyóuxì)	N.	online game
12.	病毒	病毒	bìngdú	N.	virus

	TRADITIONAL	SIMPLIFIED	PINYIN		
13.	軟件 (軟體)	软件 (软体)	ruǎnjiàn (ruǎntǐ)	N.	software
14.	硬件 (硬體)	硬件 (硬体)	yìngjiàn (yìngtǐ)	N.	hardware
15.	發短信 (送簡訊)	发短信 (送简讯)	fā duǎnxìn (sòng jiǎnxùn)	V.O.	to send a short (cell phone) message
16.	通	通	tōng	M.W.	(measure word for telephone conversation)
17.	休息	休息	xiūxi	V.	to rest
18.	睡覺	睡觉	shuìjiào	V.O.	to sleep
19.	不客氣	不客气	búkèqi		(in reply to thank you) you're welcome
20.	不謝	不谢	búxiè		(in reply to thank you) you're welcome

語文知識　LANGUAGE LINK

The Sentence Patterns provide models that will help you with the Language in Use section. In both sections, pay attention to the grammar points, vocabulary, and expressions.

句型　Sentence Patterns

A: 喂！
　Wéi!

B: 喂！
　Wéi!

A: 請問友朋在嗎?
　Qǐngwèn Yǒupéng zài ma?

B: <u>Situation 1</u>: 在，請等一下兒。
　　　　　　　　Zài, qǐng děng yíxiàr.

　<u>Situation 2</u>: 我就是。
　　　　　　　　Wǒ jiù shì.

　<u>Situation 3</u>: 對不起，他不在。
　　　　　　　　Duìbuqǐ, tā bú zài.

A: 你在做什麼?
Nǐ zài zuò shénme?

B: 我在上網。
Wǒ zài shàngwǎng.

A: 你在忙嗎?
Nǐ zài máng ma?

B: 沒有,我正在看電視呢。
Méiyǒu, wǒ zhèngzài kàn diànshì ne.

課文　Language in Use: 他正在打電話 Tā zhèngzài dǎ diànhuà

Telephone Situation 1: 在,請等一下兒
Zài, qǐng děng yíxiār

陳愛文:　喂!我是愛文。請問友朋在嗎?
Wéi! Wǒ shì Àiwén. Qǐngwèn Yǒupéng zài ma?

方書程:　在,他在他的房間。請等一下兒。喂!友朋!你的電話。
Zài, tā zài tā de fángjiān. Qǐng děng yíxiàr. Wèi! Yǒupéng, nǐ de diànhuà.

張友朋:　知道了!謝謝!
Zhīdào le! Xièxie!

張友朋:　喂!我是友朋,你是愛文吧!
Wéi! Wǒ shì Yǒupéng, nǐ shì Àiwén ba!

陳愛文:　對,是我。你在忙嗎?
Duì, shì wǒ. Nǐ zài máng ma?

張友朋:　沒有。我正在看電視呢。你在做什麼?
Méiyǒu. Wǒ zhèngzài kàn diànshì ne. Nǐ zài zuò shénme?

陳愛文:　我在上網。
Wǒ zài shàngwǎng.

<u>**Telephone Situation 2:**</u>   我就是
Wǒ jiù shì

陳愛文：   喂！
Wéi!

張友朋：   喂！
Wéi!

陳愛文：   請問友朋在嗎？
Qǐngwèn Yǒupéng zài ma?

張友朋：   我就是。請問您是哪位？
Wǒ jiù shì. Qǐngwèn nín shì nǎ wèi?

陳愛文：   我是愛文。
Wǒ shì Àiwén.

<u>**Telephone Situation 3:**</u>   不在，請留言
Bú zài, qǐng liúyán

陳愛文：   喂！請問友朋在嗎？
Wéi! Qǐngwèn Yǒupéng zài ma?

丁明：   對不起，他不在。他在上課。
Duìbuqǐ, tā bú zài. Tā zài shàngkè.

陳愛文：   請問他什麼時候回來？
Qǐngwèn tā shénme shíhou huílai?

丁明：   今天晚上。你要不要留言？
Jīntiān wǎnshàng. Nǐ yào bú yào liúyán?

陳愛文：   好的。我是愛文。我的電話是(一四二)二六八九七五三。
Hǎo de. Wǒ shì Àiwén. Wǒ de diànhuà shì yī sì èr èr liù bā jiǔ qī wǔ sān.

　　　　　　請他回來以後給我打電話。謝謝！
Qǐng tā huílai yǐhòu gěi wǒ dǎ diànhuà. Xièxie!

丁明：   不謝。再見。
Búxiè. Zàijiàn.

注釋　LANGUAGE NOTES

喂

喂 means "Hello!" It is generally used as a telephone greeting. When making or answering a phone call, it is pronounced as [wéi] to soften the tone and sound polite.

吧

吧 is a particle used at the end of a statement to indicate assumption on the part of the speaker.

你是愛文吧!　You must be Aiwen!

位

位 is a measure word for people. It is used for being polite. 哪位 means "which person."

你是哪位?　　May I know who is calling?

留言

留言 literally means "keep/stay words." In practice it means "leave a message." In Taiwan, people also use 留話 for "leave a message."

回來以後給我打電話(給我回電話/回電)

給 means "to give." "回來以後給我打電話" means "Give me a call (when person) comes back." Chinese people also use 回電話 or 回電 to refer to returning a phone call.

語法 GRAMMAR

The Progressive Aspect of an Action 在/正在

The progressive aspect of an action indicates that someone or something is currently in the process of doing something. This is similar to the English "-ing." The main structural pattern is "Subject + 在 + Verb Phrase + 呢." However, there are some options which are listed below:

Pattern				Example (I am watching TV.)
Subject	在	VP	(呢)	我在看電視 (呢)。
	正			我正看電視 (呢)。
	正在			我正在看電視 (呢)。
			呢	我看電視呢。

- Negative pattern:

Pattern					Example (I am not watching TV.)
Subject	沒有	在	VP	(呢)	我沒有在看電視 (呢)。
	沒				我沒在看電視 (呢)。
	不				我不在看電視 (呢)。

- Asking questions:

Pattern	Example	
	Question	Answer
Subject 在做什麼(呢)? *What is Subject doing?*	你哥哥在做什麼(呢)?	我哥哥(正)在看電視(呢)。 我哥哥看電視呢。 我哥哥沒在做什麼。
Subject 在 VP 嗎? *Is Subject V-ing?*	你在看電視嗎?	(是)，我在看電視。 (沒有)，我沒有在看電視。 (不)，我不在看電視。

Summary: Ways of Asking Questions

Type of question	Structure	Usage	Example
Yes-no question	嗎	turn a sentence into a question	你忙<u>嗎</u>?
Affirmative-negative questions	A 不 A 有沒有	a choice type of question	你忙<u>不忙</u>? 你<u>有沒有</u>哥哥?
"Wh"-questions — request more specific questions what who which where when how . . .	什麼 什麼時候	What When	你叫<u>什麼</u>名字? 他<u>什麼時候</u>回來?
	誰	Who	他是<u>誰</u>?
	哪 哪國人 哪兒 哪位 哪年(L10)#	Which Which nationality Where Which year Which person (polite)	你是<u>哪國人</u>? 你住<u>哪兒</u>? 你是<u>哪位</u>? 今年是<u>哪年</u>?
	幾 幾點(L10) 幾月幾日/號 (L10)	How many (under 10) What time What month and day	你有<u>幾</u>個室友? 你<u>幾點</u>回來? 今天是<u>幾月幾日/號</u>?
	多少 多少號	How many (over 10)	你有<u>多少</u>書? 你的電話是<u>多少號</u>?
Tag question	A 不 A 是嗎? 好嗎? 行嗎? 怎麼樣?	Ask for confirmation or making a suggestion	你是小美，<u>對不對</u>? 你是中國人，<u>是嗎</u>? 你給我打電話，<u>好嗎</u>? 我們去吃飯，<u>行嗎</u>? 我們吃韓國菜，<u>怎麼樣</u>?
Other	呢	Information has been shared. "How about N?"	**A:** 你好嗎? **B:** 我很好，你<u>呢</u>?

Note: # L10 means it will be introduced in Lesson 10.

補充課文 ━○○○━ SUPPLEMENTARY PRACTICE

This selection will help you test your comprehension of the grammar and vocabulary you have learned in this lesson. Be prepared to answer questions about the meaning of the passage.

今天我給小謝打電話的時候，他不在，他室友接了電話。他室友說他正在上課，他問我要不要留言，我說麻煩他回來以後給我打電話，我有事找他。晚上小謝回來了，他給我回電的時候，我正在看電視呢。我問他你在忙嗎? 你正在做什麼呢? 他說他正在上網呢!

Notes: 接 [jiē]: to receive

了 [le]: an aspect particle indicating an action completed

麻煩 [máfan]: trouble somebody to do something

回來 [huílai]: to return

有事 [yǒushì]: have some matters to attend to

找 [zhǎo]: to look for

練習   ACTIVITIES

I. Pinyin Exercises

9-1   Listen to the instructor. Mark "√" after the Pinyin if it is correct, or write in the correct Pinyin:

1. shíhuò _____   2. fángjiān _____   3. zhīdòu _____

4. diānhuà _____   5. diānsì _____   6. zhèngzài _____

7. shàngwáng _____   8. wǎngshàng _____   9. jīngtiān _____

10. liúyán _____   11. děn _____   12. zhàijiàn _____

9-2   Listen to the instructor, then fill in the Pinyin final for each of the following:

1. d _____   2. x _____   3. w _____   4. w _____

5. d _____   6. d _____   7. k _____   8. w _____

9. h _____   10. y _____   11. z _____   12. m _____

9-3　Read the following Chinese poem, paying special attention to the tones and rhythm:

Dēng Guànquèlóu (Wáng Zhīhuàn)	登鸛鵲樓 (王之渙)	On the Stork Pagoda (Wang, Zhihuan)
Báirì yī shān jìn,	白日依山盡，	White sun disappears from the mountains,
Huánghé rù hǎi liú.	黃河入海流。	Yellow River flows into the sea.
Yù qióng qiān lǐ mù,	欲窮千里目，	If one desires to expand the eye's view for a thousand miles,
Gèng shàng yì céng lóu.	更上一層樓。	Climb up another story of the pagoda.

II. Character Exercises

9-4　Read the following words and phrases:

看	正在
看書	正在上課
看電視	正在考試
看電腦	正在睡覺
看電影	正在看中文小說
看小說	正在學西班牙語

Now try to use the following characters to make words, phrases, and then sentences:

1. 打　　2. 電　　3. 等　　4. 知　　5. 忙　　6. 看

7. 做　　8. 位　　9. 時　　10. 晚　　11. 要　　12. 給

9-5　Indicate the number of strokes in each of the following characters, then create as many phrases as you can with each character:

	Number of strokes	Phrases
Example 有	6	有手機，沒有電話，有事兒， 沒有事兒……
1. 在		
2. 上		
3. 要		

III. Grammar Exercises

9-6 Substitution exercises:

1. 你在做什麼呢?
   我(正)在<u>打電話</u>呢。

休息
上網
看電視
做功課
看法國小說
跟朋友一起吃飯

2. 喂! 請問文中在嗎?
   <u>我就是。請問你是哪位</u>?

在。請等一下兒。
喂! 文中，你的電話。
對不起，他不在。你要不要留言?
對不起，你打錯了。
[dǎ cuò] dial a wrong number

9-7 Complete the sentences in their progressive forms with the phrases given, then change these sentences into their negative forms:

1. 我 ＿＿＿＿ 。　　　(忙)
2. 他 ＿＿＿＿ 。　　　(上課)
3. 她 ＿＿＿＿ 。　　　(吃飯)
4. 文中 ＿＿＿＿ 朋友。　(介紹)
5. 小美 ＿＿＿＿ 中文。　(說)
6. 于英 ＿＿＿＿ 功課。　(做)

9-8 Look at the pictures below and describe what the people are doing.

1.

2.

3.

4.

5.

6.

IV. Communicative Activities

9-9 Situational dialogue:

Situation 1:
You have a Chinese friend from Shanghai.
She/He is a new student and is looking for an
apartment/house. Please say a little bit about
your apartment when she/he calls you on
your cell phone.

Hints:
1. Topics to cover:
   • Greetings.
   • Ask about/Describe the apartment/house, rent,
     condition, and facilities.

2. Words and expressions to use:

請問是 …… 嗎?	住在哪兒?	房間大嗎?	有電話嗎?
我就是。	住在公寓。	房間很小。	有電話。

Situation 2:

You are going to have lunch with 小文. Call to invite another friend to join you.

Hints:

1. Topics to cover:
   - Greetings; ask about the friend's recent studies.
   - Talk about what you are doing right now.
   - Invite the friend to have lunch and discuss which restaurant you would like to go to.

2. Words and expressions to use:

   正在做什麼?   認識不認識 ...?
   去不去?   跟 ... 一起

Situation 3:

The friend you are calling is not at home. Please leave a message.

Hints:

1. Topics to cover:
   - Greetings; ask where your friend is right now.
   - Leave a short message with the roommate (invite your friend to visit your teacher, to lunch, or to look for an apartment with you, etc.).
   - Chat about your studies with the roommate for a while.

2. Words and expressions to use:

   請問......在嗎?   什麼時候回來?   謝謝。
   對不起,他/她不在。   要不要留言?   不客氣。

文化點滴 CULTURE LINK

手機在中國 [Shǒujī zài Zhōngguó]
Cell Phones in China
A Symbol of Fashion

Cell phones have become very popular recently in China. As well as being a status symbol, many children use them as a daily communication tool, and they are also status symbols.

Today you will see many different brands and styles of cell phones in China. The smaller in size and the newer in style, the more fashionable they are. They are especially popular among young girls and business people.

Many young people do not care too much about the features of their cell phones as long as they are small and stylish. It is very common to see young people wearing a small cell phone on a necklace. You may also see a cell phone with a tiny, artistically made light attached to a girl's shoulder bag or purse. Whenever there is an incoming call, the light flashes. What a sight!

Nowadays many business people have two or three cell phones and increasingly more young people have two cell phones turned on 24/7 for worldwide communication. The cost of cell phone calls in Mainland China is quite high, so many subscribers simply use the short messaging service, feature of the phone. They do not answer or call back directly from their phone, but wait until they get to a desk phone to do so. This is not as common in Hong Kong or Taiwan, where cell phone service is comparatively inexpensive.

139

**If you don't have a cell phone while you are in China, look for a public
telephone sign 公用電話 [gōngyòng diànhuà] such as this one. The sign above
is for a public restroom 公共衛生間 [gōnggòng wèishēng jiān].**

Questions:

1. What are the similarities and differences in the way cell phones are
used in China and the U.S.?

2. What would you advise your professor to do when someone's cell phone
rings in class?

趣味中文   FUN WITH CHINESE

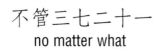

不管三七二十一
no matter what

bù	guǎn	sān	qī	èrshíyī
不	管	三	七	二十一
don't	care	three	seven	twenty-one

不管三七二十一

This slang literally means "Don't care if three times seven is twenty-one."
It is used as a metaphor to show a determined mind.

Question:

Are there any sayings in English that include numbers? Can you give some examples?

行動吧！　LET'S GO!

電話卡　**Telephone Card**

明正 received a pager message from his friend. To call his friend back he will need to insert his prepaid telephone card (IC telephone card) into the slot on a public telephone.

Useful words and expressions:

卡 [kǎ]: card
電信 (电信) [diànxìn]: telecommunications
磁卡 [cíkǎ]: magnetic card
換 (换) [huàn]: to change
欣-欣喜 [xīnxǐ]: happy, joy
集團 (集团) [jítuán]: organization
公司 [gōngsī]: company
發行 (发行) [fāxíng]: to issue, publish
技術 (技术) [jìshù]: technology
更 [gèng]: even more
先進 (先进) [xiānjìn]: advance and improve
正面 [zhèngmiàn]: the front side
反面 [fǎnmiàn]: the reverse side

(正面)

(反面)

Questions:

1. For what amount is 明正's prepaid phone card?

2. What company issued this IC telephone card?

3. What does the phrase 用心換欣 mean? What implications might it have on a telephone card?

4. What does the phrase 技術更先進 mean?

復習 **Review**

給朋友打電話

Call your Chinese friend and invite her/him to do something with you. Practice greetings, talking about somebody else, setting up the time, etc.

Useful words and expressions:

"A 不 A" pattern:　e.g. 認識不認識，想不想
Tag question:　　　e.g. 是嗎，好嗎，怎麼樣
正在 …… 呢

Picture Description

Use 正在 to describe the pictures below (at least eight sentences).
Be creative!

(1)

(2)

(3)

(4)

(5)

(6)

(7)

(8)

Character Writing

Pay attention to stroke order.

<u>Situation:</u> 寫便條 [xiě biàntiáo] Write a note

You would like to invite your friend, 小明, to eat out with you. You went to his dorm and he wasn't in. You would like to leave a note for him. (Use one character for each blank.)

小明：

　　你好，我是 _____ (your name)。我來找你的 ____ ____ (When I came)，你不 ____ (You were not in)。你室友在，他 ____ 在 ____ 電 ____ 呢 (He was watching TV)。他說你正在學校 ____ ____ (on the Internet)。我問他你 什麼時候 ____ ____ (when you would be back)，他說今天 ____ ____ (tonight)。

　　你 ____ 不 ____ 跟我 ____ ____ 去 ____ ____ (Do you want to go out to eat)?　我們去吃 ____ ____ ____ ，____ ____ ____ (Let's go eat Chinese food. How does that sound)?　請你回來 ____ ____ ，____ 我 ____ 電話。(Please call me when you return)。你 ____ ____ 我的 ____ ____ 號碼嗎 (Do you know my cell phone number)?　號碼是 ____ ____ ____ ____ ____ ____ ____ ____ ____ ____ (142) 268-9753。

　　____ ____ (Thank you)，____ ____ (Bye-bye)!

_____ (Your name)

____ ____ 月 ____ 日 (Nov. 5) ____ ____ 點 ____ ____ ____ 分 (11:27)

我每天七點半起床
I Get Up at 7:30 Every Day

第十課
LESSON

教學目標　OBJECTIVES

- Give times and dates in Chinese
- Describe your daily schedule
- Write letters in Chinese

University life is a time for learning, making friends, trying new things, having fun, and preparing for your future career.

生詞 VOCABULARY

核心詞 Core Vocabulary

	TRADITIONAL	SIMPLIFIED	PINYIN		
1.	每天	每天	měitiān		every day
2.	半	半	bàn	Adj.	half
3.	起床	起床	qǐchuáng	V.	to get up
4.	大學	大学	dàxué	N.	college, university
5.	生活	生活	shēnghuó	N.	life
6.	學期	学期	xuéqī	N.	semester
7.	門	门	mén	M.W.	(measure word for school courses)
8.	點	点	diǎn	M.W.	o'clock (point on clock)
9.	睡覺	睡觉	shuìjiào	V.O.	to go to bed; to sleep
10.	就	就	jiù	Adv.	as early as; already
11.	才	才	cái	Adv.	(used before a verb to indicate that something is rather late by general standards, or something has just happened)
12.	刻	刻	kè	M.W.	a quarter (of an hour)
13.	分	分	fēn	N.	minute
14.	然後	然后	ránhòu	Adv.	then, after that, afterwards
15.	圖書館	图书馆	túshūguǎn	N.	library
16.	下午	下午	xiàwǔ	N.	afternoon
17.	喜歡	喜欢	xǐhuān	V.	to like
18.	打球	打球	dǎqiú	V.O.	to play basketball/badminton/ tennis/table tennis
19.	寫	写	xiě	V.	to write
20.	信	信	xìn	N.	letter
21.	電子郵件	电子邮件	diànzǐ yóujiàn	N.	e-mail

TRADITIONAL	SIMPLIFIED	PINYIN		
22. 地址	地址	dìzhǐ	N.	address
23. 祝	祝	zhù	V.	to wish
24. 年	年	nián	N.	year
25. 月	月	yuè	N.	month
26. 日	日	rì	N.	day

專名　Proper Nouns

TRADITIONAL	SIMPLIFIED	PINYIN		
1. 小明	小明	Xiǎomíng	N.	(name) Xiaoming
2. 學文	学文	Xuéwén	N.	(name) Xuewen

補充詞　Supplementary Vocabulary

TRADITIONAL	SIMPLIFIED	PINYIN		
1. 點鐘	点钟	diǎnzhōng	M.W.	o'clock
2. 鐘頭	钟头	zhōngtóu	N.	hour
3. 小時	小时	xiǎoshí	N.	hour
4. 分鐘	分钟	fēnzhōng	N.	minute
5. 秒	秒	miǎo	M.W.	second
6. 過	过	guò	V.	to pass
7. 差	差	chà	V.	to lack, to be short of
8. 早	早	zǎo	Adj.	early
9. 晚	晚	wǎn	Adj.	late
10. 熬夜	熬夜	áoyè	V.O.	to burn the midnight oil
11. 刷牙	刷牙	shuāyá	V.O.	to brush your teeth
12. 洗臉	洗脸	xǐliǎn	V.O.	to wash your face
13. 洗澡	洗澡	xǐzǎo	V.O.	to take a bath

語文知識 LANGUAGE LINK

The Sentence Patterns provide models that will help you with the Language in Use section. In both sections, pay attention to the grammar points, vocabulary, and expressions.

句型 Sentence Patterns

A: 現在幾點?
Xiànzài jǐdiǎn?

B: 十點五分。
Shídiǎn wǔ fēn.

Note: 現在 [xiànzài]: now

A: 你每天幾點起床,
Nǐ měitiān jǐdiǎn qǐchuáng,

幾點睡覺?
jǐdiǎn shuìjiào?

B: 我每天七點半起床,
Wǒ měitiān qīdiǎn bàn qǐchuáng,

十二點半睡覺。
shíèrdiǎn bàn shuìjiào.

A: 今天是幾月幾號?
Jīntiān shì jǐ yuè jǐ hào?

B: 十一月二十日。
Shíyī yuè èrshí rì.

NOVEMBER
20

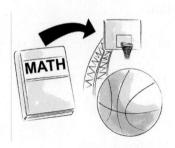

A: 下課以後,你有事兒嗎?
Xiàkè yǐhòu, nǐ yǒushèr ma?

B: 有,我有事兒,我去看書,
Yǒu, wǒ yǒushèr, wǒ qù kànshū,

然後去打球。
ránhòu qù dǎqiú.

課文　Language in Use: 我的大學生活 Wǒ de dàxué shēnghuó

小明:
Xiǎomíng:

你好!
Nǐhǎo!

這個學期我很忙，有五門課。你知道我每天幾點起床、
Zhège xuéqī wǒ hěnmáng, yǒu wǔ mén kè. Nǐ zhīdào wǒ měitiān jǐdiǎn qǐchuáng,

幾點睡覺嗎? 我七點半就起床，晚上十二點半以後才睡覺。
jǐdiǎn shuìjiào ma? Wǒ qīdiǎn bàn jiù qǐchuáng, wǎnshàng shí'èrdiǎn bàn yǐhòu cái shuìjiào.

每天都很忙。九點一刻去上課，十點二十分下課。然後，
Měitiān dōu hěnmáng. Jiǔdiǎn yí kè qù shàngkè, shídiǎn èrshí fēn xiàkè. Ránhòu,

我去圖書館看書。下午下課以後，我喜歡去打球。每天都有
wǒ qù túshūguǎn kànshū. Xiàwǔ xiàkè yǐhòu, wǒ xǐhuān qù dǎqiú. Měitiān dōu yǒu

很多功課。
hěnduō gōngkè.

這是我的大學生活，你呢? 給我寫信吧。我的電子郵件地址是:
Zhè shì wǒde dàxué shēnghuó, nǐ ne? Gěi wǒ xiěxìn ba. Wǒde diànzǐ yóujiàn dìzhǐ shì:

xuewen376@zhongwen.edu
xuewen376@zhongwen.edu

祝
Zhù

好
Hǎo

學文
Xuéwén

二〇〇三年十一月二十日
èr líng líng sān nián shí yī yuè èr shí rì

注釋 LANGUAGE NOTES

五門課

The word 門 as a noun means "door." It is also used as a measure word for counting school courses. 五門課 means "five courses."

點

點 refers to the hour when expressing clock time. 點鐘 [diǎnzhōng] is also used. For example,

三點　　　three o'clock
三點鐘　　three o'clock

鐘 standing alone means "clock."
For example, "這個鐘很好。" This clock is good.

吧　(For Suggestion)

吧 is a particle used at the end of a statement to turn it into a friendly suggestion: "You might . . ." or "Let's . . ." (When the subject is 我們 "we"). For example,

你學中文吧。　　　　　　You might study Chinese.
我們一起去學中文吧!　　Let's go study Chinese together!

Note that in Lesson 9 we learned that 吧 is also used for assumption.
For example, 你是愛文吧!　　You must be Aiwen!

語法 GRAMMAR

How to Tell the Time

- The words 點 (hour), 分 (minute), 半 (half hour), and 刻 (quarter hour) are used to tell the time as illustrated below:

Time	Chinese expressions	Notes
9:00	九點(鐘)	• For o'clock, 鐘 [zhōng] can be used.
9:08	九點〇八分/九點八分/九點過八分	• 過 [guò] means "pass." It is only used when the time passed is within 10 minutes.
9:15	九點十五分/九點一刻	
9:30	九點三十分/九點半	
9:45	九點四十五分/九點三刻	
9:58	九點五十八分/差兩分十點	• 差 [chà] means "lack." As with 過, it is used within 10 minutes of its reference time.

- Expressing A.M. and P.M.:

Morning	Noon	Afternoon	Night
早上 [zǎoshang] (around 7:00–9:00 A.M.) 7:00 A.M. 早上七點	中午 [zhōngwǔ] 12:20 中午十二點二十分	下午 [xiàwǔ] 1:30 P.M. 下午一點半	晚上 [wǎnshang] 8:35 P.M. 晚上八點三十五分
上午 [shàngwǔ] (roughly after 9:00 A.M.) 10:15 A.M. 上午十點一刻		4:10 P.M. 下午四點十分	

- Expressing day and year:

The day before yesterday	Yesterday	Today	Tomorrow	The day after tomorrow
前天 qiántiān	昨天 zuótiān	今天 jīntiān	明天 míngtiān	後天 hòutiān
The year before last year	**Last year**	**This year**	**Next year**	**The year after next year**
前年 qiánnián	去年 qùnián	今年 jīnnián	明年 míngnián	後年 hòunián

Note: When giving the year, say the numbers individually. For example, 二〇〇五年
This is pronounced èr líng líng wǔ nián.

- Expressing months and days:

January 一月	February 二月	March 三月	April 四月
May 五月	June 六月	July 七月	August 八月
September 九月	October 十月	November 十一月	December 十二月
the first of the month 一號(日)	the sixth 六號(日)	October 17th 十月十七號(日)	December 25th 十二月二十五號(日)

Note: 日 means "day." 號 means "number." Both 日 and 號 can be used to refer to the day of the
　　　 month. For example, October 3rd 十月三號/十月三日
　　　 號 is mostly used in speaking, while 日 is mostly used in writing.

- Pattern:

When telling the time, the Chinese always begins with the larger unit of time.
Time phrases can occur either before or after the subject.

二○○三年七月八日上午十點二十分。	It is 10:20 A.M., 8th July, 2003.
Subject　Time　VP	我　今天上午　十點半上課。 subject　time
Time　Subject　VP	昨天晚上　我　十一點五十分睡覺。 time　　　subject

- Asking questions

	現在幾點? 現在是什麼時候?	What time is it now?
Asking the time	昨天你幾點起床? 昨天你什麼時候起床?	What time did you get up yesterday?
Asking the month and day	今天是幾月幾號?	What month and day is it today?
Asking the year	今年是哪年?	What year is it?

Adverbs 就 and 才

就 and 才 are adverbs that occur before a verb, stressing the time and expectation of an event. 就 is used when the speaker wants to say that an event was or will be carried out sooner than expected, 才 conveys the opposite feeling, that of "belatedness."

就 and 才 should be used after time expressions. For example,

(1) 我今天七點起床。　　I got up at 7:00 today.
(2) 我今天七點就起床。　I got up at 7:00 today.　　　　　→ early
(3) 我今天七點才起床。　I didn't get up until 7:00 today.　→ too late

Example (1) is a simple statement. Example (2) indicates that I got up at 7 o'clock, which is early, while example (3) indicates that I got up at 7 o'clock, which is late.

The aspect 了 can only co-occur with 就, not with 才. 呢 and 的 can only occur with 才, not 就. For example,

(4) 他十二點四十分就來了。　　He came as early as 12:40.
(5) 他十二點四十分才來呢/的。　He didn't come until 12:40.

The action happened sooner than expected in example (4), but later than expected in example (5).

Grammar Summary 語法小結

1. Summary: Chinese word order

- Modifier + Modified

  Chinese sentences generally consist of a subject and a predicate. The basic rule of word order is that all modifiers, adjectives, adverbs, or relative clauses occur before the element they modify.

Subject		Predicate
我的	室友	學中文。
My	roommates	studies Chinese
Modifier	**Modified**	**VP**

Subject			Predicate
我的	室友的	哥哥	學中文。
My	roommate's	brother	studies Chinese
Modifier	**Modifier**	**Modified**	**VP**

Subject			Predicate	
我的	室友的	哥哥	也	學中文。
My	roommate's	brother	also	studies Chinese
Modifier	**Modifier**	**Modified**	**Modifier**	**VP**

Subject			Predicate	
我的	室友的	哥哥	也在大學	學中文。
My	roommate's	brother	also at the university	studies Chinese
Modifier	**Modifier**	**Modified**	**Modifier**	**VP**

Subject			Predicate	
我的	室友的	哥哥姐姐	也都在大學	學中文。
My	roommate's	brother and sister	also all at the university	studies Chinese
Modifier	**Modifier**	**Modified**	**Modifier**	**VP**

- Prepositional phrase (PP, as modifier) precedes the verb phrase (VP, modified). The places, objects, and recipients are specified before the action.

Pattern	Example		Meaning
在 + place + VP	我在圖書館 PP (Modifier)	看書。 VP (Modified)	I study in the library.
跟 + somebody + VP	我跟他們 PP (Modifier)	說中文。 VP (Modified)	I speak Chinese with them.
給 + somebody + VP	我給朋友 PP (Modifier)	寫信。 VP (Modified)	I write a letter to my friend.

- Wh- questions in Chinese:
  The word order of wh- questions in Chinese (e.g. 誰，什麼，哪，幾，少) is that the question word occurs where the expected answer would be.

Question word	Question	Answer
誰 什麼 哪 幾 多少	他是誰? 你學什麼? 你是哪國人? 你幾點上課? 你有多少中文書?	他是王老師。 我學工程。 我是美國人。 我十點二十分上課。 我有二十本中文書。

- When talking about time, addresses, or places, Chinese progresses from larger units to smaller ones.

Larger unit → smaller unit
Date   今天是二〇〇三年十一月二十日。
Time   現在是下午五點十二分。
Address   中國上海市100084中山路8號 他家在中國北京。

- Subject + Time + VP/Time + Subject + VP

<u>我們</u>　　　<u>今天下午</u>　　去吃中國菜。
subject　　　　time

<u>今天下午</u>　　<u>我們</u>　　　去吃中國菜。
time　　　　　　subject

2. Summary: Measure words

- Number + Measure word + Noun

Number	Measure word	Feature	Noun
一 二(兩) 三 四 五 六 七 八 九 十	本	for bound items	書，雜誌 [zázhì] (magazine)
	輛	for vehicles	車
	個	for people, buildings and characters	室友，圖書館，漢字 朋友，姐姐
	隻	animals	狗，貓
	位	people (polite form)	老師
	門	courses	課

補充課文 ─○○○─ SUPPLEMENTARY PRACTICE

This selection will help you test your comprehension of the grammar and vocabulary you have learned in this lesson. Be prepared to answer questions about the meaning of the passage.

正生： 喂！請問歡歡在嗎？

室友： 在，請等一下兒。喂，歡歡，你的電話。

歡歡： 知道了，謝謝。

　　　　喂！我是歡歡，請問你是哪位？

正生： 我是正生，好久沒跟你聯絡了。怎麼樣？你最近都在忙
　　　　什麼呢？

歡歡： 我這個學期很忙，我上五門課，每天都有很多功課。忙死了！

正生： 你每天幾點起床，幾點睡覺呢？

歡歡： 我每天七點半就起床，晚上十二點半以後才睡覺。你呢？
　　　　你的大學生活怎麼樣？

正生： 這個學期我有四門課，不太忙，我每天十點一刻去上課，
　　　　十一點二十分下課，然後，我喜歡去圖書館看書，下午下課
　　　　以後，我常和朋友一起去打球。

歡歡： 你常看你的電子郵件嗎？

正生： 常看，我每天都看我的電子郵件。

歡歡： 我的電子郵件地址是：huanhuan@zhongwen.edu 。
　　　　有空常給我寫電子郵件吧！

正生： 好，就這樣，再見！

歡歡： 再見！

Notes: 好久 [hǎojiǔ]: long time
　　　　　聯絡 [liánluò]: to contact
　　　　　最近 [zuìjìn]: recently
　　　　　忙死了 [mángsǐle]: extremely busy
　　　　　就這樣 [jiùzhèyàng]: that's it; that's all

練習　ACTIVITIES

I. Pinyin Exercises

10-1 Draw lines between the matching items and read aloud:

1.

地址	diànzǐ
學期	yóujiàn
每天	ránhòu
起床	xǐhuān
睡覺	qǐchuáng
喜歡	xiěxìn
然後	dǎqiú
寫信	dìzhǐ
電子	měitiān
郵件	xuéqī
打球	shuìjiào

2.

才	jiù
刻	zhù
幾	bàn
日	mén
半	cái
就	jǐ
點	nián
祝	diǎn
門	kè
月	rì
年	yuè

10-6 Fill in the blanks with one or two versions of the following times:

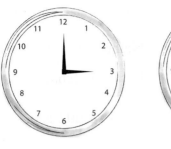   

_____   _____   _____   _____
_____   _____   _____   _____

_____   _____   _____   _____
_____   _____   _____   _____

_____   _____   _____   _____
_____   _____   _____   _____

10-7 Fill in the blanks with one of the following:

就　　　　　　才　　　　　　然後

1. 我常常在下午三點一刻去圖書館看書，_____ 四點回宿舍。

2. 小明這個學期很忙，他沒有空。他考試以後 _____ 可以給哥哥寫信。

3. 文中每天很早 _____ 起床。他七點 _____ 起床，_____ 八點去學校。

4. 今天我有事兒，一點半 _____ 吃午飯。

Note: 早 [zǎo]: early

IV. Communicative Activities

10-8 Situational dialogues:

Situation 1:

You want to play tennis with 李文中. There are two open times for the court right now. Ask for 文中's schedule to find out a suitable time to play together.

<table>
<tr><td colspan="2" align="center">李文中</td><td>*Notes:* 網球 [wǎngqiú]: (tennis)</td></tr>
<tr><td>12:45–1:15</td><td>去吃中飯</td><td>2:30–3:30</td></tr>
<tr><td>1:30–2:20</td><td>上中文課</td><td>4:30–5:30</td></tr>
<tr><td>2:30–3:30</td><td>上數學課</td><td></td></tr>
</table>

Hints:

1. Topics to cover:
   - Greetings.
   - Chat about this semester's courses, then suggest that you do some exercise together.

2. Words and expressions to use:

   忙不忙?　功課多不多?
   下課以後，我們一起......怎麼樣?
   ......吧。　是嗎?　幾點......?

Situation 2:

You are calling one of your good friends in another city to describe your current university life.

Hint:

Words and expressions to use:

就/才　每天...(睡覺、起床、上課)

Notes: 刷牙 [shuāyá]: to brush one's teeth
　　　　洗臉 [xǐliǎn]: to wash one's face
　　　　洗澡 [xǐzǎo]: to take a bath

從......到......　然後　早上　上午　中午　下午　過　差　半　刻

生詞 VOCABULARY

核心詞 Core Vocabulary

TRADITIONAL	SIMPLIFIED	PINYIN		
1. 紅	红	hóng	Adj.	red
2. 茶	茶	chá	N.	tea
3. 還是	还是	háishì	Conj.	or
4. 綠	绿	lǜ	Adj.	green
5. 服務員	服务员	fúwùyuán	N.	waiter/waitress
6. 坐	坐	zuò	V.	to sit
7. 小姐	小姐	xiǎojiě	N.	miss
8. 先生	先生	xiānsheng	N.	mister
9. 先	先	xiān	Adv.	first
10. 喝	喝	hē	V.	to drink
11. 杯	杯	bēi	M.W.	cup
12. 冰	冰	bīng	N.	ice
13. 可樂	可乐	kělè	N.	cola
14. 瓶	瓶	píng	M.W.	bottle
15. 啤酒	啤酒	píjiǔ	N.	beer
16. 面	面	miàn	N.	noodle
17. 餃子	饺子	jiǎozi	N.	dumpling (crescent shaped)
18. 盤	盘	pán	M.W.	plate
19. 炒	炒	chǎo	V.	to stir fry
20. 十	十	shí	Num.	ten
21. 碗	碗	wǎn	M.W.	bowl
22. 湯	汤	tāng	N.	soup
23. 雙	双	shuāng	M.W.	pair
24. 筷子	筷子	kuàizi	N.	chopstick

專名 Proper Nouns

	TRADITIONAL	SIMPLIFIED	PINYIN		
1.	張正然	张正然	Zhāng Zhèngrán	N.	(name) Zhengran Zhang
2.	孫信美	孙信美	Sūn Xìnměi	N.	(name) Xinmei Sun
3.	楊歡	杨欢	Yáng Huān	N.	(name) Huan Yang

補充詞 Supplementary Vocabulary

	TRADITIONAL	SIMPLIFIED	PINYIN		
1.	飯館	饭馆	fànguǎn	N.	restaurant
2.	餐廳	餐厅	cāntīng	N.	restaurant
3.	餐館	餐馆	cānguǎn	N.	restaurant
4.	飯店	饭店	fàndiàn	N.	restaurant, hotel
5.	菜單	菜单	càidān	N.	menu
6.	白飯	白饭	báifàn	N.	steamed rice
7.	飲料	饮料	yǐnliào	N.	drink
8.	果汁	果汁	guǒzhī	N.	juice
9.	橙汁	橙汁	chéngzhī	N.	orange juice
10.	柳橙汁 (柳丁汁)	柳橙汁 (柳丁汁)	liǔchéngzhī (liǔdīngzhī)	N.	tangerine juice
11.	咖啡	咖啡	kāfēi	N.	coffee
12.	點菜	点菜	diǎncài	V.O.	to order food
13.	小費	小费	xiǎofèi	N.	tip
14.	買單	买单	mǎidān	V.O.	to pay the bill
15.	結賬 (結帳)	结账 (结帐)	jiézhàng	V.O.	to settle the account
16.	酸	酸	suān	Adj.	sour
17.	甜	甜	tián	Adj.	sweet

TRADITIONAL	SIMPLIFIED	PINYIN		
18. 苦	苦	kǔ	Adj.	bitter
19. 辣	辣	là	Adj.	spicy
20. 鹹	咸	xián	Adj.	salty
21. 清淡	清淡	qīngdàn	Adj.	plain
22. 燙	烫	tàng	Adj.	burning hot
23. 涼	凉	liáng	Adj.	cool

常見食品 [Chángjiàn shípǐn]   Common Foods

TRADITIONAL	SIMPLIFIED	PINYIN		
1. 餛飩	馄饨	húntun	N.	wonton
2. 春捲	春卷	chūnjuǎn	N.	spring roll
3. 魚	鱼	yú	N.	fish
4. 蝦	虾	xiā	N.	shrimp
5. 海鮮	海鲜	hǎixiān	N.	seafood
6. 青菜	青菜	qīngcài	N.	vegetable
7. 豬肉	猪肉	zhūròu	N.	pork
8. 牛肉	牛肉	niúròu	N.	beef
9. 雞肉	鸡肉	jīròu	N.	chicken
10. 豆腐	豆腐	dòufu	N.	bean curd
11. 甜點	甜点	tiándiǎn	N.	dessert
12. 餅乾	饼干	bǐnggān	N.	cracker
13. 蛋糕	蛋糕	dàngāo	N.	cake
14. 沙拉	沙拉	shālā	N.	salad
15. 麵包	面包	miànbāo	N.	bread

常見水果 [Chángjiàn shuǐguǒ]   Common Fruits

	TRADITIONAL	SIMPLIFIED	PINYIN		
1.	蘋果	苹果	píngguǒ	N.	apple
2.	香蕉	香蕉	xiāngjiāo	N.	banana
3.	桃子	桃子	táozi	N.	peach
4.	梨子	梨子	lízi	N.	pear
5.	西瓜	西瓜	xīguā	N.	watermelon
6.	草莓	草莓	cǎoméi	N.	strawberry
7.	葡萄	葡萄	pútao	N.	grape

語文知識   LANGUAGE LINK

The Sentence Patterns provide models that will help you with the Language in Use section. In both sections, pay attention to the grammar points, vocabulary, and expressions.

句型   Sentence Patterns

A: 你要紅茶還是綠茶?
　　Nǐ yào hóngchá háishì lǜchá?

B: 我要紅茶。
　　Wǒ yào hóngchá.

A: 你想點什麼?
　　Nǐ xiǎng diǎn shénme?

B: 我們點一杯可樂、一瓶啤酒、
　　Wǒmen diǎn yìbēi kělè, yìpíng píjiǔ,

　　一盤炒飯、三碗湯和
　　yìpán chǎofàn, sānwǎn tāng hé

　　二十個餃子。
　　èrshíge jiǎozi.

課文　Language in Use: 你要紅茶還是綠茶?
Nǐ yào hóngchá háishì lǜchá?

服務員：　請問，幾位?
　　　　　Qǐngwèn, jǐ wèi?

張正然：　三位。
　　　　　Sān wèi.

服務員：　好，請跟我來。請坐。
　　　　　Hǎo, qǐng gēn wǒ lái. Qǐngzuò.

張正然、孫信美、楊歡：　謝謝!
　　　　　　　　　　　　　Xièxie!

服務員：　小姐，先生，請問，你們想先喝點兒什麼?
　　　　　Xiǎojiě, xiānsheng, qǐngwèn, nǐmen xiǎng xiān hē diǎr shénme?

孫信美：　我喜歡喝茶。
　　　　　Wǒ xǐhuān hē chá.

服務員：　你要紅茶還是綠茶?
　　　　　Nǐ yào hóngchá háishì lǜchá?

孫信美：　我要一杯冰紅茶。
　　　　　Wǒ yào yìbēi bīng hóngchá.

楊歡：　　我要一杯可樂。
　　　　　Wǒ yào yìbēi kělè.

張正然：　我要一瓶啤酒。
　　　　　Wǒ yào yìpíng píjiǔ.

服務員：　好，一杯冰紅茶、一杯可樂、一瓶啤酒。請等一下。
　　　　　Hǎo, yìbēi bīng hóngchá, yìbēi kělè, yìpíng píjiǔ. Qǐng děng yíxià.

張正然：　對了，你們喜歡吃飯還是吃麵?
　　　　　Duì le, nǐmen xǐhuān chīfàn háishì chīmiàn?

孫信美：　我都喜歡。
　　　　　Wǒ dōu xǐhuān.

楊歡：　　我想吃餃子。
　　　　　Wǒ xiǎng chī jiǎozi.

服務員：　這是您的冰紅茶、可樂、還有啤酒。你們要點菜嗎？
　　　　　Zhè shì nín de bīng hóngchá, kělè, háiyǒu píjiǔ. Nǐmen yào diǎncài ma?

張正然：　好，我們點一盤炒飯、一盤炒麵和二十個餃子吧。
　　　　　Hǎo, wǒmen diǎn yìpán chǎofàn, yìpán chǎomiàn hé èrshí ge jiǎozi ba.

孫信美：　我們還要三碗湯。對了，我們也要三雙筷子，謝謝！
　　　　　Wǒmen háiyào sānwǎn tāng. Duìle, wǒmen yě yào sānshuāng kuàizi, xièxie!

注釋　LANGUAGE NOTES

服務員

In Mainland China, this term is used for anyone who provides service, mainly waiters and waitresses. In Taiwan, people use 服務生 instead of 服務員.

位

As was explained previously, 位 is another measure word for people. It is usually used to be courteous to guests or to show respect. In a restaurant, the waiter/waitress usually politely asks "幾位？" and the customers reply with a phrase, such as "三位" (three of us) or "五位" (five of us). In this situation, the word "位" is only a response to the question and has nothing to do with courtesy or politeness.

點

點 is used to order (dishes, wine, music pieces, etc.)
Similar to 點, 要 can also be used to order food.

餃子

Instead of 餃子, 水餃 is more commonly used in Taiwan.

語法 GRAMMAR

還是

還是 is a conjunction corresponding to "or" in English. It is used to connect two alternatives in an alternative question (a question of the form "A or B"?). These two alternatives can be noun phrases, verb phrases, adjective phrases, etc., for example,

你要紅茶還是綠茶?	Would you like black tea or green tea?
你想打電話還是寫信?	Do you want to make a phone call or write a letter?
你今天上午上課還是下午上課?	Do you have class in the morning or in the afternoon?
誰是中國人,你還是他?	Who is Chinese, you or he?

量詞 (Measure Words/Classifiers) (3)

Words identifying containers can also be used as measure words. Here are some examples,

Measure word		Example		
杯	一杯冰紅茶	yì*bēi* bīnghóngchá	a *glass* of iced tea
瓶	兩瓶啤酒	liǎng*píng* píjiǔ	two *bottles* of beer
盤	三盤炒飯	sān*pán* chǎofàn	three *plates* of fried rice
碗	四碗酸辣湯	sì*wǎn* suānlàtāng	four *bowls* of hot and sour soup

Also,

Measure word		Example		
壺	一壺咖啡	yì*hú* kāfēi	a *pot* of coffee
盒	兩盒巧克力	liǎng*hé* qiǎokèlì	two *boxes* of chocolate
桶	三桶水	sān*tǒng* shuǐ	three *buckets* of water
罐	四罐可樂	sì*guàn* kělè	four *cans* of Coke
箱	五箱書	wǔ*xiāng* shū	five *cases* of books
袋	六袋花生	liù*dài* huāshēng	six *bags* of peanuts

補充課文 —◇◇◇— SUPPLEMENTARY PRACTICE

This selection will help you test your comprehension of the grammar and vocabulary you have learned in this lesson. Be prepared to answer questions about the meaning of the passage.

　　今天我們下課以後都餓了，我們就約了幾個朋友一起去中國飯館吃飯。服務員小姐看到我們很親切地說"歡迎光臨"，然後問我們想喝點兒什麼飲料。我要了一杯冰紅茶，楊歡要了一杯可樂，正然喜歡喝啤酒，他要了一瓶啤酒。

　　服務員小姐還問我們想吃麵還是想吃飯，我們看了看菜單，有很多好吃的東西，最後我們點了一盤炒飯，一盤炒麵，二十個餃子和三碗湯。我們不太習慣用叉子，比較喜歡用筷子，我們就跟服務員小姐要了三雙筷子。我們一面吃飯一面聊天，大家吃得又飽又高興。

Notes: 餓 [è]: hungry
了 [le]: an aspect particle indicating completion of an action
約 [yuē]: to make an appointment, invite
看到 [kàndào]: to see; to catch sight of
親切 [qīnqiè]: cordial; warm
歡迎光臨 [huānyíng guānglín]: welcome
然後 [ránhòu]: then
飲料 [yǐnliào]: beverage
還 [hái]: also
菜單 [càidān]: menu
好吃 [hǎochī]: yummy; delicious
最後 [zuìhòu]: finally
習慣 [xíguàn]: to get used to
叉子 [chāzi]: fork
一面 ... 一面 ... [yímiàn . . . yímiàn . . .]: adverb indicating two simultaneous actions
聊天 [liáotiān]: chat
又 ... 又 ... [yòu]: both . . . and
得 [de]: 得 is used in the "degree of complement" sentence to tell how an action is performed
飽 [bǎo]: to be full
高興 [gāoxìng]: happy

練習 ACTIVITIES

I. Pinyin Exercises

11-1 Listen to the instructor pronounce the Pinyin below. Mark "√" after the Pinyin if correct, or write in the correct Pinyin:

1. fānguǎn _____
2. lùchá _____
3. píjǔ _____
4. kuāzi _____
5. kěliè _____
6. xiānsheng _____
7. kēchá _____
8. fúwùyuán _____
9. jīwéi _____
10. jiǎozǐ _____
11. bīnhóngchā _____
12. chǎofàn _____

11-2 Listen to the instructor and fill in each blank with the correct Pinyin:

1. qǐng _____
2. _____ shì
3. _____ chá
4. _____ cài
5. liǎng _____ chá
6. sān _____ fàn
7. xiǎo _____
8. yǐn _____
9. yì _____ kuàizi
10. sìwǎn _____
11. kā _____
12. bái _____
13. chǎo _____
14. _____ yào
15. cài _____
16. _____ cài

11-3 Read the following Chinese poem, paying special attention to the tones and rhythm:

Mǐn Nóng (Lǐ Shēn)	**憫農** (李紳)
Chú hé rì dāng wǔ,	除禾日當午，
Hàn dī hé xià tǔ.	汗滴禾下土。
Shéi zhī pán zhōng cān,	誰知盤中餐，
Lìlì jiē xīnkǔ.	粒粒皆辛苦。

Gratefulness to Peasants
(Li, Shen)

Hoeing the crops under the hot sun,
Sweat drips onto the soil beneath the crops.
Who realizes the rice in the bowl
Is every grain produced from hard labor?

II. Character Exercises

11-4 Read the following words, phrases, and sentences:

茶	想
紅茶	想吃飯
冰紅茶	想吃炒飯
一杯冰紅茶	他想吃一盤炒飯
喝一杯冰紅茶	他想吃一盤蝦炒飯
她要喝一杯冰紅茶	他想吃一盤還是兩盤蝦炒飯

Note: 蝦 [xiā]: shrimp

Now try to use the following characters to make words, phrases, and then sentences:

1. 館   2. 服   3. 坐   4. 喝   5. 紅   6. 綠

7. 可   8. 瓶   9. 酒   10. 麵   11. 湯   12. 筷

11-5 Insert the proper measure word into the phrases below:

1. 三　小　說   2. 兩　車   3. 那　啤　酒

4. 這　炒　飯   5. 多　少　餃　子   6. 三　狗

7. 兩　綠　茶   8. 一　老　師   9. 一　工　程　課

10. 一　啤　酒   11. 四　餛　飩　湯   12. 幾　筷　子

III. Grammar Exercises

11-6 Substitution exercises:

1. 你想<u>喝茶</u>還是<u>喝咖啡</u>？
   我想<u>喝茶</u>。

喝紅茶	喝綠茶
喝可樂	喝啤酒
吃炒飯	吃炒麵
看小說	看電視
做功課	上網
學工程	學電腦

2. 請問，你想喝什麼？
   我要<u>一杯可樂</u>。

吃	二十個餃子
點	一盤炒麵
喝	一瓶啤酒
喝	一杯冰紅茶
喝	一杯綠茶

11-7 Fill in the blanks with the words below. Some words may be used more than once.

跟　想　要　還是

1. 你喜歡吃飯 _____ 吃麵?
2. 請 ____ 我來。
3. 你 ____ 喝什麼?
4. 我 ____ 二十個餃子。
5. 李文中常 ____ 丁明說中文。
6. 吃晚飯以後,你 ____ 上網 _____ 看電視?

11-8 Combine the words or phrases in parentheses with the sentences and the word "還是" to make alternative questions:

For example,　　今天下午他有課。　　　　　(法語　　　　　工程)
　　　　　　→ 今天下午他有法語課還是工程課?

1. 他喜歡學習。　　　　　　　　　(在圖書館　　　　在宿舍)
2. 楊歡要去圖書館。　　　　　　　(六點半　　　　　七點)
3. 李先生是老師。　　　　　　　　(日文　　　　　　中文)
4. 她要一杯茶。　　　　　　　　　(紅　　　　　　　綠)

IV. Communicative Activities

11-9 Situational dialogues:

<u>Situation 1:</u>
Your classmates are visiting you in your apartment. Please act as a good host.

Hints:
1. Topics to cover:
   • Greetings.
   • Ask what your friends would like to eat and drink.
   • Chat about your hobbies, your apartment, your studying schedule, etc.

2. Words and expressions to use:

喜歡...　　　　　...還是...
想吃/喝...　　　　...吧

Situation 2:
You and several international students are eating together in a Korean restaurant.

Hints:
1. Topics to cover:
   - Greetings.
   - Discuss what kinds of food and drink you like and place an order.
   - Get to know some new friends.
   - Ask about foods in other countries.

2. Words and expressions to use:

喜歡...	...還是...	想吃/喝...
您貴姓?	哪國人?	學什麼?
有沒有...?	是不是...?	

Situation 3:
Discuss with your friend what to do after class.

Hints:
1. Topics to cover:
   - Meet the friend on campus and greet each other.
   - Chat for a while about each other's courses this semester and ask about your mutual friends.
   - Discuss what you want to do after class: practice Chinese, visit friends, go to a restaurant, etc.

2. Words and expressions to use:

你好嗎?	忙嗎?	是...還是...?
...難嗎?	喜歡	看朋友

文化點滴　CULTURE NOTES

中國菜系介紹 [Zhōngguó càixì jièshào]
Chinese Food (1)

Chinese food is among the best-known cuisines in the world. It is abundant in variety, delicious in taste, and pleasing to the eye. Chinese food is also considered to be healthy.

Chinese people have studied the art of cooking for over 3,000 years. It would not be surprising today if you were served at a restaurant in China with 一雞三味 [yìjī sānwèi] (one chicken with three different flavors), 一鴨四吃 [yìyā sìchī] (one Peking roast duck in four or five courses) or 一魚二燒 [yìyú èrshāo] (one fish served in two cooking styles). Chinese cooking places emphasis on 色 [sè], 香 [xiāng], and 味 [wèi] (color, flavor, and taste). From simple family meals to the most elaborate banquets (usually over 18 courses), every mouthful manages to combine nutrition, aesthetics, and history.

There are eight styles of Chinese cuisine. They are 魯菜 [Lǔcài] (Shandong style), 川菜 [Chuāncài] (Sichuan style), 淮陽菜 [Huáiyángcài] (Yangzhou style), 粵菜 [Yuècài] (Cantonese style), 閩菜 [Mǐncài] (Fujian style), 浙菜 [Zhècài] (Zhejiang style), 皖菜 [Wǎncài] (Anhui style), and 湘菜 [Xiāngcài] (Hunan style). Both the 川菜 and 湘菜 are hot and spicy, whereas 淮陽菜 and 浙菜 are a sweet and

A common Chinese breakfast, 粥 [zhōu] (porridge), 醬菜 [jiàngcài] (pickles) and 蛋 [dàn] (eggs).

A banquet feast with fancy decorations.

At Chinese traditional markets 菜市場 [càishìchǎng] you can find processed meat, chicken, pickles, fish balls, baked goods, desserts, vegetables, and seafood.

light in flavor with fresh, tender ingredients. The characteristics of 粵菜 are very special and unique ingredients, consisting mostly of fresh seafood with an emphasis on the "original flavor." 點心 [diǎnxīn] (dim sum), a Cantonese-style brunch with dozens of varieties of light appetizers, is very popular among Chinese both at home and abroad.

Chinese food commonly uses a lot of ingredients with purported healing properties, including ginger, green onion, garlic, cinnamon, yam, eggs, vinegar, mung beans, and rice wine. All ingredients are categorized into groups of three different nature — hot, cold, and neutral. The combination of ingredients is based on Daoist yin-yang theory to strive for balance. Chinese people are interested in 食療 [shíliáo] (medical treatment with food). They have known for centuries that sea cucumbers strengthen bones and protect against aging. Bitter melon clears the blood. Carp is good for the gallbladder and spleen, as well as for pregnant women and their fetuses. Pig's feet and chicken broth help blood circulation. With these ideas in mind, Chinese people often use herbal medicine together with certain ingredients in their stir-fry dishes and soups to help meet the body's needs.

Food is an extremely important part of people's lives in China. In the Qing Dynasty, there were approximately 2,000 people working to provide food for the emperor and his family. Dining partners have always been a symbol of one's social status. Today, food still plays a great role in the social life of Chinese people. "Business is done at the dining table" is a common saying in China.

Dining in China is often associated with hospitality as well. Chinese usually treat their guests to abundant food of great variety.

Questions:

1. What kind of food do you like best? What do you think are the major differences between Chinese food and Western food?

2. Do you often go to Chinese restaurants? Describe one of your favorite Chinese dishes.

Chinese Food (2)

Western-brand foods are also popular in China, Taiwan, and Hong Kong:

麥當勞		[Màidāngláo]	McDonald's
肯德基	炸雞	[Kěndéjī zhájī]	Kentucky Fried Chicken
必勝客	匹薩	[Bìshèngkè pǐsà]	Pizza Hut
星巴克	咖啡	[Xīngbākè kāfēi]	Starbucks Coffee

趣味中文　FUN WITH CHINESE

> 飯後百步走，活到九十九。
> Take a walk after each meal and you will live to be 99 years old.

fàn	hòu	bǎi	bù	zǒu	huó	dào	jiǔshíjiǔ
飯	後	百	步	走	活	到	九十九
meal	after	hundred	step	walk	live	to	ninety-nine

Questions:

1. Do you know any similar sayings in a language other than Chinese?

2. Can you give an example?

行動吧！　LET'S GO!

小吃　Chinese Snacks

1. While traveling in China, 小中 saw the following interesting shop signs. Read the signs and answer the following questions.

Useful words and expressions:

小吃 [xiǎochī]: snacks
左邊 (左边) [zuǒbiān]: left side
右邊 (右边) [yòubiān]: right side
餡 (馅) [xiàn]: food filling
熊 [xióng]: bear
之父 [zhīfù]: father of
快餐 [kuàicān]: fast food
店名 [diànmíng]: name of a shop

Question:

左邊的店名叫什麼，賣什麼？右邊的店呢？

2. 小中 also visited Taiwan. During his stay there his Chinese friends took him out to eat at the following places. They ate several dishes at each place.

Useful words and expressions:

發財(发财) [fācái]: get rich

排骨 [páigǔ]: ribs or pork chop

香菇 [xiānggū]: mushroom

炸醬麵(炸酱面) [zhájiàng miàn]:
  noodles with spicy bean sauce

鍋貼(锅贴) [guōtiē]:
  fried dumpling

魚丸(鱼丸) [yúwán]:
  fish ball

十二月十八日星期一　　十二月二十二日星期日

Questions:

1. 左邊的店名叫什麼？

2. 他們十二月十八日星期一吃什麼？十二月二十二日星期日呢？

3. 你想點些什麼？

我可以借你的車嗎?
May I Borrow Your Car?

- Make a request
- Express wishes, obligations, capabilities, possibilities, or permissions

Meeting friends at the Guangzhou airport in China.

Have a good trip back to the U.S. 浦東 [Pǔdōng] International Airport in Shanghai.

Taxis are plentiful and are a convenient way to get around the city.

生詞 VOCABULARY

核心詞 Core Vocabulary

	TRADITIONAL	SIMPLIFIED	PINYIN		
1.	可以	可以	kěyǐ	Aux.	can, may
2.	借	借	jiè	V.	to borrow
3.	明天	明天	míngtiān	N.	tomorrow
4.	用	用	yòng	V.	to use
5.	得	得	děi	Aux.	must; have to
6.	機場	机场	jīchǎng	N.	airport
7.	接	接	jiē	V.	to pick up
8.	妹妹	妹妹	mèimei	N.	younger sister
9.	玩	玩	wán	V.	to play, have fun
10.	飛機	飞机	fēijī	N.	airplane
11.	到	到	dào	V.	to arrive
12.	手排擋 (手排)	手排挡 (手排)	shǒupáidǎng (shǒupái)	N.	manual transmission
13.	開	开	kāi	V.	to drive
14.	應該	应该	yīnggāi	Aux.	should
15.	問題	问题	wèntí	N.	problem; question
16.	白	白	bái	Adj.	white
17.	色	色	sè	N.	color
18.	停	停	tíng	V.	to park
19.	停車場	停车场	tíngchēchǎng	N.	parking lot
20.	這次	这次	zhècì	Pron.	this time
21.	練習	练习	liànxí	V.	to practice

TRADITIONAL	SIMPLIFIED	PINYIN		
22. 這樣	这样	zhèyàng	Pron.	thus, in this way
23. 就	就	jiù	Adv.	(connects two clauses, the first being the premise of the second)
24. 能	能	néng	Aux.	can, may, be able to
25. 進步	进步	jìnbù	V.	to improve

專名 Proper Nouns

TRADITIONAL	SIMPLIFIED	PINYIN		
1. 于影	于影	Yú Yǐng	N.	(name) Ying Yu
2. 王本樂	王本乐	Wáng Běnlè	N.	(name) Benle Wang
3. 上海	上海	Shànghǎi	N.	Shanghai
4. 洛杉磯	洛杉矶	Luòshānjī	N.	Los Angeles

補充詞 Supplementary Vocabulary

TRADITIONAL	SIMPLIFIED	PINYIN		
1. 自動排擋 (自排)	自动排挡 (自排)	zìdòngpáidǎng (zìpái)	Adj.	automatic transmission

語文知識 LANGUAGE LINK

The Sentence Patterns provide models that will help you with the Language in Use section. In both sections, pay attention to the grammar points, vocabulary, and expressions.

句型 Sentence Patterns

A: 我可以借你的車嗎?
Wǒ kěyǐ jiè nǐde chē ma?

B: 可以。
Kěyǐ.

A: 你要去接誰？
   Nǐ yào qù jiē shéi?

B: 我要去接我妹妹。
   Wǒ yào qù jiē wǒ mèimei.

A: 你會不會開車？
   Nǐ huìbuhuì kāi chē?

B: 我不會開車。
   Wǒ bú huì kāi chē.

課文   Language in Use: 我可以借你的車嗎？   Wǒ kěyǐ jiè nǐde chē ma?

于影：   本樂，明天下午你用不用車？
         Běnlè, míngtiān xiàwǔ nǐ yòngbuyòng chē?

王本樂： 我不用。你有什麼事兒嗎？
         Wǒ bú yòng. Nǐ yǒu shénme shèr ma?

于影：   我得去機場接人，可以借你的車嗎？
         Wǒ děi qù jīchǎng jiē rén, kěyǐ jiè nǐde chē ma?

王本樂： 可以。你要去接誰？
         Kěyǐ. Nǐ yào qù jiē shéi?

于影：   我妹妹和她男朋友。他們從上海坐飛機去
         Wǒ mèimei hé tā nán péngyou. Tāmen cóng Shànghǎi zuò fēijī qù

         洛杉磯玩兒，明天會到我這兒來。
         Luòshānjī wár, míngtiān huì dào wǒ zhèr lái.

王本樂： 我的車是手排擋的，你會不會開？
         Wǒ de chē shì shǒupáidǎng de, nǐ huìbuhuì kāi?

于影：   應該沒問題。我爸爸的車也是手排擋的，我常開他的車。
         Yīnggāi méi wèntí. Wǒ bàba de chē yěshì shǒupáidǎng de, wǒ cháng kāi tāde chē.

王本樂： 我的車是白色的，車號是
Wǒ de chē shì báisè de, chēhào shì

BD5730，停在五號停車場。
BD wǔ qī sān líng, tíng zài wǔ hào tíngchē chǎng.

于影： 知道了。謝謝！
Zhīdào le. Xièxie!

王本樂： 不謝。你妹妹他們會說英文嗎？
Búxiè. Nǐ mèimei tāmen huì shuō Yīngwén ma?

于影： 會一點兒，這次他們想多學習一點兒英文。
Huì yìdiǎr, zhècì tāmen xiǎng duō xuéxí yìdiǎr Yīngwén.

王本樂： 太好了，我得跟他們多練習一點兒中文。
Tàihǎo le, wǒ děi gēn tāmen duō liànxí yìdiǎr Zhōngwén.

這樣，我的中文就能進步了。
Zhèyàng, wǒde Zhōngwén jiù néng jìnbù le.

注釋 LANGUAGE NOTES

坐

坐 means "sit." When its object is a means of transportation, 坐 means "to take." For example, 坐飛機 means "to take an airplane."

手排擋 (手排)

手排擋 literally means "hand handle gear." It refers to a manual transmission. In Taiwan, 手排 is commonly used.

這樣

這樣 is a phrase meaning "in this way."

就

就 here is used as a conjunction meaning "then."

語法   GRAMMAR

Optative Verbs   (能願動詞)：要，想，應該，得，能，可以，會

Optative Verbs are placed before the main verb to express one's wish, desire, obligation, capability, possibility, or permission. Following are the commonly used optative verbs.

Optative verbs	Meaning	Examples	Negation
要 [yào]	1. want, will, to be going to	我要去機場。	不想 (irregular negation)
	2. have to, should	你要多練習中文。	不用 (irregular negation)
想 [xiǎng]	want, intend, would like to	他們想多說英文。 我想吃餃子。	不想
應該 [yīnggāi]	should, ought to, to be supposed to	你應該在宿舍學習。 你應該多休息。	不應該
得 [děi]	have to, to be required to	我得去機場接人。	不用 (irregular negation)
能 [néng]	1. have the ability to	我能開手排擋的車。	不會 (irregular negation)
	2. can (depending on circumstances)	他明天能來上課。	不能
	3. permission — may	我能借他的車。	不能
可以 [kěyǐ]	1. permission — may	我可以借他的車。	不能 (irregular negation) 不可以
	2. can (depending on circumstances)	他明天可以來。	不能 (irregular negation)
會 [huì]	1. know how to, have the ability to	你會開車。	不會
	2. be likely to	他明天會來。	不會

從 ... 去(到) ...

從 ... 去(到)...(from . . . to . . .) is a common pattern which is used to describe the movement of something from one place (or time) to another. Note that when describing an event, Chinese word order begins with the starting point, then proceeds to the means, to the arriving point, and then to the action. This reflects the temporal sequence of the event. For example,

Place:

	從 Place 1	坐 N	去 (到) Place 2	
他們	從上海	坐飛機	去 (到)洛杉磯	玩。
Subj.	Place 1	Means	Place 2	VP

They, from Shanghai, took an airplane, arrived in Los Angeles, and had fun.

Time:　這學期是從一月到五月。
This semester is from January to May.

多　VP　(學習，練習)

多 can be placed before a verb to indicate doing more of the verb. For example,

你要多學習。	You need to study more.
你應該多練習漢字 [hànzì]。	You should practice characters more.
請多吃一點兒。	Please eat a little bit more.
我要多睡一點兒。	I want to sleep a little more.

補充課文 ○○○ **SUPPLEMENTARY PRACTICE**

This selection will help you test your comprehension of the grammar and vocabulary you have learned in this lesson. Be prepared to answer questions about the meaning of the passage.

　　我妹妹和她男朋友要來美國度假，他們要先從上海坐飛機去洛杉磯玩兒，然後再到我這兒來。我得去機場接他們，可是我沒有車，我就跟本樂借車。本樂的車是手排擋的，他問我會不會開。我告訴他我雖然比較喜歡開自排的車，但是我以前也常開手排的車，所以應該沒問題。

　　妹妹他們這次來，除了想好好地玩兒以外，他們也想多瞭解美國文化，多學一點兒英文。本樂說他也可以趁這個機會跟他們多練習一點兒中文，這樣，他的中文就能進步了。我覺得這是一個好主意。

Notes: 度假 [dùjià]: to spend one's vacation
雖然...但是... [suīrán ... dànshì ...]: though ..., ... but
瞭解 [liǎojiě]: to understand
趁 [chèn]: to take advantage of
覺得 [juéde]: to think

告訴 [gàosù]: to tell
以前 [yǐqián]: before
除了...以外... [chúle ... yǐwài ...]: besides
文化 [wénhuà]: culture
機會 [jīhuì]: opportunity
主意 [zhǔyì]: idea

練習 ACTIVITIES

I. Pinyin Exercises

12-1 Listen to the instructor, then write the correct Pinyin for the following characters:

1. 機場 _____
2. 可以 _____
3. 這次 _____
4. 手排擋 _____
5. 飛機 _____
6. 白色 _____
7. 問題 _____
8. 停車場 _____
9. 進步 _____
10. 應該 _____
11. 練習 _____
12. 這樣 _____

12-2 Listen to the instructor, then fill in each blank with the correct Pinyin:

1. ____ 練習 ____ ____ 進步
2. 我 ____ 去 ____ 人
3. ____ 紐約到 ____ ____
4. 還不 ____ ____ 車
5. 想 ____ ____ 色的車
6. 我 ____ 上 ____ 車

12-3 Read the following Chinese poem, paying special attention to the tones and rhythm:

Lè Yóuyuán (Lǐ Shāngyǐn)	樂遊原 (李商隱)	Wandering about the Pleasant Plateau (Li, Shangyin)
Xiàng wǎn yì bú shì,	向晚意不適,	Feeling slightly sad near dusk,
Qū chē dēng gǔyuán.	驅車登古原。	I drive up to the ancient plateau.
Xīyáng wúxiàn hǎo,	夕陽無限好,	The sunset is endlessly beautiful,
Zhǐshì jìn huánghūn.	只是近黃昏。	But dusk is drawing near.

II. Character Exercises

12-4 Read the following words and phrases:

到	車
到機場	開車
從學校到機場	練習開車
從學校到機場接人	應該練習開車
能從學校到機場接人	應該多練習開車
你能從學校到機場去接人嗎	你們都應該多練習開車

Now try to use the following characters to make words, phrases, and then sentences:

1. 借   2. 用   3. 玩   4. 飛   5. 接   6. 色
7. 停   8. 會   9. 排   10. 次   11. 得   12. 進

12-5 Match the following traditional characters with their equivalent simplified forms:

| 應 | 機 | 習 | 進 | 飛 | 場 | 開 | 樣 |

(1)　(2)　(3)　(4)　(5)　(6)　(7)　(8)

习　场　机　开　应　进　样　飞

III. Grammar Exercises

12-6 Substitution exercises:

1. 你會不會<u>開車</u>？
   我會<u>開車</u>。

| 寫小說 |
| 用電腦 |
| 說法文 |
| 寫電子郵件 |
| 開飛機 |

2. 你現在能<u>打電話</u>嗎？
   我現在能<u>打電話</u>。

| 喝啤酒 |
| 看電視 |
| 上網 |
| 看中國文學書 |
| 跟我一起喝咖啡 |

3. 王老師要從<u>洛杉磯</u>到<u>紐約</u><u>看朋友</u>。

公寓	圖書館	看書
英國	日本	學習
家	學校	打球
六點	八點	跟朋友吃飯

12-7 Match the Chinese sentences with their English translations. Pay attention to the optative verbs.

1. 我今天得開車去學校。　　　A. I should drive to school today.

2. 我今天要開車去學校。　　　B. I will drive to school today.

3. 我今天應該開車去學校。　　C. I am likely to drive to school today.

4. 我今天能開車去學校。　　　D. I have to drive to school today.

5. 我今天會開車去學校。　　　E. I am able to drive to school today.

1. | 他不可以打手機。 |　A. | He doesn't want to use the cell phone. |

2. | 他不會打手機。 |　B. | He shouldn't use the cell phone. |

3. | 他不用打手機。 |　C. | He is not allowed to use the cell phone. |

4. | 他不想打手機。 |　D. | He doesn't know how to use the cell phone. |

5. | 他不應該打手機。 |　E. | He doesn't need to use the cell phone. |

12-8 Complete the sentences with the following optative words or their negative forms (e.g. 不用), "要、想、應該、得、能、可以、會":

1. 我今天不 ＿＿＿＿ 上課。我 ＿＿＿＿ 不 ＿＿＿＿ 跟你一起去打球？

2. 你 ＿＿＿＿ 多休息。

3. 坐飛機不 ＿＿＿＿ 打手機。

4. A： 七月你 ＿＿＿＿ 去上海玩兒嗎？

   B： 我不 ＿＿＿＿ 去。我從六月到九月都 ＿＿＿＿ 在洛杉磯學習。

5. 我很 ＿＿＿＿ 看電影。可是我明天早上六點就 ＿＿＿＿ 開車去機場接朋友，今天晚上不 ＿＿＿＿ 太晚睡覺。

6. 今天下午我 ＿＿＿＿ 借你的數學書用一下，＿＿＿＿ 嗎？

7. A： 你 ＿＿＿＿ 不 ＿＿＿＿ 說德語？

   B： ＿＿＿＿ 說一點兒。

8. 不 ＿＿＿＿ 開夜車。這樣你 ＿＿＿＿ 很累。

   Note: 開夜車 [kāiyèchē]: to burn the midnight oil

IV. Communicative Activities

12-9 Situational dialogues:

Situation 1:
You are going to travel to China next month. Your friend has a guide book on Chinese. Please borrow this book from your friend.

Hints:
1. Topics to cover:
   - Greetings.
   - Tell your friend you want to borrow the guide book on China.
   - Talk about the good scenic spots and delicious food in China.
   - Discuss and determine a possible travel route.

2. Words and expressions to use:

很好玩兒/很美　　從 …坐 … 到/去…
多吃點兒　　　　要/得/應該/可以去…
喜歡…

Situation 2:

Your friend is borrowing your car to pick up a TV he/she bought from the store. Describe your car to your friend.

Hints:
1. Topics to cover:
   - Greetings.
   - Chat about the TV and the car.
   - Discuss your route.

2. Words and expressions to use:

有事兒嗎?　　要/想 …　　　　拿[ná] pick up stuff, (items)
會不會　　　　紅/綠/白色的
沒問題　　　　知道了　　　　應該/能/可以 …　　從 … 到 …

Situation 3:

You are considering taking a Chinese course next semester. You are in the professor's office to ask whether the course will suit you.

Hints:
1. Topics to cover:
   - Greetings.
   - Chat for a while about the courses you are taking this semester.
   - Discuss your course schedule for the next semester and your current knowledge of Chinese.
   - Find out whether you should take the course.

2. Words and expressions to use:

忙嗎?　　　　　　會說/看/寫一點兒 … 應該 …　　多練習…

… 點鐘要/得上 … 課　能/可以

文化知識 ⊙─⊙─⊙ Culture Link

文化點滴　CULTURE NOTES

中國的汽車工業 [Zhōngguó de qìchē gōngyè]
China's Auto Industry
China on Wheels

China's domestic auto industry celebrated its 50th anniversary in 2003. In 1953 a truck named 解放 [Jiěfàng] (Liberation) and a limousine named 紅旗 [Hóngqí] (Red Flag) were first produced at China's First Auto Manufacturer in 長春 [Chángchūn] (Changchun), 吉林省 [Jílín Shěng] (Jilin Province). China's first sedan, branded as 上海 [Shànghǎi] (Shanghai), was also produced that year at Shanghai Auto Manufacturer.

Since the late 1980s many world-renowned auto manufacturers have established facilities in China to take advantage of the largest potential auto market in the world. Now China has Volkswagen and Audi in Changchun; Ford, Chrysler, Suzuki, and Hyundai in 北京 [Běijīng] (Beijing); Toyota in 天津 [Tiānjīn] (Tianjin); Honda and Volvo in 廣州 [Guǎngzhōu] (Guangzhou); and Volkswagen and GMC in Shanghai. The auto market in China is now filled with almost all Chinese-made and joint venture-manufactured cars and has only a small number of imported cars. By 2007, 27% of China's auto market will be open to imported cars, as required by the WTO. In October 2003 the first 2,500 BMW sedans from a joint venture at 瀋陽 [Shěnyáng] (the city of Shenyang) became available to the Chinese auto market. According to an agreement signed in September 2003, China will supply the domestic market with joint-venture Mercedes Benz sedans in 2005.

The auto market for individual Chinese started in the early 1990s when only the wealthy could afford to buy used cars from some foreign embassies and consulates in Beijing. In October 1998 the Central Bank of China started to issue auto loans to individuals for the purchase of cars. The automobile loan business expanded very rapidly. The total loan amount grew from 400 million Yuan RMB (approximately US$50 million) in 1998 to 140 billion Yuan RMB (approximately US$17.5 billion) by 2002. The number of family cars increased eight times in the ten years from 1993 to 2003, and now there are over 7.7 million family cars in China. However, that number accounts for only 10% of all cars in China as compared to a substantially higher average percentage of family cars in other parts of the world. Millions of Chinese are carrying "pocket licenses," forming a gigantic pool of potential customers for the automobile market in China.

As roads in China are not yet ready to support a large number of cars, China has restricted the purchase of private cars for the time being. As a result, a vehicle license plate today may cost as much as US$15,000 at an auction. Also, an annual parking permit in major cities like Shanghai or Beijing costs from 1,000 to 6,000 Yuan RMB (US$125 to $750). That is one reason why you hear people say that you might be able to afford to buy a new car in China, but not to use it. In China, after the purchase of a car, there are also many other additional costs for maintenance, road and bridge tolls, vehicle taxes, insurance, gas, parking, and annual inspection.

Cars also serve as a symbol of one's social status in China.

Auto detailing shops are available for car owners.

A privately owned car on the streets of Guangdong Province 粵 [Yuè]. Do you know how much the license plate costs?

Early morning in Shanghai, privately owned cars on the street.

Small, utilitarian minivans are a popular choice for businesses and families in Taiwan.

This mini truck is owned by a scooter business in Taiwan. It is used for delivering equipment and scooters.

Questions:

1. Some people say that with a large population of 1.3 billion, it is not appropriate for China to encourage its people to purchase their own cars. Do you agree with them? Why or why not?

2. How would you comment on the mentality among some Chinese that owning a car is a sign of high social status? Do you agree? Why or why not?

趣味中文   FUN WITH CHINESE

有借有還，再借不難。
If one borrows something and then returns it, it will make borrowing easier the next time.

yǒu	jiè	yǒu	huán	zài	jiè	bù	nán
有	借	有	還	再	借	不	難
have	borrow	have	return	again	borrow	not	difficult

有借有還，再借不難

Question:

How would you comment on this Chinese saying? Do you know any similar sayings in another culture?

行動吧！　LET'S GO!

停車標誌和汽車出售
Parking Sign and Car for Sale

正明 is interested in the signs below. Take a look at them, and then answer the questions.

Useful words and expressions:

車位(车位) [chēwèi]:
　parking space

每 [měi]: every

收費(收费) [shōufèi]:
　to collect a fee

電洽(电洽) [diànqià]:
　to contact via phone

覺得(觉得) [juéde]: to think

已 [yǐ]: already

滿(满) [mǎn]: full

小時(小时) [xiǎoshí]: hour

售 [shòu]: for sale

找 [zhǎo]: to look for

貴(贵) [guì]: expensive

This ad is from the window of the car on the left.

Questions:

1. 正明在找什麼？

2. 這個停車場怎麼收費？你覺得貴不貴？

3. 是誰要賣車？這輛車是自排的嗎？

4. 手機的號碼是多少？

復習 Review

LESSON 11 AND LESSON 12

Conversation

Form pairs. Ask your partner the following questions. Then report the information you collect in class.

1. 你喜歡吃飯還是吃麵?
2. 你喜歡在圖書館還是在宿舍看書?
3. 你喜歡給朋友打電話還是寫電子郵件?
4. 你會開車嗎?
5. 你會開自排擋的車還是手排擋的車?
6. 畢業以後你想去中國工作嗎?
7. 我們從這裡到洛杉磯應該開車還是坐飛機?

Situational Dialogues

You go to a Chinese restaurant. Chat with the waitress/waiter, then order drinks and dishes.

Useful expressions: 還是; measure words: 杯 瓶 盤 碗 雙; 點 (to order), 多 + VP . . . (一點兒); optative verbs: 可以, 要, 想, 應該, 能, 會, 得; time sequence: 從 place 坐 N 到 place

Traditional and Simplified Characters

Read each character aloud. Write its traditional form. Then make a phrase and a sentence using the character.

For example, 学 → 學 → 學生 → 我是學生。

L11: 务 ( )   乐 ( )   面 ( )   盘 ( )   汤 ( )   双 ( )

L12: 场 ( )   飞 ( )   应 ( )   会 ( )   习 ( )   进 ( )

我想買一件襯衫
I Want to Buy a Shirt

教學目標 OBJECTIVES

- Go shopping
- Talk about clothing, colors, and prices
- Provide opinions

Shopping malls, street malls, department stores, and traditional markets are common in Mainland China and Taiwan. They are usually crowded.

生詞 VOCABULARY

核心詞 Core Vocabulary

	TRADITIONAL	SIMPLIFIED	PINYIN		
1.	買	买	mǎi	V.	to buy
2.	件	件	jiàn	M.W.	(measure word for clothes)
3.	襯衫	衬衫	chènshān	N.	shirt
4.	店員	店员	diànyuán	N.	salesman, saleswoman
5.	條	条	tiáo	M.W.	(measure word for skirts/pants)
6.	裙子	裙子	qúnzi	N.	skirt
7.	或者	或者	huòzhě	Conj.	or, either . . . or . . .
8.	褲子	裤子	kùzi	N.	pants
9.	黃	黄	huáng	Adj.	yellow
10.	不錯	不错	búcuò		not bad, pretty good
11.	比較	比较	bǐjiào	Adv.	relatively
12.	穿	穿	chuān	V.	to wear
13.	黑	黑	hēi	Adj.	black
14.	試試	试试	shìshi	V.	to try
15.	幫	帮	bāng	V.	to help
16.	好看	好看	hǎokàn	Adj.	good-looking
17.	讓	让	ràng	V.	to let, allow
18.	覺得	觉得	juéde	V.	to think, feel
19.	錢	钱	qián	N.	money
20.	塊	块	kuài	N.	dollar
21.	張	张	zhāng	M.W.	(measure word for piece of paper)
22.	電影	电影	diànyǐng	N.	movie
23.	票	票	piào	N.	ticket

專名　Proper Nouns

TRADITIONAL	SIMPLIFIED	PINYIN		
1. 毛愛紅	毛爱红	Máo Àihóng	N.	(name) Aihong Mao
2. 方子英	方子英	Fāng Zǐyīng	N.	(name) Ziying Fang

補充詞　Supplementary Vocabulary

TRADITIONAL	SIMPLIFIED	PINYIN		
1. 貴	贵	guì	Adj.	expensive
2. 便宜	便宜	piányi	Adj.	inexpensive
3. 賣	卖	mài	V.	to sell
4. 號	号	hào	N.	size
5. 幾號	几号	jǐ hào		what size
6. 特大	特大	tè dà	Adj.	extra large
7. 大	大	dà	Adj.	large
8. 中	中	zhōng	Adj.	medium
9. 小	小	xiǎo	Adj.	small
10. 特小	特小	tè xiǎo	Adj.	extra small

貨幣 [Huòbì]　Currency

TRADITIONAL	SIMPLIFIED	PINYIN		
1. 人民幣	人民币	Rénmínbì	N.	currency of the People's Republic of China
2. 新台幣	新台币	Xīntáibì	N.	currency of Taiwan (New Taiwan dollars)
3. 港幣	港币	Gǎngbì	N.	currency of Hong Kong
4. 美金	美金	Měijīn	N.	U.S. dollar
5. 歐元	欧元	Ōuyuán	N.	euro

錢幣表達方法 [Qiánbì biǎodá fāngfǎ]   **Ways to Express Money in Chinese**

Written form:

	TRADITIONAL	SIMPLIFIED	PINYIN		
1.	元	元	yuán	N.	dollar
2.	角	角	jiǎo	N.	(10 角 = 1 元)
3.	分	分	fēn	N.	(100 分 = 10 角 = 1 元)

Spoken form:

	TRADITIONAL	SIMPLIFIED	PINYIN		
4.	塊	块	kuài	N.	dollar
5.	毛	毛	máo	N.	(10 毛 = 1 塊)
6.	分	分	fēn	N.	(100 分 = 10 毛 = 1 塊)

常見衣服 [Chángjiàn yīfu]   **Common Items of Clothing**

Measure Word: 件

	TRADITIONAL	SIMPLIFIED	PINYIN		
1.	上衣	上衣	shàngyī	N.	upper-clothing
2.	大衣	大衣	dàyī	N.	overcoat
3.	外套	外套	wàitào	N.	coat
4.	背心	背心	bèixīn	N.	vest
5.	西裝	西裝	xīzhuāng	N.	suit
6.	夾克衫 (夾克)	夹克衫 (夹克)	jiákèshān (jiákè)	N.	jacket
7.	毛衣	毛衣	máoyī	N.	sweater
8.	T-恤衫 (T-恤)	T-恤衫 (T-恤)	tīxùshān (tīxù)	N.	T-shirt
9.	內衣	内衣	nèiyī	N.	underwear

Measure Word (Classifier): 條(条)

TRADITIONAL	SIMPLIFIED	PINYIN		
10. 長褲	长裤	chángkù	N.	long pants
11. 短褲	短裤	duǎnkù	N.	shorts
12. 牛仔褲	牛仔裤	niúzǎikù	N.	jeans
13. 內褲	内裤	nèikù	N.	underpants
14. 裙子	裙子	qúnzi	N.	skirt
15. 迷你裙	迷你裙	mínǐqún	N.	miniskirt

Measure Word (Classifier): 雙(双)

TRADITIONAL	SIMPLIFIED	PINYIN		
16. 鞋子	鞋子	xiézi	N.	shoes
17. 皮鞋	皮鞋	píxié	N.	leather shoes
18. 球鞋	球鞋	qiúxié	N.	sneakers
19. 拖鞋	拖鞋	tuōxié	N.	slippers
20. 涼鞋	凉鞋	liángxié	N.	sandals
21. 靴子	靴子	xuēzi	N.	boots
22. 襪子	袜子	wàzi	N.	socks

常見飾品 [Chángjiàn shìpǐn]　Common Accessories

TRADITIONAL	SIMPLIFIED	PINYIN		
1. 手錶	手表	shǒubiǎo	N.	watch
2. 耳環	耳环	ěrhuán	N.	earrings
3. 手鐲	手镯	shǒuzhuó	N.	bracelet
4. 戒指	戒指	jièzhi	N.	ring
5. 項鏈	项链	xiàngliàn	N.	necklace
6. 眼鏡	眼镜	yǎnjìng	N.	glasses

TRADITIONAL	SIMPLIFIED	PINYIN		
7. 帽子	帽子	màozi	N.	hat
8. 手套	手套	shǒutào	N.	gloves
9. 手絹	手绢	shǒujuàn	N.	handkerchief
10. 領帶	领带	lǐngdài	N.	necktie
11. 圍巾	围巾	wéijīn	N.	scarf

常見穿衣動作 [Chángjiàn chuānyī dòngzuò]　Common Actions for Clothes

TRADITIONAL	SIMPLIFIED	PINYIN		
1. 穿	穿	chuān	V.	to wear, put on (regular clothes)
2. 穿上	穿上	chuānshàng	V.C.	to put on (regular clothes)
3. 戴	戴	dài	V.	to wear, put on (accessories)
4. 戴上	戴上	dàishàng	V.C.	to put on (accessories)
5. 脫	脱	tuō	V.	to take off (regular clothes)
6. 脫下	脱下	tuōxià	V.C.	to take off (regular clothes)
7. 摘	摘	zhāi	V.	to take off (accessories)
8. 摘下	摘下	zhāixià	V.C.	to take off (accessories)

常見顏色 [Chángjiàn yánsè]　Common Colors

TRADITIONAL	SIMPLIFIED	PINYIN		
1. 紅色	红色	hóngsè	Adj.	red
2. 白色	白色	báisè	Adj.	white
3. 黑色	黑色	hēisè	Adj.	black
4. 黃色	黄色	huángsè	Adj.	yellow
5. 綠色	绿色	lǜsè	Adj.	green
6. 藍色	蓝色	lánsè	Adj.	blue

	TRADITIONAL	SIMPLIFIED	PINYIN		
7.	紫色	紫色	zǐsè	Adj.	purple
8.	粉紅色	粉红色	fěnhóngsè	Adj.	pink
9.	橙色 (橘色)	橙色 (橘色)	chéngsè (júsè)	Adj.	orange
10.	灰色	灰色	huīsè	Adj.	gray
11.	棕色 (咖啡色)	棕色 (咖啡色)	zōngsè (kāfēisè)	Adj.	brown
12.	金黃色	金黄色	jīnhuángsè	Adj.	gold
13.	銀灰色	银灰色	yínhuīsè	Adj.	silver
14.	深色	深色	shēnsè	Adj.	dark
15.	深藍色	深蓝色	shēnlánsè	Adj.	dark blue
16.	淺色	浅色	qiǎnsè	Adj.	light
17.	淺綠色	浅绿色	qiǎnlǜsè	Adj.	light green
18.	彩色	彩色	cǎisè	Adj.	multicolored

語文知識　LANGUAGE LINK

The Sentence Patterns provide models that will help you with the Language in Use section. In both sections, pay attention to the grammar points, vocabulary, and expressions.

句型　Sentence Patterns

A: 你想買什麼？
　　Nǐ xiǎng mǎi shénme?

B: 我想買一件襯衫。
　　Wǒ xiǎng mǎi yíjiàn chènshān.

A: 你幫我看看，我穿裙子
Nǐ bāng wǒ kànkan, wǒ chuān qúnzi

好看還是穿褲子好看?
hǎokàn háishì chuān kùzi hǎokàn?

B: 我覺得你穿裙子好看。
Wǒ juéde nǐ chuān qúnzi hǎokàn.

A: 這條裙子多少錢?
Zhètiáo qúnzi duōshǎo qián?

B: 十五塊。
Shíwǔ kuài.

課文   Language in Use: 我想買一件襯衫 Wǒ xiǎng mǎi yíjiàn chènshān

店員：   兩位小姐想買什麼?
Liǎngwèi xiǎojiě xiǎng mǎi shénme?

毛愛紅：   我想買一件襯衫。
Wǒ xiǎng mǎi yíjiàn chènshān.

方子英：   我想買一條裙子或者褲子。
Wǒ xiǎng mǎi yìtiáo qúnzi huòzhě kùzi.

店員：   這件黃襯衫怎麼樣?
Zhèjiàn huáng chènshān zěnmeyàng?

毛愛紅：   還不錯。可是我比較喜歡穿黑色的，有沒有黑色的?
Hái búcuò. Kěshì wǒ bǐjiào xǐhuān chuān hēisède, yǒuméiyǒu hēisède?

店員：   有，在這兒，你試試!
Yǒu, zài zhèr, nǐ shìshi!

方子英：   愛紅，來，你幫我看看，我穿裙子好看還是
Àihóng, lái, nǐ bāng wǒ kànkan, wǒ chuān qúnzi hǎokàn háishì

穿褲子好看?
chuān kùzi hǎokàn?

毛愛紅：　你穿穿，讓我看看。我覺得你穿這條裙子好看。
　　　　　Nǐ chuānchuan, ràng wǒ kànkan. Wǒ juéde nǐ chuān zhètiáo qúnzi hǎokàn.

方子英：　請問，這條裙子多少錢？
　　　　　Qǐngwèn, zhètiáo qúnzi duōshǎo qián?

店員：　　十五塊。
　　　　　Shíwǔ kuài.

方子英：　好，我買了。
　　　　　Hǎo, wǒ mǎile.

毛愛紅：　我要買這件黑襯衫。
　　　　　Wǒ yào mǎi zhèjiàn hēi chènshān.

店員：　　對了，小姐，這張電影票是你的嗎？
　　　　　Duì le, xiǎojiě, zhèzhāng diànyǐngpiào shì nǐde ma?

方子英：　是的，這張電影票是我的。謝謝！我們等一下
　　　　　Shìde, zhèzhāng diànyǐngpiào shì wǒde. Xièxie! Wǒmen děngyíxià

　　　　　要去看電影。
　　　　　yào qù kàn diànyǐng.

注釋 LANGUAGE NOTES

不錯

不錯 literally means "not wrong." It means "good" in Chinese.

好看

好看 means "good-looking." 好 is often used together with a verb to form a new adjective to mean "good to + V," or "easy to + V." For example,

好吃	delicious (good to eat)
好聽 [tīng]	beautiful sounding (good to hear)
好玩	funny, interesting (good to play)
好喝	delicious to drink (good to drink)

Also,

好寫	easy to write
好說	easy to say
好懂 [dǒng]	easy to understand
好念 [niàn]	easy to read

覺(得)

When 覺 is pronounced as [jué] it means "to feel" or "to think." When 覺 is pronounced as [jiào] in 睡覺 it means "to sleep."

得 (Pronunciation in 得 "must" and 覺得)

When 得 is pronounced as [děi] it means "must" or "have to." When 得 is pronounced as [de] in 覺得 it means "to think" or "to feel."

多少錢

How much (money) is it?

語法 GRAMMAR

Conjunction 或者

或者 is another conjunction meaning "or", similar to 還是. However, while 還是 is only used in alternative questions, 或者 can be used in statements. Here are some examples:

A: 你想買襯衫還是T-恤衫?   Would you like to buy a shirt or a T-shirt?
B: 我想買一條裙子或者褲子。   I want to buy a skirt or a pair of pants.
A: 你喜歡黑色的還是藍色的?   Do you like black or blue?
B: 我喜歡紅色或者白色的。   I like red or white.

量詞 (Measure Words/Classifiers) (4): 件，條，張

In previous lessons we have studied the following measure words:

Measure word	Usage	Example
本	For book-like things	一本書 一本詞典 [cídiǎn] (dictionary) 一本雜誌 [zázhì] (magazine)
輛	For vehicles	一輛汽車 [qìchē] (car) 一輛自行車 [zìxíngchē] (bicycle)
隻	For animals	一隻狗 一隻貓
門	For courses	五門課
個	For people and things in general	兩個人
位	A courteous measure word used for guests	三位客人 [kèrén] (guest)
張	For sheet-like things	四張票 [piào] (ticket) 五張桌子 [zhuōzi] (table)

In this lesson, 雙 is introduced as a special measure word for certain things in pairs, for example,

Measure word	Usage	Example
雙	For pairs of certain things	一雙筷子
		一雙眼睛 [yǎnjīng] (eyes)
		兩雙鞋 [xié] (shoes)
		三雙襪子 [wàzi] (socks)

Note: Not all things in pairs take 雙 as the measure words. Here are some other examples:

Measure word	Usage	Example
副 [fù]: pair	For pairs of certain things (usually for accessories)	一副手套　[shǒutào] (gloves)
對 [duì]: pair		一對耳環　[ěrhuán] (earrings)

This lesson also introduces two measure words used for clothing, 件 and 條.

件 is generally used for upper body clothing, but sometimes it can also be used for clothing in general. For example,

Measure word	Usage	Example
件	For clothing in general	一件襯衫
		一件大衣　[dàyī] (overcoat)
		一件運動衫 [yùndòngshān] (sports shirt)
		一件T-恤衫 [tīxùshān] (T-shirt)
		一件夾克衫 [jiákèshān] (jacket)
		一件滑雪衫 [huáxuěshān] (winter coat)

條 is a measure word used for long-shaped clothing, such as 褲子 and 裙子. For example,

Measure word	Usage	Example
條	For long-shaped items	一條褲子
		一條長褲　[chángkù] (long pants)
		一條牛仔褲 [niúzǎikù] (jeans)
		一條裙子

Duplication of Verbs

Many verbs can be duplicated in spoken Chinese to indicate a quick action — "to do a little bit of something" or to do something in a relaxed way. Here are some examples:

試試	to have a try	看看	to have a look
穿穿	to try on	聽聽 [tīngting]	to listen for a little while
寫寫	to write a little	說說	to say a little
想想	to think a little	走走	to take a walk

If the verb is disyllabic, the duplication is as follows:

介紹介紹　to give a little introduction　　　學習學習　to study a little

Basically, verbs expressing active actions or behaviors can be duplicated. Those that indicate status or existence cannot be duplicated. Sometimes, a duplicated verb expression may have "一" in between, such as,

看一看　試一試　想一想　穿一穿

Notes:
a. Only monosyllabic verbs can take 一 in between when duplicated.
b. The duplicated syllable is always pronounced in the neutral tone.

Such verbs may also be followed by 一下(兒). This has the same effect as duplication.

看看	=	看一看	=	看一下(兒)
想想	=	想一想	=	想一下(兒)
介紹介紹	=	(NA)	=	介紹一下(兒)
學習學習	=	(NA)	=	學習一下(兒)

補充課文 ⊸⚬⚬— SUPPLEMENTARY PRACTICE

This selection will help you test your comprehension of the grammar and vocabulary you have learned in this lesson. Be prepared to answer questions about the meaning of the passage.

　　上個週末，我和子英一起去購物中心逛街，買東西。我想買一件襯衫，子英想買一條裙子或者褲子。我們到了一家服飾店，我先挑了一件黃色和一件黑色的襯衫。我試穿了一下，照照鏡子，覺得黑色的比較適合我，所以我就買了那件黑襯衫。

　　子英也拿了一條裙子和一條褲子，然後就到試衣間穿穿，她要我幫她看看，我看了以後，覺得她穿裙子比較好看，最後她決定買那條裙子，店員小姐說那條裙子十五塊錢。我們買了衣服以後，就去看電影了。

Notes: 週末 [zhōumò]: weekend　　　　　購物中心 [gòuwù zhōngxīn]: shopping center
　　　　逛街 [guàngjiē]: to go shopping　　東西 [dōngxi]: thing; stuff
　　　　到 [dào]: to arrive　　　　　　　家 [jiā]: measure word for shops
　　　　服飾店 [fúshìdiàn]: clothing shop　挑 [tiāo]: to choose; to pick
　　　　試穿 [shìchuān]: to try on　　　　照 [zhào]: to reflect; to mirror
　　　　鏡子 [jìngzi]: mirror　　　　　　適合 [shìhé]: to suit
　　　　試衣間 [shìyījiān]: dressing room　最後 [zuìhòu]: finally, at last
　　　　決定 [juédìng]: to decide

練習 ACTIVITIES

I. Pinyin Exercises

13-1 Listen to the instructor and write down the sentences in Pinyin:

1. _____

2. _____

3. _____

4. _____

5. _____

13-2 Matching game: Work in groups of three. Prepare three stacks of cards. One stack should have pictures of T-shirts, jackets, shirts, sports shirts, pants, skirts, jeans, shoes, socks, and caps. The second stack should have the words for these items in Pinyin, and the third stack has a price written on each card. One person plays the role of a customer and makes requests for what he/she wants to buy. Another plays the role of the store assistant and picks out the card with the picture that matches the request and gives the price, then the third picks out the cards with the Pinyin and the price. After finishing one round, change roles and continue with the same game.

Useful words and expressions:

件，條，雙，頂 [dǐng] (measure word/classifier for hats)

襯衫，褲子，T-恤衫，運動衫，裙子，襪子 [wàzi] (socks)，
帽子 [màozi] (hat, cab)，運動鞋，夾克衫，牛仔褲

13-3 Read the following Chinese poem, paying special attention to the tones and rhythm:

Jué Jù **(Dù Fǔ)**	**絕句** **(杜甫)**
Liǎngge huánglí míng cuìliǔ, Yìháng báilù shàng qīngtiān. Chuāng hán Xīlǐng qiānqiū xuě, Mén bó Dōngwú wànlǐ chuán.	兩個黃鸝鳴翠柳， 一行白鷺上青天。 窗含西嶺千秋雪， 門泊東吳萬里船。

A Quatrain
(Du, Fu)

Two golden orioles are singing on the green willow trees,
White egrets are flying in a line in the blue sky.
Looking out of my window I see the snow-capped Western Mountains,
At my door are parked eastward-going ships that have traveled thousands of miles.

II. Character Exercises

13-4 Read the following words, phrases, and sentences:

襯衫	好看
一件襯衫	裙子好看
一件白襯衫	紅裙子好看
一件白色的襯衫	這條紅裙子好看
買一件白色的襯衫	穿這條紅裙子好看
想買一件白色的襯衫	你穿這條紅裙子好看
我想買一件白色的襯衫	我覺得你穿這條紅裙子好看
我想買一件白色的或者黑色的襯衫	我覺得你穿這條紅裙子比較好看

Now try to use the following characters to make words, phrases, and then sentences:

1. 店　　2. 幫　　3. 褲　　4. 黃　　5. 錯　　6. 票

7. 黑　　8. 試　　9. 讓　　10. 錢　　11. 塊　　12. 張

13-5 Identify the radical of each of the following characters and write out the meaning of the radical in English. Then give as many examples of characters with the same radical as you can.

For example,

嗎　口　mouth　呢　吃　喝　和

1. 衫　☐　_____　_____

2. 買　☐　_____　_____

3. 黃　☐　_____　_____

4. 黑　☐　_____　_____

5. 錢　☐　_____　_____

6. 件　☐　_____　_____

7. 試　☐　_____　_____

8. 覺　☐　_____　_____

9. 塊　☐　_____　_____

10. 票　☐　_____　_____

III. Grammar Exercises

13-6 Substitution exercises:

1. 你想買什麼?
   我想買一<u>件</u><u>襯衫</u>。

件	運動衫
件	T恤衫
件	毛衣
條	長褲
條	裙子
雙	鞋子

2. 你想做什麼?
   我想<u>買</u><u>一件襯衫</u>或者<u>一件大衣</u>。

看	中國電影	美國電影
吃	春捲	餃子
穿	皮鞋	運動鞋
開	美國車	韓國車
去	中國飯館	日本飯館

3. 你覺得這<u>碗</u><u>湯</u>怎麼樣?
   我覺得這<u>碗</u><u>湯</u>很<u>好喝</u>。

盤	炒飯	好吃
個	漢字	好寫
個	句子	好說
部	電影	好玩
條	裙子	好看

Notes: 漢字 [hànzì]: characters
句子 [jùzi]: sentence
部 [bù]: measure word for 電影

4. 這件<u>運動衫</u><u>不貴</u>
   多少錢?
   <u>二十五塊八毛九分</u>。

大衣	很便宜	五十六塊
皮鞋	很貴	四十三塊九毛五分
襪子	很好	兩塊二毛六分

13-7 Insert an appropriate measure word in each of the following:

1. 兩 _____ 書   2. 五 _____ 車票   3. 三 _____ 襯衫

4. 一 _____ 皮鞋   5. 四 _____ 裙子   6. 六 _____ 牛仔褲

13-8 Complete the following sentences with duplication of the verb phrases given:

1. 這件襯衫我穿太大了，你 _____ 吧 。(to have a try)

2. 這是誰的車? 我來 _____ 車號 。(to have a look)

3. 這是我的室友。 來，你們 _____ 。(to get to know each other)

4. 這首歌很好聽，你也 _____ 。(to listen to it)

5. 你知道這本書嗎? 我來給你 _____ 。
   (to give you a little introduction)

   Notes: 首 [shǒu]: measure word for song
   　　　歌 [gē]: song
   　　　聽 [tīng]: to listen

13-9 Answer the following questions, using the word 或者 in your answer:

1. 先生，您想買什麼?

   _____

2. 子英，你喜歡黑色的襯衫嗎?

   _____

3. 愛紅，你說我穿什麼好看?

   _____

4. 于信，你今天晚上做什麼?

   _____

IV. Communicative Activities

13-10 猜猜他/她是誰? (Play "Guess the classmate")

Divide the class into groups. Each group secretly decides on a classmate for the other groups to guess. Each member of the group says one or two sentences to describe the person, and then the other groups try to guess who the person is. For example,

　　　他(她)今天穿一件白襯衫，黑褲子……
　　　你們猜猜他/她是誰?

Note: 猜 [cāi]: to guess

13-11 In groups of three, act out the following scenario:

It is your first week in China. You go shopping with your friend Fang Mingming. You see a T-shirt and a pair of blue jeans. You like the style but are not sure of the color. You ask Fang Mingming for suggestions and he gives you a lot of good ones regarding your selection.

Words and expressions to use:

式樣 [shìyàng] (style)   合適 [héshì] (suitable, fit)
試試   覺得   怎麼樣
還是   或者   比較

文化點滴　CULTURE NOTES

中國的傳統服飾
[Zhōngguó de chuántǒng fúshì]
Chinese Traditional Dress

The most typical representative items of traditional Chinese clothing are the 旗袍 [qípáo] for women, and the 唐裝 [tángzhuāng] and traditional vests and suits for both genders. The material is usually silk with either patterned or picturesque embroidery on it. At first glance these clothes all look alike when compared to Western dress. It is this simplicity that people value in traditional Chinese clothing. Without using much cloth, the clothing accents the shape of the body to create an elegant and neat look.

This beautiful and delicate Qipao is made of silk and has the lucky colors of silver, red, and gold as well as lucky flowers and the phoenix embroidered on it.

Ladies in qipao and tangzhuang.

A gentleman in tangzhuang.

Chinese traditional dress is frequently worn to celebrate cultural festivals.

Around the 17th century, noble Manchurian men and women wore long, loose, tube-shaped robes. Each generation made subtle changes until the 1930s when it truly became the 旗袍 we associate with Chinese culture today. The choice of having sleeves or no sleeves, as well as certain differences in the collars and lengths of the dresses, all show the progression. The 1930s was a period of strong Western influence, and it was at this time that the 旗袍 became internationally popular.

An additional type of common clothing is the Chinese traditional suit. This is less formal and is unisex in shape. The only distinction between male and female suits is color. Men usually wear dark colors, while women prefer pastels. This outfit consists of loose pants and a shirt all made out of the same type of cloth. For children, an embroidered vest would sometimes accompany this suit.

Today, Western-style clothing is much more common in China. Chinese traditional dress is usually worn during cultural festivals. Parents also often dress their young children in traditional outfits. 旗袍 and 唐裝 are also often seen in Chinese TV programs and movies that depict the 30s. Another example would be traditional wedding banquets, where the 旗袍 and 唐裝 are popular among the newlyweds as well as the guests. In Chinese culture, red symbolizes good luck, so red outfits are very common.

Questions:

1. Besides red, what other lucky colors do you think Chinese people like to wear on happy occasions?

2. Have you ever seen any unique clothes worn by Chinese minorities? If so, describe them to your classmates.

3. Have you seen any movies where people wear traditional Chinese clothes?

趣味中文   FUN WITH CHINESE
. . . .

> ## 情人眼裡出西施。
> Any woman becomes a beauty in the eyes of her lover.
> Love makes one blind to all imperfections.

qíngrén	yǎn	lǐ	chū	Xīshī
情人	眼	裡	出	西施
lover	eye	inside	come out	Xishi

西施 [Xīshī] is the name of a
famous beauty in Chinese history.
She lived in the 越國 [Yuèguó] Yue
state in the 春秋 [Chūnqiū] Spring
and Autumn period
(722 to 484 B.C.).

Questions:

1. Do you know of any other famous beauties in Chinese history?

2. Can you think of any stories that are examples of
   情人眼裡出西施?

3. How do you feel about the imperfections of your boyfriend or
   girlfriend?

行動吧！ LET'S GO!

購物： 錢幣， 收據和發票
Shopping: Bill, Receipt, and Invoice

1. Below are samples of currency in 人民幣, 新台幣 and 港幣:

Useful words and expressions:

正面 [zhèngmiàn]: front side
樣本(样本) [yàngběn]: sample
反面 [fǎnmiàn]: reverse

(正面樣本)　　　　　　　（反面樣本)

Questions:

1. What are the names of the central banks in China and Taiwan?

2. Do you notice any similarities or differences in these samples?

2. 在台灣，這是美英去超市買菜付錢以後收銀員
   給她的一張統一發票：

Useful words and expressions:

統一發票(统一发票) [tǒngyī fāpiào]: name of the receipts
   commonly used in Taiwan

合計(合计) [héjì]: total

超市 [chāoshì]: supermarket

收銀員(收银员) [shōuyínyuán]: cashier

收銀機(收银机) [shōuyínjī]: cashier machine

便利商店 [biànlì shāngdiàn]: convenience store

收執聯(收执联) [shōuzhílián]: to receive and keep a sheet
   receipt

稅(税) [shuì]: tax

Questions:

1. 這個超市叫什麼？

2. 美英一共 [yígòng] (in total) 花了多少錢？

14

我今年二十歲
I Am 20 This Year

教學目標　OBJECTIVES

- Say the days of the week
- Extend/accept an invitation
- Talk about people's birthdays

Eating cake at home, going out to eat at a steak house, and singing songs at KTV are all fun ways to celebrate birthdays.

生詞 VOCABULARY

核心詞 Core Vocabulary

	TRADITIONAL	SIMPLIFIED	PINYIN		
1.	歲	岁	suì	N.	age, years
2.	有空	有空	yǒukòng	V.O.	to have free time
3.	星期	星期	xīngqī	N.	week
4.	過	过	guò	V.	to spend (life, time); to celebrate (e.g. birthday)
5.	生日	生日	shēngrì	N.	birthday
6.	為	为	wèi	Prep.	(indicates the object of one's act of service)
7.	舞會	舞会	wǔhuì	N.	dance party
8.	參加	参加	cānjiā	V.	to participate; to join
9.	一定	一定	yídìng	Aux.	certainly; surely
10.	做	做	zuò	V.	to make; to do
11.	蛋糕	蛋糕	dàngāo	N.	cake
12.	送	送	sòng	V.	to give as a present
13.	棒	棒	bàng	Adj.	wonderful
14.	不客氣。	不客气。	búkèqi		You are welcome.
15.	多大	多大	duōdà		how old
16.	地圖	地图	dìtú	N.	map

補充詞 Supplementary Vocabulary

	TRADITIONAL	SIMPLIFIED	PINYIN		
1.	日曆	日历	rìlì	N.	calendar
2.	月曆	月历	yuèlì	N.	monthly calendar
3.	慶生	庆生	qìngshēng	V.O.	to celebrate a birthday
4.	禮物	礼物	lǐwù	N.	gift
5.	蠟燭	蜡烛	làzhú	N.	candle
6.	祝你生日快樂。	祝你生日快乐。	Zhù nǐ shēngrì kuàilè.		Happy birthday to you.

三　　　　月

星期一	星期二	星期三	星期四	星期五	星期六	星期日
		1	2	3	4	5
6	7	8	9	10	11	12
13	14	15	16	17	18	19
20	21	22	23	24	25	26
27	28	29	30	31		

語文知識 LANGUAGE LINK

The Sentence Patterns provide models that will help you with the Language in Use section. In both sections, pay attention to the grammar points, vocabulary, and expressions.

句型 Sentence Patterns

A: 今天是星期幾?
Jīntiān shì xīngqī jǐ?

B: 今天是星期六。
Jīntiān shì xīngqī liù.

A: 你今年多大？
Nǐ jīnnián duō dà?

B: 我今年二十歲。
Wǒ jīnnián èrshí suì.

A: 你的生日是幾月幾號？
Nǐ de shēngrì shì jǐ yuè jǐ hào?

B: 我的生日是十月三號。
Wǒ de shēngrì shì shí yuè sān hào.

課文　Language in Use: 我今年二十歲 Wǒ jīnnián èrshí suì

方子英： 愛紅，二月十八日你有沒有空？
Àihóng, èr yuè shíbā rì nǐ yǒuméiyǒu kòng?

毛愛紅： 二月十八日那天是星期幾？
Èr yuè shíbā rì nàtiān shì xīngqī jǐ?

方子英： 星期六。
Xīngqī liù.

毛愛紅： 我有空。有什麼事兒嗎？
Wǒ yǒu kòng. Yǒu shénme shèr ma?

方子英： 那天我過生日，我男朋友要為我
Nàtiān wǒ guò shēngrì, wǒ nánpéngyou yào wèi wǒ

　　　　 開一個生日舞會，我想請你參加。
kāi yíge shēngrì wǔhuì, wǒ xiǎng qǐng nǐ cānjiā.

毛愛紅： 謝謝你，我一定去。還有誰會去？
Xièxie nǐ, wǒ yídìng qù. Hái yǒu shéi huì qù?

方子英： 我們想請我們的同學和朋友都參加。
Wǒmen xiǎng qǐng wǒmen de tóngxué hé péngyou dōu cānjiā.

毛愛紅： 我會做蛋糕。我送你一個生日蛋糕，怎麼樣？
Wǒ huì zuò dàngāo. Wǒ sòng nǐ yíge shēngrì dàngāo, zěnmeyàng?

方子英： 太棒了！謝謝你！
Tàibàngle! Xièxie nǐ!

毛愛紅：　不客氣。你今年多大？
　　　　　Búkèqi. Nǐ jīnnián duō dà?

方子英：　我今年二十歲。你呢？你的生日是幾月幾號？
　　　　　Wǒ jīnnián èrshí suì. Nǐ ne? Nǐ de shēngrì shì jǐ yuè jǐ hào?

毛愛紅：　我的生日是十月三號，我今年二十二歲。你的舞會在哪兒開？
　　　　　Wǒ de shēngrì shì shí yuè sān hào, wǒ jīnnián èrshíèr suì. Nǐ de wǔhuì zài nǎr kāi?

方子英：　在我男朋友的家，這是他的地址。你知道怎麼去嗎？
　　　　　Zài wǒ nánpéngyou de jiā, zhè shì tāde dìzhǐ. Nǐ zhīdào zěnme qù ma?

毛愛紅：　沒問題！我有地圖。星期六下午五點見。
　　　　　Méi wèntí! Wǒ yǒu dìtú. Xīngqīliù xiàwǔ wǔdiǎn jiàn.

方子英：　再見。
　　　　　Zàijiàn.

注釋　LANGUAGE NOTES

開舞會(晚會/派對)

開 here means "to hold (a party)," 開舞會 means "to hold a dance party." For parties, the following terms are commonly used: 晚會 [wǎnhuì] and 派對 [pàiduì].

太棒了

太棒了 is a phrase meaning "Great!," "Terrific!" "棒" here is an adjective meaning "good," "great." It is similar to "太好了！"

不客氣

不客氣 is a phrase meaning "You are welcome." It is similar to 不謝.

多大

多大 means "How old?" It is generally used to ask the age of adults and children over ten years old. For young children under ten years old, 幾歲 ("How old?") is commonly used. For older people, it is appropriate to use "您多大年紀[niánjì] (age)?"

地址(住址)

For "address," both 地址 and 住址 are commonly used. When writing an address, Chinese word order progresses from the larger unit to the smaller unit. For example,

中國北京市中山路12號　　No. 12, Zhongshan Road, Beijing, China

語法 GRAMMAR

Days of the Week

The ways to express the days of the week in Chinese are illustrated below:

Monday	Tuesday	Wednesday	Thursday	Friday	Saturday	Sunday
星期一	星期二	星期三	星期四	星期五	星期六	星期日 星期天
週一	週二	週三	週四	週五	週末 [zhōumò] weekend	

- 禮拜 [lǐbài] is also commonly used for indicating the days of the week.

  For example, 禮拜一, 禮拜五, and 禮拜天.

- 星期幾 and 禮拜幾 mean "Which day of the week?"

  For Chinese, a week starts on Monday instead of Sunday.

Expressing Dates, Year, Month, and Days of the Week

前天 the day before yesterday	昨天 yesterday	今天 today	明天 tomorrow	後天 the day after tomorrow
前年 the year before last year	去年 last year	今年 this year	明年 next year	後年 the year after next year
上上個星期 the week before last week	上個星期 last week	這個星期 this week	下個星期 next week	下下個星期 the week after next week
上上個月 the month before last month	上個月 last month	這個月 this month	下個月 next month	下下個月 the month after next month

Preposition 為

為 is a preposition meaning "for." Together with its object it forms a prepositional phrase (P.P.), which occurs before a verb phrase (V.P.). For example,

他　為我　開一個晚會。　　He is having a party for me.
　　P.P.　V.P.

補充課文 ━○○○━ **SUPPLEMENTARY PRACTICE**

This selection will help you test your comprehension of the grammar and vocabulary you have learned in this lesson. Be prepared to answer questions about the meaning of the passage.

二月十八日　　　　　星期六　　　　天氣：晴

　　今天我真高興，我過了一個很難忘的二十歲生日。我男朋友在他家為我舉辦了一個慶生會，他還邀請了很多朋友來參加，我收到了很多禮物，愛紅還為我做了一個生日蛋糕，太棒了！

　　每個人都祝我生日快樂，為我唱生日快樂歌，我許了一個願，吹了蠟燭，然後切蛋糕給大家吃。

　　我們一起唱卡拉 OK，聽流行音樂，跳舞，聊天……很好玩！

　　啊！我的二十歲生日，真特別！

Notes: 天氣 [tiānqì]: weather
晴 [qíng]: sunny
難忘 [nánwàng]: unforgettable
舉辦 [jǔbàn]: to hold
慶生會 [qìngshēnghuì]: birthday party
邀請 [yāoqǐng]: to invite
收到 [shōudào]: to receive
生日快樂歌 [shēngrì kuàilè gē]: happy birthday song
許願 [xǔyuàn]: to make a wish
吹 [chuī]: to blow
蠟燭 [làzhú]: candle
切 [qiē]: to cut; to slice
卡拉OK [kǎlā ōukēi]: karaoke
流行音樂 [liúxíng yīnyuè]: popular music
特別 [tèbié]: special

練習 ACTIVITIES

I. Pinyin Exercises

14-1 Listen to the phrases and write them down in Pinyin:

1. _____   2. _____   3. _____   4. _____

5. _____   6. _____   7. _____   8. _____

14-2 Listen to the instructor and fill in each blank with the correct Pinyin:

Àimíng: Zhège _____ shì wǒde _____ . Wǒ yào kāi yígè _____ .

Nǐ néng lái ma?

Xiǎoyīng: Tài hǎo le! Wǒ _____ qù. Nǐ jīnnián _____ ?

Àimíng: Wǒ èrshíyī _____ . Nǐde shēngrì shì _____ ?

Xiǎoyīng: Wǒde shēngrì shì _____ . Wǒ jīnnián _____ suì.

14-3 Read the following Chinese poem, paying special attention to the tones and rhythm:

Xiāng Sī (**Wáng Wéi**)	相思 (王維)
Hóngdòu shēng nánguó, Chūn lái fā jǐ zhī. Yuàn jūn duō cǎi xié, Cǐ wù zuì xiāngsī.	紅豆生南國， 春來發幾枝。 願君多採擷， 此物最相思。

Remembrance
(Wang, Wei)

The red bean grows in the southern lands,
In spring its slender twigs bloom.
Gather more of them, I hope,
Of loving remembrance they evince.

II. Character Exercises

14-4 Read the following words, phrases, and sentences:

號 幾 號 幾 月 幾 號 今 天 是 幾 月 幾 號	舞 會 生 日 舞 會 我 的 生 日 舞 會 參 加 我 的 生 日 舞 會 請 參 加 我 的 生 日 舞 會 請 你 參 加 我 的 生 日 舞 會 我 請 你 參 加 我 的 生 日 舞 會 我 想 請 你 參 加 我 的 生 日 舞 會
地 址 家 的 地 址 我 家 的 地 址 這 是 我 家 的 地 址 這 是 我 男 朋 友 家 的 地 址	

Now try to use the following characters to make words, phrases, and then sentences:

1. 歲　　2. 空　　3. 星　　4. 過　　5. 為　　6. 定
7. 做　　8. 蛋　　9. 送　　10. 棒　　11. 客　　12. 圖

14-5 From the dialogue in Language in Use, find words that have the following radicals:

宀		土		木	
米		月		力	
門		辵(辶)		厶	

14-6 Match the following characters with their English definitions:

地址	to join	送	birthday
舞會	surely	歲	years old
蛋糕	cakes	客氣	week
參加	dance party	星期	to give
一定	address	生日	to be polite

Questions:

1. 你是屬什麼的?　　What's your sign?
2. 你的生肖個性怎麼樣?　What kind of personality is your sign supposed to have?
3. 準不準?　　Is that an accurate description of your personality?

Notes: 屬 [shǔ]: to belong to
　　　個性 [gèxìng]: personality
　　　準 [zhǔn]: accurate

趣味中文　FUN WITH CHINESE

女大十八變。
A girl changes quickly in physical appearance from childhood to adulthood.

nǚ	dà	shíbā	biàn
女	大	十八	變
girl	big/grow up	eighteen	change

Chinese people usually use 女大十八變 to show
their admiration of the changing appearance of a girl, or
their surprise at seeing a girl grow up to become a young lady.

Questions:

1. Has your appearance changed much as you have grown? Can your friends or relatives who haven't seen you for a long time still recognize you?

2. Can you apply "女大十八變" to some movie stars you are familiar with?

行動吧！ LET'S GO!

慶祝賀詞
Common Phrases for Congratulations and Best Wishes

Read the following congratulatory phrases, which Chinese people use often on various social occasions.

1. 祝你生日快樂 [Zhù nǐ shēngrì kuàilè]: Wishing you a happy birthday.

2. 福如東海，壽比南山 [fú rú dōnghǎi, shòu bǐ nánshān]: happiness as immense as the Eastern Sea; life span as lofty as the Southern Mountain (commonly heard in relation to the birthday of someone aged 60 or older).

3. 永浴愛河 [yǒng yù àihé]: bathe in the river of love forever (used for newlyweds).

4. 步步高陞 [bùbù gāoshēng]: to get promotions step by step.

5. 金榜題名 [jīnbǎng tímíng]: to emerge successful from a competitive examination.

6. 學業進步 [xuéyè jìnbù]: to make progress in one's studies.

7. 恭賀新禧 [gōnghè xīnxǐ]: best wishes for a happy new year.

8. 事事如意 [shìshì rúyì]: everything will go well and smoothly.

9. 祝你好運 [zhù nǐ hǎo yùn]: wishing you good luck.

10. 吉祥如意 [jíxiáng rúyì]: hope things go well and smoothly.

生詞 VOCABULARY

核心詞 Core Vocabulary

	TRADITIONAL	SIMPLIFIED	PINYIN		
1.	前邊	前边	qiánbiān	N.	in front of
2.	參觀	参观	cānguān	V.	to visit
3.	歡迎	欢迎	huānyíng	V.	to welcome
4.	裡邊	里边	lǐbiān	N.	inside
5.	廚房	厨房	chúfáng	N.	kitchen
6.	公用	公用	gōngyòng	Adj.	for public use, communal
7.	旁邊	旁边	pángbiān	N.	beside, nearby
8.	客廳	客厅	kètīng	N.	living room
9.	走	走	zǒu	V.	to walk
10.	對面	对面	duìmiàn	N.	opposite
11.	餐廳	餐厅	cāntīng	N.	dining room
12.	洗澡間	洗澡间	xǐzǎojiān	N.	bathroom; restroom
13.	臥室	卧室	wòshì	N.	bedroom
14.	中間	中间	zhōngjiān	N.	middle
15.	桌子	桌子	zhuōzi	N.	table
16.	上邊	上边	shàngbiān	N.	on top of; above; over
17.	後邊	后边	hòubiān	N.	behind, at the back
18.	公園	公园	gōngyuán	N.	park
19.	真	真	zhēn	Adv.	really

專名　Proper Nouns

TRADITIONAL	SIMPLIFIED	PINYIN		
1. 田進	田进	Tián Jìn	N.	(name) Jin Tian
2. 梁園生	梁园生	Liáng Yuánshēng	N.	(name) Yuansheng Liang
3. 包志中	包志中	Bāo Zhìzhōng	N.	(name) Zhizhong Bao

補充詞　Supplementary Vocabulary

TRADITIONAL	SIMPLIFIED	PINYIN		
1. 左邊	左边	zuǒbiān	N.	on the left
2. 右邊	右边	yòubiān	N.	on the right
3. 門	门	mén	N.	door
4. 書桌	书桌	shūzhuō	N.	desk
5. 窗戶	窗户	chuānghu	N.	window
6. 椅子	椅子	yǐzi	N.	chair
7. 衣櫥	衣橱	yīchú	N.	wardrobe
8. 床	床	chuáng	N.	bed
9. 教室	教室	jiàoshì	N.	classroom
10. 雜誌	杂志	zázhì	N.	magazine
11. 亂	乱	luàn	Adj.	messy
12. 整齊	整齐	zhěngqí	Adj.	tidy
13. 乾淨	干净	gānjìng	Adj.	clean
14. 髒	脏	zāng	Adj.	dirty
15. 整理	整理	zhěnglǐ	V.	to arrange, put in order

注釋 LANGUAGE NOTES

洗澡間(洗手間, 廁所)

洗澡 means "to take a bath." 間 means "room." 洗澡間 is "bathroom."
洗手間 [xǐshǒujiān], which literally means "wash hands room," and 廁所 [cèsuǒ] are also common terms for the restroom or bathroom.

有的

有的 means "some (of the) N." Thus 有的(書) means "some books."

語法 GRAMMAR

Position Words

A position word is used to specify a relative location. The following are examples of position words:

Position words	English	Position words	English
前邊/前面	front	後邊/後面	back
上邊/上面	top	下邊/下面	under, beneath
裡邊/裡面	inside	外邊/外面	outside
左 [zuǒ] (left) 邊	left	右 [yòu] (right) 邊	right
旁邊	beside		
中間	middle		
對面	opposite		

- The suffix 邊 literally means "side." It is usually interchangeable with 面.
- However, in 左邊, 右邊, and 旁邊 the 邊 cannot be replaced with 面.
- 面 literally means "face." 對面 means "opposite, face to face."

- In Chinese, the word order for specifying a location is different from that of English. For example,

圖書館	在宿舍的	前邊。	The library is in front of the dorm.
	The reference point (landmark)	location	

State the reference point (宿舍) first, then specify the location (前邊).

- 的 can be either present or not. Therefore we can use both 宿舍前邊 or 宿舍的前邊

- 裡邊 means "inside." It is never used with a place word that is a geographical name, building, or organization. For example,

他在北京學中文。　　　　　He studies Chinese in Beijing.
他在銀行 [yínháng] 工作。　He works in a bank.

Sentences Expressing Location and Existence with 在, 有, and 是

在, 有, and 是 are commonly used to indicate location and existence. Some of their sentence patterns are shown below:

Pattern	Example	English
N. (definite) + 在 + Place	圖書館在宿舍(的)前邊。	The library is in front of the dorm. (focus on location)
Place + 有 + N. (indefinite)	宿舍(的)前邊有一個圖書館。	There is a library in front of the dorm. (focus on existence)
Place + 是 + N. (definite or indefinite)	宿舍(的)前邊是圖書館。	In front of the dorm is the library. (focus on identification)

Notes: Example of definite noun: the library.
　　　　Example of indefinite noun: a library.

Example	English	Situation
這兒有廁所嗎?	Is there a bathroom here?	(e.g., when traveling and asking someone whether there is a bathroom)
廁所在哪兒?	Where is the bathroom?	(e.g., at a friend's house, asking for the location of the bathroom)
這兒是廁所嗎?	Is this the bathroom?	(e.g., to identify whether this is or isn't a bathroom)

補充課文 ⟶⟵ **SUPPLEMENTARY PRACTICE**

This selection will help you test your comprehension of the grammar and vocabulary you have learned in this lesson. Be prepared to answer questions about the meaning of the passage.

今天下午我和包志中去看田進。田進住在學校的宿舍裡，他常常說他的宿舍很不錯，所以我們今天去看看，他非常高興。

田進的臥室不太大，可是很明亮。他的客廳很大。臥室和客廳的中間有一個洗澡間。廚房在臥室的旁邊，客廳的對面是餐廳。廚房和餐廳都是公用的，雖然不大，可是很乾淨。

田進的書桌上有很多書，有的是他的，有的是他朋友的。他不常在宿舍看書，他喜歡去圖書館學習。圖書館離他的宿舍很近，就在宿舍的前邊，那兒也很安靜。圖書館的後邊還有一個很大的公園，每天有很多人在那兒鍛煉，打太極拳。田進有時候也喜歡去那兒打球。

田進非常喜歡他的宿舍，我和包志中也都覺得田進的宿舍真的很不錯。

Notes: 明亮 [míngliàng]: bright
雖然......可是...... [suīrán . . . . . . kěshì . . . . . .]: although . . . (but) . . .
乾淨 [gānjìng]: clean
鍛煉 [duànliàn]: to exercise
安靜 [ānjìng]: quiet
打 [dǎ]: to play
太極拳 [tàijíquán]: tai chi

練習   **ACTIVITIES**

I. Pinyin Exercises

15-1 Listen to the instructor and circle the correct Pinyin:

1. a. gòngyòng chǔfàng
   b. gǒngyōng chùfáng
   c. gōngyòng chúfáng

2. a. kètīng/cāntīng
   b. kétīng/càntīng
   c. kètíng/cántìng

3. a. túshūguán
   b. túshūguǎn
   c. tūshúguàn

4. a. hǒubiàn
   b. hòubiān
   c. hōubián

5. a. cánguàn
   b. cànguàn
   c. cānguān

6. a. dìzhǐ
   b. dīzhǐ
   c. dǐzhì

15-2 Listen to the dialogue from Language in Use, and then use Pinyin to answer the following questions:

1. Tián Jìn de sùshè yǒuméiyǒu chúfáng?

   _____

2. Tián Jìn de fángjiān zài chúfáng de nǎbiān?

   _____

3. Kètīng hé wòshì de zhōngjiān shì shénme?

   _____

4. Tián Jìn chángcháng zài nǎr xuéxí?

   _____

5. Gōngyuán zài nǎr? Tián Jìn cháng qù nàr zuò shénme?

   _____

15-3 Read the following Chinese poem, paying special attention to the tones and rhythm:

Wàng Lúshān Pùbù **(Lǐ Bó/Lǐ Bái)**	望廬山瀑布 (李白)
Rì zhào xiānglú shēng zǐyān, Yáo kàn pùbù guà qiánchuān. Fēi liú zhí xià sānqiān chǐ, Yí shì yínhē luò jiǔ tiān.	日照香爐生紫煙， 遙看瀑布掛前川。 飛流直下三千尺， 疑是銀河落九天。
Viewing the Waterfall on Mount Lu **(Li, Bo)**	
The sunshine on the incense burner produces a purple cloud, Looking from afar the waterfall is like a huge curtain hanging high. Its torrent rushes down three thousand feet from above, I feel as if the Milky Way fell from the sky.	

Note: 李白 Lǐ Bái is pronounced as Lǐ Bó in Classical Chinese.

II. Character Exercises

15-4 Read the following words, phrases, and sentences:

宿舍	旁邊
我的宿舍	在旁邊
參觀我的宿舍	在客廳旁邊
來參觀我的宿舍	臥室在客廳旁邊
歡迎來參觀我的宿舍	我的臥室在客廳旁邊
歡迎你們來參觀我的宿舍	我的臥室在客廳和餐廳旁邊

Now try to use the following characters to make words, phrases, and then sentences:

1. 前   2. 裡   3. 房   4. 公   5. 間   6. 面
7. 洗   8. 臥   9. 桌   10. 後   11. 園   12. 真

15-5 Identify the radicals of the following characters, then give an example, selected from Language in Use, of a character with the same radical:

For example,   嗎 ____口____   ____呢____

1. 邊 _____ _____   2. 廚 _____ _____
3. 洗 _____ _____   4. 園 _____ _____

15-6 Match the traditional characters with their simplified equivalents:

歡   園   邊   廳   廚   觀   後

观   欢   后   边   园   厅   厨

III. Grammar Exercises

15-7 Substitution exercises:

1. 我們的<u>房間</u>在<u>客廳</u>的<u>右邊</u>。

圖書館	公園	前邊
廚房	客廳	後邊
洗澡間	臥室	旁邊
書房	餐廳	左邊
字典	書桌	上邊
車庫	客廳	下邊

Notes: 書房 [shūfáng]: study room   字典 [zìdiǎn]: dictionary
書桌 [shūzhuō]: desk   車庫 [chēkù]: garage
左邊 [zuǒbiān]: left

2. <u>宿舍</u>的<u>後邊</u>有<u>一個公園</u>。

書桌	上邊	一本字典
臥室	後邊	一個洗澡間
客廳	旁邊	一個廚房
椅子	下邊	一個球
床	旁邊	一個衣櫥
炒飯	前邊	一雙筷子

Note: 衣櫥 [yīchú]: closet

3. <u>臥室</u>的<u>旁邊</u>是<u>洗澡間</u>。

中國飯館	後邊	公園
停車場	左邊	宿舍
機場	前邊	商店
宿舍和圖書館	中間	停車場
書房和客廳	中間	廁所

Note: 廁所 [cèsuǒ]: bathroom, restroom

15-8 Fill in the blanks with 有，在，or 是：

1. 臥室 _____ 客廳的右邊。

2. 臥室的前邊 _____ 書房。

3. 客廳 _____ 臥室和廚房的中間。

4. 飯廳的後邊 _____ 廚房。

5. 洗澡間 _____ 洗衣房的後邊，臥室的右邊。

Notes: 洗衣房 [xǐyīfáng]: laundry room
　　　　右邊 [yòubiān]: right

IV. Communicative Activities

15-9 Situational dialogue:

Your friend has just arrived at your place. He has enrolled to study at your university. Before he came he asked you to help him find an apartment. You have found a very nice one-bedroom apartment for him. Tell him everything you know about this apartment. The following pictures can serve as clues.

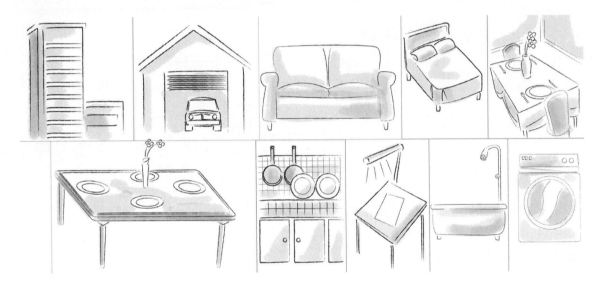

Useful expressions:

有 是 在   前邊 旁邊 對面

不錯   乾淨 [gānjìng] (clean)

大 小

文化點滴　CULTURE NOTES

風水[Fēngshuǐ] Feng Shui
The Chinese Art of Placement

風水 [fēng shuǐ] (winds and waters) in its literal sense refers to the topography of the earth, its mountains, valleys, and waterways whose shape and size, direction, and levels are created by the continuous interactions of these two powerful forces of nature.

The goal of 風水 is to maintain harmony and balance between 陰 [yīn] and 陽 [yáng] in the universe and in nature. According to Chinese culture, all living things are interrelated by the cosmic energy known as 氣 [qì]. 氣 is the invisible flow of energy that circulates through the earth and sky, bringing the life force with it. The practice of 風水 is concerned with harnessing this vital energy to maximize the positive effects that it bestows. It is believed that we can influence our fate and fortune by enhancing and directing the flow of 氣.

風水, which originated over 4,000 years ago, is the ancient Chinese art of placement. The farmers in southern China developed certain 風水 principles because of their dependence on the earth and the forces governing it. They learned that living in harmony with nature made life much easier. Building homes on hills protected them from floods and also made it easier for them to defend themselves from attackers. Homes were also built to face the south, so that they would not face the storms of yellow dust that blew down from Mongolia. Besides, facing the south exposed them to the winter sunshine so that they would be bright and warm during the cold months but comparatively cool in summer. In addition to being used by farmers, 風水 also played a vital role in ancient Chinese burials, important because of the tradition of ancestor veneration in Chinese culture. It was thought that ancestors made happy with good 風水 guiding the placement of their tombs would shower the blessings of prosperity, honor, long life, and healthy offspring on the living.

In the family home, good 風水 positioning is believed to facilitate harmonious relationships between husband and wife, foster good health, attract abundance and prosperity, and help to build good reputations.

In Chinese cultures, where family life and honor are important, good 風水 is seen as helping husbands and wives beget many good and loving children, who will bring honor to the family name.

In business, following 風水 rules in the selection and design of the premises is thought to create opportunities for growth, raise one's business profile and standing in the community, attract customers, and increase profits and turnover. It is also believed that adhering to good 風水 practices in business will help ensure loyal employees and smooth working relationships.

It is said that a fish tank will bring good luck. These two homes, one in Hong Kong and one in Taiwan, have fish tanks placed to provide decoration and improve Feng shui.

八卦 [bāguà] (The Eight Trigrams) is used to help measure a location's Feng shui.

This is a classy residential building in Hong Kong. Why is there a hole in the building? It is said that the structure continually collapsed while being built. The builder consulted with a Feng shui master and learned that there was a dragon who lived nearby and the mansion was blocking its way. The builder was told to leave a hole for the dragon to pass through.

To Chinese communities the world over, 風水 has been a common mystical practice for centuries, which blends ancient wisdom with cultural traditions. It is the art of living in harmony with our environment for health, wealth, and happiness. It has also attained popularity in many Western countries where its benefits are now being increasingly recognized.

Questions:

1. Do you believe in 風水? Will you consult a 風水 master when you buy a house?

2. Do you think 風水 is a superstition or a science?

趣味中文　FUN WITH CHINESE

有緣千里來相會，無緣對面不相識。

If it is fated, even those separated by one thousand *li* will meet each other. If it is not fated, even those who are face to face will not know each other.

yǒu	yuán	qiān	lǐ	lái	xiāng	huì,
有	緣	千	里	來	相	會，
have	fate	thousand	kilometer	come	mutually	meet,

wú	yuán	duìmiàn	bù	xiāng	shí.
無	緣	對面	不	相	識。
no	fate	face to face	no	mutually	know.

The concept of fate or destiny is very important in Chinese culture. This saying shows how Chinese people emphasize the importance of their acquaintances. It is usually used to refer to couples who are meant to be together, or to remind people that friends are very precious.

Questions:

1. Do you know where your classmates come from? Are you all "有緣千里來相會"?

2. Can you think of any movie in which the characters come to meet each other from thousands of miles away?

行動吧! LET'S GO!

北京觀光景點   Scenic Spots in Beijing

東東 just returned from visiting Beijing. He is showing you some of the scenic spots that he has visited. Ask the location of some of the spots, such as 十三陵在北京市的哪一邊? 北京的南邊有什麼? 北邊是故宮嗎?

Useful words and expressions:

觀光(观光) [guānguāng]: sightseeing
景點(景点) [jǐngdiǎn]: scenic spots
名勝(名胜) [míngshèng]: a scenic spot
故宮(故宫) [Gùgōng]: the Imperial Palace
頤和園(颐和园) [Yí Hé Yuán]: the Yi He Garden (the Summer Palace)
十三陵(十三陵) [Shísān Líng]: the Thirteen Emperors' Tombs
天壇(天坛) [Tiān Tán]: the Altar of Heaven
東邊(东边) [dōng biān]: east side
東南邊(东南边) [dōngnán biān]: southeast side
東北邊(东北边) [dōngběi biān]: northeast side
南邊(南边) [nán biān]: south side
西邊(西边) [xī biān]: west side
西南邊(西南边) [xīnán biān]: southwest side
西北邊(西北边) [xīběi biān]: northwest side
北邊(北边) [běi biān]: north side

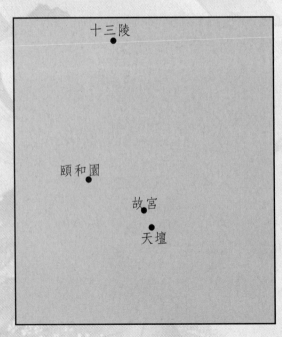

北京觀光景點地圖

她打籃球打得很好
She Plays Basketball Very Well

教學目標 OBJECTIVES

- Describe how an action is performed
- Talk about hobbies and exercises

to run 跑步 *[pǎobù]*

martial arts 功夫 *[gōngfu]*

to play the violin 拉小提琴 *[lā xiǎotíqín]*

Do you have any of these hobbies? How good are you at them?

Warm-up Exercises

1. Instructor leads the students in reading aloud the Chinese term for each activity
2. Instructor asks students about their hobbies. Use 得 to ask how well they do them. For example,

A: 你的愛好 [àihào] 是什麼？　（你喜歡做什麼？）
B: 我喜歡跑步 [pǎobù] 。
A: 你跑步跑得怎麼樣?
B: 我跑得很快 。

self-defense **防身術** *[fángshēn shù]*

to read **看書** *[kànshū]*

to draw **畫畫** *[huàhuà]*

to play ball **打球** *[dǎqiú]*

to use a computer 打電腦 [dǎ diànnǎo]

to sing 唱歌 [chànggē]

to eat 吃東西 [chī dōngxi]

to swim 游泳 [yóuyǒng]

生詞 VOCABULARY

核心詞 Core Vocabulary

	TRADITIONAL	SIMPLIFIED	PINYIN		
1.	籃球	篮球	lánqiú	N.	basketball
2.	得	得	de	Part.	(used between a verb or an adjective and its complement to indicate result, possibility, or degree)
3.	倆	俩	liǎ		(colloquial) two people
4.	教練	教练	jiàoliàn	N.	coach, trainer
5.	教	教	jiāo	V.	to teach; to coach
6.	游泳	游泳	yóuyǒng	V.O.	to swim
7.	非常	非常	fēicháng	Adv.	very
8.	快	快	kuài	Adj.	fast
9.	體育館	体育馆	tǐyùguǎn	N.	gymnasium
10.	游泳池	游泳池	yóuyǒngchí	N.	swimming pool
11.	健身房	健身房	jiànshēnfáng	N.	gym
12.	鍛煉	锻炼	duànliàn	V.	to exercise
13.	現在	现在	xiànzài	Adv.	now
14.	昨天	昨天	zuótiān	N.	yesterday
15.	球賽	球赛	qiúsài	N.	ball game; match
16.	作業	作业	zuòyè	N.	homework
17.	包	包	bāo	V.	to wrap
18.	慢	慢	màn	Adj.	slow

補充詞 Supplementary Vocabulary

	TRADITIONAL	SIMPLIFIED	PINYIN		
1.	社團	社团	shètuán	N.	organization
2.	俱樂部	俱乐部	jùlèbù	N.	club
3.	球季	球季	qiújì	N.	season (of a sport)

運動項目 [Yùndòng xiàngmù]　**Sports Items**

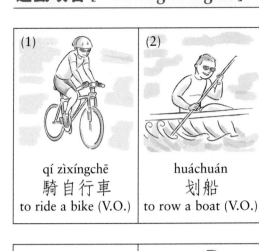

(1) qí zìxíngchē 騎自行車 to ride a bike (V.O.)	(2) huáchuán 划船 to row a boat (V.O.)	(3) qiánshuǐ 潛水 to dive (V.O.)	(4) yóuyǒng 游泳 to swim (V.O.)	(5) diàoyú 釣魚 to fish (V.O.)

(6) huáxuě 滑雪 to snow ski (V.O.)	(7) huábīng 滑冰 to skate (V.O.)	(8) bīngqiú 冰球 ice hockey	(9) páshān 爬山 to climb a mountain (V.O.)	(10) yuǎnzú 遠足 hiking

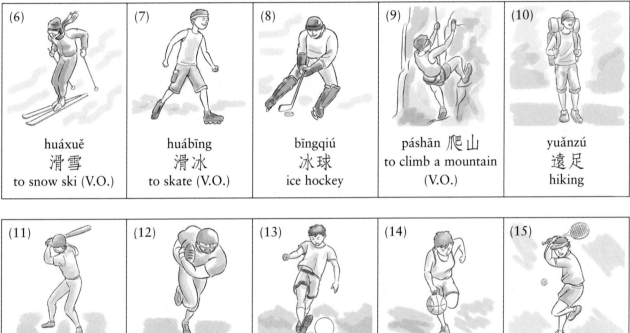

(11) bàngqiú 棒球 baseball	(12) gǎnlǎnqiú 橄欖球 football	(13) zúqiú 足球 soccer	(14) lánqiú 籃球 basketball	(15) wǎngqiú 網球 tennis

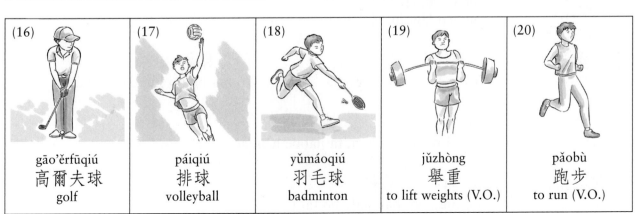

(16) gāo'ěrfūqiú 高爾夫球 golf	(17) páiqiú 排球 volleyball	(18) yǔmáoqiú 羽毛球 badminton	(19) jǔzhòng 舉重 to lift weights (V.O.)	(20) pǎobù 跑步 to run (V.O.)

語文知識 LANGUAGE LINK

The Sentence Patterns provide models that will help you with the Language in Use section. In both sections, pay attention to the grammar points, vocabulary, and expressions.

句型　Sentence Patterns

A: 你游泳游得怎麼樣？
Nǐ yóuyǒng yóude zěnmeyàng?

B: 我游泳游得非常快。
Wǒ yóuyǒng yóude fēicháng kuài.

A: 你做飯做得好不好？
Nǐ zuòfàn zuòde hǎobuhǎo?

B: 我做飯做得不太好。
Wǒ zuòfàn zuòde bútàihǎo.

課文　Language in Use: 她打籃球打得很好 Tā dǎ lánqiú dǎde hěnhǎo

張正然：

你們倆要去哪兒？
Nǐmenliǎ yàoqù nǎr?

孫信美，楊歡：

我們去打籃球。
Wǒmen qù dǎ lánqiú.

張正然：

你們籃球打得怎麼樣？
Nǐmen lánqiú dǎde zěngmeyàng?

孫信美：

楊歡籃球打得很好。我還不太會打籃球，
Yáng Huān lánqiú dǎde hěnhǎo. Wǒ hái bú tài huì dǎ lánqiú,

她是我的教練，她教得很好。
tā shì wǒde jiàoliàn, tā jiāode hěnhǎo.

楊歡：

不行，我還打得不太好。
Bùxíng, wǒ hái dǎde bú tài hǎo.

張正然：　我不常打籃球，我常常和我室友去游泳，
Wǒ bù cháng dǎ lánqiú, wǒ chángcháng hé wǒ shìyǒu qù yóuyǒng,

他游泳游得非常快。
tā yóuyǒng yóude fēicháng kuài.

楊歡：　你們常去哪兒游泳？
Nǐmen cháng qù nǎr yóuyǒng?

張正然：　我們常去體育館裡邊的游泳池游泳，
Wǒmen cháng qù tǐyùguǎn lǐbiān de yóuyǒngchí yóuyǒng,

我們也常去健身房鍛煉。
wǒmen yě cháng qù jiànshēnfáng duànliàn.

孫信美：　你現在要不要跟我們去打籃球？
Nǐ xiànzài yàobuyào gēn wǒmen qù dǎ lánqiú?

張正然：　現在不行。我昨天看球賽看得太晚了，今天起得很晚，
Xiànzài bùxíng. Wǒ zuótiān kàn qiúsài kànde tàiwǎn le, jīntiān qǐde hěnwǎn,

現在得去做作業。
xiànzài děi qù zuò zuòyè.

楊歡：　昨天我們那兒包餃子、做中國菜。你晚上到我們
Zuótiān wǒmen nàr bāo jiǎozi, zuò Zhōngguó cài. Nǐ wǎnshàng dào wǒmen

那兒吃餃子吧。
nàr chī jiǎozi ba.

張正然：　太好了！我很喜歡吃餃子。
Tàihǎo le! Wǒ hěn xǐhuān chī jiǎozi.

你們包餃子包得快不快？
Nǐmen bāo jiǎozi bāode kuàibukuài?

孫信美：　我們包得很慢。
Wǒmen bāode hěnmàn.

楊歡：　信美很會做飯。她做飯做得很好。
Xìngměi hěn huì zuòfàn. Tā zuòfàn zuòde hěnhǎo.

注釋 LANGUAGE NOTES

得 [de, děi]

得 has two pronunciations that have different meanings and functions. 得 [de] is used for degree of complement sentences, whereas [děi] is an optative verb meaning "have to."

倆

倆 means "two people." It is used with pronouns. For example, 我們倆 (us two), 你們倆 (you two), and 他們倆 (they two).

教 [jiào, jiāo]

When 教 is used as a noun, it is pronounced as [jiào], such as 教練, 教授 [jiàoshòu] (professor), or 教育 [jiàoyù] (education). When 教 is used as a verb, it is pronounced as [jiāo].

鍛煉

鍛煉 means "exercise, work out." In Taiwan, the term 運動 [yùndòng] is more commonly used.

語法 GRAMMAR

Degree of Complement Sentences

A degree of complement sentence is used to assess or tell how an action is performed (such as how fast, how well, how soon, etc.). The word 得 is used. For example,

Single verb	Subject V. 得 Adv. Adj.
你游得怎麼樣?	How well do you swim?
我游得很快。	I swim very fast.
我游得不快。	I don't swim fast.
你游得快不快?	Do you swim fast or not?

Verb Object (V.O.)	Subject V.O.V. 得 Adv. Adj.
他打籃球打得怎麼樣?	How well does he play basketball?
他打籃球打得好不好?	Does he play basketball well or not?
他打籃球打得很好。	He plays basketball very well.
他打籃球打得不太好。	He doesn't play basketball very well.

V.: 游，說，學，吃，鍛煉，介紹，練習，參觀，學習

V.O.: 游泳，上課，教書，做飯，吃飯，開車，打球，上綱，睡覺

The object can also be placed at the beginning of a sentence for emphasis. For example,

餃子我包得很慢。

籃球他打得非常好。

補充課文 ──○○○── SUPPLEMENTARY PRACTICE

This selection will help you test your comprehension of the grammar and vocabulary you have learned in this lesson. Be prepared to answer questions about the meaning of the passage.

　　大家好！我叫孫信美。我和楊歡是好朋友。我們倆都喜歡游泳，常常一起去體育館裡邊的游泳池游泳。我不太會游泳，現在正在學。楊歡游泳游得非常好，她也是我的游泳教練。她教我教得很好，所以我學得很快。

　　張正然是楊歡的男朋友。他不常游泳，可是他特別喜歡打籃球。我們學校有一個很好的健身房，他常常跟他的室友一起去那兒打籃球。他的室友籃球打得非常好，他還是學校籃球隊的隊長。他們常常一起出去參加比賽。

　　我們四個人都是體育活動愛好者，常常去健身房鍛煉。我們有時候也一起吃飯。楊歡包餃子包得又快又好，我包餃子包得很慢，可是我做中國飯做得特別好吃，他們都喜歡吃我做的飯。

Notes: 特別 [tèbié]: especially, particularly
　　　　還 [hái]: used as an adverb, to mean "also," "as well"
　　　　隊 [duì]: team
　　　　隊長 [duìzhǎng]: team leader
　　　　參加 [cānjiā]: to participate
　　　　比賽 [bǐsài]: contest
　　　　愛好者 [àihàozhě]: one who loves (a sport, a hobby, etc.)

練習 ACTIVITIES

I. Pinyin Exercises

16-1 Listen to the instructor and select the correct Pinyin:

1. a. dǎ lánqiú
   b. dà lànqiú
   c. dá lānqiú

2. a. bāo jiàozi
   b. bāo jiǎozi
   c. bǎo jiāozi

3. a. kán qiùsài
   b. kān qiùsài
   c. kàn qiúsài

4. a. jiāo yóuyǒng   5. a. tìyùguǎn   6. a. zuō zuóyè
    b. jiáo yōuyòng   b. tǐyúguǎn   b. zuò zuòyè
    c. jiāo yòuyōng   c. tǐyùguǎn   c. zuò zuǒyè

16-2 Listen to the instructor and complete the sentences in Pinyin:

1. Nǐmen _____ zhème kuài, yào qù nǎr?

2. Yáng Huān _____ fēicháng hǎo.

3. Zhāng Zhèngrán yóuyǒng _____.

4. Wǒ zuótiān wǎnshàng _____.

5. Shéi zuò fàn _____?

16-3 Read the following Chinese poem, paying special attention to the tones and rhythm:

Fēngqiáo Yè Bó **(Zhāng Jì)**	**楓橋夜泊** **(張繼)**
Yuè luò wū tí shuāng mǎn tiān, Jiāng fēng yúhuǒ duì chóu mián. Gūsū chéngwài Hánshānsì, Yè bàn zhōngshēng dào kèchuán.	月落烏啼霜滿天， 江楓漁火對愁眠。 姑蘇城外寒山寺， 夜半鐘聲到客船。

Night Docking at Maple Bridge
(Zhang, Ji)

The moon is setting, the magpie chirping, and the sky full of frost,
Accompanied by the Maple River water and fishing candles I sleep with worries
     on my mind.
Outside Suzhou is the Hanshan Temple,
At midnight the sound of its bell reaches my boat.

II. Character Exercises

16-4 Read the following words, phrases, and sentences:

籃	快
籃球	非常快
打籃球	說得非常快
他打籃球	王老師說得非常快
他打籃球打得很好	王老師說中文說得非常快
他和他室友籃球都打得很好	王老師和方老師中文都說得非常快

Now try to use the following characters to make words, phrases, and then sentences:

1. 倆	2. 教	3. 游	4. 體	5. 池	6. 健
7. 身	8. 鍛	9. 賽	10. 業	11. 包	12. 慢

16-5 Find some characters from the lesson that begin with the same stroke as the following characters:

1. 你 ＿＿＿ ＿＿＿ ＿＿＿

2. 要 ＿＿＿ ＿＿＿ ＿＿＿ ＿＿＿

3. 室 ＿＿＿ ＿＿＿ ＿＿＿ ＿＿＿ ＿＿＿

16-6 Circle the radical of each of the following characters. Then provide the meaning of the radical and write at least two other characters that share the same radical.

For example, 快　　heart　　忙　想

游 ＿＿＿＿＿＿＿＿＿＿＿　　　球 ＿＿＿＿＿＿＿＿＿＿＿

鍛 ＿＿＿＿＿＿＿＿＿＿＿　　　籃 ＿＿＿＿＿＿＿＿＿＿＿

常 ＿＿＿＿＿＿＿＿＿＿＿　　　賽 ＿＿＿＿＿＿＿＿＿＿＿

III. Grammar Exercises

16-7 Substitution exercises:

1. 他開車開得怎麼樣?
   他開車開得很快。

游泳	好
教書	累 [lèi] tired
學電腦	慢
做飯	好
包餃子	快
吃飯	高興

   Notes: 累 [lèi]: tired
   高興 [gāoxìng]: happy

2. 你的生日過得好不好?
   我的生日過得很好。

中國菜	做	好
中文	說	好棒
功課	做	好棒
籃球	打	好棒
德國車	買	貴

   Note: 貴 [guì]: expensive

16-8 Ask questions with "得" based on the pictures, and then provide an answer:

1.

Q. _____

A. _____

游泳 [yóuyǒng]: swimming

2.

Q. _____

A. _____

籃球 [lánqiú]: basketball

3.

Q. _____

A. _____

棒球 [bàngqiú]: baseball

4.

Q. _____

A. _____

排球 [páiqiú]: volleyball

5.

Q. _____

A. _____

踢 [tī]: to kick   足球 [zúqiú]: soccer

16-9 Complete the following sentences with "得" and an expression to indicate the degree of complement (clues are provided):

1. 我媽媽做飯 (fast) _____
2. 楊歡打籃球 (well) _____
3. 你們做作業 (late) _____
4. 我鍛煉 (little) _____
5. 誰包餃子 (slow) _____

IV. Communicative Activities

You and your friend are chatting about your extracurricular interests. Create a dialogue. Be sure that the following words and expressions are used (but do not limit your dialogue to these words):

Useful words and expressions:

球賽 (籃球，排球 [páiqiú] (volleyball)，足球 [zúqiú] (soccer)，

棒球 [bàngqiú] (baseball)，乒乓球 [pīngpāngqiú] (table tennis)，

高爾夫球 [gāo'ěrfūqiú] (golf))

健身房　　游泳　　　鍛煉　　　體育館

社團 (俱樂部) [shètuán (jùlèbù)] (organization, club)

文化點滴　CULTURE NOTES

中國體育 [Zhōngguó tǐyù] Chinese Sport

In international sports competitions, such as 奧運會 [Àoyùnhuì] (the Olympics) and 世界錦標賽 [Shìjiè jǐnbiāosài] (World Championships), China is famous for its excellence in many events. Chinese athletes are top ranked in the world in sports such as volleyball, table tennis, basketball, gymnastics, swimming, women's soccer, and diving.

Soccer is one of the most popular sports in China. Currently, China has a professional soccer league. Famous Chinese soccer teams include 上海申花 [Shànghǎi Shēnhuā] (Shanghai Shen Hua) and 大連實德 [Dàlián Shídé] (Dalian Shi De). Whenever there is a major soccer game, Chinese fans either want to go to the stadium or to watch it on television. The games are so popular that the tickets are generally sold out. Fans even buy some tickets that might cost more than an average salesman's monthly salary! The Chinese professional soccer league has attracted talented players from other countries and has adopted foreign soccer

Exercises such as running, swimming, and using the hula hoop are popular in China.

The professional baseball league in Taiwan has many fans.

systems, resulting in growing audiences at soccer matches. Soccer analysts predict that China will have a strong soccer team in the near future. Soccer is also very popular in Hong Kong.

In Taiwan, the most popular sports are baseball and basketball. They both have professional leagues. Fans are of all ages and their favorite players become their idols. Through promotions of the American National Basketball Association (NBA) and visits from superstars such as Michael Jordan, basketball has become one of the most popular sports in Taiwan. Having the Chinese player 姚明 [Yáo Míng] in the NBA definitely attracts more Chinese fans and has opened the NBA market in China. With so many popular sports in Chinese societies, Chinese people are excited about and looking forward to the Olympics coming to Beijing in 2008!

Questions:

1. Can you introduce the Chinese sports star that you like the most?
2. What sports activities do you think Chinese people are especially good at?

趣味中文　FUN WITH CHINESE

> 臨時抱佛腳
> To embrace Buddha's feet and pray for help in time of emergency
> (i.e., to do something too late and without preparation).

lín	shí	bào	fó	jiǎo
臨	時	抱	佛	腳
encounter	time	embrace	Buddha	feet

Questions:

1. Do you know any similar sayings describing procrastinators in English?
2. Do you often do things at the last minute? If so, do you plan to change this habit?

行動吧！ LET'S GO!

公佈告示   Announcements and Notifications

The following are some common announcement and notification signs from which we can learn some survival Chinese.

Useful words and expressions:

公佈(公布) [gōngbù]: announcement

營業(营业) [yíngyè]: business operation

疏散 [shūsàn]: to disperse

安全 [ānquán]: safe

出口 [chūkǒu]: exit

輕聲(轻声) [qīngshēng]: quiet voice

意見箱(意见箱) [yìjiànxiāng]: opinion box

告示 [gàoshi]: notification

隨手關門(随手关门) [suíshǒu guānmén]: close the door after one enters or leaves a room

講話(讲话) [jiǎnghuà]: to speak

慢走 [mànzǒu]: walk slowly

同樣的(同样的) [tóngyàng de]: same, similar

信息 [xìnxī]: information

牌子 [páizi]: sign

Questions:

1. 在圖書館裡邊，我們可以看到哪些同樣的信息？

2. 你在哪兒會看到像這樣的牌子？

復習　Review

Conversation

1. You and your friend are chatting about your dormitory/apartment. Your conversation should include the following topics.

   A: 你的宿舍/公寓 [gōngyù] (apartment) 在哪兒?

   B: 你的宿舍/公寓在你的學校 [xuéxiào] (school) 的旁邊嗎?

   C: 你的床 [chuáng] (bed) 的旁邊是什麼? 客廳呢? 客廳的旁邊是廚房嗎? 你的書桌上面常常有什麼?

   D: 你住的地方 [dìfang] (place) 附近 [fùjìn] (neighborhood) 都有什麼? (商店 [shāngdiàn] (store), 飯館、圖書館、公園、飛機場、停車場...) (Use the position words: 旁邊、後邊、前邊、對面、etc. to describe.)

2. You and your friend are chatting about extracurricular activities, hobbies, and exercises. Topics to include are:

   A: 你最 [zuì] (the most) 喜歡的課外活動 [kèwài huódòng] (extracurricular activities) 是什麼?

   B: 你常在什麼時候、在哪兒做這些活動?

   C: 你常常和誰一起進行 [jìnxíng] (to do) 這些活動? 你做得怎麼樣? 你的朋友呢?

Situational Dialogue

Today is orientation day for the freshmen in your department and you have volunteered to show them around the campus. You and the freshmen are in front of the library and you are pointing out all the main campus buildings to them and telling them what their function is. (Use the map on the next page for reference.)

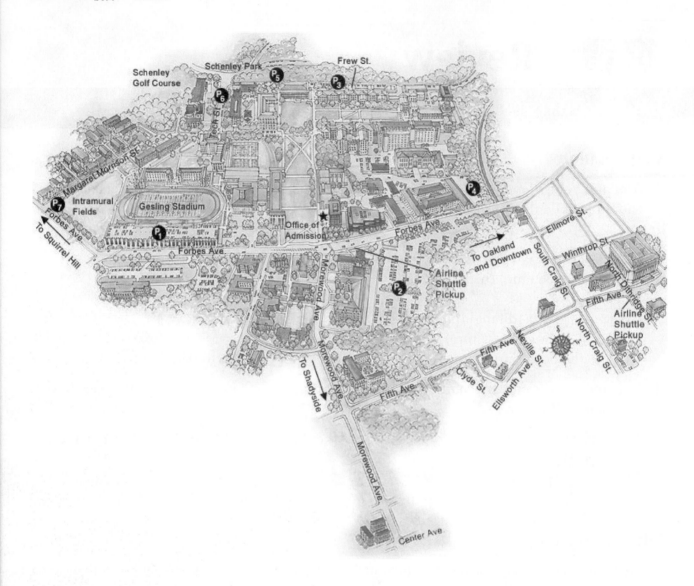

P1: 停車場   P2: 學生宿舍   P3: 中文系   P4: 書店
P5: 圖書館   P6: 商業系   P7: 中國飯館

Notes: 系 [xì]: (department)
        商業 [shāngyè]: (business)

Useful grammar points and expressions:

N. + 在 + Place; Place + 有 + N.; Place + 是 + N.; V. + 得 + Complement
Position words: 前邊, 後邊, 左邊, 右邊, 上邊, 下邊, 裡邊, 外邊, 旁邊, 中間, 對面

Traditional and Simplified Characters

Read each character aloud. Write its traditional form. Then tell a story (at least five sentences) using the following characters.

For example, 学 → 學 → 學生 → 我是一個學生, 我學......

L15: 边 (   )   观 (   )   里 (   )   厅 (   )   后 (   )
L16: 篮 (   )   练 (   )   体 (   )   赛 (   )   业 (   )

春天就要來了
Spring Is Coming Soon

- Talk about the four seasons
- Describe the weather
- Express that something will happen in the near future

There are four seasons in China. However, as China is a large country, a winter day might mean heavy snow in the north but comfortable sunshine in the south.

December in Taiwan.

December in Beijing.

July in Hong Kong.

July in Taiwan: hot and sunny.

生詞　VOCABULARY

核心詞　Core Vocabulary

	TRADITIONAL	SIMPLIFIED	PINYIN		
1.	春天	春天	chūntiān	N.	spring
2.	久	久	jiǔ	Adj.	for a long time
3.	時間	时间	shíjiān	N.	time
4.	過	过	guò	V.	to pass
5.	放	放	fàng	V.	to have, start (a vacation)
6.	春假	春假	chūnjià	N.	spring break
7.	氣候	气候	qìhòu	N.	climate
8.	夏	夏	xià	N.	summer
9.	秋	秋	qiū	N.	autumn
10.	冬	冬	dōng	N.	winter
11.	其中	其中	qízhōng		among (whom, which)
12.	最	最	zuì	Adv.	(indicates the superlative degree)
13.	暖和	暖和	nuǎnhuo	Adj.	warm
14.	短	短	duǎn	Adj.	short
15.	有時候	有时候	yǒushíhou	Adv.	sometimes
16.	熱	热	rè	Adj.	hot
17.	華氏	华氏	huáshì	N.	Fahrenheit
18.	百	百	bǎi	Num.	hundred
19.	度	度	dù	N.	degree
20.	極	极	jí	Adv.	extremely
21.	刮風	刮风	guāfēng	V.O.	(wind) to blow

TRADITIONAL	SIMPLIFIED	PINYIN		
22. 下雨	下雨	xiàyǔ	V.O.	to rain
23. 冷	冷	lěng	Adj.	cold
24. 雪	雪	xuě	N.	snow
25. 見面	见面	jiànmiàn	V.O.	to meet each other

專名　Proper Nouns

TRADITIONAL	SIMPLIFIED	PINYIN		
1. 小玲	小玲	Xiǎo Líng	N.	(name) Xiao Ling

補充詞　Supplementary Vocabulary

TRADITIONAL	SIMPLIFIED	PINYIN		
1. 天氣	天气	tiānqì	N.	weather
2. 四季	四季	sìjì	N.	four seasons
3. 放假	放假	fàngjià	V.O.	to have holidays
4. 寒假	寒假	hánjià	N.	winter holiday
5. 暑假	暑假	shǔjià	N.	summer holiday
6. 假期	假期	jiàqī	N.	holiday
7. 攝氏	摄氏	shèshì	N.	centigrade
8. 長	长	cháng	Adj.	long
9. 氣溫	气温	qìwēn	N.	temperature
10. 上升	上升	shàngshēng	V.	to increase
11. 下降	下降	xiàjiàng	V.	to decrease

語文知識 LANGUAGE LINK

The Sentence Patterns provide models that will help you with the Language in Use section. In both sections, pay attention to the grammar points, vocabulary, and expressions.

句型 Sentence Patterns

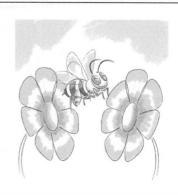

A: 春天就要來了。
Chūntiān jiùyào lái le.

B: 太好了！我們快要放春假了。
Tài hǎo le! Wǒmen kuàiyào fàng chūnjià le.

A: 春夏秋冬，其中
Chūn xià qiū dōng, qízhōng

你最喜歡哪一個？
nǐ zuì xǐhuān nǎ yíge?

B: 我最喜歡春天。你呢？
Wǒ zuì xǐhuān chūntiān. Nǐ ne?

A: 這兒的夏天熱不熱？
Zhèr de xiàtiān rèburè?

B: 這兒的夏天熱極了！
Zhèr de xiàtiān rè jí le!

課文 Language in Use: 春天就要來了! Chūntiān jiùyào lái le!

小玲,
Xiǎolíng,

好久不見。
Hǎojiǔ bújiàn.

你現在怎麼樣? 時間過得真快, 春天就要來了, 我們也
Nǐ xiànzài zěnmeyàng? Shíjiān guòde zhēnkuài, chūntiān jiùyào lái le, wǒmen yě

快要放春假了。
kuàiyào fàng chūnjià le.

我們這兒的氣候春夏秋冬都有。其中我最喜歡春天,
Wǒmen zhèr de qìhòu chūn xià qiū dōng dōuyǒu. Qízhōng wǒ zuì xǐhuān chūntiān,

很暖和, 可是很短。夏天有時候很熱, 最熱的時候, 會到華氏
hěn nuǎnhuo, kěshì hěnduǎn. Xiàtiān yǒushíhou hěn rè, zuì rè de shíhou, huì dào huáshì

一百度, 熱極了。秋天有時候會刮風、下雨。這兒的冬天非常冷,
yìbǎi dù, rè jí le. Qiūtiān yǒushíhou huì guāfēng, xiàyǔ. Zhèr de dōngtiān fēicháng lěng,

常常下雪。
chángcháng xiàxuě.

放春假的時候我想去你那兒玩玩, 我們很快就要見面了!
Fàng chūnjià de shíhou wǒ xiǎng qù nǐ nàr wánwan, wǒmen hěnkuài jiùyào jiànmiàn le!

祝
Zhù

好!
Hǎo!

大中
Dàzhōng

二〇〇四年三月十日
èr líng líng sì nián sān yuè shí rì

練習 ACTIVITIES

I. Pinyin Exercises

17-1 Listen to the instructor. Mark "√" if the Pinyin is correct, or write the correct Pinyin if it is incorrect:

1. cūntiān _____
2. shíjiā _____
3. fàngjià _____
4. qìhòu _____
5. jízhōng _____
6. shíhòu _____
7. huáshì _____
8. xiàoyǔ _____
9. shèxì _____
10. shuòshì _____
11. qízhōng _____
12. sàjiàng _____

17-2 Listen to the instructor and fill in each blank with the correct Pinyin:

1. 很快 ____ 考試了，我忙 ____ 了。
2. 我 ____ 沒有回家了，放 ____ 的 ____ 我想回家看看。
3. 北京的 ____ 春夏秋冬都有，____ 我比較喜歡 ____。
4. 香港的 ____ 很 ____，有時候非常 ____，還會 ____、____。
5. ____ 就要來了，____ 就要 ____ 了。

   Notes: 北京 [Běijīng]: Beijing
   香港 [Xiānggǎng]: Hong Kong

17-3 Read the following Chinese poem, paying special attention to the tones and rhythm:

Zǎo Fā Báidìchéng **(Lǐ Bó/Lǐ Bái)**	**早發白帝城** **(李白)**
Zhāo cí Báidì cǎiyún jiān,	朝辭白帝彩雲間，
Qiānlǐ jiānglíng yírì huán.	千里江陵一日還。
Liǎng'àn yuánshēng tí bú zhù,	兩岸猿聲啼不住，
Qīngzhōu yǐ guò wàn chóng shān.	輕舟已過萬重山。

Departing Baidi at Dawn **(Li, Bo/Li, Bai)**
At dawn I depart Baidi amid the colorful clouds, After a day I reach Jiangling, a thousand miles away. On the riverbanks monkey calls ring endlessly, My little boat has already passed ten thousand mountains.

Note: 李白 Lǐ Bái is pronounced as Lǐ Bó in Classical Chinese.

II. Character Exercises

17-4 Read the following words, phrases, and sentences:

就	最
就要	最快
就要到了	游得最快
就要到上海了	游泳游得最快
飛機就要到上海了	教練游泳游得最快
飛機很快就要到上海了	王教練游泳游得最快

Now try to use the following characters to make words, phrases, and then sentences:

1. 春　　2. 久　　3. 放　　4. 氣　　5. 其　　6. 暖

7. 短　　8. 熱　　9. 華　　10. 度　　11. 風　　12. 雨

17-5 Write the following adjectives in Chinese:

1. warm _____　　2. hot _____　　3. cold _____

4. (time) long _____　　5. short _____　　6. fast _____

7. slow _____　　8. difficult _____　　9. many _____

10. few _____　　11. big _____　　12. small _____

III. Grammar Exercises

17-6 Substitution exercises:

1. 我們什麼時候去游泳?
   馬上就要去了。

上課
打球
中國飯館
看電影
參加舞會
買襯衫

   Note: 馬上 [mǎshàng]: immediately

2. 誰打球打得最好?
   他打球打得最好。

包餃子	慢
開車	快
做蛋糕	好
學習	久
吃飯	少

17-7 Match the second part of the sentence with its first part:

1. 天氣熱極了，　　　　　A. 其中我最喜歡紅色的那條。

2. 這兒的裙子都很好看，　B. 有時候她會請我們去她家吃飯。

3. 他們認識的時間很短，　C. 我想坐飛機去中國玩兒。

4. 她的中國菜做得不錯，　D. 夏天就要到了。

5. 就要放春假了，　　　　E. 才不到一個月。

17-8 Rewrite the following sentences using the pattern of "就/快要…了":

For Example,　　春天來了。　→　春天就要來了。
　　　　　　　　　　　　　　　　春天快要來了。

1. 小玲明天和大中見面。

　_____

2. 我的朋友下個月從加拿大回美國。

　_____

3. 爸爸等一會兒給我打電話。

　_____

4. 我們下午去公園玩兒。

　_____

5. 楊老師下個學期教我們中文。

　_____

6. 同學們下課以後去游泳。

　_____

IV. Communicative Activities

17-9 Situational dialogues:

<u>Situation 1:</u>
You and your roommate will be picked up by another friend to attend a party together. Your friend's car will arrive soon, but your roommate is still trying on his/her best suit/dress for the party.

Hints:

1. Topics to cover:
   - Talk about the time of the party and your friend's arrival time.
   - Ask your roommate to be quick.
   - Help him/her select which clothing to wear.

2. Words and expressions to use:

就/快要...了　　　　　　　　快一點兒
這件/條還是那件/條好看...　　我覺得　　比較/最

Situation 2:

Your professor is going to teach in China next week. You and your friend are planning to see him/her off at the airport.

Hints:

1. Topics to cover:
   - Chat about your professor's schedule for the trip.
   - Talk about the weather of the city he/she is visiting.
   - Discuss when and how to get to the airport.

2. Words and expressions to use:

熱/冷極了　　坐/開車去　　從...到...
就/快要...了　　教什麼?　　有沒有...?

Situation 3:

Your sister's son will turn six next week and will attend school soon. Give your sister some ideas about what to get him as a present.

Hints:

1. Topics to cover:
   - Greeting.
   - Chat about your nephew's birthday.
   - Make some suggestions about what kind of birthday present would be good.

2. Words and expressions to use:

幾歲?　　就/快要...了,是嗎?　　應該...
喜歡　　買自行車/衣服/書/蛋糕　　好極了

行動吧！ LET'S GO! ....

天氣預報   **Weather Forecast**

書文 is visiting 上海 for a week. He is looking for a weather forecast in the newspaper.

Useful words and expressions:

預報(预报) [yùbào]: forecast

氣象報告(气象报告)[qìxiàng bàogào]: weather forecast
(term used in Taiwan)

紫外線(紫外线) [zǐwàixiàn]: ultraviolet rays

轉(转) [zhuǎn]: to turn

強 [qiáng]: strong

弱 [ruò]: weak

風力(风力) [fēnglì]: wind power

微風(微风) [wēifēng]: breeze

傘(伞) [sǎn]: umbrella

抹 [mǒ]: to apply to

防曬油(防晒油) [fángshài yóu]: sunscreen

溫差 [wēnchā]: temperature difference

上海今日天氣

九月十八日	星期一	天氣：晴	最高氣溫：28度	最低氣溫：26度

一週天氣預告

日期	週	天氣	最高氣溫	最低氣溫	風力	紫外線
九月十九日	週二	陰轉晴	22 度	19 度	微風	中弱
九月二十日	週三	晴	26 度	23 度	輕	中強
九月二十一日	週四	多雲	23 度	20 度	輕	弱
九月二十二日	週五	晴轉陣雨	31 度	25 度	輕	中強
九月二十三日	週六	雨	21 度	18 度	輕	弱
九月二十四日	週日	晴	26 度	23 度	微風	強

Questions:

1. 今天他要穿外套嗎？

2. 書文星期五要出外旅行，他應該帶傘嗎？

3. 星期日要去海邊玩，他應該戴帽子，抹防曬油嗎？

4. 一天的溫差最大的是哪一天？

我們要坐火車去旅行
We Are Going to Take a Train Trip

- Describe means of transportation
- Talk about travel plans

Scooters are very practical and popular in Taiwan.

Double-decker bus and boats in Hong Kong.

Bicycles in China.

生詞 VOCABULARY

核心詞 Core Vocabulary

	TRADITIONAL	SIMPLIFIED	PINYIN		
1.	火車	火车	huǒchē	N.	train
2.	旅行	旅行	lǚxíng	V.	to travel
3.	離	离	lí	V.	to be off, away, from
4.	學校	学校	xuéxiào	N.	school
5.	遠	远	yuǎn	Adj.	far
6.	只要	只要	zhǐyào	Adv.	only
7.	分鐘	分钟	fēnzhōng	N.	minute
8.	騎	骑	qí	V.	to ride
9.	自行車	自行车	zìxíngchē	N.	bicycle
10.	公共汽車	公共汽车	gōnggòngqìchē	N.	bus
11.	走路	走路	zǒulù	V.O.	to walk
12.	近	近	jìn	Adj.	near
13.	西部	西部	xībù	N.	west
14.	先	先	xiān	Adv.	first
15.	風景	风景	fēngjǐng	N.	scenery
16.	船	船	chuán	N.	ship
17.	南部	南部	nánbù	N.	south
18.	聽說	听说	tīngshuō	V.	to be told; to hear of; it is said
19.	海邊	海边	hǎibiān	N.	seaside
20.	景色	景色	jǐngsè	N.	scenery; view
21.	一共	一共	yígòng	Adv.	altogether; in all
22.	租	租	zū	V.	to rent; to hire; to lease

專名　Proper Nouns

TRADITIONAL	SIMPLIFIED	PINYIN		
1. 季長風	季长风	Jì Chángfēng	N.	(name) Changfeng Ji
2. 白秋影	白秋影	Bái Qiūyǐng	N.	(name) Qiuying Bai
3. 加拿大	加拿大	Jiānádà	N.	Canada

補充詞　Supplementary Vocabulary

TRADITIONAL	SIMPLIFIED	PINYIN		
1. 海灘	海滩	hǎitān	N.	seashore
2. 東	东	dōng	N.	east
3. 北	北	běi	N.	north
4. 旺季	旺季	wàngjì	N.	busy season
5. 淡季	淡季	dànjì	N.	off-season
6. 單車 (腳踏車)	单车 (脚踏车)	dānchē (jiǎotàchē)	N.	bicycle
7. 汽車	汽车	qìchē	N.	car
8. 摩托車 (機車)	摩托车 (机车)	mótuōchē (jīchē)	N.	motorcycle, scooter
9. 出租汽車 (計程車)	出租汽车 (计程车)	chūzūqìchē (jìchéngchē)	N.	taxi
10. 火車	火车	huǒchē	N.	train
11. 公車 (巴士)	公车 (巴士)	gōngchē (bāshì)	N.	bus
12. 麵包車 (包型車)	面包车 (包型车)	miànbāochē (bāoxíngchē)	N.	minibus, van
13. 吉普車	吉普车	jípǔchē	N.	jeep
14. 跑車	跑车	pǎochē	N.	sports car
15. 大貨車	大货车	dàhuòchē	N.	truck

TRADITIONAL	SIMPLIFIED	PINYIN		
16. 四輪驅動 (四輪傳動)	四轮驱动 (四轮传动)	sìlúnqūdòng (sìlúnchuándòng)	N.	four-wheel drive
17. 越野車	越野车	yuèyěchē	N.	off-road vehicle
18. 車站	车站	chēzhàn	N.	stop; station
19. 捷運	捷运	jiéyùn	N.	MRT (Mass Rapid Transportation) in Taiwan
20. 地鐵	地铁	dìtiě	N.	subway
21. 磁浮鐵路	磁浮铁路	cífú tiělù	N.	magnetic railway
22. 天橋	天桥	tiānqiáo	N.	overhead bridge
23. 馬路	马路	mǎlù	N.	road, street
24. 地下道	地下道	dìxiàdào	N.	underground passage
25. 隧道	隧道	suìdào	N.	tunnel
26. 碼頭	码头	mǎtóu	N.	wharf; dock; pier
27. 司機	司机	sījī	N.	driver

語文知識   LANGUAGE LINK

The Sentence Patterns provide models that will help you with the Language in Use section. In both sections, pay attention to the grammar points, vocabulary, and expressions.

句型   Sentence Patterns

A: 你家離學校遠不遠？
　 Nǐ jiā lí xuéxiào yuǎnbuyuǎn?

B: 不太遠。開車只要五分鐘。
　 Bú tài yuǎn. Kāichē zhǐyào wǔ fēnzhōng.

A: 你每天怎麼來學校?
Nǐ měitiān zěnme lái xuéxiào?

B: 我常騎自行車,
Wǒ cháng qí zìxíngchē,

有時候坐公共汽車。
yǒushíhou zuò gōnggòng qìchē.

你呢?
Nǐ ne?

A: 你們怎麼去旅行?
Nǐmen zěnme qù lǚxíng?

B: 我們先坐火車,
Wǒmen xiān zuò huǒchē,

然後坐船去加拿大,
ránhòu zuò chuán qù Jiānádà,

再從加拿大坐飛機回來。
zài cóng Jiānádà zuò fēijī huílai.

課文　Language in Use: 我們要坐火車去旅行 Wǒmen yào zuò huǒchē qù lǚxíng

季長風： 秋影,你住在校外嗎? 離學校遠不遠?
Qiūyǐng, nǐ zhù zài xiàowài ma? Lí xuéxiào yuǎnbuyuǎn?

白秋影： 不太遠,開車只要五分鐘。
Bú tài yuǎn, kāichē zhǐyào wǔ fēnzhōng.

季長風： 你每天怎麼來學校?
Nǐ měitiān zěnme lái xuéxiào?

白秋影： 我常騎自行車,下雨下雪的時候就坐公共汽車,
Wǒ cháng qí zìxíngchē, xiàyǔ xiàxuě de shíhou jiù zuò gōnggòng qìchē,

有時候我也走路,可以鍛煉鍛煉。你呢?
yǒushíhou wǒyě zǒulù, kěyǐ duànlian duànlian. Nǐ ne?

季長風： 我住在宿舍,離學校很近,我每天走路來學校。
Wǒ zhùzài sùshè, lí xuéxiào hěnjìn, wǒ měitiān zǒulù lái xuéxiào.

白秋影： 對了,這個春假你要做什麼?
Duìle, zhège chūnjià nǐ yào zuò shénme?

季長風：　我要跟我的室友一起去西部旅行。
Wǒ yào gēn wǒde shìyǒu yìqǐ qù xībù lǚxíng.

白秋影：　你們怎麼去？
Nǐmen zěnme qù?

季長風：　我們想先坐火車去，路上可以看看風景。
Wǒmen xiǎng xiān zuò huǒchē qù, lùshang kěyǐ kànkan fēngjǐng.

　　　　　然後坐船去加拿大，再從加拿大坐飛機回來。你呢？
Ránhòu zuò chuán qù Jiānádà, zài cóng Jiānádà zuò fēijī huílai. Nǐ ne?

白秋影：　我很想我爸爸、媽媽和妹妹，我要先回家。
Wǒ hěn xiǎng wǒ bàba, māma hé mèimei, wǒ yào xiān huíjiā.

　　　　　然後再跟朋友開車去玩兒。
Ránhòu zài gēn péngyou kāichē qù wár.

季長風：　你們要去哪兒玩兒？
Nǐmen yào qù nǎr wár?

白秋影：　我們想去南部玩兒。聽說那兒的海邊景色很美。
Wǒmen xiǎng qù nánbù wár. Tīngshuō nàr de hǎibiān jǐngsè hěn měi.

季長風：　你們有幾個人去？
Nǐmen yǒu jǐge rén qù?

白秋影：　我們一共有五個人去，我們想租一輛車。
Wǒmen yígòng yǒu wǔge rén qù, wǒmen xiǎng zū yíliàng chē.

注釋　LANGUAGE NOTES

自行車

自行車 means "bicycle." A more colloquial form used mostly in Taiwan is 腳踏車 [jiǎotàchē], and 單車 [dānchē] is also used in Mainland China and Hong Kong. The bicycle is currently the most common means of transportation in China.

公共汽車

公共汽車 means "(public) bus." In Taiwan, it is more commonly called 公車 or 巴士 [bāshì].

路上

路上 is an idiomatic expression commonly used to mean "on the way."

語法　GRAMMAR

離

The verb 離 means "to be away from . . ." It is used in the following pattern:

  A + 離 + B + adjective phrase

For example,　宿舍　離　學校　很近。　The dorm is very close to the school.
　　　　　　中國　離　美國　很遠。　China is very far from the U.S.

Note: While English modifiers of distance such as "very close" and "very far" are placed between the names of two places, Chinese modifiers of distance are placed at the end of the sentence, as shown in the examples above.

先……(再)…… 然後……

Both 先 and 再 are adverbs, but 然後 is a conjunction. All three words are used to show sequence. Look at the following examples:

他先去吃飯，再去圖書館，然後回宿舍。
He first went to eat, then to the library and after that he went back to the dorm.

我先去找老師，然後去看你。
I will go to see the professor first, and then to see you.

Note that when you want to indicate sequence, you must use 先 first, and then 然後. If there are more than two actions involved, you need to use 再 as well. The order of the three expressions can be either 先……, 再……, 然後…… or 先……, 然後…… 再…….
For example, for the sentence "Xiaomei will go to Beijing first, then to Hong Kong, and then to Taiwan to visit her Grandma," the Chinese sentence can be either

　　小美要先去北京，再去香港，然後去台灣看奶奶。
or　小美要先去北京，然後去香港，再去台灣看奶奶。

坐, 騎　and　開

These three verbs are used for different kinds of vehicles:

Verb	Vehicle	Translation
坐 to take, to ride in	汽車	to take (ride in) a car
	長途汽車 [chángtú qìchē]	to take (ride in) a long-distance bus
	出租汽車 [chūzū qìchē] 公共汽車 [gōnggòng qìchē] 火車 飛機	to take (ride in) a taxicab to take (ride in) a (public) bus to take (ride in) a train to take (fly in) an airplane
	輪船 [lúnchuán]	to take a ship
騎 to ride	自行車	to ride a bike
	馬 [mǎ]	to ride a horse
開 to drive	車	to drive a car

補充課文 —◦◦◦— SUPPLEMENTARY PRACTICE

This selection will help you test your comprehension of the grammar and vocabulary you have learned in this lesson. Be prepared to answer questions about the meaning of the passage.

四月十日　　　　　星期六　　　　　晴

　　今天下午我去看大中。他住在校外的公寓裡，他的公寓離學校很近，開車只要五分鐘就到了。他常常騎自行車去學校，有時候也走路，他覺得走路可以鍛煉身體，下雨下雪的時候他就坐公共汽車。

　　大中跟他的室友正在上網。因為他們想在放假的時候一起去西部旅行，所以他們想看看網上有沒有便宜的火車票和飛機票。他們想先坐飛機到舊金山，在舊金山玩兩天，然後坐火車去西雅圖，一路上可以欣賞一下外邊的風景，在西雅圖再玩兩天，然後坐船去加拿大，最後再從加拿大坐飛機回來。

　　我好久沒有回家了，我很想家。放假以後我要先回家，看看我的爸爸、媽媽和妹妹。然後我想租一輛車，跟我的朋友一起開車去南部的海邊玩兒。聽說那兒的風景很美，還可以游泳、曬太陽，所以我想在那兒好好地玩兒幾天再回家。

Notes: 晴 [qíng]: sunny
公寓 [gōngyù]: apartment
便宜 [piányì]: inexpensive
舊金山 [Jiùjīnshān]: San Francisco
西雅圖 [Xīyǎtú]: Seattle
欣賞 [xīnshǎng]: to enjoy
曬太陽 [shàitàiyáng]: to get a suntan
幾: an indefinite pronoun used here to indicate "some"

練習   ACTIVITIES

I. Pinyin Exercises

18-1 Fill in the blanks with the correct Pinyin:

1. Wǒ měitiān _____ lái xuéxiào.

   a. zhǒulú   b. zǒulù   c. zhòunù

2. _____ wǒ yào gēn péngyou _____ qù wár.

   a. Chūnjià/kāichē   b. Cúnjià/kāichē   c. Chǔnjiǎ/kàichē

3. Wǒmen xià _____ xià _____ de shíhou zuò _____ qù xuéxiào.

   a. yù/xuè/gǒnggóng qìchē   b. yú/xuè/gōnggōng qīchē   c. yǔ/xuě/gōnggòng qìchē

4. Dào _____ qù kěyi kàndào hěnduō _____.

   a. xībù/fēngjǐng   b. xíbù/féngjíng   c. xìbù/fēngjìng

5. Wǒ tèbié xǐhuān _____ de _____.

   a. háibiàn/fèngjǐng   b. hāibiǎn/fēngjíng   c. hǎibiān/fēngjǐng

18-2 Read the following poem, paying special attention to the tones and rhythm:

Tí Xīlínbì **(Sū Shì)**	**題西林壁** **(蘇軾)**
Héng kàn chéng lǐng cè chéng fēng, Yuǎn jìn gāo dī gè bùtóng. Bù shí Lúshān zhēn miànmù, Zhǐ yuán shēn zài cǐ shān zhōng.	橫看成嶺側成峰， 遠近高低各不同。 不識廬山真面目， 只緣身在此山中。

Inscription on the Xilin Cliff
(Su, Shi)

Looking transversely we see a mountain ridge and sidewise a peak,
The cliff looks very different from all directions.
The true face of Mount Lushan cannot be seen,
Just because you are in the mountains.

II. Character Exercises

18-3 Read the following words and phrases:

火	走
火車	走路
坐火車	走路去學校
從上海坐火車	我每天走路去學校
從上海坐火車去北京	我每天跟我室友走路去學校
我們想從上海坐火車去北京玩兒	我每天跟我室友走路去學校上課

Now try to use the following characters to make words, phrases, and then sentences:

1. 旅　　2. 離　　3. 遠　　4. 只　　5. 騎　　6. 汽

7. 近　　8. 西　　9. 景　　10. 船　　11. 聽　　12. 租

18-4 Write the following phrases in characters:

1. Zhù zài xiào wài ＿＿＿＿＿＿＿　　2. Zū yíliàng chē＿＿＿＿＿＿＿

3. Zuò fēijī ＿＿＿＿＿＿＿　　4. Qí zìxíngchē ＿＿＿＿＿＿＿

5. Zuò chuán qù wán＿＿＿＿＿＿＿　　6. Xībù fēngjǐng ＿＿＿＿＿＿＿

7. Lí xuéxiào hěnjìn ＿＿＿＿＿＿＿　　8. Kāichē lǚxíng ＿＿＿＿＿＿＿

9. Hǎibiān jǐngsè ＿＿＿＿＿＿＿　　10. Zuò huǒchē ＿＿＿＿＿＿＿

18-5 Group the following characters according to how many components they have:

騎　自　遠　離　風　西　海　租　船　景　近
汽　行　旅　先　路　春　部　雪　假　機　開

1.　　One component

＿＿＿＿＿＿＿＿＿＿＿＿＿＿＿＿＿＿

2.　　Two components

＿＿＿＿＿＿＿＿＿＿＿＿＿＿＿＿＿＿

＿＿＿＿＿＿＿＿＿＿＿＿＿＿＿＿＿＿

＿＿＿＿＿＿＿＿＿＿＿＿＿＿＿＿＿＿

＿＿＿＿＿＿＿＿＿＿＿＿＿＿＿＿＿＿

3.　　Three components

＿＿＿＿＿＿＿＿＿＿＿＿＿＿＿＿＿＿

＿＿＿＿＿＿＿＿＿＿＿＿＿＿＿＿＿＿

III. Grammar Exercises

18-6 Substitution exercises:

1. 宿舍離學校很近。

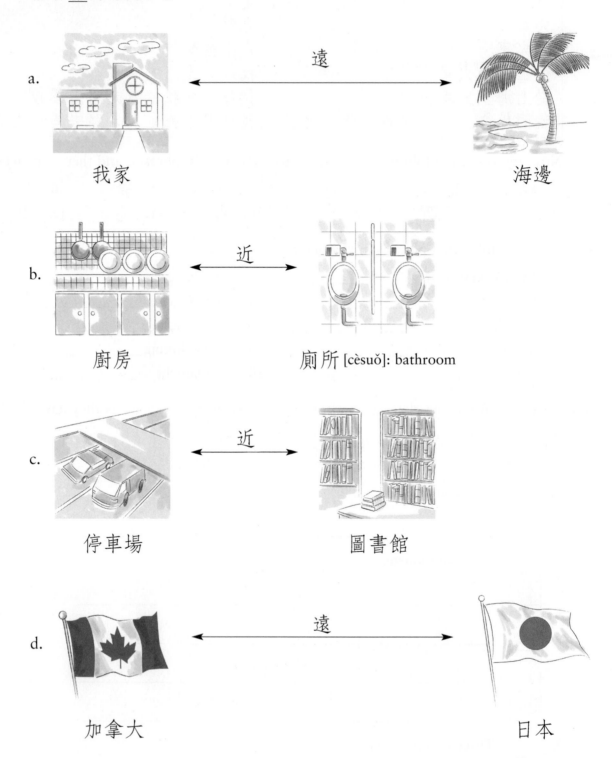

a. 我家   遠   海邊

b. 廚房   近   廁所 [cèsuǒ]: bathroom

c. 停車場   近   圖書館

d. 加拿大   遠   日本

2. 我<u>先</u>去飯館吃飯，<u>再</u>去喝咖啡 [kāfēi]: coffee，<u>然後</u>回家。

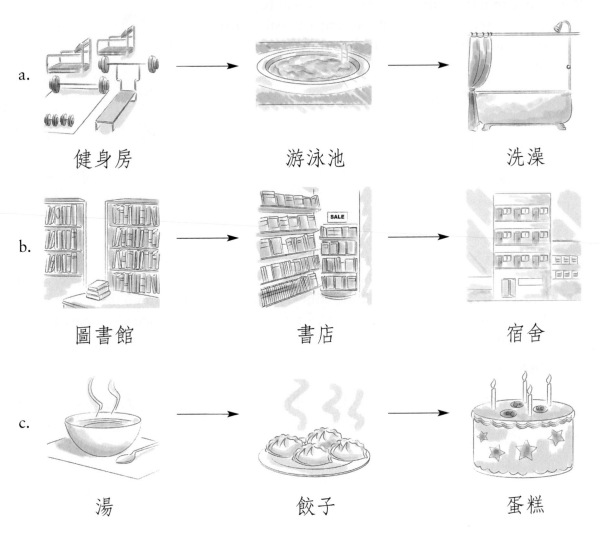

a.　　　健身房　　　　　　游泳池　　　　　　洗澡

b.　　　圖書館　　　　　　書店　　　　　　　宿舍

c.　　　湯　　　　　　　　餃子　　　　　　　蛋糕

18-7 Fill in each blank with 坐, 開, 騎, 租:

1. 我每天 ＿＿＿＿＿＿ 公共汽車來學校。

2. 你 ＿＿＿＿＿＿ 車 ＿＿＿＿＿＿ 得快嗎?

3. A: 他會不會 ＿＿＿＿＿＿ 自行車?

　　B: 會。他 ＿＿＿＿＿＿ 得很好。

4. ＿＿＿＿＿＿ 火車比較慢，可是很舒服。

5. 我們應該 ＿＿＿＿＿＿ 一輛麵包車，我的汽車太小了。

IV. Communicative Activities

18-8 In one month your summer vacation will begin. You and your friend are discussing a possible trip to Canada. Your discussion should include (but not be limited to) the following:

1. Time of the trip

2. Route

3. How to travel

4. Vehicles

18-9 You and a few of your friends are planning to travel during the summer. You are now discussing the specifics of your plan. Form groups of two or three and work out a detailed plan for your travel, including where to go, when to go, how to go, and why. While giving your suggestions, try to refer to your or someone else's past travel experiences.

Useful words and expressions:

離……遠/近， 先……然後……再……， 東/南/西/北部， 只要， 一共， 聽說， 覺得， 坐(船/火車/飛機/出租汽車, etc.)， 風景/景色， 海邊， 租

文化知識 ⟡⟡⟡ Culture Link

文化點滴　CULTURE NOTES

中國的交通標誌與規則
[Zhōngguó de jiāotōng biāozhì yǔ guīzé]
Traffic in China
Traffic Signs and Rules in China

The traffic rules and regulations in China are basically the same as those in other countries of the world. People in China also drive on the right side of the road, as in the U.S.

However, 交通標誌 [jiāotōng biāozhì] (traffic signs) in China are not always the same as those in the U.S. When driving in China, one must pay attention to the following differences.

 Stop signs/Traffic lights: Before stop signs or traffic lights, there is frequently very little warning before the stopping point.

 Pedestrian signs: A series of lines painted in white (like a zebra) on roads indicates a crossing for pedestrians.

 Merge signs: Before the merge point on highways, there are signs indicating 200 meters, 100 meters and 50 meters, informing the driver of the distance to the merge point.

 Street signs: Street name signs in China contain large characters arranged horizontally and are located at each street corner. Most of the signs are made of enamel with a white background and blue Chinese characters.

 Highway signs: The signs for newly built interstate highways in China are all bilingual, in both Chinese and English.

 Speed limit signs: In cities or towns in China, there are no speed limit signs, because drivers are not able to drive their vehicles faster than 50 kph (30 mph) due to the narrow streets or high volume of bicycles and pedestrians in the streets. The speed limit on interstate highways is 80–120 kph (50–75 mph).

Question:

Do you believe Interpretation 1, 2, or 3? Why?

行動吧！ LET'S GO!

. . . .

火車和飛機票 Train and Airplane Tickets

While in China 小謝 took a train and then an airplane to Beijing. Below are his train ticket, airport fee receipt, and boarding pass. Read them and then answer the questions.

火車票　　　　機場管理費收據

飛機登機牌

Useful words and expressions:

(I) 火車(火车):

廣州東(广州东) [Guǎngzhōu dōng]: refers to the East Train Station in Guangzhou city, a city in Guangdong Province in southern China

深圳 [Shēnzhèn]: a city next to Hong Kong in Guangdong Province

全價(全价) [quán jià]: total price

空調(空调) [kōngtiáo]: air conditioning

一等 [yīděng]: first class

軟座(软座) [ruǎnzuò]: soft seat

硬座 [yìngzuò]: hard seat

準高速(准高速) [zhǔn gāosù]: close to high speed

使用 [shǐyòng]: to use

有效 [yǒuxiào]: to be valid

(II) 機場管理費(机场管理费):

民航 [mínháng]: civil aviation

管理 [guǎnlǐ]: to manage, maintain

建設費(建设费) [jiànshè fèi]: development fee

整 [zhěng]: exact

當地(当地) [dāngdì]: this place

當日(当日) [dāngrì]: on this day

(III) 飛機(飞机):

登機牌(登机牌) [dēngjī pái]: boarding pass

到達站(到达站) [dàodá zhàn]: destination

登機口(登机口) [dēngjīkǒu]: gate

航班號 [hángbān hào]: flight number

艙位 [cāngwèi]: class

登機時間(登机时间) [dēngjī shíjiān]: boarding time

日期 [rìqī]: date

座位 [zuòwèi]: seat

登機閘口(登机闸口) [dēngjī zhákǒu]: boarding gate

關閉(关闭) [guānbì]: to close

Questions:

1. 他先從哪兒坐火車到哪兒去，然後他再坐飛機去北京？

2. 火車有空調嗎？他坐的是什麼座 (軟坐還是硬座)？

3. 小謝付了多少錢的機場管理費？

4. 當地、當日的口語怎麼說？

5. 小謝是什麼時候的班機？他的登機口在哪兒？

復習   Review

Conversation

Form pairs and chat about the following topics. Then report the information you collect to the class.

1. 你喜歡這裡的氣候嗎？為什麼？
2. 春夏秋冬四季 [sìjì] (four seasons) 裡面，你比較喜歡哪一個？為什麼？
3. 很快就要放暑假了，你有什麼計劃 [jìhuà] (plan) 呢？
4. 你每天怎麼去學校？坐公車還是開車去？騎自行車還是走路去？
5. 你是不是快要畢業了？你學了很多門課，其中你最喜歡哪一門？為什麼？

Situational Dialogue

Your friend is travelling to China next week. You are planning to see him/her off at the airport. And since you've been to China before, you are going to relate your experience to him/her. Chat about the schedule for the trip the weather, the cities you like and dislike, etc.

Useful expressions:

就/快要...了；   從...到...；   我覺得；   比較/最；
...極了；有沒有；   坐/開車去；   喜歡；   應該

Traditional and Simplified Characters

Read each character aloud. Write its traditional form. Then tell a story (at least five sentences) using the following characters.

For example,   学 → 學 → 學生 → 我是一個學生，我學......

L17: 热 (   )   机 (   )   华 (   )   欢 (   )   会 (   )
L18: 离 (   )   远 (   )   骑 (   )   风 (   )   听 (   )

第十九課
LESSON

19

我感冒了
I Caught a Cold

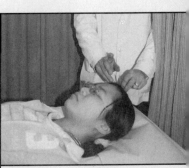

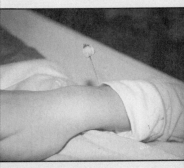

針灸 *[zhēnjiǔ] acupuncture is a popular therapy for curing headache, back pain, joint pain, and arthritis. Treatments are commonly administered at a Chinese medicine hospital.*

腳底按摩 *[jiǎodǐ ànmó] foot massage is believed to be able to detect and cure diseases of the inner organs.*

教學目標 OBJECTIVES

- Describe the symptoms of an illness
- Describe something that has happened

生詞 VOCABULARY

核心詞 Core Vocabulary

	TRADITIONAL	SIMPLIFIED	PINYIN		
1.	感冒	感冒	gǎnmào	N.	cold, flu
2.	餓	饿	è	Adj. V.	hungry to starve
3.	好像	好像	hǎoxiàng	V.	to be like; to seem
4.	舒服	舒服	shūfu	Adj.	comfortable; well
5.	頭疼	头疼	tóuténg	V.	to have a headache
6.	發燒	发烧	fāshāo	V.O.	to have a fever
7.	咳嗽	咳嗽	késòu	V.	to cough
8.	生病	生病	shēngbìng	V.O.	to fall ill
9.	考試	考试	kǎoshì	N.	exam
10.	復習	复习	fùxí	V.	to review
11.	所以	所以	suǒyǐ	Conj.	therefore; consequently
12.	醫生	医生	yīshēng	N.	doctor
13.	吃藥	吃药	chīyào	V.O.	to take medicine
14.	地	地	de	Part.	(attached to an adjective to transform the whole unit into an adverb)
15.	休息	休息	xiūxi	V.	to rest
16.	準備	准备	zhǔnbèi	V.	to prepare
17.	筆記	笔记	bǐjì	N.	notes
18.	感謝	感谢	gǎnxiè	V.	to thank; to be grateful

專名　Proper Nouns

TRADITIONAL	SIMPLIFIED	PINYIN		
1. 歐陽迎	欧阳迎	Ōuyáng Yíng	N.	(name) Ying Ouyang
2. 唐志信	唐志信	Táng Zhìxìn	N.	(name) Zhixin Tang

補充詞　Supplementary Vocabulary

TRADITIONAL	SIMPLIFIED	PINYIN		
1. 醫務室 (醫護室)	医务室 (医护室)	yīwùshì (yīhùshì)	N.	clinic
2. 打針	打针	dǎzhēn	V.O.	to give or receive an injection
3. 護士	护士	hùshi	N.	nurse
4. 醫院	医院	yīyuàn	N.	hospital
5. 診所	诊所	zhěnsuǒ	N.	clinic
6. 嚴重	严重	yánzhòng	Adj.	severe
7. 厲害	厉害	lìhài	Adj.	severely; very much
8. 體溫	体温	tǐwēn	N.	body temperature
9. 流感 (流行性感冒)	流感 (流行性感冒)	liúgǎn (liúxíngxìng gǎnmào)	N.	flu
10. 預防針	预防针	yùfángzhēn	N.	immunization shot
11. 流感疫苗	流感疫苗	liúgǎn yìmiáo	N.	flu shot

語文知識   LANGUAGE LINK

The Sentence Patterns provide models that will help you with the Language in Use section. In both sections, pay attention to the grammar points, vocabulary, and expressions.

句型   Sentence Patterns

A: 你吃飯了嗎?
Nǐ chīfàn le ma?

B: 還沒有呢。我不餓。
Hái méiyǒu ne. Wǒ bú è.

A: 你怎麼了? 好像不舒服。
Nǐ zěnme le? Hǎoxiàng bù shūfu.

B: 我感冒了。我頭疼發燒,
Wǒ gǎnmào le. Wǒ tóuténg fāshāo,

還有一點兒咳嗽。
háiyǒu yìdiǎr késòu.

A: 你看醫生了沒有?
Nǐ kàn yīshēng le méiyǒu?

B: 看了。我也吃藥了。
Kàn le. Wǒ yě chīyào le.

可是還沒有好呢。
Kěshì hái méiyǒu hǎo ne.

課文　Language in Use: 我感冒了 Wǒ gǎnmào le

唐志信：　歐陽迎，你吃飯了嗎？
　　　　　Ōuyáng Yíng, nǐ chīfàn le ma?

歐陽迎：　還沒有呢。我不餓。
　　　　　Hái méiyǒu ne. Wǒ bú è.

唐志信：　你怎麼了？好像不舒服。
　　　　　Nǐ zěnme le? Hǎoxiàng bù shūfu.

歐陽迎：　我感冒了。我頭疼發燒，還有一點兒咳嗽。
　　　　　Wǒ gǎnmào le. Wǒ tóuténg fāshāo, háiyǒu yìdiǎr késòu.

唐志信：　你怎麼生病了呢？
　　　　　Nǐ zěnme shēngbìng le ne?

歐陽迎：　這幾天我有很多考試，每天都在復習，
　　　　　Zhè jǐ tiān wǒ yǒu hěnduō kǎoshì, měitiān dōu zài fùxí,

　　　　　睡覺睡得太少，所以就病了。
　　　　　shuìjiào shuì de tàishǎo, suǒyǐ jiù bìng le.

唐志信：　你看醫生了沒有？
　　　　　Nǐ kàn yīshēng le méiyǒu?

歐陽迎：　看了。我也吃藥了。可是還沒有好呢。
　　　　　Kàn le. Wǒ yě chīyào le. Kěshì hái méiyǒu hǎo ne.

唐志信：　你應該在家好好地休息。不應該來上課。
　　　　　Nǐ yīnggāi zàijiā hǎohǎo de xiūxi. Bù yīnggāi lái shàngkè.

歐陽迎：　你說得很對。可是我有很多考試。我得好好地準備。
　　　　　Nǐ shuō de hěnduì. Kěshì wǒ yǒu hěnduō kǎoshì. Wǒ děi hǎohǎo de zhǔnbèi.

唐志信：　這是我上課的筆記，借給你看看。
　　　　　Zhèshì wǒ shàngkè de bǐjì, jiè gěi nǐ kànkan.

歐陽迎：　非常感謝！好吧，我現在就回家休息。
　　　　　Fēicháng gǎnxiè! Hǎo ba, wǒ xiànzài jiù huíjiā xiūxi.

唐志信：　好，我開車送你回去。你得好好地睡覺。
　　　　　Hǎo, wǒ kāichē sòng nǐ huíqù. Nǐ děi hǎohǎo de shuìjiào.

注釋 LANGUAGE NOTES

怎麼了

怎麼了 is a common phrase meaning "What happened?" "What's wrong?"

生病了

"I am sick" can be expressed by either 我病了 "I am sick" or 我生病了 (literally "I produced sickness").

地

地 [dì] can be a noun meaning "ground, earth" such as in 地圖 and 地址. 地 [de] can also be attached to an adjective to transform the whole unit into an adverb, such as 慢慢地 (slowly).

語法 GRAMMAR

The Aspect Particle 了

The aspect particle 了 is usually used in the following situations:

A. Completion of an action: 了 is placed after a verb or at the end of a sentence to indicate the completion of an action.

了: indicate the completion of an action	Pattern	Example
(1) question	V._了嗎, V._了沒有	你看醫生了嗎? Did you go to see a doctor? 你看醫生了沒有? Did you go to see a doctor?
(2) Positive answer	V. 了, or sentence end 了	我看了醫生。 I saw the doctor. 我看醫生了。 I saw the doctor.
(3) Negative answer	(1) 沒有 V. (to negate a completion aspect, indicating that an action didn't take place) (2) 還沒有 ___ 呢 (to indicate a planned action)	我沒有參加旅行。 I didn't go on the trip. 你們去旅行了嗎? Have you gone on your trip yet? 我們還沒有去旅行呢。 We haven't gone on our trip yet.

- 了 must **not** be regarded as a "past tense" marker. It is an aspect particle indicating action completion. In Chinese, to indicate the present, past, and future tenses, time words are often used, such as 去年, 現在, and 明天.
- Note that 了 is not used in negations in the completion of an action usage.
- Note that when 了 is followed by a quantified object, it is preferred to place 了 after the verb.

  e.g., 我看了兩次醫生。
  e.g., 我買了三本中文書。

B. New situation: 了 is also used at the end of a sentence to express a situation that has changed.

	Pattern	Example
了: new situation	Sentence end 了	你會開車了嗎? Do you know how to drive? 我會開車了。 I can drive now.
	不… V. 了 (not doing V. any more)	他不吸煙 [xīyān] 了。 He does not smoke any more. 他不喝酒了。 He does not drink any more.

Note: When 了 is placed at the end of a sentence, it may be used to indicate the completion of an action or the change of a situation. For example, the sentence 他去北京了 can mean "He went to Beijing" (i.e., he did the action) or "He is in Beijing now", depending on the context.

的, 得, and 地

的, 得, and 地 are all pronounced as [de] but have different meanings and functions.

Pattern	Features	Examples
的 + N.	Possessive, structure 的	我的車 my car 上課的筆記 notes taken in class 他是一個認真的學生。 He is a conscientious student.
V. + 得 + Adv./Adj.	Used in a degree of complement sentences	他說中文說得很快。 He speaks Chinese very fast. 他寫漢字寫得很認真。 He writes the characters conscientiously.
Adj. + 地	Manner adverbial, combines with an adjective, similar to "-ly" in English, used before a verb to indicate the attitude or manner of an action	他慢慢地吃飯。 He eats slowly. 他認真地寫漢字。 He writes the characters conscientiously.

Notes: 認真 [rènzhēn]: conscientious; serious
　　　　漢字 [hànzì]: Chinese characters

補充課文 ⚬⚬⚬ SUPPLEMENTARY PRACTICE

This selection will help you test your comprehension of the grammar and vocabulary you have learned in this lesson. Be prepared to answer questions about the meaning of the passage.

　　歐陽迎是我中文班的同學。今天她好像有點兒不舒服,臉色很不好,中飯也沒有吃,原來她感冒了。又是頭疼又是發燒,還有一點兒咳嗽。

　　這幾天她太忙了。這個學期她選了六門課,每門課都有很多功課,前幾天剛寫完了兩個報告,還有幾個考試。每天晚上她都要開夜車,復習到很晚,睡覺睡得太少,每天平均才睡四個小時。這兩天天氣也不太好,一會兒熱,一會兒冷,又常常下雨,所以她感冒了。

　　我想送她去醫院,她說前天她已經看了醫生,也吃了點兒藥。醫生說她應該在家裡好好地休息,多喝水,多睡覺。可是她得準備考試,沒有時間休息,所以她的病好得很慢。我覺得她應該好好地睡一覺。我告訴她我有上課的筆記,可以借給她。然後我就開車送她回家了,我也給她買了一些吃的東西,她非常感激。

Notes: 臉色 [liǎnsè]: complexion
原來 [yuánlái]: It turned out that . . . ; apparently
報告 [bàogào]: report
開夜車 [kāiyèchē]: to burn the midnight oil
平均 [píngjūn]: on average
醫院 [yīyuàn]: hospital
感激 [gǎnjī]: to appreciate

練習 ACTIVITIES

I. Pinyin Exercises

19-1 Listen to the instructor. Mark "√" if the Pinyin is correct, or write the correct Pinyin if it is incorrect.

1. gǎngmào _____	2. shūfù _____	3. tóuténg _____
4. késuò _____	5. kǒushì _____	6. shēngbìn _____
7. zhǔnbèi _____	8. yìshēng _____	9. xūxi _____
10. yánzhèng _____	11. chīyòu _____	12. suǒyǐ _____

19-2 Fill in each blank with the correct Pinyin:

1. 暖和 ____   老師和學生 ____
2. 地圖 ____   好好地休息 ____
3. 睡覺 ____   覺得 ____
4. 得去接人 ____   游泳游得很快 ____
5. 教中文 ____   籃球教練 ____

19-3 Read the following Chinese poem, paying special attention to the tones and rhythm:

Xún Yǐnzhě Bú Yù (**Jiǎ Dǎo**)	**尋隱者不遇** (賈島)
Sōng xià wèn tóngzǐ, Yán shī cǎi yào qù. Zhǐ zài cǐ shān zhōng, Yún shēn bù zhī chù.	松下問童子, 言師採藥去。 只在此山中, 雲深不知處。

Seeking the Hermit but Not Found
(**Jia, Dao**)

Beneath a pine tree I inquire of a young servant,
He says his master has gone to collect herbs.
"He is somewhere in the mountains,
But I can't tell where he is for the clouds are so deep."

II. Character Exercises

19-4 Read the following words, phrases, and sentences:

像	地
好像	好好地
好像病了	好好地休息
好像生病了	應該好好地休息
怎麼好像生病了	應該在家好好地休息
怎麼好像生病了呢	我覺得你應該在家好好地休息

Now try to use the following characters to make words, phrases, and then sentences:

1. 感　　2. 餓　　3. 舒　　4. 疼　　5. 燒　　6. 咳

7. 病　　8. 考　　9. 所　　10. 準　　11. 醫　　12. 記

19-5 Write down the simplified forms for the following traditional characters.

1. 餓 _____　　2. 頭 _____　　3. 發 _____　　4. 燒 _____

5. 復 _____　　6. 準 _____　　7. 備 _____　　8. 醫 _____

9. 藥 _____　　10. 筆 _____　　11. 還 _____　　12. 記 _____

III. Grammar Exercises

19-6 Substitution exercises:

1. 你吃飯了嗎?
   我還沒有吃飯呢。

看球賽
跟朋友見面
坐火車去玩兒
去機場接妹妹
買襯衫
參加晚會

2. 你打電話了沒有?
   我打電話了。

知道	怎麼去機場
看	電影
回	宿舍
打	籃球
包	餃子

3. 你會<u>游泳</u>了嗎?
   我會<u>游泳</u>了。

說中文
騎自行車
做中國菜
用電腦
寫漢字

Notes: 電腦 [diànnǎo]: computer
　　　　漢字 [hànzì]: Chinese characters

4. **A:** <u>你</u><u>做作業</u>了嗎?
   B: <u>我</u><u>做</u>了。你呢?
   A: <u>我</u>(還)沒有<u>做</u>。

王老師	教第二十課	李老師
你爸爸	去北京	你哥哥
你的朋友	吃藥	他的朋友
媽媽	吃飯	姐姐
妹妹	睡覺	弟弟

19-7 Fill in the blanks with 的, 得, or 地:

1. 那個穿紅色裙子 ＿＿＿ 人是我妹妹。
2. 他很快 ＿＿＿ 吃了飯。
3. 這個公園 ＿＿＿ 景色很美。
4. 我的德文說 ＿＿＿ 不好。
5. 考試以後我要好好 ＿＿＿ 玩玩。
6. 小文走路走 ＿＿＿ 很慢。

19-8 Form pairs.

1. Take turns reading the following passage.
2. Take turns asking and answering the questions.

田進：　　明明，你學開車了沒有?
方明明：　我還沒有學呢。你教我怎麼樣?
田進：　　行，沒問題。
方明明：　對了，昨天我給你打電話了，可是你不在。
田進：　　我去參加晚會了。
方明明：　什麼晚會?
田進：　　中文課的中文晚會。
方明明：　我忘了! 你們都做了什麼?
田進：　　我們吃餃子，<u>唱歌</u>，<u>跳舞</u>，還看了<u>功夫表演</u>。
　　　　　很有意思。
方明明：　你們唱中文歌了嗎?
田進：　　唱了，還是<u>新</u>的<u>流行歌曲</u>呢!

方明明：　你會唱中國歌了沒有？
田　進：　　我會了。我們還看了一個叫《英雄》的中國電影。
　　　　　　棒極了！
方明明：　你們喝啤酒了沒有？
田　進：　　以前我喜歡喝啤酒，可是我女朋友不喜歡我喝酒，
　　　　　　所以我現在已經不喝了。

Useful words:

忘 [wàng]: forget　　　　　　　　酒 [jiǔ]: wine, alcoholic beverage
唱歌 [chànggē]: to sing　　　　　功夫 [gōngfu]: martial arts
跳舞 [tiàowǔ]: to dance　　　　　流行歌曲 [liúxíng gēqǔ]: popular songs
表演 [biǎoyǎn]: to perform; performance　以前 [yǐqián]: before
新 [xīn]: new　　　　　　　　　　已經 [yǐjīng]: already
英雄 [yīngxióng]: hero

Questions:

1. 他們是誰？
2. 方明明要田進教他什麼？
3. 田進昨天為什麼 [wèishénme] (why) 不在家？
4. 他們在中文晚會做了什麼？
5. 田進會唱中國歌了嗎？
6. 他們看了什麼電影？
7. 電影怎麼樣？
8. 田進以前喜歡做什麼？現在呢？為什麼？

IV. Communicative Activities

19-9 Situational dialogues:

Situation 1:

Your roommate has just come back from a trip to China.
Please chat with him/her about his/her experience.

Hints:

1. Topics to cover:
   - Greetings.
   - Discuss your roommate's impression of China.
   - Talk about your roommate's experience in China,
     including eating, seeing different scenic spots,
     shopping for clothes or gifts.

2. Words and expressions to use:

怎麼樣?　　　　……了嗎/了沒有?
覺得　　　想　　吃/參觀/買...了

Situation 2:

Your classmate has been practicing for a basketball game for several days. Because the weather has been cold and he/she didn't wear warm clothes after practice, he/she caught a cold. Ask about your classmate's illness.

Hints:

1. Topics to cover:
   • Greetings.
   • Ask what is the matter when you see that your classmate doesn't look well.
   • Show your concern and give suggestions.

2. Words and expressions to use:

怎麼了　　　　是不是……　　　　……了嗎/了沒有?
打球……得　　沒有很快……穿　暖和　衣服　　　所以
藥　　　　　　醫生　　　　　　　想……　　　　應該……

Situation 3:

You return from a Chinese student's party, and your friend asks about it. Give your friend some information about the party.

Hints:

1. Topics to cover:
   • Greetings.
   • Tell him/her about your new Chinese friends.
   • Describe what you did at the party.

2. Words and expressions to use:

參加　　介紹　　中國學生　　認識　　中國朋友
中國菜　　包　　餃子　　　　電影　　了

文化知識 ∞∞∞ Culture Link

文化點滴　CULTURE NOTES

中醫中藥 [Zhōngyī Zhōngyào]
Traditional Chinese Medicine and Pharmacology

Traditional Chinese medicine and pharmacology form a unique scientific system. In ancient times, traditional medicine and drugs were the only means to treat illnesses and protect the health of Chinese people. Today, many Chinese still have faith in traditional Chinese medicine and pharmacology, even though Western medicine has been practiced in China for years. Some believe that traditional Chinese medicine provides permanent cure for an illness, while Western medicine merely alleviates the symptoms.

Traditional Chinese medicine and pharmacology, taking the ancient Daoist ideas of 陰陽 [yīnyáng] (yin-yang) and 五行 [wǔxíng] (wu xing: the five elements) as a theoretical basis, strive to explain the various physiological and pathological phenomena and their interactions. Together, these ideas form a complete scientific system, unique in both theory and practice, containing interconnected elements of physiology, pathology, and pharmacology for the prevention, diagnosis, and treatment of diseases.

The Daoist 陰陽 concept has become the theoretical premise of traditional Chinese medicine. According to the 陰陽 concept, excitement suggests that the human body is in the state of 陽, while the state of 陰 inevitably results in depression. 陽 predominates during the day and turns into 陰 after dark. The human body is regarded as the universe in miniature. When the 陰 and 陽 elements in a person's body are well balanced, the person is in good health. A person falls sick when the balance is disrupted.

Like the 陰陽 concept, the concept of 五行 constitutes a fundamental theoretical premise of traditional Chinese medicine. Each vital organ of the human body is seen as belonging, by nature, to one of the five elements: earth, wood, metal, fire, and water. The five vital organs, the heart, the liver, the spleen, the lungs, and the kidneys are interlocked in a generative-subjugating relationship. It is believed that a pathological change in any of the vital organs will result in an abnormal function of other organs.

Street-side traditional Chinese pharmacies are common in China.
The concepts of 陰 [yīn], 陽 [yáng], and the balance of 氣 [qì] are the essence of Chinese medicine.

Chinese herbal medicine is becoming popular outside Chinese communities.

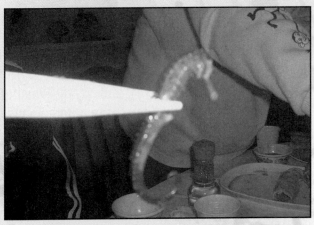

The sea horse is an ingredient used in Chinese medicine.

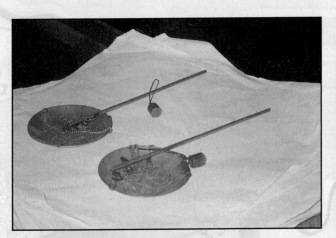

A tiny balancing scale is used to measure the herbal ingredients in Chinese medicine. The white square paper sheets are commonly used to wrap the ingredients after weighing.

A mortar and pestle are used to grind the medicine or mix the ingredients.

The traditional Chinese pharmacy consists mainly of natural medicinal materials — plants, animal parts, minerals of medicinal value, some chemical compounds, and biological drugs. For over 4,000 years, Chinese people have used herbal medicine to treat diseases. Hundreds of pharmacological works were compiled in ancient times and the most important is 本草綱目 [Běncǎogāngmù] (The Compendium of Material Medica) by 李時珍 [Lǐ Shízhēn] (Li, Shizhen) (1518–1593) of the Ming Dynasty. So far, specialists in traditional Chinese medicine have identified the therapeutic value of more than 8,000 medicinal materials, of which over 6,000 are plants.

Traditional Chinese medicine attaches great importance to the prevention of diseases, and Chinese people believe prevention of diseases is more important than treatment. To live a long, healthy life, Chinese people are faithful to traditional ways of maintaining physical and mental soundness by leading a regulated life, eating the type of diet that best fits their body conditions, and doing 氣功 [qìgōng] (*qigong*), 太極拳 [tàijíquán] (*tai chi*), and 武術 [wǔshù] (*martial arts*) exercises. 氣功 is a general term referring to different sets of regulated and controlled breathing exercises and is generally believed to allow the body and mind to regulate their functions in a completely natural state of relaxation and ease. 武術, or 功夫 [gōngfu] (*kung fu*) as it is better known in the West, was in fact a kind of martial art for hand-to-hand combat in ancient times. In modern times, however, people practice 武術 just for exercise. 武術 and 氣功 are closely linked, hence the saying "without proper training in 氣功, one will never master the art of 武術." A typical example of this combination is the Chinese shadow boxing known as 太極拳, which features high concentration of the mind and slow, regulated breathing accompanying rhythmical motions of the arms, legs, and body.

The other important way Chinese people keep fit is to cook food with herbs. This is sometimes called 食療 [shíliáo] "treatment of diseases by food." For example, pears steamed with crystal rock sugar can cure bronchitis. Of course, acupuncture and moxibustion are also major ways of treating illnesses in traditional Chinese medicine.

Questions:

1. What's your opinion about the Daoist concept and traditional Chinese medicine?

2. Have you ever tried traditional Chinese medicine? Did it work?

3. Do you practice martial arts (kung fu) or any other hand-to-hand combat skill, e.g., boxing, karate, tae kwon do, tai chi, judo . . . ? Why?

4. Do you know any 食補 [shí bǔ] ("treatment of diseases by food") recipes?

趣味中文　FUN WITH CHINESE

良藥苦口，忠言逆耳。
Good medicines are bitter, good advice is never pleasant to the ear.

liáng	yào	kǔ	kǒu,	zhōng	yán	nì	ěr.
良	藥	苦	口，	忠	言	逆	耳。
good	medicine	bitter	mouth,	loyal	words	against	ear.

良藥苦口

忠言逆耳

Question:

Do you believe "良藥苦口，忠言逆耳"? Why or why not?

行動吧！　LET'S GO!

西瓜霜潤喉片
Watermelon Frost Throat Lozenges

When 王中 visited his relatives in Beijing he got a sore throat. His aunt gave him some medicine. Let's study it.

Suggested procedure:

(1) Skim through to see how much of it you can understand.
(2) Study the useful words and expressions and then try to translate them into English.
(3) What are the spoken forms of items such as 良, 與, 服藥, 含服, 至, etc.?
(4) Use your own words to retell the information. Try to use spoken forms instead of written forms.

Useful words and expressions:

西瓜 [xīguā]: watermelon

中藥(中药) [zhōngyào]: Chinese medicine

潤喉片(润喉片) [rùnhóu piàn]: throat lozenge

品種(品种) [pǐnzhǒng]: variety, assortment

咽喉 [yānhóu]: throat

良藥(良药) [liángyào]: good medicine

與 [yǔ]: (written form) and

雙重(双重) [shuāngchóng]: double

霜 [shuāng]: frost

名牌 [míngpái]: famous brand

產品(产品) [chǎnpǐn]: product

國家(国家) [guójiā]: country, nation

保護(保护) [bǎohù]: to protect

新一代 [xīnyídài]: new generation

口腔 [kǒuqiāng]: oral cavity

治療(治疗) [zhìliáo]: to treat, cure

預防(预防) [yùfáng]: to prevent

作用 [zuòyòng]: effect

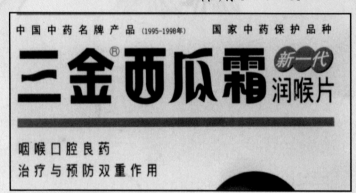

(5) Translate the information below into English:

New words:

主要 [zhǔyào]: main

薄荷腦(薄荷脑) [bòhenǎo]: menthol; peppermint camphor

利 [lì]: to benefit

消腫(消肿) [xiāozhǒng]: to reduce the swelling

嘶啞(嘶哑) [sīyǎ]: hoarse

用量 [yòngliàng]: dosage

服 [fú]: to take (medicine)

成分 [chéngfèn] ingredient

功能 [gōngnéng]: function

主治 [zhǔzhì]: main cure

咽 [yàn]: to swallow

止痛 [zhǐtòng]: to relieve pain

防治 [fángzhì]: to prevent

用法 [yòngfǎ]: usage

含 [hán]: to keep in the mouth

a. 主要成分：西瓜霜，冰片，薄荷腦等

b. 功能主治：清音利咽，消腫止痛，用於防治咽喉腫痛，聲音嘶啞，喉嚨痛等

c. 用法用量：含服，每小時含二至四片

我把小謝帶來了...
I've Brought Xiao Xie Over . . .

- Rent an apartment
- Indicate the direction of a movement
- Describe an event and its cause

Safe and peaceful residence, special phone line: 9310278, apartment building management and maintenance company

She wants to walk over.
她想走過去。（走 [zǒu] to walk）

Warm-up Exercises:

琳琳寶寶 [Línlin bǎobao] (Baby Linlin) on the move. You will learn to use directional complements (see grammar notes) to describe what 琳琳寶寶 can do or wants to do. Instructor may lead the students (use the grammar notes as a reference) to say these actions, then students may try on their own. For example, photo (1) 站: 她想站起來 。

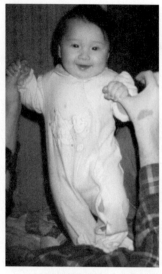

(1) Stand up (站 [zhàn] to stand)

(2) Walk over (走 [zǒu] to walk)

(3) Crawl over (爬 [pá] to crawl)

(4) Slide down (滑 [huá] to slide)

(5) Crawl in and out (爬 [pá] to crawl)

(6) Jump on (跳 [tiào] to jump)

(7) Run back and forth (跑 [pǎo] to run)

(8) It's such fun she doesn't want to come down.

Now try to use 把 [bǎ] and directional complements to describe what 琳琳寶寶 does below:

(9) **Put stuff in her mouth** (放 [fàng] to put)

(10) **Pick up the shoes and put them on** (撿 [jiǎn] to pick; 穿 [chuān] to put on)

(11) **Hold the cup and drink the water** (拿 [ná] to hold; 喝 [hē] to drink)

(12) **Push little sister back and forth** (推 [tuī] to push)

生詞 VOCABULARY

核心詞 Core Vocabulary

	TRADITIONAL	SIMPLIFIED	PINYIN		
1.	把	把	bǎ	Prep.	(introduces the object of a verb)
2.	帶來	带来	dàilái	V.C.	to bring over
3.	啊	啊	a	Int.	(used at the end of a sentence to indicate surprise)
4.	進	进	jìn	V.	to enter
5.	搬	搬	bān	V.	to move
6.	出	出	chū	V.	to be out
7.	出去	出去	chūqù	V.C.	to go out
8.	過來	过来	guòlái	V.C.	to come over
9.	做飯	做饭	zuòfàn	V.O.	to cook
10.	吸煙	吸烟	xīyān	V.O.	to smoke
11.	沒關係	没关系	méiguānxi		no problem
12.	以前	以前	yǐqián	N.	before; previously
13.	但是	但是	dànshì	Conj.	but
14.	女朋友	女朋友	nǚpéngyou	N.	girlfriend
15.	必須	必须	bìxū	Aux.	must
16.	第一天	第一天	dìyītiān	N.	first day
17.	付	付	fù	V.	to pay
18.	房租	房租	fángzū	N.	rent
19.	樓上	楼上	lóushàng	N.	upstairs
20.	馬上	马上	mǎshàng	Adv.	immediately

專名 Proper Nouns

TRADITIONAL	SIMPLIFIED	PINYIN		
1. 常天	常天	Cháng Tiān	N.	(name) Tian Chang
2. 夏中明	夏中明	Xià Zhōngmíng	N.	(name) Zhongming Xia
3. 謝進學	谢进学	Xiè Jìnxué	N.	(name) Jinxue Xie

補充詞 Supplementary Vocabulary

TRADITIONAL	SIMPLIFIED	PINYIN		
1. 房東	房东	fángdōng	N.	landlord
2. 房客	房客	fángkè	N.	tenant
3. 簽約	签约	qiānyuē	V.O.	to sign a contract
4. 租屋	租屋	zūwū	V.O.	to rent a house

語文知識 LANGUAGE LINK

The Sentence Patterns provide models that will help you with the Language in Use section. In both sections, pay attention to the grammar points, vocabulary, and expressions.

句型 Sentence Patterns

A: 我把我朋友帶來了。
Wǒ bǎ wǒ péngyou dài lái le.

B: 快請他進來。
Kuài qǐng tā jìnlái.

A: 我們這兒有一個人搬出去了，
Wǒmen zhèr yǒu yíge rén bān chūqù le,

你要不要搬進來？
nǐ yàobuyào bān jìnlái?

B: 太好了！我可以先過去看看嗎？
Tài hǎo le! Wǒ kěyǐ xiān guòqù kànkan ma?

A: 請你下來幫我把桌子
Qǐng nǐ xiàlái bāng wǒ bǎ zhuōzi

搬上去，好嗎?
bān shàngqu, hǎo ma?

B: 好的，我馬上下去。
Hǎo de, wǒ mǎshàng xiàqu.

課文   Language in Use: 我把小謝帶來了... Wǒ bǎ Xiǎo Xiè dài lái le ...

常天: 中明，我回來了。我把車開回來了，還把小謝也帶來了。
Zhōngmíng, wǒ huílái le. Wǒ bǎ chē kāi huílái le, hái bǎ Xiǎo Xiè yě dàilái le.

夏中明: 是小謝啊! 快請他進來。
Shì Xiǎo Xiè a! Kuài qǐng tā jìnlái.

謝進學: 我聽說你們這兒有一個人搬出去了，我想搬進來，
Wǒ tīngshuō nǐmen zhèr yǒu yíge rén bān chūqù le, wǒ xiǎng bān jìnlái,

所以過來看看。
suǒyǐ guòlái kànkan.

常天: 你不想住宿舍了，是不是?
Nǐ bù xiǎng zhù sùshè le, shìbushì?

謝進學: 是的。宿舍太小了，我想搬出來住。這兒可以不可以做飯?
Shì de. Sùshè tài xiǎo le, wǒ xiǎng bān chūlái zhù. Zhèr kěyǐbukěyǐ zuòfàn?

夏中明: 可以，我們有廚房。
Kěyǐ, wǒmen yǒu chúfáng.

謝進學: 太好了! 我很喜歡做飯。搬出來以後就可以常常
Tài hǎo le! Wǒ hěn xǐhuān zuòfàn. Bān chūlái yǐhòu jiù kěyǐ chángcháng

做飯了。
zuòfàn le.

夏中明: 你吸煙嗎? 我們這兒不能吸煙。
Nǐ xīyān ma? Wǒmen zhèr bùnéng xīyān.

謝進學： 沒關係。以前我吸煙，但是我女朋友說我不應該吸煙，
　　　　 Méiguānxi. Yǐqián wǒ xīyān, dànshì wǒ nǚpéngyou shuō wǒ bù yīnggāi xīyān,

　　　　 所以我現在不吸煙了。
　　　　 suǒyǐ wǒ xiànzài bù xīyān le.

夏中明： 還有，我們必須在每個月的第一天付房租。
　　　　 Háiyǒu, wǒmen bìxū zài měigeyuè de dìyītiān fù fángzū.

謝進學： 沒問題！
　　　　 Méi wèntí!

常天： 喂，小謝，我在樓上，你要不要上來看看？中明，
　　　　 Wèi, Xiǎo Xiè, wǒ zài lóushàng, nǐ yàobuyào shànglái kànkan? Zhōngmíng,

　　　　 你把小謝帶上來看看吧。
　　　　 nǐ bǎ Xiǎo Xiè dài shànglái kànkan ba.

夏中明： 常天，我們現在還不能上去。你得先下來幫我把
　　　　 Chángtiān, wǒmen xiànzài hái bùnéng shàngqu. Nǐ děi xiān xiàlái bāng wǒ bǎ

　　　　 這張桌子搬上去。
　　　　 zhèzhāng zhuōzi bān shàngqu.

常天： 好的，我馬上下去。
　　　　 Hǎode, wǒ mǎshàng xiàqu.

注釋 LANGUAGE NOTES

小謝

小謝 literally means "Little Xie." Here it refers to 謝進學.
In Mainland China, 老 (old) or 小 (young, little) + surname is a friendly and informal way to address familiar people who are older or younger than you.

吸煙

吸煙 [xīyān] and 抽煙 [chōuyān] are both common terms used for "smoke a cigarette."

但是　and　可是

Both 但是 and 可是 mean "but." 可是 is more colloquial than 但是.

必須

必須 is an optative verb meaning "must," "be required to."

序數

第 is used for ordinal numbers. For example, 第一 (the first), 第二 (the second), 第三 (the third), and 第一天 (the first day).

語法 GRAMMAR

Directional Complement　趨向補語 (DC)

A. The simple directional complement (simple DC)

來 and 去 are often attached to a verb to form a simple directional complement to indicate the direction of a motion. When the motion is towards the speaker, 來 is used. When the motion is away from the speaker, 去 is used. The following are some examples of simple directional complements.

Motion verbs + 來/去

Motion verbs	上 upward	下 downward	進 enter	出 outward	回 return	過 cross	起 up	搬 move	帶 take with
來	上來	下來	進來	出來	回來	過來	起來	搬來	帶來
去	上去	下去	進去	出去	回去	過去		搬去	帶去

- 起 can only be combined with 來, forming 起來

Verb + Object (e.g., place, people) + 來/去

他<u>回</u>宿舍<u>去</u>了。
你們都<u>進</u>客廳<u>去</u>吧！
我<u>帶</u>我女朋友<u>來</u>了。

B. Compound directional complement (Compound DC)

The simple directional complements 上來(去), 下來(去), 進來(去), 出來(去), 回來(去), 過來(去), and 起來 may be attached to other verbs to function as complements indicating the direction of movement. They are called compound directional complements.

Their combination possibilities are illustrated below:

Common action verbs:			
走 [zǒu] to walk	跑 [pǎo] to run	跳 [tiào] to jump	坐 [zuò] to sit
站 [zhàn] to stand	搬 [bān] to move	帶 [dài] to bring	
拿 [ná] to take	掉 [diào] to fall	撿 [jiǎn] to pick	
上來/上去：	坐上來	坐下去	跑上來	跑下去	
下來/下去：	走下來	走下去	跳下來	跳下去	掉下去
進來/進去：	走進來	走進去	拿進來	拿進去	
出來/出去：	搬出來	搬出去	帶進來	帶出去	
回來/回去：	跑回來	拿回來	跑回去	拿回去	
過來/過去：	帶過來	搬過來	帶過去	搬過去	
起來：	站起來	跳起來	拿起來	撿起來	

- The verbs such as 走, 跑, 跳, 拿 (walk, run, jump, pick) state the action.
- The simple directional complement indicates the direction of the action in relation to a location. It also can indicate the direction of the motion towards or away from the speaker.

Verb + Object (e.g., person, thing) + simple DC

他	要搬	桌子	過來。
Subject	V.	Object	simple DC

他	帶	一瓶酒	回來	了。
	V.			

Note: 起來 has an idiomatic usage. Its object should be placed as below:

他<u>拿起來</u>一本書。
他<u>拿起</u>書<u>來</u>。

把　Sentences

把 sentences are used to stress the effects of an action upon its object. Their structure is illustrated below:

Subject + 把 + Object + Verb-complement

The following are some characteristics of 把 sentences:

- Used most often with action verbs.
- The object must be definite.
- The verb must incorporate a complement.
- Commonly occurs in imperative sentences. For example, 把飯吃了！(Eat your meal!); 把他帶來！(Bring him over!); 把車開回來！(Drive the car back!)
- The common complements involved with 把 structures are:

  a. degree of complement 他把這個字寫得很好。
  b. 了 may be used as complement for a 把 structure to indicate completion of an action. 我把湯喝了。
  c. directional complement 我要把那張桌子搬過去。
  d. resultative complement (will be introduced later) 他把我的杯子打破 [dǎpò] (break) 了。
  e. duration and frequency complements (will be introduced later) 他把這個漢字寫了十遍。

把　Sentences and the Directional Complement

Group A	Group B
我帶來我的室友了。	我把我室友帶來了。
我搬來那張桌子了。	我把那張桌子搬來了。
我帶我的手機過去了。	我把我的手機帶過去了。

- With the directional complement, if there is a definite object of the action, the 把 structure (Group B) is preferred.
- The examples in Group A are not often used. They simply describe an event. However, the examples in Group B also imply that the location of the object has been changed due to (related to) the subject. That is, the subject is the cause of the change.

把　Construction

The 把 construction is also called a "disposal" construction. That is, the 把 sentence usually indicates that the object is disposed of, dealt with, or affected by the subject. Choosing a 把 construction or a non- 把 construction is not an easy task. However, there are some guidelines listed below:

I. Situations in which the 把 construction is usually **preferred**:

1. The speaker wants to emphasize that an action has caused the object to change position or change from one state to another.

e.g., (a) 我吃了那包藥。　　　I took that medicine.
　　　(b) 我把那包藥吃了。　　I took that medicine.

Example (a) is a simple statement of fact. Example (b) emphasizes that the medicine has been taken by the subject and is gone.

2. If there is a long or complicated direct object, a 把 construction is preferred.

　　e.g., 我把我媽媽昨天從藥房買回來的那包藥吃了。

3. The 把 construction is preferred in imperative sentences (commands).

　　e.g., 把那包藥吃了!

II. Situations in which the 把 construction is obligatory
(there is no corresponding non- 把 construction):

---

1. With some resultative complements (結果補語) (introduced in a later lesson).

　　Subject 把 Object V. + 成 (into/to); V. + 做 (as); V. + 在; V. + 到

　　e.g., 寫成 [xiěchéng]: to write A as B
　　　他把那個故事寫成小說了。　　　He wrote that story as a novel.

　　e.g., 當做 [dàngzuò]: to treat as
　　　我把她當作自己的女兒。　　　I treated her as my own daughter.

　　e.g., 停在 [tíngzài]: to park
　　　我把我的車停在河邊。　　　I parked my car by the river.

　　e.g., 放到 [fàngdào]: to put, place
　　　我把你的書放到桌上。　　　I placed your book on the desk.

2. If a sentence has a plural object and the adverb 都, the 把 construction must be used.

　　e.g., 我把我們的書都賣 [mài] (to sell) 了。　　I sold all our books.

III. Verbs that cannot be used in the 把 construction:

There are certain verbs that do not allow a "disposal" explanation. Therefore they cannot be used in the 把 construction. The following is a sample list of verbs that are incompatible with the 把 construction:

1. Intransitive verbs: 來 (to come), 去 (to go), 跑 (to run), 走 (to walk), 旅行 (to travel), 畢業 (to graduate), 工作 (to work), 站 (to stand), 坐 (to sit)

2. Existence verbs: 是 (to be), 在 (to be at), 有 (to have)

3. Emotion verbs: 喜歡 (to like), 愛 (to love), 怕 [pà] (to fear)

4. Sensory perception verbs: 會 (to be able to), 知道 (to know), 認識 (to recognize), 覺得 [juéde] (to think, to feel), 希望 [xīwàng] (to hope), 看見 [kànjiàn] (to see), 聽見 [tīngjiàn] (to hear)

5. Others: 歡迎 (to welcome), 贊成 [zànchéng] (to approve)

補充課文 ⟨⚬⚬⚬⟩ SUPPLEMENTARY PRACTICE

This selection will help you test your comprehension of the grammar and vocabulary you have learned in this lesson. Be prepared to answer questions about the meaning of the passage.

四月二十日　　　　　星期三　　　　　多雲

今天常天開車把我帶到他住的地方去了。他和夏中明一起住在校外的一個公寓樓裡。前幾天他們樓上有一個人搬出去了，昨天常天把這個消息告訴了我。我很想去看看，如果那兒很好，我也想搬過去。我不想住在宿舍裡了。宿舍太小，又不能做飯。我喜歡自己做飯，我做飯也做得很好。

中明告訴我他們那兒有廚房，常天把我帶上去看了一下，我覺得還不錯，不大也不小，也很乾淨。中明還告訴我他們那兒不能吸煙。不過這對我來說沒關係，因為我現在已經不吸煙了。其實吸煙真的很不好，我女朋友也說我不應該吸煙，所以我就把煙戒了。

常天說他們必須每個月的第一天付房租，這也沒問題，我一定會按時付房租的。

我想明天給房東打電話，希望我能早一點兒搬過去。

Notes: 多雲 [duōyún]: cloudy
　　　　對我來說 [duì wǒ lái shuō]: to me
　　　　沒關係 [méiguānxi]: it doesn't matter
　　　　其實 [qíshí]: as a matter of fact
　　　　戒(煙) [jiè(yān)]: to quit (smoking)
　　　　按時 [ànshí]: on time, punctually
　　　　房東 [fángdōng]: landlord
　　　　希望 [xīwàng]: to hope

練習 ACTIVITIES

I. Pinyin Exercises

20-1 Listen to the instructor, then write the Pinyin for the following expressions:

1. 吸煙 _____
2. 沒關係 _____
3. 必須 _____
4. 搬出去 _____
5. 付房租 _____
6. 走過來 _____

20-2 Listen to the instructor and fill in each blank with the correct Pinyin:

1. _____面_____雨了，我們進_____吧！
2. 我_____來了，我也_____晚飯_____回來了。
3. 我_____在_____飯呢，很好_____，你們_____來_____吧！
4. 我以_____很_____歡_____煙，_____是_____在不吸煙了。
5. 我們_____在_____個_____的_____一天_____房_____。

20-3 Read the following Chinese poem, paying special attention to the tones and rhythm:

Huí Xiāng ǒu Shū (**Hè Zhīzhāng**)	**回鄉偶書** **(賀知章)**
Shào xiǎo lí jiā lǎo dà huí, Xiāngyīn wú gǎi bìnmáo shuāi. Értóng xiāngjiàn bù xiāngshí, Xiào wèn kè cóng hé chù lái.	少小離家老大回， 鄉音無改鬢毛衰。 兒童相見不相識， 笑問客從何處來。

Returning Home
(He, Zhizhang)

I left home young, returned old,
My accent changed not, although my hair grew thin.
The youngsters see me, but don't know me,
With smiles they ask where I come from.

II. Character Exercises

20-4 Read the following words and phrases:

帶	第
帶來	第一
帶回來	第一次出去
把朋友帶回來	第一次搬出去
把朋友帶回來了	我第一次搬出去
我把我朋友從學校帶回來了	這是我第一次搬出去

Now try to use the following characters to make words, phrases, and then sentences:

1. 吸   2. 關   3. 但   4. 付   5. 租   6. 必

7. 進   8. 樓   9. 幫   10. 馬   11. 搬   12. 出

20-5 Write down the simplified forms for the following traditional characters:

1. 帶 _____   2. 關 _____   3. 系 _____   4. 進 _____

5. 歡 _____   6. 須 _____   7. 樓 _____   8. 馬 _____

III. Grammar Exercises

20-6 Substitution exercises:

1. 你<u>帶</u>了什麼<u>回來</u>?
   我<u>帶</u>了<u>一個蛋糕</u><u>回來</u>。

買	一瓶可樂	回來
借	兩本書	回來
搬	一張桌子	進來
拿	一條裙子	上去
送	一張電影票	出去

2. 你要他做什麼了?
   我要他把<u>那瓶藥</u><u>拿過來</u>。

那碗飯	買回來
他寫的信	寄出去
這個月的房租	付出去
那張桌子	搬過去
這碗湯	喝下去

Note: 寄 [jì]: to mail

20-7 Directional complement:

A. 訪客 *(A visitor)*: Fill in the blanks with 來 or 去

小花： 明明，這就是我的宿舍，外面有點兒冷，我們進＿＿＿吧！
小雪，我回＿＿＿了，我也把明明帶＿＿＿了。

小雪： 我在樓上，我正在看電影呢，很有意思 [yǒuyìsi] (interesting)，你們一起上＿＿＿看看吧！

明明： 我們等一下再上＿＿＿。

小花： 對了，秋雨在她的房間，我去叫她。
秋雨，請出＿＿＿，明明來了。

秋雨： 我知道了，我正在打電話，我馬上就出＿＿＿見她。

明明： 秋雨，我把你要的書帶＿＿＿了。

秋雨： 太好了，謝謝。

小花： 小雪，我們都在樓下，請你下＿＿＿，好嗎?

小雪： 好，我馬上下＿＿＿。

小花： 啊! 你最後[zuìhòu] (finally) 總算 [zǒngsuàn] (at long last) 下＿＿＿了。

B. Answer the following questions:

1. 小花回去的時候，小雪正在做什麼?
2. 秋雨在哪兒? 她正在做什麼? 她什麼時候出來?
3. 明明把什麼東西帶去給秋雨了?
4. 小雪最後 [zuìhòu] (finally) 下去了嗎?

20-8 Rewrite the following sentences using "把":

1. 我介紹我的老師給他了。
2. 我帶來了我的中文書。
3. 他穿上那件襯衫了。
4. 小方帶來了這盤炒麵。
5. 爸爸給我了那張地圖。
6. 她搬去了那張桌子。
7. 他帶去了他的中文作業。
8. 我室友搬來了他的電腦。

20-9 Picture description: Form groups of three. Use 把 and directional complements to tell a story (at least ten sentences).

Useful words and expressions:

釣魚 [diàoyú]: to go fishing   釣魚竿 [diàoyúgān]: fishing pole
水桶 [shuǐtǒng]: bucket   取水 [qǔshuǐ]: to fetch water
石頭 [shítou]: stone   樹 [shù]: tree
滑 [huá]: to slide   爬 [pá]: to climb
跳 [tiào]: to jump   掉 [diào]: to fall
挖土 [wātǔ]: to dig the earth

上去   下去   過來   過去

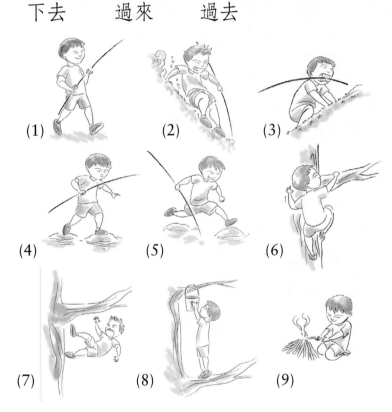

(1)   (2)   (3)

(4)   (5)   (6)

(7)   (8)   (9)

IV. Communicative Activities

20-10 Form pairs. Fill in the blanks with 把 and a directional complement:

A.1. 昨天我的好朋友要從紐約＿＿＿ ＿＿＿看我，昨天下課以後，
                        (come over)

我從教室走＿＿＿ ＿＿＿以後就＿＿＿宿舍＿＿＿了。
        (go out)   (return)

當 [dāng] (when) 我要開門＿＿＿ ＿＿＿的時候，我的鑰匙
                        (enter)

[yàoshi] (key) 不見了，我＿＿＿ ＿＿＿ ＿＿＿。
                    (cannot enter)

2. 我＿＿＿我的背包 [bēibāo] (backpack) ＿＿＿ ＿＿＿ ＿＿＿
(pick up)

看看，還是沒有。所以又＿＿＿ ＿＿＿教室
(return to)

＿＿＿。我＿＿＿ ＿＿＿ ＿＿＿以後，＿＿＿桌子
(run and enter)

搬＿＿＿ ＿＿＿又搬＿＿＿ ＿＿＿，我也＿＿＿書
(move the table back and forth)

＿＿＿ ＿＿＿ ＿＿＿看看，又＿＿＿ ＿＿＿ ＿＿＿，
(pick up the books)　　　　　　　(put it down)

還是沒找到 (cannot find it)　。

3. 後來 (later)，老師＿＿＿ ＿＿＿了，她＿＿＿ ＿＿＿
(enter)　　　　　　　　(come over)

問我怎麼了？我告訴她我從宿舍
＿＿＿ ＿＿＿ ＿＿＿找我的鑰匙 (key)　。
(run back)

老師＿＿＿她的書＿＿＿ ＿＿＿ ＿＿＿，裡面有
(pick up her book)

一把鑰匙(a key)

4. 那是我的鑰匙 (key)，我高興 [gāoxìng]
(happy) 地＿＿＿ ＿＿＿ ＿＿＿，原來 [yuánlái]
(jump up)

(adverb: indicating discovery of the truth) 我交 [jiāo]
(to submit) 作業的時候，不小心 (carelessness)＿＿＿

鑰匙 (key) 也交＿＿＿ ＿＿＿了。我說了謝謝，
(hand it in)

馬上又 [yòu] (again) ＿＿＿ ＿＿＿宿舍＿＿＿了。
(run back)

B. Form pairs and act out the situation above.

復習 Review

LESSON 19 AND LESSON 20

Conversation

Make a phone call to invite your friend to your dorm to prepare for next week's exam. Your friend is sick and has to see a doctor. Try to include the following questions in the conversation:

1. 喂，請問……在嗎? (You may refer to Lesson 9 "打電話" for phone manners)
2. ……去我宿舍一起復習準備考試好嗎?
3. 我生病了(不舒服、頭疼、發燒、感冒、咳嗽……)
4. 你怎麼生病了呢?
5. 你看醫生了沒有? 吃藥了沒有?

Situational Dialogues

You and your friends are chatting about your dorm. Try to include the following questions in the conversation:

1. 你住哪兒? 離學校近不近?
2. 你的宿舍/公寓 [gōngyù] (apartment) 怎麼樣? 好不好? 你想搬出來嗎?
   想搬到什麼地方?
3. 你們每個月什麼時候付房租? 房東(landlord)怎麼樣?
4. 你喜歡做飯嗎?

Traditional and Simplified Characters

Read each simplified character aloud. Then write the corresponding traditional character beside it. Finally make a phrase and a sentence using the character.

For example,　学 → 學 → 學生 → 我是學生。

L19: 头 (　) 发 (　) 烧 (　) 医 (　) 药 (　) 准 (　) 备 (　) 笔 (　)

L20: 带 (　) 进 (　) 烟 (　) 关 (　) 系 (　) 须 (　) 楼 (　) 马 (　)

暑假你要做什麼?
What Will You Do During the Summer Vacation?

教學目標 OBJECTIVES

- Talk about plans
- Express blessings and wishes

Graduation day at a university.

Computer company internships are popular.

College students find part-time jobs at places such as fast-food restaurants, coffee shops, and learning centers.

生詞 VOCABULARY

核心詞 Core Vocabulary

	TRADITIONAL	SIMPLIFIED	PINYIN		
1.	暑假	暑假	shǔjià	N.	summer vacation
2.	畢業	毕业	bìyè	V.	to graduate
3.	決定	决定	juédìng	V.	to decide
4.	申請	申请	shēnqǐng	V.	to apply
5.	研究生院	研究生院	yánjiūshēngyuàn	N.	graduate school
6.	國外	国外	guówài	N.	overseas, abroad
7.	留學	留学	liúxué	V.O.	to study abroad
8.	找	找	zhǎo	V.	to seek; look for
9.	打工	打工	dǎgōng	V.O.	to work for others; to be employed
10.	家	家	jiā	M.W.	(measure word for company, enterprise, store, etc.)
11.	公司	公司	gōngsī	N.	company
12.	實習	实习	shíxí	N.	internship
13.	電腦	电脑	diànnǎo	N.	computer
14.	暑期	暑期	shǔqī	N.	summer
15.	班	班	bān	N.	class
16.	一面	一面	yímiàn	Adv.	at the same time
17.	有意思	有意思	yǒuyìsi	Adj.	interesting, enjoyable
18.	愉快	愉快	yúkuài	Adj.	happy
19.	一路平安	一路平安	yílùpíng'ān		have a pleasant journey
20.	好運	好运	hǎoyùn		good luck

專名 Proper Nouns

TRADITIONAL	SIMPLIFIED	PINYIN		
1. 程海華	程海华	Chéng Hǎihuá	N.	(name) Haihua Cheng
2. 白秋雨	白秋雨	Bái Qiūyǔ	N.	(name) Quiyu Bai
3. 加州	加州	Jiāzhōu	N.	California

補充詞 Supplementary Vocabulary

TRADITIONAL	SIMPLIFIED	PINYIN		
1. 大學生	大学生	dàxuéshēng	N.	college students
2. 研究生	研究生	yánjiūshēng	N.	graduate students
3. 博士生	博士生	bóshìshēng	N.	doctoral students
4. 學位	学位	xuéwèi	N.	degree
5. 學士	学士	xuéshì	N.	bachelor's degree
6. 碩士	硕士	shuòshì	N.	master's degree
7. 博士	博士	bóshì	N.	doctoral degree
8. 簡歷 (履歷表)	简历 (履历表)	jiǎnlì (lǚlìbiǎo)	N.	resumé

語文知識 LANGUAGE LINK

The Sentence Patterns provide models that will help you with the Language in Use section. In both sections, pay attention to the grammar points, vocabulary, and expressions.

句型 Sentence Patterns

A: 畢業以後你想做什麼?
Bìyè yǐhòu nǐ xiǎng zuò shénme?

B: 我想申請研究生院。
Wǒ xiǎng shēnqǐng yánjiūshēngyuàn.

A: 今年暑假你要做什麼?
Jīnnián shǔjià nǐ yào zuò shénme?

B: 我要去一家公司做暑期實習。
Wǒ yào qù yìjiā gōngsī zuò shǔqī shíxí.

A: 你去中國做什麼?
Nǐ qù Zhōngguó zuò shénme?

B: 我想在那兒一面旅行,
Wǒ xiǎng zài nàr yímiàn lǚxíng,

一面學中文。
yímiàn xué Zhōngwén.

A: 祝你工作愉快!
Zhù nǐ gōngzuò yúkuài!

B: 祝你一路平安! 祝你好運!
Zhù nǐ yílùpíng'ān! Zhù nǐ hǎoyùn!

課文   Language in Use: 暑假你要做什麼? Shǔjià nǐyào zuò shénme?

程海華: 秋雨,我問你,你明年就要畢業了,畢業以後你想做什麼?
Qiūyǔ, wǒ wèn nǐ, nǐ míngnián jiùyào bìyè le, bìyè yǐhòu nǐ xiǎng zuò shénme?

白秋雨: 我還沒有決定呢。可是我很喜歡學習,我可能會
Wǒ hái méiyǒu juédìng ne. Kěshì wǒ hěn xǐhuān xuéxí, wǒ kěnéng huì

申請研究生院,或者去國外留學。你呢?
shēnqǐng yánjiūshēngyuàn, huòzhě qù guówài liúxué. Nǐ ne?

你什麼時候畢業?
Nǐ shénme shíhou bìyè?

程海華: 我還有兩年才畢業呢。畢業以後我想去找工作。
Wǒ háiyǒu liǎngnián cái bìyè ne. Bìyè yǐhòu wǒ xiǎng qù zhǎo gōngzuò.

白秋雨：　我們就要放暑假了，今年暑假你要做什麼？
Wǒmen jiùyào fàng shǔjià le, jīnnián shǔjià nǐ yào zuò shénme?

程海華：　我要去打工。我要去一家公司實習。
Wǒ yào qù dǎgōng. Wǒ yào qù yìjiā gōngsī shíxí.

白秋雨：　在哪兒？是什麼工作？
Zài nǎr? Shì shénme gōngzuò?

程海華：　在加州，是一家電腦公司。你呢？暑假你要做什麼？
Zài Jiāzhōu, shì yìjiā diànnǎo gōngsī. Nǐ ne? Shǔjià nǐ yào zuò shénme?

白秋雨：　我要去中國，我申請了去上海的暑期班學習，
Wǒ yào qù Zhōngguó, wǒ shēnqǐng le qù Shànghǎi de shǔqībān xuéxí,

　　　　　我想一面學中文，一面在中國旅行。
wǒ xiǎng yímiàn xué Zhōngwén, yímiàn zài Zhōngguó lǚxíng.

程海華：　那一定很有意思。你什麼時候去？
Nà yídìng hěn yǒuyìsi. Nǐ shénme shíhou qù?

白秋雨：　下個星期。
Xiàge xīngqī.

程海華：　這麼快！你到中國以後要常常給我寫電子郵件。
Zhème kuài! Nǐ dào Zhōngguó yǐhòu yào chángcháng gěi wǒ xiě diànzǐ yóujiàn.

白秋雨：　沒問題。我祝你工作愉快！
Méi wèntí. Wǒ zhù nǐ gōngzuò yúkuài!

程海華：　我也祝你一路平安！祝你好運！
Wǒ yě zhù nǐ yílùpíng'ān! Zhù nǐ hǎoyùn!

Useful words and expressions:

念書(念书) [niànshū]:
to study

回答 [huídá]: answer

問題(问题) [wèntí]: question

廣州市(广州市)
[Guǎngzhōu shì]: Guangzhou
city

服務業(服务业) [fúwù yè]:
service business

發票(发票) [fāpiào]: invoice;
receipt

查詢(查询) [cháxún]:
to check

報銷 (报销) [bàoxiāo]:
reimbursement

名稱(名称) [míngchēng]:
title

收款人 [shōukuǎn rén]:
person who received the
remittance

金額(金额) [jīn'é]: amount

付錢(付钱) [fùqián]: to pay

成績單(成绩单)
[chéngjìdān/chéngjīdān]:
transcript

以下 [yǐxià]: the following

廣東省(广东省) [Guǎngdōng
shěng]: Guangdong Province
in southern China

定額(定额) [dìng'é]:
a fixed amount or number

發票聯(发票联) [fāpiào
lián]: invoice; receipt

顧客(顾客) [gùkè]: customer

憑證(凭证) [píngzhèng]: proof

人民幣(人民币) [rénmínbì]:
name of currency used in
Mainland China

單位(单位) [dānwèi]: unit

營業(营业) [yíngyè]: business
operation

查驗(查验) [cháyàn]: to
examine

支票 [zhīpiào]: check

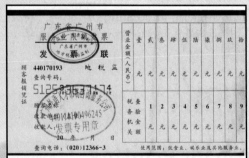

Questions:

1. 小紅一共付了多少錢?

2. Translate the following sentence: 使用範圍: 飲食業,
娛樂業及其他服務業.

3. What are the equivalent spoken forms for the written expressions:
金額, 收款人, and 及?

4. 小紅's father wrote an amount on a check as 捌佰陸拾貳元.
How much is that?

第二十二課
LESSON
22

我到上海了
I Have Arrived in Shanghai

- Exchange e-mails
- Describe your current situation

Several views of metropolitan Shanghai

小籠包 *[xiǎolóngbāo] Little steamed buns*

生詞　VOCABULARY

核心詞　Core Vocabulary

	TRADITIONAL	SIMPLIFIED	PINYIN		
1.	對不起	对不起	duìbuqǐ		I'm sorry; Excuse me.
2.	因為	因为	yīnwèi	Conj.	because
3.	不過	不过	búguò	Conj.	but; however
4.	認真	认真	rènzhēn	Adj.	conscientious; serious
5.	已經	已经	yǐjīng	Adv.	already
6.	美麗	美丽	měilì	Adj.	beautiful
7.	城市	城市	chéngshì	N.	city
8.	到處	到处	dàochù	N.	everywhere
9.	新	新	xīn	Adj.	new
10.	大樓	大楼	dàlóu	N.	tall building
11.	地方	地方	dìfang	N.	place
12.	活動	活动	huódòng	N.	activity
13.	比如	比如	bǐrú	Conj.	for example
14.	京劇	京剧	jīngjù	N.	Peking Opera
15.	書法	书法	shūfǎ	N.	calligraphy
16.	東西	东西	dōngxi	N.	thing
17.	最	最	zuì	Adv.	most; the highest degree
18.	小籠包	小笼包	xiǎolóngbāo	N.	little steamed buns with stuffing
19.	機會	机会	jīhuì	N.	opportunity
20.	嚐嚐	尝尝	chángchang	V.	to have a taste
21.	開始	开始	kāishǐ	V.	to start; to begin
22.	高興	高兴	gāoxìng	Adj.	happy

TRADITIONAL	SIMPLIFIED	PINYIN		
23. 收到	收到	shōudào	V.C.	to receive
24. 看來	看来	kànlái		it seems
25. 開心	开心	kāixīn	Adj.	happy
26. 同事	同事	tóngshì	N.	colleague
27. 熱心	热心	rèxīn	Adj.	warm-hearted
28. 老闆	老板	lǎobǎn	N.	boss
29. 一些	一些	yìxiē	Adj.	some
30. 學到	学到	xuédào	V.C.	to learn and master
31. 來信	来信	láixìn	V.O.	to write a letter (to the speaker)
32. 保重	保重	bǎozhòng		take care

補充詞　Supplementary Vocabulary

TRADITIONAL	SIMPLIFIED	PINYIN		
1. 心想事成	心想事成	xīnxiǎngshìchéng		Every wish comes true.
2. 健康	健康	jiànkāng	Adj.	healthy
3. 順利	顺利	shùnlì	Adj.	smooth

語文知識　LANGUAGE LINK

The Sentence Patterns provide models that will help you with the Language in Use section. In both sections, pay attention to the grammar points, vocabulary, and expressions.

句型　Sentence Patterns

A: 上海怎麼樣?
Shànghǎi zěnmeyàng?

B: 上海是一個非常美麗的
Shànghǎi shì yíge fēicháng měilìde

城市, 到處都是新的大樓。
chéngshì, dàochù dōu shì xīnde dàlóu.

A: 你們在那兒做了什麼?
Nǐmen zài nàr zuò le shénme?

B: 我們參加了一些活動，比如:
Wǒmen cānjiā le yìxiē huódòng, bǐrú:

看京劇、寫書法等等。
kàn jīngjù, xiě shūfǎ děngděng.

A: 這兒的同事都很熱心，常常
Zhèr de tóngshì dōu hěn rèxīn, chángcháng

教我很多東西，老闆也不錯。
jiāo wǒ hěnduō dōngxi, lǎobǎn yě búcuò.

B: 很好! 你要認真地工作，
Hěn hǎo! Nǐ yào rènzhēn de gōngzuò,

才能學到一些東西。
cái néng xué dào yìxiē dōngxi.

課文　Language in Use: 我到上海了 Wǒ dào Shànghǎi le

海華:
Hǎihuá:

你好! 今天是六月十五號，我一個星期以前就到上海了。
Nǐhǎo! Jīntiān shì liù yuè shíwǔ hào, wǒ yíge xīngqī yǐqián jiù dào Shànghǎi le.

對不起，因為太忙了，所以今天才給你寫電子郵件。
Duìbuqǐ, yīnwèi tài máng le, suǒyǐ jīntiān cái gěi nǐ xiě diànzǐ yóujiàn.

我們每天都有很多課，功課也不少。不過老師教得很好，
Wǒmen měitiān dōu yǒu hěnduō kè, gōngkè yě bùshǎo. Búguò lǎoshī jiāode hěnhǎo,

也很認真。我們每天都說中文。我的中文進步得很快，
yě hěn rènzhēn. Wǒmen měitiān dōu shuō Zhōngwén. Wǒde Zhōngwén jìnbù de hěnkuài.

現在我已經能說很多中文了。
Xiànzài wǒ yǐjīng néng shuō hěnduō Zhōngwén le.

上海是一個非常美麗的城市，到處都是新的大樓。
Shànghǎi shì yíge fēicháng měilìde chéngshì, dàochù dōu shì xīnde dàlóu.

我們參觀了一些地方，也參加了一些活動，比如: 看京劇、
Wǒmen cānguān le yìxiē dìfang, yě cānjiā le yìxiē huódòng, bǐrú: kàn jīngjù,

寫書法等等，都很有意思。還有，上海有很多好吃的東西，
xiě shūfǎ děngděng, dōu hěn yǒuyìsi. Háiyǒu, Shànghǎi yǒu hěnduō hǎochī de dōngxi,

其中我最喜歡吃的是小籠包，你有機會應該嚐嚐。
qízhōng wǒ zuì xǐhuān chī de shì xiǎolóngbāo. Nǐ yǒu jīhuì yīnggāi chángchang.

你開始實習了嗎？忙不忙？有空請給我寫電子郵件。
Nǐ kāishǐ shíxí le ma? Mángbumáng? Yǒukòng qǐng gěi wǒ xiě diànzǐ yóujiàn.

祝
Zhù

好！
Hǎo!

秋雨
Qiūyǔ

二〇〇四年六月十五日
Èr líng líng sì nián liù yuè shíwǔ rì

秋雨：
Qiūyǔ:

你好！很高興收到你的電子郵件。看來你在上海過得很開心。
Nǐhǎo! Hěn gāoxìng shōudào nǐde diànzǐ yóujiàn. Kànlái nǐ zài Shànghǎi guòde hěn kāixīn.

我現在在洛杉磯，已經開始實習了。這兒的同事都很好，也很
Wǒ xiànzài zài Luòshānjī, yǐjīng kāishǐ shíxí le. Zhèr de tóngshì dōu hěnhǎo, yě hěn

熱心，常常教我很多東西，老闆也不錯。我的工作有時候忙，
rèxīn, chángcháng jiāo wǒ hěnduō dōngxi, lǎobǎn yě búcuò. Wǒde gōngzuò yǒushíhou máng,

有時候不太忙，我想我得認真地工作，才能學到一些東西。
yǒushíhou bútàimáng. Wǒ xiǎng wǒ děi rènzhēn de gōngzuò, cái néng xué dào yìxiē dōngxi.

好了，不多寫了。有空請多來信，多保重。
Hǎo le, bù duō xiě le. Yǒukòng qǐng duō lái xìn. Duō bǎozhòng.

祝
Zhù

好！
Hǎo!

海華
Hǎihuá

二〇〇四年六月十七日
Èr líng líng sì nián liù yuè shíqī rì

注釋 LANGUAGE NOTES

等等

等等 means et cetera, and is usually used after a list of people or things. Sometimes one character 等 is used instead of two.

還有

還有 (and, also, in addition) is used to introduce additional information.

來信

來信 can be used as a noun to mean "a letter coming from . . ." 來 is used here to indicate that this is said from the speaker's point of view, which means the letter is coming to the speaker. If the letter is going away from the speaker, then 去信 should be used.

語法 GRAMMAR

比如

This is an expression equivalent to "for example" or "for instance" or "such as" in English. It is used to introduce specific examples. For example,

我們的晚會有很多活動，比如：唱歌、跳舞、寫毛筆字等等。
他會說很多語言，比如：英文，中文，法文，西班牙文。

Summary of Measure Words in Chinese

In modern Chinese a numeral is never used immediately before a noun as in English. A measure word is always placed between a numeral or a demonstrative pronoun 這/那 and a noun. There are many measure words in Chinese, and different measure words are required for different nouns. The following is a list of the measure words we have learned so far:

Category	Measure word (Classifier)	Example
Measure words for people	個: used for all people 位: only used in a polite way	e.g., 六千多個學生 幾位客人? 兩位，請進。
Measure words for things (definite)	個: the most commonly used measure word for things in general; used for cups, buildings, characters, etc.	e.g., 一個杯子，那個電話，三個專業 一個公園，一個圖書館， 五個漢字
	本: used for bound items (book-like things)	e.g., 這本漢英詞典，兩本中文書， 三本英文雜誌

Category	Measure word (Classifier)	Example
	張: generally used for sheet-like things with a flat surface	e.g., 一張床，這張報紙，三張電影票，那張桌子
	隻: generally used for animals	e.g., 一隻狗，六隻貓
	門: used for subjects and courses as well as special skills	e.g., 六門課 這門手藝 [shǒuyì] (skill)
	輛: used for vehicles	e.g., 這輛汽車，那輛公共汽車，三輛自行車
	家: used for a facility such as a company, a hospital, a factory, or a TV station	e.g., 一家公司， 這家電視臺 [diànshìtái] (TV station)， 一家醫院 [yīyuàn] (hospital)
	點, 分, 秒 [miǎo] (second), 刻: used for time	e.g., 三點二十分 (3:20) 五點一刻 (5:15) 十二點三十分零 [líng] (zero) 六秒 [miǎo] (second) (12:30:06)
	元/塊, 角/毛: used for money	e.g., 八十元七角三分 (¥80.73) 九塊四毛六分 (¥9.46)
	件: used for clothing, especially for upper body clothing	e.g., 一件襯衫 (a shirt) 兩件運動衫 [yùndòngshān] (sports wear)
	條: used for things of long and slim shape	e.g., 一條褲子 (a pair of pants) 三條裙子 (three skirts)
	雙, 副 and 對: used for things in pairs	e.g., 一雙運動鞋 (a pair of sports shoes) 一雙手 (a pair of hands) 一雙筷子 (a pair of chopsticks) 一雙眼睛 [yǎnjīng] (a pair of eyes) 一副手套 [shǒutào] (a pair of gloves) 一副眼鏡 [yǎnjìng] (a pair of eyeglasses) 一副耳環 [ěrhuán] (a pair of earrings) 一副手鐲 [shǒuzhuó] (a pair of bracelets) 一對姐妹 [jiěmèi] (sisters) (two sisters) 一對夫妻 [fūqī] (a couple — husband and wife)
	碗, 盤, and, 杯: refer to containers, used for food or drinks	e.g., 一碗湯 (a bowl of soup) 兩盤炒麵 (two plates of fried noodles) 三杯啤酒 (three glasses of beer)

Category	Measure word (Classifier)	Example
Things (indefinite)	一點兒: means a little, used to indicate quantity (used before a noun)	e.g., A: 你會說中文嗎？ B: 我會說一點兒。
	一下兒, 一會兒: means a little, used to indicate a brief action (used after a verb)	e.g., A: 你來一下兒，好嗎？ B: 好，我馬上就來。 or: 請等一會兒。
Things (plural)	些	e.g., 我們參觀了一些城市 他們收到了一些電子郵件。

Note: Measure words can be used in reduplication to indicate "each and every," but this usage is limited to single-syllable measure words only. For examples,

他們個個都是好學生。 　　　(每個人)
這兒的書本本都很好看。 　　　(每本)

Summary of Conjunctions in Chinese

Conjunctions are used to connect nouns/pronouns, verbs, adjectives, adverbs, numerals, and even clauses to indicate grammatical relationships. We have learned the following conjunctions so far:

Category	Conjunction	Example
和: – used to indicate a parallel relationship	– usually to connect two nouns, pronouns, and nominal phrases *Note:* 和 can never be used to connect two sentences/clauses.	e.g., 我爸爸和媽媽都是中國人。(N. 和 N.) 我們點一盤餃子和一碗湯吧。(NP. 和 NP.)
可是, 但是, 不過: – used to indicate transition, similar to "but," "however," "nevertheless." – can be used interchangeably	– usually used to introduce a clause that bears a meaning contrary to what might have been expected based on the previous clause, often used together with 雖然 [suīrán] (although) *Note:* While in English "although" and "so" are not used together, 雖然 and 但是/可是/不過 are often used together as a pair of conjunctions.	e.g., 中國文學不太難，可是功課不少。 我打球打得不太好，但是我很喜歡打球。 今天氣溫 [qìwēn] (temperature) 不太高，不過很舒服。 The temperature today is not very high, but very pleasant.

Category	Conjunction	Example
所以: – used to indicate causality, meaning "so" or "therefore" in English	– equivalent to "so" or "therefore" in English, often used together with 因為 as a pair of conjunctions *Note:* While in English "because" and "so" are never used together, in Chinese 因為 and 所以 can and often are used together in one sentence. Sometimes 因為 can be omitted if the cause-effect relationship between the first and the second clauses is very clear.	e.g., (因為)冬天太冷，所以我不喜歡冬天。 (因為)她常常鍛煉，所以她的身體 [shēntǐ] (body)很好。
還是, 或者: – used to indicate alternatives – can be translated as "or" in English	還是 is used in a question while 或者 is used in a statement	e.g., 你去體育館還是健身房？你每天走路還是坐公共汽車來學校？ 我想明天或者後天搬過來。 今年暑假我想去北京或者上海暑期班學習。
然後: – used to indicate succession and order of things	– often used together with 先 and 再 *Note:* When using 先, 再, and 然後, 先 always comes first, but 再, and 然後 can be reversed.	e.g., 我想先回家，再去洛杉磯看朋友，然後去公司實習。 廣東 [Guǎngdōng] (Canton, a province in southern China) 人都喜歡先喝湯，然後吃飯。
一面……一面…… (一邊…… 一邊……): – used for simultaneous actions	– usually connects two verbs or verb phrases to indicate that two actions are happening at the same time	e.g., 他一面吃飯一面看電視。 我喜歡一面做功課一面聽音樂 [tīng yīnyuè] (listen to music)。

補充課文 ─◦◦◦─ SUPPLEMENTARY PRACTICE

This selection will help you test your comprehension of the grammar and vocabulary you have learned in this lesson. Be prepared to answer questions about the meaning of the passage.

(打電話)

秋雨：　喂，你好！請問海華在嗎？

海華：　我就是。你是秋雨吧？

秋雨：　對，是我。

海華：　你在哪兒？

秋雨：　我在上海。我一個星期以前就到了。對不起，因為太忙了，
　　　　所以到現在才給你打電話。

海華：　沒關係。你在那兒好嗎？

秋雨：　很好，可是太忙了。我們每天都有很多課，功課也不少。

海華：　你們的老師怎麼樣？

秋雨：　老師很不錯，教得很認真。

海華：　你現在中文一定進步得很快吧？

秋雨：　還不錯，我們每天都說中文。我現在已經可以說很多了。

海華：　太好了。你覺得上海怎麼樣？

秋雨：　我很喜歡上海。上海非常漂亮。我們去了很多地方玩兒，
　　　　還看了京劇，寫了書法，參加了很多活動，很有意思。
　　　　對了，這兒有很多好吃的東西。

海華：　真的？那你最喜歡吃什麼？

秋雨：　我最喜歡吃小籠包。真的很好吃。有機會你一定要嚐嚐。

海華：　好的。看來你在上海過得很開心。

秋雨：　你呢？你在洛杉磯還好嗎？

海華：　還可以。我已經開始實習了，老闆還不錯，同事們都很好，
　　　　也很熱心，還教了我不少東西。

秋雨：　工作忙不忙？

海華：　有時候忙，有時候不太忙。我想多學一些東西，所以得
　　　　認真地工作。

秋雨：　有志者事竟成。祝你成功！

海華：　謝謝。好，就這樣。請多保重。

秋雨：　我也要掛電話了。再見！

海華：　再見！

Notes: 漂亮 [piàoliang]: pretty

有志者事竟成。[Yǒuzhìzhě shì jìng chéng]: Where there is a will, there is a way.

成功 [chénggōng]: success

就這樣 [jiùzhèyàng]: that's it; that's all

掛 [guà]: to hang up (the phone)

練習　ACTIVITIES

I. Pinyin Exercises

22-1 Listen to the instructor, then write out the Pinyin:

1. _____　　2. _____

3. _____　　4. _____

5. _____　　6. _____

22-2 Listen to the instructor and then write out the short dialogues in Pinyin:

1. _____
_____

2. _____
_____

3. _____
_____

4. _____
_____

5. _____
_____

22-3 Read the following Chinese poem, paying special attention to the tones and rhythm:

Gǔyuán Cǎo **(Bái Jūyì)**	**古原草** **(白居易)**
Lílí yuán shàng cǎo,	離離原上草，
Yí suì yì kū róng.	一歲一枯榮。
Yěhuǒ shāo bú jìn,	野火燒不盡，
Chūnfēng chuī yòu shēng.	春風吹又生。

Grass on the Old Grassland
(Bai, Juyi)

The grass is growing in full bloom on the grassland,
Every year it withers and grows again.
Wild fire will not burn it dead,
It grows again with the coming of spring wind.

II. Character Exercises

23-4 Read the following words, phrases, and sentences:

城	嚐
城市	嚐嚐
大城市	嚐嚐小籠包
是一個大城市	應該嚐嚐小籠包
上海是一個大城市	有機會應該嚐嚐小籠包
上海是一個美麗的大城市	你有機會應該嚐嚐小籠包

Now try to use the following characters to make words, phrases, and then sentences:

1. 麗   2. 處   3. 新   4. 方   5. 比   6. 京

7. 東   8. 始   9. 高   10. 收   11. 闆   12. 保

22-5 Group the following words according to their meanings (e.g., place, food, activity, adjective, verb, conjunction):

認真	保重	熱心	不過	開心	同事	活動	書法
東西	高興	小籠包	地方	上海	京劇	所以	收到
老闆	美麗	來信	嚐嚐	城市	努力	吸煙	參觀

Group 1: _____

Group 2: _____

Group 3: _____

Group 4: _____

Group 5: _____

Group 6: _____

Group 7: _____

Group 8: _____

Group 9: _____

22-6 Circle the radicals of the following characters:

For example, 劇

1. 認   2. 保   3. 籠   4. 麗   5. 理   6. 機   7. 愉   8. 體

III. Grammar Exercises

22-7 Fill in each blank with an appropriate measure word using to the clues:

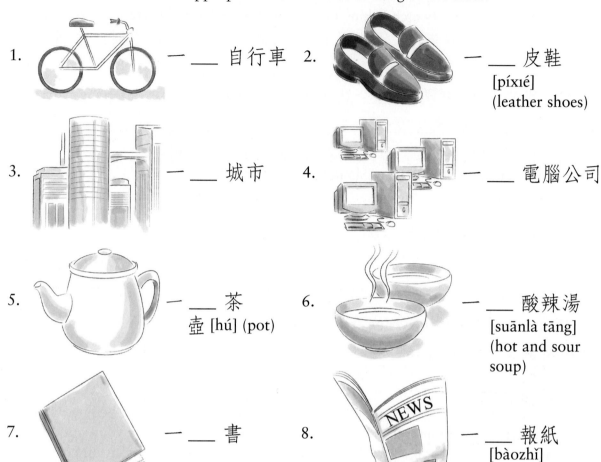

1. 一＿＿ 自行車　　2. 一＿＿ 皮鞋
[píxié]
(leather shoes)

3. 一＿＿ 城市　　4. 一＿＿ 電腦公司

5. 一＿＿ 茶
壺 [hú] (pot)　　6. 一＿＿ 酸辣湯
[suānlà tāng]
(hot and sour
soup)

7. 一＿＿ 書　　8. 一＿＿ 報紙
[bàozhǐ]
(newspaper)

22-8 Connect the sentences by using appropriate conjunctions:

因為......所以......，一面......一面......，可是，
先......再......然後......，還是

1. 方明正在看電腦。方明正在打手機。

_____

2. 上海很美麗，我很想去上海看看。

_____

3. 現在已經是四月了，天氣還是很冷。

_____

4. 你要去北京的暑期班嗎? 你要去公司實習嗎?

_____

5. 八點我起床，九點我上課，十點我去吃午飯。

_____

22-9 Use 比如 to complete the following sentences with the help of the clues:

For example,   我們參加了很多活動......
(watch Peking Opera, practice calligraphy, etc.)

→ 我們參加了很多活動，比如：看京劇，寫書法
    等等。

1. 我喜歡吃中國菜......   (hot and sour soup, fried rice, dumplings, etc.)

   _____

2. 我很想去中國看看，特別 [tèbié] (especially) 想去......
   (big cities such as Beijing, Shanghai, and Hong Kong)

   _____

3. 我對很多活動有興趣......
   (swimming, playing basketball, bicycling, etc.)

   _____

IV. Communicative Activities

22-10 Situational dialogues:

Situation 1:
Your best friend 司馬 [Sīmǎ] 學文 is now studying Chinese in Beijing, China, and you are doing an internship at a company in New York. This is your second week at work. You are talking with 學文 on the phone. Your conversation covers the following topics:

1. You ask 學文 about his life and studies in Beijing.
2. 學文 tells you about his classes and his teachers.
3. You tell him how you feel about your work at the company.
4. You encourage each other to do a good job in both studies and work.
5. You promise that you will e-mail each other as often as possible.

In your conversation you should use (but are not limited to) the following words and expressions:

對不起　　因為　　一個星期
功課　　　喜歡　　開心
還是　　　每天　　機會
參觀　　　認真　　雖然
常常　　　活動　　參加
熱心　　　比如　　同事
一面......一面......

文化知識 ⊶○○⊷ Culture Link

文化點滴　CULTURE NOTES

京劇; 書法
Peking Opera; Chinese Calligraphy

京劇 (Peking Opera)

京劇 originated in the 安徽 [Ānhuī] (Anhui) and 湖北 [Húběi] (Hubei) Provinces of China in the 18th century; it is now known as China's national opera. In fact, in Taiwan it is referred to as 國劇 [guójù] (national opera). 京劇 can be divided into two types, 文戲 [wénxì] (civil pieces), which are characterized by singing, and 武戲 [wǔxì] (martial pieces), which feature acrobatics and stunts. Some operas are a combination of both.

The repertoire of 京劇 includes historical subjects, comedic performances, tragedies, and farces. Two groups of musicians, a string section and a percussion section, accompany the singing. The 二胡 [èrhú], a two-stringed instrument played with a bow, is the backbone of the orchestra. The operatic dialogues and monologues are recited in Peking dialect, and some of the words are pronounced in a special fashion unique to Peking Opera.

Main instruments: Chinese fiddle, two-stringed violin, and pipa.

There are established movements in the opera that are used by the performers to portray emotions. Such movements include, for instance, smoothing of a beard, raising a foot, jerking a sleeve, or adjusting a hat.

In general there are four roles within the 京劇: 生 [shēng] (male), 旦 [dàn] (female), the 淨 [jìng] (painted face), and 丑 [chǒu] (the clown). These roles are further classified by age and profession. The male role can be divided into three categories: old, young, and martial arts expert. The female role is divided into four categories: young or middle-aged, innocent or dissolute, martial arts expert, and old woman. The painted-face role represents open-minded men with brightly colored faces. The clown role is marked by white on the ridge of his nose. The clown can have a number of personalities, from a light-hearted, humorous character to an evil, crafty character. These personalities are revealed by the way each character sings and moves. For example, the personality of the painted-face character is indicated by the color his face is painted: red indicates uprightness and loyalty; white represents craftiness and cunning; blue represents vigor and courage; yellow represents intelligence; black represents honesty; and brown represents stubbornness.

Rehearsing before the show.

Costuming is a very extravagant part of the opera; all the costumes are based on Ming Dynasty dress. They are very colorful and very expensive in appearance. Props for the stage are relatively simple. Often there are just a table and a few chairs on the stage. Common props include a cloth wall, tents, parasols, a whip, paddles, and a few weapons. Someone holding a whip and walking around can represent a person riding a horse. A few soldiers may represent a huge army on stage. Performers also use their eyes and facial expressions to help convey more specific meanings.

Examples of costumes and stage props.

Since its birth 200 years ago, 京劇 survives today. There are a number of schools in China and Taiwan dedicated to training children to be future performers in the Peking Opera.

書法 (Calligraphy)

書法 is considered the highest form of art in China. Together with painting, it is the best embodiment of Chinese philosophy around the world. The Daoist theory of yin-yang is well integrated into the best works of calligraphy. Balance and harmony are essential for a masterpiece. Many calligraphers are at the same time scholars and artists. Very often they incorporate poems in their calligraphic art as well.

For a calligrapher, the most important tools are the 文房四寶 [wénfángsìbǎo] (the four treasures of the study room), an expression that refers to paper, writing brush, ink slab, and ink stick.

文房四寶 [wénfángsìbǎo] (the four treasures of the study room) paper, writing brush, ink slab, and ink stick. A calligraphy master writes Chinese lunar new year couplets by request.

Chinese calligraphy has five basic styles, the earliest being 篆書 [zhuànshū] (Seal Style). Later styles include 隸書 [lìshū] (Official Style), 楷書 [kǎishū] (Standard Style), 行書 [xíngshū] (Running Style) and 草書 [cǎoshū] (Grass/Cursive Style). Today, the most commonly used style for official documents is 楷書, and 行書 is used most by people in daily life.

Students being introduced to calligraphy.

Calligraphy is used for *Gualian* (couplets), mottos, and calligraphy paintings. These are common interior decorations for Chinese.

The following are examples by Yi Qing of the five major styles of Chinese calligraphy:

Zhuanshu (Seal Style)	Lishu (Official Style)	Kaishu (Regular Style)	Xingshu (Running Style)	Caoshu (Grass/Cursive Style)
篆書	隸書	楷書	行草	

Questions:

1. Have you ever seen Peking Opera?

2. If yes, where, when, and what did you think of it?

3. If not, from what you learned from the textbook, do you think Peking Opera is similar to Western opera? Why or why not?

4. Do you know any other performing art? Introduce it to the class.

5. Have you ever tried calligraphy? Do you want to learn it?

趣味中文　FUN WITH CHINESE

心想事成
Whatever one wishes, it will come true.

xīn	xiǎng	shì	chéng
心	想	事	成
mind	think	matter	successful

Question:

Do you believe "心想事成"? Why or why not?

行動吧! LET'S GO!

標語 Slogan

1. 小民 is studying in Beijing. He is also doing a work-study assignment at the new technology development area in 中關村. Below are several slogan posters he saw in 中關村. Translate the slogans into English.

Useful words and expressions:

海淀中關村(海淀中关村) [Hǎidiàn Zhōngguāncūn]:
   Zhongguan village in the Haidian area, famous for its devotion to developing advanced technology, similar to Silicon Valley in California.

人類(人类) [rénlèi]: human being
必須 [bìxū]: must
增長(增长) [zēngzhǎng]: growth
資源(资源) [zīyuán]: resources
回收 [huíshōu]: to recycle
地球 [dìqiú]: the Earth
控制 [kòngzhì]: to control
環保(环保) [huánbǎo]: environmental protection

(1)   (2)   (3)

用你自己的話, 說說標語(1) (2) (3)是什麼意思?

2. 林榮圈 [Lín Róngquān] is a taxi driver for the 開心 taxi company in Taiwan. He is taking a passenger from the airport to Taipei. Below is the receipt he needs to fill out for his passenger. Use the following information to fill out the receipt:

Fare: NT $800, 開心車行, 電話: (02) 2675-8983

Useful words and expressions:

計程車(计程车) [jìchéngchē]: taxi
收據(收据) [shōujù]: receipt
車資(车资) [chēzī]: fare
車行(车行) [chēháng]: taxi company
駕駛人(驾驶人) [jiàshǐrén]: driver
撥(拨) [bō]: to dial
意見(意见) [yìjiàn]: opinion
下列 [xiàliè]: the following
監理處(监理处) [jiānlǐchù]: Department of Management
   and Supervision
市政府 [shìzhèngfǔ]: city government
警察局 [jǐngchájú]: police bureau
駕駛員(驾驶员) [jiàshǐyuán]: driver
新台幣(新台币) [xīntáibì]: name of currency used in Taiwan
搭乘 [dāchéng]: to take a vehicle
職業工會(职业工会) [zhíyè gōnghuì]: occupational association

計 程 車 收 據	謝謝您的搭乘，如有任何意見，請撥下列交通服務電話：
車　資　新台幣　　　　元	
車行名稱	台北市監理處　2767-8217
電　話	台北市政府警察局　2394-9007（日）
車　號　　04 ~ 190	2321-9166（夜）
駕駛人	台北區監理所　2688-6052
姓　名　　林學邁	基隆監理站　2451-7239
	台北市汽車駕駛員職業工會　2659-9999
	90. 5. 500,000

Translate the receipt:

_____

_____

_____

_____

復習　Review

Conversation

I. Form pairs. The semester will end in about two weeks. You and your roommate are discussing your plans for the summer. Remember, you will need to include the following topics in your conversation (Remember to use 了 as appropriate):

1. 去年夏天你原來 [yuánlái] (originally) 想做什麼? 後來你做了什麼?
2. 今年暑假你想做什麼?
3. 你要去哪兒實習/學習?

II. It is summer now. You are doing an internship at a company in New Jersey and your good friend 文華 is studying Chinese in Beijing, China. You are now talking to her over the phone and telling her about your internship. Include the following topics in your conversation:

1. 你在什麼公司實習? 你是不是很喜歡你實習的公司?
2. 你覺得你實習的工作有意思嗎?
3. 你的老闆怎麼樣? 同事呢?
4. 實習完 [wán] (finish) 了以後你想做什麼?

Hints: The following vocabulary items and conjunctions should be used:

實習, 申請, 決定, 老闆, 同事
因為……所以……, 雖然……不過/可是/但是……, 還是, 或者,
先……再……然後……, 一面……一面……

III. You have just come back from your summer study in Shanghai. Your best friend 白雪 is also considering participating in a summer study abroad program next year. Therefore, you are talking to her about your experience in Shanghai. Remember to include the following:

1. 你是什麼時候到上海的? 你去上海做什麼?
2. 你在上海忙嗎? 每天有什麼活動?
3. 你覺得上海是一個什麼樣的城市? 你喜歡不喜歡上海? 為什麼?
4. 你在中國旅行了嗎? 去了什麼地方?

Hints: Please use the following vocabulary and conjunctions, and use 了 at the appropriate places:

暑期班, 星期, 活動, 最, 參觀, 忙, 城市, 文化 [wénhuà] culture
因為……所以……, 雖然……不過/可是/但是……, 還是, 或者,
先……再……然後……, 一面……一面……

Measure Words

Fill in each blank with an appropriate measure word:

　　我到上海已經三_____星期了。我們暑期班一共有三十六_____學生。其中有十五_____美國人，還有韓國人和日本人。

　　我們每天都很忙。上午有四_____課，從八_____上課到十一_____三十_____下課。下午有講座 [jiǎngzuò] (lecture)，我有時候去聽_____，有時候我們一起坐公共汽車去參觀上海的一些地方，或者去買東西。上_____星期三我去了一_____商店 [shāngdiàn] (store) 買了一_____紅襯衫，兩_____黑裙子和一_____運動鞋 [yùndòngxié] (sneaker)，很便宜，一共五十六_____七_____九_____ (¥56.79)。

　　我們都住在外國學生宿舍。我的宿舍裡有一_____床，一_____書桌。書桌上有很多書、幾_____字典 [zìdiǎn] (dictionary) 和一_____電話。我還有兩_____玩具狗 [wánjù gǒu] (toy dog)。

　　學校裡有三_____校車 [xiàochē] (school bus)，很方便 [fāngbiàn] (convenient)。我們也有兩_____食堂 [shítáng] (cafeteria)，我們常常在那裡吃飯。我常常點一_____湯，一_____菜，有時候我也喜歡喝一_____中國茶。

　　我在上海過得很快樂。

Traditional and Simplified Characters

Circle the radical of each of the following characters and then match the character with its simplified form:

認　處　熱　動　劇　實　觀　麗

动　剧　观　丽　处　认　实　热

Small Report

Talk about your experiences such as work study, courses, or study abroad.

Useful words and expressions:

工作：　公司，實習，申請，找工作，打工，履歷表 [lǚlìbiǎo] (resume)，上班，老闆，同事，機會

上課：　留學，暑期班，功課，上課，教，活動，參觀，進步，京劇，書法，新，地方，旅行

生詞表 VOCABULARY LIST

Lesson 1

你	好	是	學生	學	嗎	我	呢
也	他	不	老師				

Lesson 2

您	貴	姓	請問	請	問	的	英文
名字	中文	叫	什麼	她	誰	同學	

專名

李文中	吳小美	于英

補充詞

漢語	英語

Lesson 3

哪	國	人	很	對了	法國	美國	英國
中國	說	會	一點兒	兒	法文	和	

補充詞

德國	德國人	德語(德文)		韓國	韓國人	韓語(韓文)
加拿大	加拿大人			泰國	泰國人	泰語(泰文)
日本	日本人	日語(日文)				
西班牙	西班牙人		西班牙語(西班牙文)			

Lesson 4

那	書	這	本	文學	工程	難	太
可是	功課	多	我們	們	少		

補充詞

系	數學	計算機(電腦)	專業(主修)		輔修	容易
忙	累	作業	考試	有點兒	還好	

Lesson 5

朋友	來	介紹	一下	室友	有	幾	兩
個	他們	都	常	跟			

專名

王紅	丁明	方小文

補充詞

沒有	女朋友	男朋友	認識

Lesson 6

家	大家	從	在	一	四	爸爸	媽媽
姐姐	工作	工程師	男	男朋友	沒有	輛	車
隻	狗	愛					

專名

紐約

補充詞

自我介紹		自己	兄弟姐妹		哥哥	妹妹	弟弟
女	女朋友	孩子	寵物	貓			

Lesson 7

住	哪兒	宿舍	多少	號	房間	大	電話
小	號碼	二	三	五	六	七	八
九	手機	校外					

專名

陳愛文	張友朋

補充詞

校內	公寓	房子	十	○

Lesson 8

認識	去	上課	下課	以後	事兒	想	回
一起	吃	飯	吃飯	菜	今天	下次	怎麼樣
行	再見	再	見				

專名

韓國　日本

補充詞

名片　休息　早飯　午飯(中飯)　晚飯　宵夜

Lesson 9

正在	打電話	喂	等一下兒	等	知道	了
謝謝	吧	對	忙	看	電視	做	上網
我就是	位	留言(留話)	對不起	時候	回來	晚上
要	給					

補充詞

佔線	打錯了	小說	電影	網絡(網路)	網吧(網咖)
網站	網頁	聊天室	電腦遊戲	在線遊戲(線上遊戲)
病毒	軟件(軟體)	硬件(硬體)	發短信(送簡信)
通	休息	睡覺	不客氣　不謝

Lesson 10

每天	半	起床	大學	生活	學期	門	點
睡覺	就	才	刻	分	然後	圖書館	下午
喜歡	打球	寫	信	電子郵件		地址	祝
年	月	日					

專名

小明　學文

補充詞

點鐘	鐘頭	小時	分鐘	秒	過	差	早
晚	熬夜	刷牙	洗臉	洗澡			

Lesson 11

紅	茶	還是	綠	服務員	坐	小姐	先生
先	喝	杯	冰	可樂	瓶	啤酒	麵
餃子	盤	炒	十	碗	湯	雙	筷子

專名

張正然　孫信美　楊歡

補充詞

飯館	餐廳	餐館	飯店	菜單	白飯	飲料單	果汁
橙汁	柳橙汁(柳丁汁)		咖啡	點菜	小費	買單	
結賬(結帳)		酸	甜	苦	辣	鹹	清淡
燙	涼						

Lesson 12

可以	借	明天	用　　得	機場	接　應該	妹妹題
玩	飛機	到	手排擋(手排)	開	這樣	問就
白	色	停	停車場　這次	練習		
能	進步					

專名

于影　王本樂　上海　洛杉磯

補充詞

自動排擋(自排)

Lesson 13

買	件	襯衫	店員	條	裙子	或者	褲子
黃	不錯	比較	穿	黑	試試	幫	好看
讓	覺得	錢	塊	張	電影	票	

專名

毛愛紅　方子英

補充詞

貴	便宜	賣	號	幾號	特大	大	中
小	特小						

Lesson 14

歲	有空	星期	過	生日	為	舞會	參加
一定	做	蛋糕	送	棒	不客氣	多大	地圖

補充詞

日曆	月曆	慶生	禮物	蠟燭	祝你生日快樂

Lesson 15

前邊	參觀	歡迎	裡邊	廚房	公用	旁邊	客廳
走	對面	餐廳	洗澡間	臥室	中間	桌子	上邊
後邊	公園	真					

專名

田進	梁園生	包志中

補充詞

左邊	右邊	門	書桌	窗戶	椅子	衣櫥	床
教室	雜誌	亂	整齊	乾淨	髒	整理	

Lesson 16

籃球	得	倆	教練	教	游泳	非常	快
體育館	游泳池	健身房	鍛煉	現在	昨天	球賽	作業
包	慢						

補充詞

社團	俱樂部	球季

Lesson 17

春天	久	時間	過	放	春假	氣候	夏熱
秋	氏	其中	最	暖和	短	有時候	雪
華氏	百	度	極	刮風	下雨	冷	
見面	冬						

專名

小玲

補充詞

天氣	四季	放假	寒假	暑假	假期	攝氏	長
氣溫	上升	下降					

Lesson 18

火車	旅行	離	學校	遠	只要	分鐘	騎
自行車	公共汽車		走路	近	西部	先	風景
船	南部	聽說	海邊	景色	一共	租	

專名

季長風　白秋影　加拿大

補充詞

海灘	東	北	旺季	淡季	單車(腳踏車)		汽車
機車(摩拖車)		出租汽車(計程車)	火車	公車(巴士)			
麵包車(包型車)		吉普車	跑車	大貨車	四輪驅動(四輪傳動)		
越野車	車站	捷運	地鐵	磁浮鐵路		天橋	馬路
地下道	隧道	碼頭	司機				

Lesson 19

感冒	餓	好像	舒服	頭疼	發燒	咳嗽	生病
考試	復習	所以	醫生	吃藥	地	休息	準備
筆記	感謝						

專名

歐陽迎　唐志信

補充詞

醫務室(醫護室)	打針	護士	醫院	診所	嚴重	厲害
體溫	流感(流行性感冒)		預防針	流感疫苗		

Lesson 20

把	帶來	啊	進	搬	出	出去	過來
做飯	吸煙	沒關係	以前	但是	女朋友	必須	第一天
付	房租	樓上	馬上				

專名

常天	夏中明	謝進學

補充詞

房東	房客	簽約	租屋

Lesson 21

暑假	畢業	決定	申請	研究生院		國外	留學
找	打工	家	公司	實習	電腦	暑期	班
一面	有意思	愉快	一路平安		好運		

專名

程海華	白秋雨	加州

補充詞

大學生	研究生	博士生	學位	學士	碩士	博士
簡歷(履歷表)						

Lesson 22

對不起	因為	不過	認真	已經	美麗	城市	到處
新	大樓	地方	活動	比如	京劇	書法	東西
最	小籠包	機會	嚐嚐	開始	高興	收到	看來
開心	同事	熱心	老闆	一些	學到	來信	保重

補充詞

心想事成	健康	順利

繁簡體字對照表
TRADITIONAL/SIMPLIFIED CHARACTER TABLE

繁體字：[fán tǐ zì]　traditional character (or: complex character)
簡體字：[jiǎn tǐ zì]　simplified character

第一課　Lesson 1

繁：	學	嗎	師
簡：	学	吗	师

第二課　Lesson 2

繁：	貴	請	問	麼	誰
簡：	贵	请	问	么	谁

第三課　Lesson 3

繁：	國	對	說	會	點	兒
簡：	国	对	说	会	点	儿

第四課　Lesson 4

繁：	書	這	難	課	們
簡：	书	这	难	课	们

第五課　Lesson 5

繁：	來	紹	幾	兩	個
簡：	来	绍	几	两	个

第六課　Lesson 6

繁：	從	媽	沒	輛	車	隻	愛
簡：	从	妈	没	辆	车	只	爱

第七課　Lesson 7

繁：	號	間	電	話	碼	機
簡：	号	间	电	话	码	机

第八課　Lesson 8

| 繁： | 認 | 識 | 後 | 飯 | 樣 | 見 |
| 簡： | 认 | 识 | 后 | 饭 | 样 | 见 |

第九課　Lesson 9

| 繁： | 謝 | 視 | 網 | 時 | 給 |
| 簡： | 谢 | 视 | 网 | 时 | 给 |

第十課　Lesson 10

| 繁： | 門 | 覺 | 圖 | 館 | 歡 | 寫 | 郵 |
| 簡： | 门 | 觉 | 图 | 馆 | 欢 | 写 | 邮 |

第十一課　Lesson 11

| 繁： | 紅 | 還 | 綠 | 務 | 員 | 樂 | 麵 | 餃 | 盤 | 湯 | 雙 |
| 簡： | 红 | 还 | 绿 | 务 | 员 | 乐 | 面 | 饺 | 盘 | 汤 | 双 |

第十二課　Lesson 12

| 繁： | 場 | 飛 | 擋 | 開 | 應 | 該 | 題 | 練 | 習 | 進 |
| 簡： | 场 | 飞 | 挡 | 开 | 应 | 该 | 题 | 练 | 习 | 进 |

第十三課　Lesson 13

| 繁： | 買 | 襯 | 條 | 褲 | 黃 | 錯 | 較 | 試 | 幫 | 讓 | 錢 |
| 簡： | 买 | 衬 | 条 | 裤 | 黄 | 错 | 较 | 试 | 帮 | 让 | 钱 |

| 繁： | 塊 | 張 |
| 簡： | 块 | 张 |

第十四課　Lesson 14

| 繁： | 歲 | 過 | 為 | 參 | 氣 |
| 簡： | 岁 | 过 | 为 | 参 | 气 |

第十五課　Lesson 15

| 繁： | 邊 | 觀 | 裡 | 廚 | 廳 | 臥 | 園 |
| 簡： | 边 | 观 | 里 | 厨 | 厅 | 卧 | 园 |

第十六課   Lesson 16

繁：	籃	倆	體	鍛	煉	現	賽	業
簡：	篮	俩	体	锻	炼	现	赛	业

第十七課   Lesson 17

繁：	熱	華	極	風
簡：	热	华	极	风

第十八課   Lesson 18

繁：	離	遠	鐘	騎	聽
簡：	离	远	钟	骑	听

第十九課   Lesson 19

繁：	餓	頭	發	燒	復	醫	藥	準	備	筆	記
簡：	饿	头	发	烧	复	医	药	准	备	笔	记

第二十課   Lesson 20

繁：	帶	煙	關	係	須	樓	馬
簡：	带	烟	关	系	须	楼	马

第二十一課   Lesson 21

繁：	畢	決	實	腦	運
簡：	毕	决	实	脑	运

第二十二課   Lesson 22

繁：	經	麗	處	動	劇	東	籠	嚐	興	闆
簡：	经	丽	处	动	剧	东	笼	尝	兴	板

第一課　你好!

Mary:	你好!
John:	你好!
Mary:	你是學生嗎?
John:	我是學生。你呢?
Mary:	我也是學生。
John:	他呢? 他是學生嗎?
Mary:	他不是學生。他是老師。

第一课　你好!

Mary:	你好!
John:	你好!
Mary:	你是学生吗?
John:	我是学生。你呢?
Mary:	我也是学生。
John:	他呢? 他是学生吗?
Mary:	他不是学生。他是老师。

第二課　您貴姓?

Mary:	你好! 請問您貴姓?
John:	我姓李，我的英文名字是 John Lee, 中文名字是李文中。你呢，請問你叫什麼名字?
Mary:	我叫 Mary, 我的英文名字是 Mary Wood, 中文名字是吳小美。
John:	她呢? 她是誰?
Mary:	她是我的同學于英。

第二课　您贵姓?

Mary:	你好! 请问您贵姓?
John:	我姓李，我的英文名字是 John Lee, 中文名字是李文中。你呢，请问你叫什么名字?
Mary:	我叫 Mary, 我的英文名字是 Mary Wood, 中文名字是吴小美。
John:	她呢? 她是谁?
Mary:	她是我的同学于英。

第三課　你是哪國人?

李文中：小美，你好嗎?
吳小美：我很好。對了，文中，你是哪國人?
李文中：我是法國人，你呢? 你是美國人嗎?
吳小美：不是，我不是美國人，我是英國人。
李文中：老師呢?
吳小美：他是中國人。他說中文。
李文中：你會說中文嗎?
吳小美：我會說一點兒中文，我也會說法文和英文。

第三课　你是哪国人?

李文中：小美，你好吗?
吳小美：我很好。对了，文中，你是哪国人?
李文中：我是法国人，你呢? 你是美国人吗?
吳小美：不是，我不是美国人，我是英国人。
李文中：老师呢?
吳小美：他是中国人。他说中文。
李文中：你会说中文吗?
吳小美：我会说一点儿中文，我也会说法文和英文。

第四課　你學什麼?

吳小美：文中，那是你的書嗎?
李文中：那是我的書。
吳小美：那是一本什麼書?
李文中：那是一本英文書。
吳小美：這本呢? 這是一本什麼書?
李文中：這是一本中文書。
吳小美：對了，你學什麼?
李文中：我學英國文學，你呢?
吳小美：我學工程。
李文中：工程難嗎?
吳小美：不太難，可是功課很多。
李文中：我們的功課也不少。

第四课　你学什么?

吴小美：文中，那是你的书吗?
李文中：那是我的书。
吴小美：那是一本什么书?
李文中：那是一本英文书。
吴小美：这本呢? 这是一本什么书?
李文中：这是一本中文书。
吴小美：对了，你学什么?
李文中：我学英国文学，你呢?
吴小美：我学工程。
李文中：工程难吗?
吴小美：不太难，可是功课很多。
李文中：我们的功课也不少。

第五課　這是我朋友

吴小美：文中，來! 我來介紹一下。這是我室友，王紅。這是我朋友，
　　　　文中。
李文中：你好!
王　紅：你好! 你有室友嗎?
李文中：有，我有室友。
王　紅：你有幾個室友?
李文中：我有兩個室友。
王　紅：他們都是誰?
李文中：他們是丁明和方小文。他們都是中國人。我常跟他們說中文。

第五课　这是我朋友

吴小美：文中，来! 我来介绍一下。这是我室友，王红。这是我朋友，
　　　　文中。
李文中：你好!
王　红：你好! 你有室友吗?
李文中：有，我有室友。
王　红：你有几个室友?
李文中：我有两个室友。
王　红：他们都是谁?
李文中：他们是丁明和方小文。他们都是中国人。我常跟他们说中文。

第六課　我的家

大家好! 我叫吳小美。我是從紐約來的。我學工程。我來介紹一下我的家。我家在紐約,有四個人:爸爸、媽媽、姐姐和我。爸爸是英國人,媽媽是美國人,他們都在紐約工作。爸爸是工程師,媽媽是老師,我和姐姐都是學生。姐姐有男朋友,我沒有。我們有兩輛車,一隻狗。我的家很好。我很愛我的家。

第六课　我的家

大家好! 我叫吴小美。我是从纽约来的。我学工程。我来介绍一下我的家。我家在纽约,有四个人:爸爸、妈妈、姐姐和我。爸爸是英国人,妈妈是美国人,他们都在纽约工作。爸爸是工程师,妈妈是老师,我和姐姐都是学生。姐姐有男朋友,我没有。我们有两辆车,一只狗。我的家很好。我很爱我的家。

第七課　你住哪兒?

陳愛文: 友朋,你住在哪兒?
張友朋: 我住宿舍。
陳愛文: 多少號?
張友朋: 三一四號。
陳愛文: 你的房間大嗎? 有沒有電話?
張友朋: 房間很小。有電話。
陳愛文: 你的電話號碼是多少?
張友朋: (一四二)二六八九三七五。
陳愛文: 你有手機嗎?
張友朋: 有。號碼是(一四二) 五一二六八三七。你也住宿舍嗎?
陳愛文: 不,我不住宿舍,我住校外。

第七课　你住哪儿?

陈爱文: 友朋,你住在哪儿?
张友朋: 我住宿舍。
陈爱文: 多少号?
张友朋: 三一四号。
陈爱文: 你的房间大吗? 有没有电话?
张友朋: 房间很小。有电话。
陈爱文: 你的电话号码是多少?
张友朋: (一四二)二六八九三七五。
陈爱文: 你有手机吗?
张友朋: 有。号码是(一四二) 五一二六八三七。你也住宿舍吗?
陈爱文: 不,我不住宿舍,我住校外。

第八課　你認識不認識他?

張友朋：愛文，你去哪兒?
陳愛文：是你，友朋，我去上課。你呢?
張友朋：我也去上課。下課以後你有事兒嗎?
陳愛文：我沒有事兒。我想回宿舍，有什麼事兒嗎?
張友朋：你認識不認識我的朋友小文?
陳愛文：我認識他。我們一起上英國文學課。
張友朋：下課以後我跟他一起去吃飯，你去不去?
陳愛文：太好了! 去哪兒吃飯?
張友朋：你想不想吃韓國菜?
陳愛文：想。可是我也想吃日本菜。
張友朋：我們今天吃韓國菜，下次吃日本菜，怎麼樣?
陳愛文：行。下課以後再見。
張友朋：再見。

第八课　你认识不认识他?

张友朋：爱文，你去哪儿?
陈爱文：是你，友朋，我去上课。你呢?
张友朋：我也去上课。下课以后你有事儿吗?
陈爱文：我没有事儿。我想回宿舍，有什么事儿吗?
张友朋：你认识不认识我的朋友小文?
陈爱文：我认识他。我们一起上英国文学课。
张友朋：下课以后我跟他一起去吃饭，你去不去?
陈爱文：太好了! 去哪儿吃饭?
张友朋：你想不想吃韩国菜?
陈爱文：想。可是我也想吃日本菜。
张友朋：我们今天吃韩国菜，下次吃日本菜，怎么样?
陈爱文：行。下课以后再见。
张友朋：再见。

第九課　他正在打電話

Situation 1: 在，請等一下兒

陳愛文：喂！我是愛文。請問友朋在嗎？
方書程：在，他在他的房間。請等一下兒。喂！友朋！你的電話。
張友朋：知道了！謝謝！
張友朋：喂！我是友朋，你是愛文吧！
陳愛文：對，是我。你在忙嗎？
張友朋：沒有。我正在看電視呢。你在做什麼？
陳愛文：我在上網。

Situation 2: 我就是

陳愛文：喂！
張友朋：喂！
陳愛文：請問友朋在嗎？
張友朋：我就是。請問您是哪位？
陳愛文：我是愛文。

Situation 3: 不在，請留言

陳愛文：喂！請問友朋在嗎？
丁　明：對不起，他不在。他在上課。
陳愛文：請問他什麼時候回來？
丁　明：今天晚上。你要不要留言？
陳愛文：好的。我是愛文。我的電話是(一四二)二六八九七五三。請他
　　　　回來以後給我打電話。謝謝！
丁　明：不謝。再見。

第九课　他正在打电话

<u>Situation 1:</u>　在，请等一下儿

陈爱文：喂！我是爱文。请问友朋在吗？
方書程：在，他在他的房间。请等一下儿。喂！友朋！你的电话。
张友朋：知道了！谢谢！
张友朋：喂！我是友朋，你是爱文吧！
陈爱文：对，是我。你在忙吗？
张友朋：没有。我正在看电视呢。你在做什么？
陈爱文：我在上网。

<u>Situation 2:</u>　我就是

陈爱文：喂！
张友朋：喂！
陈爱文：请问友朋在吗？
张友朋：我就是。请问您是哪位？
陈爱文：我是爱文。

<u>Situation 3:</u>　不在，请留言

陈爱文：喂！请问友朋在吗？
丁　明：对不起，他不在。他在上课。
陈爱文：请问他什么时候回来？
丁　明：今天晚上。你要不要留言？
陈爱文：好的。我是爱文。我的电话是(一四二)二六八九七五三。请他
　　　　回来以后给我打电话。谢谢！
丁　明：不谢。再见。

第十課　我每天七點半起床

小明：

　　你好！

　　這個學期我很忙，有五門課。你知道我每天幾點起床、幾點睡覺嗎？我七點半就起床，晚上十二點半以後才睡覺。每天都很忙。九點一刻去上課，十點二十分下課。然後，我去圖書館看書。下午下課以後，我喜歡去打球。每天都有很多功課。

　　這是我的大學生活，你呢？給我寫信吧。我的電子郵件地址是：xuewen376@zhongwen.edu

　　　　祝

好

　　　　　　　　　　　　　　　　　　　　　　　學文

　　　　　　　　　　　　　　　　　　　　二〇〇三年十一月二十日

第十课　我每天七点半起床

小明：

　　你好！

　　这个学期我很忙，有五门课。你知道我每天几点起床、几点睡觉吗？我七点半就起床，晚上十二点半以后才睡觉。每天都很忙。九点一刻去上课，十点二十分下课。然后，我去图书馆看书。下午下课以后，我喜欢去打球。每天都有很多功课。

　　这是我的大学生活，你呢？给我写信吧。我的电子邮件地址是：xuewen376@zhongwen.edu

　　　　祝

好

　　　　　　　　　　　　　　　　　　　　　　　学文

　　　　　　　　　　　　　　　　　　　　二〇〇三年十一月二十日

第十一課　你要紅茶還是綠茶？

服務員：請問，幾位？
張正然：三位。
服務員：好，請跟我來。請坐。
張正然，孫信美，楊歡：　謝謝！
服務員：小姐，先生，請問，你們想先喝點兒什麼？
孫信美：我喜歡喝茶。
服務員：你要紅茶還是綠茶？
孫信美：我要一杯冰紅茶。
楊　歡：我要一杯可樂。
張正然：我要一瓶啤酒。
服務員：好，一杯冰紅茶、一杯可樂、一瓶啤酒。請等一下。
張正然：對了，你們喜歡吃飯還是吃麵？
孫信美：我都喜歡。
楊　歡：我想吃餃子。
服務員：這是您的冰紅茶、可樂、還有啤酒。你們要點菜嗎？
張正然：好，我們點一盤炒飯、一盤炒麵和二十個餃子吧。
孫信美：我們還要三碗湯。對了，我們也要三雙筷子，謝謝！

第十一课　你要红茶还是绿茶？

服务员：请问，几位？
张正然：三位。
服务员：好，请跟我来。请坐。
张正然，孙信美，杨欢：　谢谢！
服务员：小姐，先生，请问，你们想先喝点儿什么？
孙信美：我喜欢喝茶。
服务员：你要红茶还是绿茶？
孙信美：我要一杯冰红茶。
杨　欢：我要一杯可乐。
张正然：我要一瓶啤酒。
服务员：好，一杯冰红茶、一杯可乐、一瓶啤酒。请等一下。
张正然：对了，你们喜欢吃饭还是吃面？
孙信美：我都喜欢。
杨　欢：我想吃饺子。
服务员：这是您的冰红茶、可乐、还有啤酒。你们要点菜吗？
张正然：好，我们点一盘炒饭、一盘炒面和二十个饺子吧。
孙信美：我们还要三碗汤。对了，我们也要三双筷子，谢谢！

第十二課   我可以借你的車嗎?

于　　影: 本樂，明天下午你用不用車?
王本樂: 我不用。你有什麼事兒嗎?
于　　影: 我得去機場接人，可以借你的車嗎?
王本樂: 可以。你要去接誰?
于　　影: 我妹妹和她男朋友。他們從上海坐飛機去洛杉磯玩兒，
　　　　　明天會到我這兒來。
王本樂: 我的車是手排擋的，你會不會開?
于　　影: 應該沒問題。我爸爸的車也是手排擋的，我常開他的車。
王本樂: 我的車是白色的，車號是BD5730,停在五號停車場。
于　　影: 知道了。謝謝!
王本樂: 不謝。你妹妹他們會說英文嗎?
于　　影: 會一點兒，這次他們想多學習一點兒英文。
王本樂: 太好了，我得跟他們多練習一點兒中文。這樣，我的中文就能
　　　　　進步了。

第十二课   我可以借你的车吗?

于　　影: 本乐，明天下午你用不用车?
王本乐: 我不用。你有什么事儿吗?
于　　影: 我得去机场接人，可以借你的车吗?
王本乐: 可以。你要去接谁?
于　　影: 我妹妹和她男朋友。他们从上海坐飞机去洛杉矶玩儿，
　　　　　明天会到我这儿来。
王本乐: 我的车是手排挡的，你会不会开?
于　　影: 应该没问题。我爸爸的车也是手排挡的，我常开他的车。
王本乐: 我的车是白色的，车号是BD5730,停在五号停车场。
于　　影: 知道了。谢谢!
王本乐: 不谢。你妹妹他们会说英文吗?
于　　影: 会一点儿，这次他们想多学习一点儿英文。
王本乐: 太好了，我得跟他们多练习一点儿中文。这样，我的中文就能
　　　　　进步了。

第十三課　我想買一件襯衫

店　員：兩位小姐想買什麼?
毛愛紅：我想買一件襯衫。
方子英：我想買一條裙子或者褲子。
店　員：這件黃襯衫怎麼樣?
毛愛紅：還不錯。可是我比較喜歡穿黑色的，有沒有黑色的?
店　員：有，在這兒，你試試!
方子英：愛紅，來，你幫我看看，我穿裙子好看還是穿褲子好看?
毛愛紅：你穿穿，讓我看看。我覺得你穿這條裙子好看。
方子英：請問，這條裙子多少錢?
店　員：十五塊。
方子英：好，我買了。
毛愛紅：我要買這件黑襯衫。
店　員：對了，小姐，這張電影票是你的嗎?
方子英：是的，這張電影票是我的。謝謝! 我們等一下要去看電影。

第十三课　我想买一件衬衫

店　员：两位小姐想买什么?
毛爱红：我想买一件衬衫。
方子英：我想买一条裙子或者裤子。
店　员：这件黄衬衫怎么样?
毛爱红：还不错。可是我比较喜欢穿黑色的，有没有黑色的?
店　员：有，在这儿，你试试!
方子英：爱红，来，你帮我看看，我穿裙子好看还是穿裤子好看?
毛爱红：你穿穿，让我看看。我觉得你穿这条裙子好看。
方子英：请问，这条裙子多少钱?
店　员：十五块。
方子英：好，我买了。
毛爱红：我要买这件黑衬衫。
店　员：对了，小姐，这张电影票是你的吗?
方子英：是的，这张电影票是我的。谢谢! 我们等一下要去看电影。

第十四課　我今年二十歲

方子英：愛紅，二月十八日你有沒有空?
毛愛紅：二月十八日那天是星期幾?
方子英：星期六。
毛愛紅：我有空。有什麼事兒嗎?
方子英：那天我過生日，我男朋友要為我開一個生日舞會，我想請你參
　　　　加。
毛愛紅：謝謝你，我一定去。還有誰會去?
方子英：我們想請我們的同學和朋友都參加。
毛愛紅：我會做蛋糕。我送你一個生日蛋糕，怎麼樣?
方子英：太棒了! 謝謝你!
毛愛紅：不客氣。你今年多大?
方子英：我今年二十歲。你呢? 你的生日是幾月幾號?
毛愛紅：我的生日是十月三號，我今年二十二歲。你的舞會在哪兒開?
方子英：在我男朋友的家，這是他的地址。你知道怎麼去嗎?
毛愛紅：沒問題! 我有地圖。星期六下午五點見。
方子英：再見。

第十四课　我今年二十岁

方子英：爱红，二月十八日你有没有空?
毛爱红：二月十八日那天是星期几?
方子英：星期六。
毛爱红：我有空。有什么事儿吗?
方子英：那天我过生日，我男朋友要为我开一个生日舞会，我想请你参
　　　　加。
毛爱红：谢谢你，我一定去。还有谁会去?
方子英：我们想请我们的同学和朋友都参加。
毛爱红：我会做蛋糕。我送你一个生日蛋糕，怎么样?
方子英：太棒了! 谢谢你!
毛爱红：不客气。你今年多大?
方子英：我今年二十岁。你呢? 你的生日是几月几号?
毛爱红：我的生日是十月三号，我今年二十二岁。你的舞会在哪儿开?
方子英：在我男朋友的家，这是他的地址。你知道怎么去吗?
毛爱红：没问题! 我有地图。星期六下午五点见。
方子英：再见。

第十五課 圖書館在宿舍前邊

(Situation: 今天是宿舍參觀日，在學生宿舍)

田　進：你們好！歡迎你們來看我的宿舍。請跟我來。
梁園生：田進，你的宿舍裡邊有沒有廚房？
田　進：有廚房，是公用的。
包志中：你的房間在哪兒？
田　進：我的房間在旁邊，從這兒走。來，請進。這是客廳，客廳的對
　　　　面是一個餐廳。
梁園生：洗澡間呢？
田　進：洗澡間在客廳和臥室的中間。你看，這是我的臥室。
包志中：桌子上邊的中文書都是你的嗎？
田　進：有的是我的，有的是我朋友的。
包志中：你常在宿舍學習嗎？
田　進：不，我不常在宿舍學習，我常去圖書館學習。
梁園生：圖書館在哪兒？
田　進：圖書館在宿舍前邊。圖書館的後邊還有一個公園。我常去那兒
　　　　打球。
梁園生，包志中：你們的宿舍真不錯。

第十五课 图书馆在宿舍前边

(Situation: 今天是宿舍参观日，在学生宿舍)

田　进：你们好！欢迎你们来看我的宿舍。请跟我来。
梁园生：田进，你的宿舍里边有没有厨房？
田　进：有厨房，是公用的。
包志中：你的房间在哪儿？
田　进：我的房间在旁边，从这儿走。来，请进。这是客厅，客厅的对
　　　　面是一个餐厅。
梁园生：洗澡间呢？
田　进：洗澡间在客厅和卧室的中间。你看，这是我的卧室。
包志中：桌子上边的中文书都是你的吗？
田　进：有的是我的，有的是我朋友的。
包志中：你常在宿舍学习吗？
田　进：不，我不常在宿舍学习，我常去图书馆学习。
梁园生：图书馆在哪儿？
田　进：图书馆在宿舍前边。图书馆的后边还有一个公园。我常去那儿
　　　　打球。
梁园生，包志中：你们的宿舍真不错。

第十六課　她打籃球打得很好

張正然：你們倆要去哪兒?
孫信美，楊歡：　我們去打籃球。
張正然：你們籃球打得怎麼樣?
孫信美：楊歡籃球打得很好。我還不太會打籃球，她是我的教練，她教
　　　　得很好。
楊　歡：不行，我還打得不太好。
張正然：我不常打籃球，我常常和我室友去游泳，他游泳游得非常快。
楊　歡：你們常去哪兒游泳?
張正然：我們常去體育館裡邊的游泳池游泳，我們也常去健身房鍛煉。
孫信美：你現在要不要跟我們去打籃球?
張正然：現在不行。我昨天看球賽看得太晚了，今天起得很晚，
　　　　現在得去做作業。
楊　歡：昨天我們那兒包餃子、做中國菜。你晚上到我們那兒吃餃子
　　　　吧。
張正然：太好了! 我很喜歡吃餃子。你們包餃子包得快不快?
孫信美：我們包得很慢。
楊　歡：信美很會做飯。她做飯做得很好。

第十六课　她打篮球打得很好

张正然：你们俩要去哪儿?
孙信美，杨欢：　我们去打篮球。
张正然：你们篮球打得怎么样?
孙信美：杨欢篮球打得很好。我还不太会打篮球，她是我的教练，她教
　　　　得很好。
杨　欢：不行，我还打得不太好。
张正然：我不常打篮球，我常常和我室友去游泳，他游泳游得非常快。
杨　欢：你们常去哪儿游泳?
张正然：我们常去体育馆里边的游泳池游泳，我们也常去健身房锻炼。
孙信美：你现在要不要跟我们去打篮球?
张正然：现在不行。我昨天看球赛看得太晚了，今天起得很晚，
　　　　现在得去做作业。
杨　欢：昨天我们那儿包饺子、做中国菜。你晚上到我们那儿吃饺子
　　　　吧。
张正然：太好了! 我很喜欢吃饺子。你们包饺子包得快不快?
孙信美：我们包得很慢。
杨　欢：信美很会做饭。她做饭做得很好。

第十七課　春天就要來了

小玲：

　　好久不見。

　　你現在怎麼樣? 時間過得真快，春天就要來了，我們也快要放春假了。

　　我們這兒的氣候春夏秋冬都有。其中我最喜歡春天，很暖和，可是很短。夏天有時候很熱，最熱的時候，會到華氏一百度，熱極了。秋天有時候會刮風、下雨。這兒的冬天非常冷，常常下雪。

　　放春假的時候我想去你那兒玩玩，我們很快就要見面了!

　　　　祝

好!

大中

二〇〇四年三月十日

第十七课　春天就要来了

小玲：

　　好久不见。

　　你现在怎么样? 时间过得真快，春天就要来了，我们也快要放春假了。

　　我们这儿的气候春夏秋冬都有。其中我最喜欢春天，很暖和，可是很短。夏天有时候很热，最热的时候，会到华氏一百度，热极了。秋天有时候会刮风、下雨。这儿的冬天非常冷，常常下雪。

　　放春假的时候我想去你那儿玩玩，我们很快就要见面了!

　　　　祝

好!

大中

二〇〇四年三月十日

第十八課　我們要坐火車去旅行

季長風：秋影，你住在校外嗎? 離學校遠不遠?
白秋影：不太遠，開車只要五分鐘。
季長風：你每天怎麼來學校?
白秋影：我常騎自行車，下雨下雪的時候就坐公共汽車，有時候我也走
　　　　路，可以鍛煉鍛煉。你呢?
季長風：我住在宿舍，離學校很近，我每天走路來學校。
白秋影：對了，這個春假你要做什麼?
季長風：我要跟我的室友一起去西部旅行。
白秋影：你們怎麼去?
季長風：我們想先坐火車去，路上看看風景。然後坐船去加拿大，再從
　　　　加拿大坐飛機回來。你呢?
白秋影：我很想我爸爸、媽媽和妹妹，我要先回家。然後再跟朋友開車
　　　　去玩兒。
季長風：你們要去哪兒玩兒?
白秋影：我們想去南部玩兒。聽說那兒的海邊景色很美。
季長風：你們有幾個人去?
白秋影：我們一共有五個人去，我們想租一輛車。

第十八课　我们要坐火车去旅行

季长风：秋影，你住在校外吗? 离学校远不远?
白秋影：不太远，开车只要五分钟。
季长风：你每天怎么来学校?
白秋影：我常骑自行车，下雨下雪的时候就坐公共汽车，有时候我也走
　　　　路，可以锻炼锻炼。你呢?
季长风：我住在宿舍，离学校很近，我每天走路来学校。
白秋影：对了，这个春假你要做什么?
季长风：我要跟我的室友一起去西部旅行。
白秋影：你们怎么去?
季长风：我们想先坐火车去，路上看看风景。然后坐船去加拿大，再从
　　　　加拿大坐飞机回来。你呢?
白秋影：我很想我爸爸、妈妈和妹妹，我要先回家。然后再跟朋友开车
　　　　去玩儿。
季长风：你们要去哪儿玩儿?
白秋影：我们想去南部玩儿。听说那儿的海边景色很美。
季长风：你们有几个人去?
白秋影：我们一共有五个人去，我们想租一辆车。

第十九課　我感冒了

唐志信：歐陽迎，你吃飯了嗎?
歐陽迎：還沒有呢。我不餓。
唐志信：你怎麼了? 好像不舒服。
歐陽迎：我感冒了。我頭疼發燒，還有一點兒咳嗽。
唐志信：你怎麼生病了呢?
歐陽迎：這幾天我有很多考試，每天都在復習，睡覺睡得太少，所以就
　　　　病了。
唐志信：你看醫生了沒有?
歐陽迎：看了。我也吃藥了。可是還沒有好呢。
唐志信：你應該在家好好地休息。不應該來上課。
歐陽迎：你說得很對，可是我有很多考試。我得好好地準備。
唐志信：這是我上課的筆記，借給你看看。
歐陽迎：非常感謝! 好吧，我現在就回家休息。
唐志信：好，我開車送你回去。你得好好地睡覺。

第十九课　我感冒了

唐志信：欧阳迎，你吃饭了吗?
欧阳迎：还没有呢。我不饿。
唐志信：你怎么了? 好像不舒服。
欧阳迎：我感冒了。我头疼发烧，还有一点儿咳嗽。
唐志信：你怎么生病了呢?
欧阳迎：这几天我有很多考试，每天都在复习，睡觉睡得太少，所以就
　　　　病了。
唐志信：你看医生了没有?
欧阳迎：看了。我也吃药了。可是还没有好呢。
唐志信：你应该在家好好地休息。不应该来上课。
欧阳迎：你说得很对，可是我有很多考试。我得好好地准备。
唐志信：这是我上课的笔记，借给你看看。
欧阳迎：非常感谢! 好吧，我现在就回家休息。
唐志信：好，我开车送你回去。你得好好地睡觉。

第二十課　我把小謝帶來了 . . .

常　天：中明，我回來了。我把車開回來了，還把小謝也帶來了。
夏中明：是小謝啊！快請他進來。
謝進學：我聽說你們這兒有一個人搬出去了，我想搬進來，所以過來看看。
常　天：你不想住宿舍了，是不是？
謝進學：是的。宿舍太小了，我想搬出來住。這兒可以不可以做飯？
夏中明：可以，我們有廚房。
謝進學：太好了！我很喜歡做飯。搬出來以後就可以常常做飯了。
常　天：你吸煙嗎？我們這兒不能吸煙。
謝進學：沒關係。以前我吸煙，但是我女朋友說我不應該吸煙，所以我現在不吸煙了。
夏中明：還有，我們必須在每個月的第一天付房租。
謝進學：沒問題！
常　天：喂，小謝，我在樓上，你要不要上來看看？中明，你把小謝帶上來看看吧。
夏中明：常天，我們現在還不能上去，你得先下來幫我把這張桌子搬上去。
常　天：好的，我馬上下去。

第二十课　我把小谢带来了 . . .

常　天：中明，我回来了。我把车开回来了，还把小谢也带来了。
夏中明：是小谢啊！快请他进来。
谢进学：我听说你们这儿有一个人搬出去了，我想搬进来，所以过来看看。
常　天：你不想住宿舍了，是不是？
谢进学：是的。宿舍太小了，我想搬出来住。这儿可以不可以做饭？
夏中明：可以，我们有厨房。
谢进学：太好了！我很喜欢做饭。搬出来以后就可以常常做饭了。
常　天：你吸烟吗？我们这儿不能吸烟。
谢进学：没关系。以前我吸烟，但是我女朋友说我不应该吸烟，所以我现在不吸烟了。
夏中明：还有，我们必须在每个月的第一天付房租。
谢进学：没问题！
常　天：喂，小谢，我在楼上，你要不要上来看看？中明，你把小谢带上来看看吧。
夏中明：常天，我们现在还不能上去，你得先下来帮我把这张桌子搬上去。
常　天：好的，我马上下去。

第二十一課 暑假你要做什麼?

程海華：秋雨，我問你，你明年就要畢業了，畢業以後你想做什麼?
白秋雨：我還沒有決定呢。可是我很喜歡學習，我可能會申請研究生院，
　　　　或者去國外留學。你呢? 你什麼時候畢業?
程海華：我還有兩年才畢業呢。畢業以後我想去找工作。
白秋雨：我們就要放暑假了，今年暑假你要做什麼?
程海華：我要去打工。我要去一家公司實習。
白秋雨：在哪兒? 是什麼工作?
程海華：在加州，是一家電腦公司。你呢? 暑假你要做什麼?
白秋雨：我要去中國，我申請了去上海的暑期班學習，我想一面學中文，
　　　　一面在中國旅行。
程海華：那一定很有意思。你什麼時候去?
白秋雨：下個星期。
程海華：這麼快! 你到中國以後要常常給我寫電子郵件。
白秋雨：沒問題。我祝你工作愉快!
程海華：我也祝你一路平安! 祝你好運!

第二十一课 暑假你要做什么?

程海华：秋雨，我问你，你明年就要毕业了，毕业以后你想做什么?
白秋雨：我还没有决定呢。可是我很喜欢学习，我可能会申请研究生院，
　　　　或者去国外留学。你呢? 你什么时候毕业?
程海华：我还有两年才毕业呢。毕业以后我想去找工作。
白秋雨：我们就要放暑假了，今年暑假你要做什么?
程海华：我要去打工。我要去一家公司实习。
白秋雨：在哪儿? 是什么工作?
程海华：在加州，是一家电脑公司。你呢? 暑假你要做什么?
白秋雨：我要去中国，我申请了去上海的暑期班学习，我想一面学中文，
　　　　一面在中国旅行。
程海华：那一定很有意思。你什么时候去?
白秋雨：下个星期。
程海华：这么快! 你到中国以后要常常给我写电子邮件。
白秋雨：没问题。我祝你工作愉快!
程海华：我也祝你一路平安! 祝你好运!

第二十二課　我到上海了

海華:

　　你好! 今天是六月十五號, 我一個星期以前就到上海了。對不起, 因為太忙了, 所以今天才給你寫電子郵件。

　　我們每天都有很多課, 功課也不少, 不過老師教得很好, 也很認真。我們每天都說中文, 我的中文進步得很快, 現在我已經能說很多中文了。

　　上海是一個非常美麗的城市, 到處都是新的大樓。我們參觀了一些地方, 也參加了一些活動, 比如: 看京劇、寫書法等等, 都很有意思。還有, 上海有很多好吃的東西, 其中我最喜歡吃的是小籠包, 你有機會應該嚐嚐。

　　你開始實習了嗎? 忙不忙? 有空請給我寫電子郵件。

　　　　祝

好!

　　　　　　　　　　　　　　　　　　　　　　秋雨

　　　　　　　　　　　　　　　　　　二〇〇四年六月十五日

秋雨:

　　你好! 很高興收到你的電子郵件。看來你在上海過得很開心。

　　我現在在洛杉磯, 已經開始實習了。這兒的同事都很好, 也很熱心, 常常教我很多東西, 老闆也不錯。我的工作有時候忙, 有時候不太忙, 我想我得認真地工作, 才能學到一些東西。

　　好了, 不多寫了。有空請多來信, 多保重。

　　　　祝

好!

　　　　　　　　　　　　　　　　　　　　　　海華

　　　　　　　　　　　　　　　　　　二〇〇四年六月十七日

第二十二课　我到上海了

海华：

　　你好！今天是六月十五号，我一个星期以前就到上海了。对不起，因为太忙了，所以今天才给你写电子邮件。

　　我们每天都有很多课，功课也不少，不过老师教得很好，也很认真。我们每天都说中文，我的中文进步得很快，现在我已经能说很多中文了。

　　上海是一个非常美丽的城市，到处都是新的大楼。我们参观了一些地方，也参加了一些活动，比如：看京剧、写书法等等，都很有意思。还有，上海有很多好吃的东西，其中我最喜欢吃的是小笼包，你有机会应该尝尝。

　　你开始实习了吗？忙不忙？有空请给我写电子邮件。

　　　　祝

好！

秋雨
二〇〇四年六月十五日

秋雨：

　　你好！很高兴收到你的电子邮件。看来你在上海过得很开心。

　　我现在在洛杉矶，已经开始实习了。这儿的同事都很好，也很热心，常常教我很多东西，老板也不错。我的工作有时候忙，有时候不太忙，我想我得认真地工作，才能学到一些东西。

　　好了，不多写了。有空请多来信，多保重。

　　　　祝

好！

海华
二〇〇四年六月十七日

Lesson 1   Hello!

Mary: Hello!
John: Hello!
Mary: Are you a student?
John: I'm a student. How about you?
Mary: I'm also a student.
John: How about him? Is he a student?
Mary: He is not a student. He is a teacher.

Lesson 2   What's Your Surname?

Mary: Hello. May I ask your surname?
John: My family name is Lee. My English name is John Lee. My Chinese name is
        Wenzhong Li. What's your name?
Mary: I'm Mary. My English name is Mary Wood. My Chinese name is Xiaomei Wu.
John: How about her? Who is she?
Mary: She is my classmate Ying Yu.

Lesson 3   Which Country Are You From?

Wenzhong Li: Xiaomei, how are you?
Xiaomei Wu: I'm fine. By the way, Wenzhong, which country are you from?
Wenzhong Li: I'm French. How about you? Are you American?
Xiaomei Wu: No, I'm not American. I'm British.
Wenzhong Li: How about the teacher?
Xiaomei Wu: He is Chinese. He speaks Chinese.
Wenzhong Li: Can you speak Chinese?
Xiaomei Wu: I can speak a little Chinese. I can also speak French and English.

Lesson 4   What Do You Study?

Xiaomei Wu: Wenzhong, is that your book?
Wenzhong Li: That is my book.
Xiaomei Wu: What book is that?
Wenzhong Li: That is an English book.
Xiaomei Wu: How about this book? What book is this?
Wenzhong Li: This is a Chinese book.
Xiaomei Wu: Well, what do you study?

Wenzhong Li:	I study English literature. How about you?
Xiaomei Wu:	I study engineering.
Wenzhong Li:	Is engineering difficult?
Xiaomei Wu:	Not very difficult. But there is a lot of homework.
Wenzhong Li:	We have a lot of homework too.

Lesson 5   This Is My Friend

Xiaomei Wu:	Wenzhong, come here! Let me introduce you. This is my roommate Hong Wang. This is my friend Wenzhong.
Wenzhong Li:	Hello!
Hong Wang:	Hello! Do you have roommates?
Wenzhong Li:	Yes.
Hong Wang:	How many roommates do you have?
Wenzhong Li:	I have two roommates.
Hong Wang:	Who are they?
Wenzhong Li:	They are Ming Ding and Xiaowen Fang. They are both Chinese. I often speak with them in Chinese.

Lesson 6   My Family

Hi everybody! I'm Xiaomei Wu. I'm from New York. I study engineering. Let me introduce my family. My home is in New York. There are four people in my family: father, mother, elder sister, and I. My father is British. My mother is American. They both work in New York. My father is an engineer. My mother is a teacher. My elder sister and I are both students. She has a boyfriend; I don't. We have two cars and a dog. My family is very nice. I love my family.

Lesson 7   Where Do You Live?

Aiwen Chen:	Youpeng, where do you live?
Youpeng Zhang:	I live in the dorm.
Aiwen Chen:	What's your room number?
Youpeng Zhang:	No. 314.
Aiwen Chen:	Is your room big? Is there a phone?
Youpeng Zhang:	My room is very small. There is a phone.
Aiwen Chen:	What's your phone number?
Youpeng Zhang:	(142) 268-9375
Aiwen Chen:	Do you have a cell phone?
Youpeng Zhang:	Yes. My number is (142) 512-6037. Do you live in the dorm too?
Aiwen Chen:	No, I don't live in the dorm. I live off campus.

Lesson 8　Do You Know Him?

Youpeng Zhang:	Aiwen, where are you going?
Aiwen Chen:	It's you, Youpeng. I'm going to class. How about you?
Youpeng Zhang:	I'm going to class too. Do you have any plans for after class?
Aiwen Chen:	No. I'd like to go back to the dorm. What's up?
Youpeng Zhang:	Do you know my friend Xiao Wen?
Aiwen Chen:	I know him. We take English literature together.
Youpeng Zhang:	I'm going to have dinner with him after class. Will you come?
Aiwen Chen:	Great! Where are we going?
Youpeng Zhang:	Do you want to have Korean food?
Aiwen Chen:	Yes. But I also want to have Japanese food.
Youpeng Zhang:	Let's have Korean food today. Next time we'll have Japanese food. How is that?
Aiwen Chen:	OK. See you after class.
Youpeng Zhang:	See you.

Lesson 9　He Is Making a Phone Call

Situation 1　Please Hold

Aiwen Chen:	Hello! This is Aiwen. Is Youpeng in now?
Shucheng Fang:	Yes, he is in his room. Please hold. Hey, Youpeng, the phone is for you.
Youpeng Zhang:	Got it! Thank you!
Youpeng Zhang:	Hello! This is Youpeng. You must be Aiwen!
Aiwen Chen:	Right, it's me. Are you busy?
Youpeng Zhang:	No. I'm watching TV. What are you doing?
Aiwen Chen:	I'm online.

Situation 2　Speaking

Aiwen Chen:	Hello!
Youpeng Zhang:	Hello!
Aiwen Chen:	Is Youpeng in?
Youpeng Zhang:	Speaking. May I ask who is calling?
Aiwen Chen:	It's Aiwen.

Situation 3　Please Leave a Message

Aiwen Chen:	Hello! Is Youpeng in?
Ding Ming:	Sorry, he is not here. He is in class.
Aiwen Chen:	When will he be back?
Ding Ming:	Tonight. Do you want to leave a message?
Aiwen Chen:	OK. I'm Aiwen. My phone number is (142) 268-9753. Please ask him to call back when he returns. Thank you!
Ding Ming:	My pleasure. Goodbye.

Lesson 10   I Get Up at 7:30 Every Day

Xiao Ming,

How are you?

I'm very busy this semester. I have five classes. Can you guess when I get up and go to bed every day? I get up at 7:30, and go to bed after 12:00. I'm very busy every day. I walk from the dorm to class at 9:15 every morning. Class is over at 10:20. Then I go to the library to study. In the afternoon after class, I like to play basketball. I have lots of homework every day.

This is my college life. How about you? Send me a letter. My e-mail address is xuewen376@zhongwen.edu.

Wish you all the best.

Xuewen
Nov. 20, 2003

Lesson 11   Do You Want Black Tea or Green Tea?

Waitress:	How many?
Zhenran Zhang:	Three.
Waitress:	OK. Please follow me. Sit down, please.
Zhenran Zhang, Xinmei Sun, Huan Yang:	Thank you.
Waitress:	Miss, sir, what would you like to drink?
Xinmei Sun:	I would like tea.
Waitress:	Black tea or green tea?
Xinmei Sun:	Iced black tea, please.
Huan Yang:	Coke for me, please.
Zhenran Zhang:	I'd like to have a bottle of beer.
Waitress:	OK, iced tea, Coke, and a bottle of beer. Won't be a moment.
Zhenran Zhang:	Well. Do you want to have rice or noodles?
Xinmei Sun:	I like both.
Huan Yang:	I want to have dumplings.
Waitress:	These are your iced tea, Coke, and beer. Would you like to order food?
Zhenran Zhang:	OK. Let's have one fried rice, one fried noodles, and twenty dumplings.
Xinmei Sun:	We also want soup for three. And we would like to have three pairs of chopsticks too. Thanks.

Lesson 12   May I Borrow Your Car?

Xin Yu:	Benle, will you use your car tomorrow afternoon?
Benle Wang:	No. What's up?
Xin Yu:	I need to go to the airport to pick somebody up. May I borrow your car?
Benle Wang:	Sure. Who are you picking up?
Xin Yu:	My younger sister and her boyfriend. They are flying to Los Angeles from Shanghai to do some sightseeing. They arrive tomorrow.

Benle Wang:	My car has a manual transmission. Do you know how to drive it?
Xin Yu:	There should be no problem. My dad's car also has a manual transmission. I often drove his car.
Benle Wang:	My car is white. The plate number is BD5730, and it is parked at the parking lot No. 5.
Xin Yu:	I see. Thanks!
Benle Wang:	You are welcome. Does your sister speak English?
Xin Yu:	A little bit. This time they want to learn some English.
Benle Wang:	Great! I should practice some Chinese with them. That way, my Chinese will make progress.

Lesson 13　I Want to Buy a Shirt

Sales:	What would you like to buy?
Aihong Mao:	I want to buy a shirt.
Ziying Fang:	I want to buy a skirt or pants.
Sales:	How about this yellow shirt?
Aihong Mao:	Good. But I like black better. Do you have black ones?
Sales:	Yes, here. Have a try.
Ziying Fang:	Aihong, come and have a look. Would I look good in this shirt or pants?
Aihong Mao:	Put them on and let me have a look. I think you look good in this shirt.
Ziying Fang:	How much is this shirt?
Sales:	Fifteen dollars.
Ziying Fang:	OK, I'll buy it.
Aihong Mao:	I'll take this shirt too.
Sales:	Well, miss, is this movie ticket yours?
Ziying Fang:	Yes, thank you! The ticket is mine. We are going to see a movie later.

Lesson 14　I Am 20 This Year

Ziying Fang:	Aihong, will you be free on February 18?
Aihong Mao:	What day of the week is February 18?
Ziying Fang:	It's a Saturday.
Aihong Mao:	I'll be free. Do you have anything in mind?
Ziying Fang:	It's my birthday. My boyfriend is having a party for me. I'd like to invite you.
Aihong Mao:	Thank you. I'll definitely come. Who else is coming?
Ziying Fang:	We want to invite all our classmates and friends.
Aihong Mao:	I know how to make cake. I'll make a cake for you, how's that?
Ziying Fang:	Great! Thank you!
Aihong Mao:	You're welcome. How old are you?
Ziying Fang:	I'll be twenty this year. How about you? When's your birthday?
Aihong Mao:	My birthday is October 3. I'm twenty-two. Where will the party be held?
Ziying Fang:	At my boyfriend's place. This is his address. Do you know how to get there?
Aihong Mao:	No problem. I have a map. See you at 5:00 Saturday afternoon.
Ziying Fang:	See you.

Lesson 15   The Library Is in Front of the Dorm

(At the students' dorm)

Jin Tian:	Hello! Welcome to my dorm. Please follow me.
Yuansheng Liang:	Jin Tian, is there a kitchen in your dorm?
Jin Tian:	Yes, it's shared.
Zhizhong Bao:	Where is your room?
Jin Tian:	My room is on that side. Go this way. Come, please come in! This is the living room. The dining room is on the opposite side.
Yuansheng Liang:	Where is the bathroom?
Jin Tian:	The bathroom is between the living room and the bedroom. Look, this is my bedroom.
Zhizhong Bao:	Are all the Chinese books on the table yours?
Jin Tian:	No. Some are mine, some are my friends'.
Zhizhong Bao:	Do you often study in your dorm?
Jin Tian:	No, I don't often study in the dorm. I usually go to study in the library.
Yuansheng Liang:	Where is the library?
Jin Tian:	The library is in front of the dorm. At the back of the library there is a park. I often go there to play ball.
Yuansheng Liang and Zhizhong Bao:	Your dorm is very nice.

Lesson 16   She Plays Basketball Very Well

Zhengran Zhang:	Where are you going?
Xinmei Sun and Huan Yang:	We are going to play basketball.
Zhengran Zhang:	Are you good at it?
Xinmei Sun:	Huan Yang plays very well. I'm not very good at it. She is my coach. She coaches me very well.
Huan Yang:	No, I don't play very well.
Zhengran Zhang:	I don't play basketball often. I usually go swimming with my roommate. He swims really fast!
Huan Yang:	Where do you usually go?
Zhengran Zhang:	The swimming pool in the gym. And we also exercise often in the gym.
Xinmei Sun:	Do you want to come to play basketball with us?
Zhengran Zhang:	Not now. I stayed up too late watching the game last night, so I got up very late this morning. Now I have to do homework.
Huan Yang:	Yesterday we made dumplings and Chinese food. Come to our place to eat dumplings tonight.
Zhengran Zhang:	Great. I like dumplings very much. Do you make dumplings quickly?
Xinme Sun:	No, we are very slow.
Huan Yang:	Xinmei is very good at cooking. She cooks very well.

Lesson 17   Spring Is Coming Soon

Xiao Ling:

Long time no see. How are you? Time is flying by. Spring is coming. And we will have spring break soon.

We have four seasons here. I like spring most. It's warm, but very short. In the summer, sometimes it's very hot. On the hottest days, the temperature usually reaches 100°F. So hot! In the fall, sometimes it is rainy and windy. Winter is very cold here, with lots of snow.

I plan to go to your place during spring break. We'll meet soon.

Best wishes.

Dazhong
Mar. 10, 2004

Lesson 18   We Are Going to Take a Train Trip

Ji Changfeng:	Qiuying, do you live off campus? Is it far from school?
Bai Qiuying:	Not too far. Only a five-minute drive.
Ji Changfeng:	How do you get to school each day?
Bai Qiuying:	I usually ride a bike. When it is raining or snowing, I take the bus. Sometimes I walk, which gives me some exercise. How about you?
Ji Changfeng:	I live in the dorm, which is very close to school. I walk to school every day.
Bai Qiuying:	Well, what will you do during the spring break?
Ji Changfeng:	I'll travel to the West with my roommates.
Bai Qiuying:	How will you go?
Ji Changfeng:	We want to go by train. We would like to do some sightseeing on the road. Then we'll go to Canada by boat. Finally, from Canada, we'll take a plane back home. How about you?
Bai Qiuying:	I miss my parents and sister very much. I'll go home first. Then I'll drive somewhere with my friends.
Ji Changfeng:	Where do you want to go?
Bai Qiuying:	We'd like to go to the South. It is said that the shore is beautiful there.
Ji Changfeng:	How many people will go with you?
Bai Qiuying:	There are five people. We want to rent a car.

Lesson 19   I Caught a Cold

Zhixin Tang:	Ouyang Ying, have you eaten yet?
Ouyang Ying:	Not yet. I'm not hungry.
Zhixin Tang:	What's wrong? You look sick.
Ouyang Ying:	I have a cold. I have a headache, a fever, and a bit of a cough.
Zhixin Tang:	How did you get sick?
Ouyang Ying:	I had lots of exams these past few days. Every day I revised a lot and didn't get enough sleep. So I'm sick.

Zhixin Tang:	Did you see the doctor?
Ouyang Ying:	Yes. I took pills. But it's not over yet.
Zhixin Tang:	You should stay at home and get some rest. You shouldn't come to class.
Ouyang Ying:	You are right. But I have lots of exams. I have to be well prepared.
Zhixin Tang:	These are my class notes. You may borrow them.
Ouyang Ying:	Thanks a lot. I'd better go home and get some rest.
Zhixin Tang:	OK, I'll drive you home. You should sleep well.

Lesson 20   I've Brought Xiao Xie Over . . .

Tian Chang:	Zhongming, I'm back. I drove the car back, and I also brought Xiao Xie over.
Zhongming Xia:	Oh, it's Xiao Xie! Ask him to come in.
Jinxue Xie:	I heard that one of your roommates moved out. I want to move in. So here I am to have a look.
Tian Chang:	You don't want to live in the dorm any more, right?
Jinxue Xie:	Yes. The dorm is too small. I want to move out. Can you cook here?
Zhongming Xia:	Yes. We have a kitchen.
Jinxue Xie:	Great. I like to cook. After moving out of the dorm, I could cook often.
Tian Chang:	Do you smoke? It's non-smoking here.
Jinxue Xie:	It's OK. I used to smoke, but my girlfriend said I shouldn't, so I quit.
Zhongming Xia:	And, we have to pay the rent on the 1st of each month.
Jinxue Xie:	No problem.
Tian Chang:	Hi, Xiao Xie, I'm upstairs. Don't you want to come up to have a look? Zhongming, bring Xiao Xie up here.
Zhongming Xia:	Tian Chang, we can't come up now. You'd better come down to help me move the table up first.
Tian Chang:	OK. I will come down immediately.

Lesson 21   What Will You Do During the Summer Vacation?

Haihua Cheng:	Qiuyu, let me ask you, you'll graduate next year. What will you do after graduation?
Qiuyu Bai:	I haven't decided yet. But I love to study. I'll probably apply for graduate school, or go to study abroad. How about you? When will you graduate?
Haihua Cheng:	I still have two more years to go. After graduation, I want to find a job.
Qiuyu Bai:	We'll have summer vacation soon. What will you do this summer?
Haihua Cheng:	I'll work. I have a summer internship with a company.
Qiuyu Bai:	Where? What kind of job?
Haihua Cheng:	In California, a computer company. How about you? What will you do this summer?
Qiuyu Bai:	I'll go to China. I applied for a summer class in Shanghai. I want to learn some Chinese, and at the same time do some traveling in China.
Haihua Cheng:	It must be very interesting. When will you leave?
Qiuyu Bai:	Next week.

Haihua Cheng:　So fast! E-mail me often after you arrive in China.
Qiuyu Bai:　　　No problem. Have a good time working!
Haihua Cheng:　Have a safe journey, and good luck!

Lesson 22　I Have Arrived in Shanghai

Haihua,

　　How are you? Today is June 15. I arrived in Shanghai a week ago. Sorry, I've been too busy to write you an e-mail before today.

　　We have many classes every day, and lots of homework too. The instructor is good and very conscientious. We speak Chinese every day. My Chinese has improved greatly. Now I can speak lots of Chinese.

　　Shanghai is a beautiful city, with new buildings everywhere. We visited some places, as well as attending some activities, including watching Peking Opera, writing calligraphy, etc. All very interesting! And, there is a lot of good food here. Of all the food, I love the little steamed buns the best. You should have a taste some time.

　　Have you begun your internship yet? Are you busy? When you have time, please e-mail me.

　　Best wishes.

Qiuyu
June 15, 2004

Qiuyu:

　　How are you? I was so glad to get your e-mail. It seems you are very happy in Shanghai.

　　I've begun my internship in Los Angeles. My colleagues here are all very nice and warmhearted. They are teaching me many things. The boss is nice too. I'm busy from time to time. I believe I will work hard to learn more things.

　　OK, I should stop here. Write to me more when you have time. Take care.

　　Best wishes.

Haihua
June 17, 2004

Each entry lists Pinyin, traditional character, simplified character, part of speech, English meaning, and lesson number.

Note: The letter "s" means that the entry occurs in the supplementary vocabulary to that lesson.

A

a	啊	啊	*Int.*	(used at the end of a sentence to indicate surprise)	20
āyí	阿姨	阿姨	*N.*	aunt (mother's sister)	6s
ài	愛	爱	*V.*	to love	6
áoyè	熬夜	熬夜	*V.O.*	to burn the midnight oil	10s

B

ba	吧	吧	*Part.*	(indicates an assumption or suggestion)	9
bā	八/捌	八/捌	*Num.*	eight	7
bǎ	把	把	*Prep.*	(introduces the object of a verb)	20
bàba	爸爸	爸爸	*N.*	father	6
bái	白	白	*Adj.*	white	12
báifàn	白飯	白饭	*N.*	steamed rice	11s
báisè	白色	白色	*Adj.*	white	13s
bǎi	百	百	*Num.*	hundred	17
bān	搬	搬	*V.*	to move	20
	班	班	*N.*	class	21
bàn	半	半	*Adj.*	half	10
bāng	幫	帮	*V.*	to help	13
bàng	棒	棒	*Adj.*	wonderful	14
bàngqiú	棒球	棒球	*N.*	baseball	16s
bāo	包	包	*V.*	to wrap	16
bǎozhòng	保重	保重		Take care.	22s
bēi	杯	杯	*M.W.*	cup	11
běi	北	北	*N.*	north	18s
bèixīn	背心	背心	*N.*	vest	13s
běn	本	本	*M.W.*	(measure word for book)	4
bǐjì	筆記	笔记	*N.*	notes	19
bǐjiào	比較	比较	*Adv.*	relatively	13
bǐrú	比如	比如	*Conj.*	for example	22
bìxū	必須	必须	*Aux.*	must	20

bìyè	畢業	毕业	V.	to graduate	21
biǎodì	表弟	表弟	N.	cousin (son of parents' sister or mother's brother) (younger than the speaker)	6s
biǎodìmèi	表弟妹	表弟妹	N.	cousin (wife of 表弟)	6s
biǎogē	表哥	表哥	N.	cousin (son of parents' sister or mother's brother) (older than the speaker)	6s
biǎojiě	表姐	表姐	N.	cousin (daughter of parents' sister or mother's brother) (older than the speaker)	6s
biǎojiěfu	表姐夫	表姐夫	N.	cousin (husband of 表姐)	6s
biǎomèi	表妹	表妹	N.	cousin (daughter of parents' sister or mother's brother) (younger than the speaker)	6s
biǎomèifu	表妹夫	表妹夫	N.	cousin (husband of 表妹)	6s
biǎosǎo	表嫂	表嫂	N.	cousin (wife of 表哥)	6s
bīng	冰	冰	N.	ice	11
bīngqiú	冰球	冰球	N.	ice hockey	16s
bǐnggān	餅乾	饼干	N.	cracker	11s
bìngdú	病毒	病毒	N.	virus	9s
bóbo	伯伯	伯伯	N.	uncle (father's elder brother)	6s
bómǔ	伯母	伯母	N.	aunt (wife of father's elder brother)	6s
bóshì	博士	博士	N.	doctoral degree	21s
bóshìshēng	博士生	博士生	N.	doctoral students	21s
bù	不	不	Adv.	not, no (used to form a negative)	1
búcuò	不錯	不错		not bad; pretty good	13
búguò	不過	不过	Conj.	but, however	22
búkèqi	不客氣	不客气		you're welcome; don't mention it (in reply to thank you)	9s, 14
búxiè	不謝	不谢		you're welcome; don't mention it (in reply to thank you)	9s

C

cái	才	才	Adv.	(used before a verb to indicate that something is rather late by general standards or something has just happened)	10
cǎisè	彩色	彩色	Adj.	multicolor	13s
cài	菜	菜	N.	dish	8
càidān	菜單	菜单	N.	menu	11s

cānguān	參觀	参观	V.	to visit	15
cānguǎn	餐館	餐馆	N.	restaurant	11s
cānjiā	參加	参加	V.	to participate, join	14
cāntīng	餐廳	餐厅	N.	restaurant, dining room	11s, 15
cǎoméi	草莓	草莓	N.	strawberry	11s
chá	茶	茶	N.	tea	11
chà	差	差	V.	to lack	10s
cháng	常	常	Adv.	often; frequently	5
	長	长	Adj.	long	17s
chángchang	嚐嚐	尝尝	V.	to have a try, taste	22
chángjiàn	常見	常见	Adj.	common	11s
chángkù	長褲	长裤	N.	long pants	13s
chǎo	炒	炒	V.	to stir fry	11
chē	車	车	N.	car	6
chēzhàn	車站	车站	N.	stop, station	18s
chènshān	襯衫	衬衫	N.	shirt	13
chēngwèi	稱謂	称谓	N.	form of address	6s
chéngsè (júsè)	橙色 (橘色)	橙色 (橘色)	Adj.	orange	13s
chéngshì	城市	城市	N.	city	22
chéngxùyuán (chéngshì shèjìshī)	程序員 (程式設計師)	程序员 (程式设计师)	N.	computer programmer	6s
chéngzhī	橙汁	橙汁	N.	orange juice	11s
chī	吃	吃	V.	to eat	8
chīfàn	吃飯	吃饭	V.O.	to eat, have a meal	8
chīyào	吃藥	吃药	V.O.	to take medicine	19
chǒngwù	寵物	宠物	N.	pet	6s
chū	出	出	V.	to be out	20
chūqù	出去	出去	V.C.	to go out	20
chūzūqìchē (jìchéngchē)	出租汽車 (計程車)	出租汽车 (计程车)	N.	taxi	18s
chúfáng	廚房	厨房	N.	kitchen	15
chuān	穿	穿	V.	to wear, put on (regular clothes)	13, 13s
chuānshàng	穿上	穿上	V.C.	to put on (regular clothes)	13s
chuán	船	船	N.	ship	18
chuānghu	窗戶	窗户	N.	window	15s
chuáng	床	床	N.	bed	15s
chūnjià	春假	春假	N.	spring break	17
chūnjuǎn	春捲	春卷	N.	spring roll	11s
chūntiān	春天	春天	N.	spring	17
cífú tiělù	磁浮鐵路	磁浮铁路	N.	magnetic railway	18s
cóng	從	从	Prep.	from	6

D

dǎ diànhuà	打電話	打电话	V.O.	to make a phone call	9
dǎcuòle	打錯了	打错了		to dial a wrong number	9s
dǎgōng	打工	打工	V.O.	to work for others, be employed	21
dǎqiú	打球	打球	V.O.	to play basketball/badminton/ tennis/table tennis	10
dǎzhēn	打針	打针	V.O.	to give or receive an injection	13s, 19s
dà	大	大	Adj.	big, large	7, 13s
dàhuòchē	大貨車	大货车	N.	truck	18s
dàjiā	大家	大家	Pron.	all, everybody	6
dàlóu	大樓	大楼	N.	tall building	22
dàxué	大學	大学	N.	college; university	10
dàxuéshēng	大學生	大学生	N.	college student(s)	6s, 21s
dàyī	大衣	大衣	N.	overcoat	13s
dài	戴	戴	V.	to wear, put on (accessories)	13s
dàilái	帶來	带来	V.C.	to bring over	20
dàishàng	戴上	戴上	V.C.	to put on (accessories)	13s
dānchē (jiǎotàchē)	單車 (腳踏車)	单车 (脚踏车)	N.	bicycle	18s
dàngāo	蛋糕	蛋糕	N.	cake	11s, 14
dànjì	淡季	淡季	N.	off-season	18s
dànshì	但是	但是	Conj.	but	20
dǎoyóu	導遊	导游	N.	tourist guide	6s
dào	到	到	V.	to arrive	12
dàochù	到處	到处	Adv.	everywhere	22
de	的	的	Part.	(a structural particle)	2
	得	得	Part.	(used between a verb or an adjective and its complement to indicate result, possibility or degree)	16
	地	地	Part.	(attached to an adjective to transform the whole unit into an adverb)	19
Déguó	德國	德国	N.	Germany	3s
Déguórén	德國人	德国人	N.	German (person)	3s
Déyǔ (Déwén)	德語 (德文)	德语 (德文)	N.	German (language)	3s
děi	得	得	Aux.	must; have to	12
děng	等	等	V.	to wait	9
děng yíxiàr	等一下兒	等一下儿		to wait for a moment	9
dìdi	弟弟	弟弟	N.	younger brother	6s

dìfang	地方	地方	N.	place	22
dìtú	地圖	地图	N.	map	14
dìtiě	地鐵	地铁	N.	subway	18s
dìxiàdào	地下道	地下道	N.	underground passage	18s
dìyītiān	第一天	第一天	N.	first day	20
dìzhǐ	地址	地址	N.	address	10
diǎn	點	点	M.W.	o'clock (point on clock)	10
diǎncài	點菜	点菜	V.O.	to order food	11s
diǎnzhōng	點鐘	点钟	M.W.	hour	10s
diànhuà	電話	电话	N.	phone	7
diànnǎo	電腦	电脑	N.	computer	21
diànnǎo yóuxì	電腦遊戲	电脑游戏	N.	computer game	9s
diànshì	電視	电视	N.	television	9
diànyǐng	電影	电影	N.	movie	9s, 13
diànyuán	店員	店员	N.	salesman; saleswoman	13
diànzǐ yóujiàn	電子郵件	电子邮件	N.	email	10
diàoyú	釣魚	钓鱼	V.O.	to fish	16s
dōng	冬	冬	N.	winter	17
	東	东	N.	east	18s
dōngxi	東西	东西	N.	thing	22
dòngzuò	動作	动作	N.	action	13s
dōu	都	都	Adv.	all; both	5
dòufu	豆腐	豆腐	N.	bean curd	11s
dù	度	度	N.	degree	17
duǎn	短	短	Adj.	short	17
duǎnkù	短褲	短裤	N.	shorts	13s
duànliàn	鍛煉	锻炼	V.	to exercise	16
duì	對	对	Adj.	correct, right	9
duìbuqǐ	對不起	对不起		sorry, I'm sorry; Excuse me.	9, 22
duìle	對了	对了		by the way (a phrase used to start a new topic)	3
duìmiàn	對面	对面	N.	opposite	15
duō	多	多	Adj.	many, much	4
duōdà	多大	多大		how old	14
duōshǎo	多少	多少	Pron.	how many, how much	7

E

è	餓	饿	Adj.	hungry	19
			V.	to starve	3
ér	兒	儿		(retroflex ending)	3
ěrhuán	耳環	耳环	N.	earrings	13s
èr	二/貳	二/贰	Num.	two	7

F

fā duǎnxìn (sòng jiǎnxùn)	發短信 (送簡訊)	发短信 (送简讯)	V.O.	to send a short (cell phone) message	9s
fāshāo	發燒	发烧	V.O.	to have a fever	19
Fǎguó	法國	法国	N.	France	3
Fǎwén	法文	法文	N.	French (language)	3
fàn	飯	饭	N.	cooked rice; meal	8
fàndiàn	飯店	饭店	N.	restaurant	11s
fànguǎn	飯館	饭馆	N.	restaurant	11s
fángdìchǎn gùwèn	房地產顧問	房地产顾问	N.	real estate agent	6s
fángdōng	房東	房东	N.	landlord	20s
fángjiān	房間	房间	N.	room	7
fángkè	房客	房客	N.	tenant	20s
fángzū	房租	房租	N.	rent	20
fángzi	房子	房子	N.	house; room	7s
fàng	放	放	V.	to have, start (a vacation)	17
fàngjià	放假	放假	V.O.	to have vacation	17s
fēicháng	非常	非常	Adv.	very	16
fēijī	飛機	飞机	N.	airplane	12
fēixíngyuán	飛行員	飞行员	N.	pilot	6s
fēn	分	分	N.	minute; 100 fen = 10 jiao/ 10 mao = 1 yuan/1 kuai	10, 13s
fēnzhōng	分鐘	分钟	N.	minute	10s, 18
fěnhóngsè	粉紅色	粉红色	Adj.	pink	13s
fēngjǐng	風景	风景	N.	scenery	18
fúwùyuán	服務員	服务员	N.	waiter/waitress	11
fǔxiū	輔修	辅修	N.	minor	4s
fù	付	付	V.	to pay	20
fùxí	復習	复习	V.	to review	19

G

gānjìng	乾淨	干净	Adj.	clean	15s
gǎnlǎnqiú	橄欖球	橄榄球	N.	football	16s
gǎnmào	感冒	感冒	N.	cold, flu	19
gǎnxiè	感謝	感谢	V.	to thank, be grateful	19
Gǎngbì	港幣	港币	N.	currency of Hong Kong	13s
gāo'ěrfūqiú	高爾夫球	高尔夫球	N.	golf	16s
gāoxìng	高興	高兴	Adj.	happy	22
gēge	哥哥	哥哥	N.	elder brother	6s
gè	個	个	M.W.	(the most commonly used measure word for cups, buildings, characters, etc.)	5

gěi	給	给	*Prep.*	for, to	9
			V.	to give	
gēn	跟	跟	*Prep.*	with	5
gōngchē (bāshì)	公車 (巴士)	公车 (巴士)	*N.*	bus	18s
gōngchéng	工程	工程	*N.*	engineering	4
gōngchéngshī	工程師	工程师	*N.*	engineer	6, 6s
gōnggòngqìchē	公共汽車	公共汽车	*N.*	bus	18
gōngkè	功課	功课	*N.*	homework; assignment	4
gōngsī	公司	公司	*N.*	company	21
gōngyù	公寓	公寓	*N.*	apartment	7s
gōngyòng	公用	公用	*Adj.*	for public use, communal	15
gōngyuán	公園	公园	*N.*	park	15
gōngzuò	工作	工作	*N.*	job	6
			V.	to work	6
gǒu	狗	狗	*N.*	dog	6
gūfù	姑父	姑父	*N.*	uncle (husband of father's sister)	6s
gūgu	姑姑	姑姑	*N.*	aunt (father's sister)	6s
gūmā	姑媽	姑妈	*N.*	aunt (father's sister)	6s
gūzhàng	姑丈	姑丈	*N.*	uncle (husband of father's sister)	6s
gùwèn	顧問	顾问	*N.*	consultant	6s
guāfēng	刮風	刮风	*V.O.*	to blow (wind)	17
guānyuán	官員	官员	*N.*	government official	6s
guì	貴	贵	*Adj.*	noble, honored; expensive	2, 13s
guó	國	国	*N.*	country	3
guówài	國外	国外	*N.*	overseas, abroad	21
guǒzhī	果汁	果汁	*N.*	juice	11s
guò	過	过	*V.*	to pass, to spend (life, time); celebrate (e.g., birthday)	10s, 14, 17
guòlái	過來	过来	*V.C.*	to come over	20

H

hái hǎo	還好	还好		not bad; okay	4s
háishì	還是	还是	*Conj.*	or	11
háizi	孩子	孩子	*N.*	child	6s
hǎibiān	海邊	海边	*N.*	seaside	18
hǎitān	海灘	海滩	*N.*	seashore	18s
hǎixiān	海鮮	海鲜	*N.*	seafood	11s
Hánguó	韓國	韩国	*N.*	Korea	3s, 8
Hánguórén	韓國人	韩国人	*N.*	Korean (person)	3s
hánjià	寒假	寒假	*N.*	winter vacation	17s
Hányǔ (Hánwén)	韓語 (韓文)	韩语 (韩文)	*N.*	Korean (language)	3s

Hànyǔ	漢語	汉语	N.	Chinese (language)	2s
hǎo	好	好	Adj.	good; well	1
hǎokàn	好看	好看	Adj.	good looking	13
hǎoxiàng	好像	好像	V.	to be like, seem	19
hǎoyùn	好運	好运		Good luck.	21
hào	號	号	N.	number, size	7, 13s
hàomǎ	號碼	号码	N.	number	7
hē	喝	喝	V.	to drink	11
hé	和	和	Conj.	and	3
hēi	黑	黑	Adj.	black	13
hēisè	黑色	黑色	Adj.	black	13s
hěn	很	很	Adv.	very, quite	3
hóng	紅	红	Adj.	red	11
hóngsè	紅色	红色	Adj.	red	13s
hòubiān	後邊	后边	N.	behind, at the back	15
hùshi	護士	护士	N.	nurse	6s, 19s
huábīng	滑冰	滑冰	V.O.	to skate	16s
huáchuán	划船	划船	V.O.	to row	16s
huáshì	華氏	华氏	N.	Fahrenheit	17
huáxuě	滑雪	滑雪	V.O.	to snow ski	16s
huānyíng	歡迎	欢迎	V.	to welcome	15
huáng	黃	黄	Adj.	yellow	13
huángsè	黃色	黄色	Adj.	yellow	13s
huīsè	灰色	灰色	Adj.	gray	13s
huí	回	回	V.	to return	8
huílai	回來	回来	V.C.	to return	9
huì	會	会	Aux.	can, be able to	3
húntun	餛飩	馄饨	N.	wonton	11s
huódòng	活動	活动	N.	activity	22
huǒchē	火車	火车	N.	train	18, 18s
huòbì	貨幣	货币	N.	currency	13s
huòzhě	或者	或者	Conj.	or; either . . . or . . .	13

J

jīchǎng	機場	机场	N.	airport	12
jīhuì	機會	机会	N.	opportunity	22
jīròu	雞肉	鸡肉	N.	chicken	11s
jí	極	极	Adv.	extremely	17
jípǔchē	吉普車	吉普车	N.	jeep	18s
jǐ	幾	几		how many	5
jǐ hào	幾號	几号		which size	13s
jìsuànjī	計算機	计算机	N.	computer	4s
(diànnǎo)	(電腦)	(电脑)			
jiā	家	家	N.	home; family	6

			M.W.	(measure word for company, enterprises, store, etc.)	21
Jiānádà	加拿大	加拿大	*N.*	Canada	3s
Jiānádàrén	加拿大人	加拿大人	*N.*	Canadian (person)	3s
jiātíng zhǔfù	家庭主婦	家庭主妇	*N.*	housewife	6s
Jiāzhōu	加州	加州	*N.*	California (state)	21
jiákèshān	夾克衫	夹克衫	*N.*	jacket	13s
(jiákè)	(夾克)	(夹克)			
jiàqī	假期	假期	*N.*	holiday	17s
jiǎnlì	簡歷	简历	*N.*	resume	21s
(lǚlìbiǎo)	(履歷表)	(履历表)			
jiàn	見	见	*V.*	to see	8
	件	件	*M.W.*	(measure word for clothes)	13
jiànkāng	健康	健康	*Adj.*	healthy	22s
jiànmiàn	見面	见面	*V.O.*	to meet each other	17
jiànshēnfáng	健身房	健身房	*N.*	gym	16
jiànzhùshī	建築師	建筑师	*N.*	architect	6s
jiāo	教	教	*V.*	to teach, coach	16
jiǎo	角	角	*N.*	(10 角 = 1 元)	13s
jiǎozi	餃子	饺子	*N.*	dumpling (crescent shaped)	11
jiào	叫	叫	*V.*	to call	2
jiàoliàn	教練	教练	*N.*	coach, trainer	16
jiàoshì	教室	教室	*N.*	classroom	15s
jiàoshòu	教授	教授	*N.*	professor	6s
jiàoyù gōngzuòzhě	教育工作者	教育工作者	*N.*	educator	6s
jiē	接	接	*V.*	to pick up	12
jiéyùn	捷運	捷运	*N.*	MRT (Mass Rapid Transportation) in Taiwan	18s
jiézhàng	結賬	结账	*V.O.*	to settle the account	11s
(jiézhàng)	(結帳)	(结帐)			
jiějie	姐姐	姐姐	*N.*	elder sister	6
jiè	借	借	*V.*	to borrow	12
jièshào	介紹	介绍	*V.*	to introduce	5
			N.	introduction	5
jièzhi	戒指	戒指	*N.*	ring	13s
jīnhuángsè	金黃色	金黄色	*Adj.*	gold	13s
jīntiān	今天	今天	*N.*	today	8
jìn	近	近	*Adj.*	near	18
	進	进	*V.*	to enter	20
jìnbù	進步	进步	*V.*	to improve	12
jīngjìrén	經紀人	经纪人	*N.*	agent	6s
jīngjìshī	經濟師	经济师	*N.*	economist	6s
jīngjù	京劇	京剧	*N.*	Peking opera	22
jīnglǐ	經理	经理	*N.*	manager	6s
jǐngsè	景色	景色	*N.*	scenery; view	18

jiǔ	九/玖	九/玖	*Num.*	nine	7
	久	久	*Adj.*	for a long time	17
jiù	就	就	*Adv.*	as early as; already; therefore (connects two clauses, the first being the premise of the second)	10, 12
jiùjiu	舅舅	舅舅	*N.*	uncle (mother's brother)	6s
jiùmā	舅媽	舅妈	*N.*	aunt (wife of mother's brother)	6s
jǔzhòng	舉重	举重	*V.O.*	to lift weights	16s
jùlèbù	俱樂部	俱乐部	*N.*	club	16s
juéde	覺得	觉得	*V.*	to think, feel	13
juédìng	決定	决定	*V.*	to decide	21

K

kāfēi	咖啡	咖啡	*N.*	coffee	11s
kāi	開	开	*V.*	to drive	12
kāishǐ	開始	开始	*V.*	to start, begin	22
kāixīn	開心	开心	*Adj.*	happy	22
kàn	看	看	*V.*	to look at; see; watch	9
kànlái	看來	看来		it seems	22
kǎoshì	考試	考试	*N.*	exam	4s, 19
késòu	咳嗽	咳嗽	*V.*	to cough	19
kělè	可樂	可乐	*N.*	cola	11
kěshì	可是	可是	*Conj.*	but; yet; however	4
kěyǐ	可以	可以	*Aux.*	can, may	12
kè	刻	刻	*M.W.*	a quarter (of an hour)	10
kètīng	客廳	客厅	*N.*	living room	15
kǔ	苦	苦	*Adj.*	bitter	11s
kùzi	褲子	裤子	*N.*	pants	13
kuài	快	快	*Adj.*	fast	16
	塊	块	*N.*	dollar	13, 13s
kuàijìshī	會計師	会计师	*N.*	accountant	6s
kuàizi	筷子	筷子	*N.*	chopstick	11

L

là	辣	辣	*Adj.*	spicy	11s
làzhú	蠟燭	蜡烛	*N.*	candle	14s
lái	來	来	*V.*	to come (used before a verb to indicate that one is about to do something)	5
láixìn	來信	来信	*V.O.*	to write a letter (to the speaker)	22
lánqiú	籃球	篮球	*N.*	basketball	16, 16s
lánsè	藍色	蓝色	*Adj.*	blue	13s
lǎobǎn	老闆	老板	*N.*	boss	6s, 22

lǎolao	姥姥	姥姥	N.	maternal grandmother	6s
lǎoshī	老師	老师	N.	teacher	1, 6s
lǎoye	老爺	姥爷	N.	maternal grandfather	6s
le	了	了	Part.	(indicates assumption)	9
lèi	累	累	Adj.	tired	4s
lěng	冷	冷	Adj.	cold	17
lí	離	离	V.	to be off, away, from	18
lízi	梨子	梨子	N.	pear	11s
lǐbiān	裡邊	里边	N.	inside	15
lǐwù	禮物	礼物	N.	gift	14s
lìhài	屬害	厉害	Adj.	severely, very much	19s
liǎ	倆	俩		two people (colloquial)	16
liànxí	練習	练习	V.	to practice	12
liáotiānshì	聊天室	聊天室	N.	chat room	9s
liáng	涼	凉	Adj.	cool	11s
liángxié	涼鞋	凉鞋	N.	sandles	13s
liǎng	兩	两	Num.	two	5
liàng	輛	辆	M.W.	(measure word for vehicles)	6
líng	○/零	○/零	Num.	zero	7s
lǐngdài	領帶	领带	N.	necktie	13s
liúgǎn (liúxíngxìng gǎnmào)	流感 (流行性感冒)	流感 (流行性感冒)	N.	flu	19s
liúgǎn yìmiáo	流感疫苗	流感疫苗	N.	flu shot	19s
liú xuéshēng	留學生	留学生	N.	international students	6s
liúxué	留學	留学	V.O.	to study abroad	21
liúyán (liúhuà)	留言 (留話)	留言 (留话)	V.O.	to leave a message	9
liǔchéngzhī (liǔdīngzhī)	柳橙汁 (柳丁汁)	柳橙汁 (柳丁汁)	N.	tangerine juice	11s
liù	六/陸	六/陆	Num.	six	7
lóushàng	樓上	楼上	N.	upstairs	20
luàn	亂	乱	Adj.	messy	15s
lǚxíng	旅行	旅行	V.	to travel	18
lǜ	綠	绿	Adj.	green	11
lǜsè	綠色	绿色	Adj.	green	13s
lǜshī	律師	律师	N.	lawyer	6s

M

ma	嗎	吗	Part.	(used at the end of a sentence to transform it into a question)	1
māma	媽媽	妈妈	N.	mother	6
mǎlù	馬路	马路	N.	road, street	18s
mǎshàng	馬上	马上	Adv.	immediately	20

mǎtóu	碼頭	码头	N.	wharf, dock, pier	18s
mǎi	買	买	V.	to buy	13
mǎidān	買單	买单	V.O.	to pay the bill	11s
mài	賣	卖	V.	to sell	13s
màn	慢	慢	Adj.	slow	16
máng	忙	忙	Adj.	busy	4s, 9
māo	貓	猫	N.	cat	6s
máo	毛	毛	N.	(10 毛 = 1 塊)	13s
máoyī	毛衣	毛衣	N.	sweater	13s
màozi	帽子	帽子	N.	hat	13s
méiguānxi	沒關係	没关系		No problem.	20
méiyǒu	沒有	没有	V.	to not have; be without	5s, 6
Měiguó	美國	美国	N.	the United States	3
Měijīn	美金	美金	N.	U.S. dollar	13s
měilì	美麗	美丽	Adj.	beautiful	22
měitiān	每天	每天	N.	every day	10
mèimei	妹妹	妹妹	N.	younger sister	6s, 12
men	們	们		(used after a personal pronoun or noun to show plural number)	4
mén	門	门	M.W.	(measure word for school course)	10
			N.	door	15s
mínǐqún	迷你裙	迷你裙	N.	miniskirt	13s
mìshū	祕書	秘书	N.	secretary	6s
miàn	麵	面	N.	noodle	11
miànbāo	麵包	面包	N.	bread	11s
miànbāochē (bāoxíngchē)	麵包車 (包型車)	面包车 (包型车)	N.	minibus, van	18s
miǎo	秒	秒	N.	second	10s
míngpiàn	名片	名片	N.	name card	8s
míngtiān	明天	明天	N.	tomorrow	12
míngzi	名字	名字	N.	name	2
mótuōchē (jīchē)	摩托車 (機車)	摩托车 (机车)	N.	scooter, motorcycle	18s

N

nǎ	哪	哪	Pron.	which	3
nà	那	那	Pron.	that	4
nǎinai	奶奶	奶奶	N.	grandmother	6s
nán	難	难	Adj.	difficult	4
	男	男	N.	male	6
nánbù	南部	南部	N.	south	18
nánpéngyou	男朋友	男朋友	N.	boyfriend	5s, 6
nǎr	哪兒	哪儿	Pron.	where	7

ne	呢	呢	*Part.*	(used at the end of an interrogative sentence)	1
nèikù	內褲	内裤	*N.*	underpants	13s
nèiyī	內衣	内衣	*N.*	underwear	13s
néng	能	能	*Aux.*	can	12
nǐ	你	你	*Pron.*	you	1
nián	年	年	*N.*	year	10
nín	您	您	*Pron.*	you (polite)	2
niúròu	牛肉	牛肉	*N.*	beef	11s
niúzǎikù	牛仔褲	牛仔裤	*N.*	jeans	13s
Niǔyuē	紐約	纽约	*N.*	New York	6
nuǎnhuo	暖和	暖和	*Adj.*	warm	17
nǚ	女	女	*N.*	female	6s
nǚpéngyou	女朋友	女朋友	*N.*	girlfriend	5s, 6s, 20

O

| Ōuyuán | 歐元 | 欧元 | *N.* | Euro | 13s |

P

páshān	爬山	爬山	*N.*	mountain climbing	16s
			V.O.	to climb a mountain	
páiqiú	排球	排球	*N.*	volleyball	16s
pán	盤	盘	*M.W.*	plate	11
pángbiān	旁邊	旁边	*N.*	nearby	15
pǎobù	跑步	跑步	*V.O.*	to run	16s
pǎochē	跑車	跑车	*N.*	sports car	18s
péngyou	朋友	朋友	*N.*	friend	5
píjiǔ	啤酒	啤酒	*N.*	beer	11
píxié	皮鞋	皮鞋	*N.*	leather shoes	13s
piányi	便宜	便宜	*Adj.*	inexpensive	13s
piào	票	票	*N.*	ticket	13
píng	瓶	瓶	*M.W.*	bottle	11
píngguǒ	蘋果	苹果	*N.*	apple	11s
pútao	葡萄	葡萄	*N.*	grape	11s

Q

qī	七/柒	七/柒	*Num.*	seven	7
qí	騎	骑	*V.*	to ride	18
qí zìxíngchē	騎自行車	骑自行车	*V.O.*	to ride a bike	16s
qízhōng	其中	其中		among (whom, which)	17
qǐchuáng	起床	起床	*V.O.*	to get up	10
qìchē	汽車	汽车	*N.*	car	18s

qìhòu	氣候	气候	N.	climate	17
qìwēn	氣溫	气温	N.	temperature	17s
qiānyuē	簽約	签约	V.O.	to sign a contract	20s
qián	錢	钱	N.	money	13
qiánbiān	前邊	前边	N.	in front of	15
qiánshuǐ	潛水	潜水	V.O.	to dive	16s
qiǎnlǜsè	淺綠色	浅绿色	Adj.	light green	13s
qiǎnsè	淺色	浅色	Adj.	light	13s
qīnshǔ	親屬	亲属	N.	relatives	6s
qiū	秋	秋	N.	autumn	17
qiújì	球季	球季	N.	season (of a sport)	16s
qiúsài	球賽	球赛	N.	ball game, match	16
qiúxié	球鞋	球鞋	N.	sneakers	13s
qīngcài	青菜	青菜	N.	vegetable	11s
qīngdàn	清淡	清淡	Adj.	plain	11s
qìngshēng	慶生	庆生	V.O.	to celebrate a birthday	14s
qǐng	請	请		please (polite)	2
qǐng wèn	請問	请问		may I ask	2
qù	去	去	V.	to go	8
qúnzi	裙子	裙子	N.	skirt	13

R

ránhòu	然後	然后	Adv.	then; after that; afterwards	10
ràng	讓	让	V.	to let, allow	13
rè	熱	热	Adj.	hot	17
rèxīn	熱心	热心	Adj.	warm-hearted	22
rén	人	人	N.	person	3
Rénmínbì	人民幣	人民币	N.	currency of the People's Republic of China	13s
rènshi	認識	认识	V.	to know, recognize	5s, 8
rènzhēn	認真	认真	Adj.	conscientious; serious	22
rì	日	日	N.	day	10
Rìběn	日本	日本	N.	Japan	3s, 8
Rìběnrén	日本人	日本人	N.	Japanese (person)	3s
Rìyǔ (Rìwén)	日語 (日文)	日语 (日文)	N.	Japanese (language)	3s
róngyì	容易	容易	Adj.	easy	4s
ruǎnjiàn (ruǎntǐ)	軟件 (軟體)	软件 (软体)	N.	sorftware	9s

S

| sān | 三/叁 | 三/叁 | Num. | three | 7 |
| sè | 色 | 色 | N. | color | 12 |

shālā	沙拉	沙拉	N.	salad	11s
shǎo	少	少	Adj.	few, little	4
shāngrén	商人	商人	N.	businessman	6s
shàngbiān	上邊	上边	N.	on top of, above, over	15
shàngkè	上課	上课	V.O.	to begin class; attend class	8
shàngshēng	上升	上升	V.C.	to increase	17s
shàngwǎng	上網	上网	V.O.	to be online	9
shàngyī	上衣	上衣	N.	upper clothing	13s
shèshì	攝氏	摄氏	N.	Centigrade	17s
shètuán	社團	社团	N.	organization	16s
shéi	誰	谁	Pron.	who, whom	2
shēnlánsè	深藍色	深蓝色	Adj.	dark blue	13s
shēnqǐng	申請	申请	V.	to apply	21
shēnsè	深色	深色	Adj.	dark	13s
shénme	什麼	什么	Pron.	what	2
shěnshen	嬸嬸	婶婶	N.	aunt (wife of father's younger brother)	6s
shēngbìng	生病	生病	V.O.	to fall ill	19
shēnghuó	生活	生活	N.	life	10
shēngrì	生日	生日	N.	birthday	14
shèr	事兒	事儿	N.	matter, thing, business	8
shí	十/拾	十/拾	Num.	ten	7s, 11
shíhou	時候	时候	N.	time (the duration of time); (a point in)	9
shíjiān	時間	时间	N.	time	17
shípǐn	食品	食品	N.	food	11s
shíxí	實習	实习	N.	internship	21
shì	是	是	V.	to be; yes (affirmative answer)	1
shìpǐn	飾品	饰品	N.	accessory	13s
shìshi	試試	试试	V.	to try	13
shìyǒu	室友	室友	N.	roommate	5
shōudào	收到	收到	V.C.	to receive	22
shǒubiǎo	手錶	手表	N.	watch	13s
shǒujī	手機	手机	N.	cellular phone	7
shǒujuàn	手絹	手绢	N.	handkerchief	13s
shǒupáidǎng (shǒupái)	手排擋 (手排)	手排挡 (手排)	N.	manual transmission	12
shǒutào	手套	手套	N.	gloves	13s
shǒuzhuó	手鐲	手镯	N.	bracelet	13s
shū	書	书	N.	book	4
shūfǎ	書法	书法	N.	calligraphy	22
shūfu	舒服	舒服	Adj.	comfortable, be well	19
shūshu	叔叔	叔叔	N.	uncle (father's younger brother)	6s
shūzhuō	書桌	书桌	N.	desk	15s
shǔjià	暑假	暑假	N.	summer vacation	17s, 21

shǔqī	暑期	暑期	N.	summer	21
shùxué	數學	数学	N.	mathematics	4s
shuāyá	刷牙	刷牙	V.O.	to brush teeth	10s
shuāng	雙	双	M.W.	pair	11
shuìjiào	睡覺	睡觉	V.O.	to sleep; to go to bed	9s, 10
shùnlì	順利	顺利	Adj.	smooth	22s
shuō	說	说	V.	to speak	3
shuòshì	碩士	硕士	N.	master's degree	21s
sījī	司機	司机	N.	driver	18s
sì	四/肆	四/肆	Num.	four	6
sìjì	四季	四季	N.	four seasons	17s
sìlúnqūdòng (sìlúnchuándòng)	四輪驅動 (四輪傳動)	四轮驱动 (四轮传动)	N.	four-wheel drive	18s
sòng	送	送	V.	to give as a present	14
sùshè	宿舍	宿舍	N.	dorm	7
suān	酸	酸	Adj.	sour	11s
suì	歲	岁	N.	age, years	14
suìdào	隧道	隧道	N.	tunnel	18s
suǒyǐ	所以	所以	Conj.	therefore, consequently	19

T

tā	他	他	Pron.	he, him	1
	她	她	Pron.	she, her	2
tāmen	他們	他们	Pron.	they, them	5
tài	太	太	Adv.	too	4
Tàiguó	泰國	泰国	N.	Thailand	3s
Tàiguórén	泰國人	泰国人	N.	Thai (person)	3s
Tàiyǔ (Tàiwén)	泰語 (泰文)	泰语 (泰文)	N.	Thai (language)	3s
tāng	湯	汤	N.	soup	11
tángdì	堂弟	堂弟	N.	cousin (son of father's brother) (younger than the speaker)	6s
tángdìmèi	堂弟妹	堂弟妹	N.	cousin (wife of 堂弟)	6s
tánggē	堂哥	堂哥	N.	cousin (son of father's brother) (older than the speaker)	6s
tángjiě	堂姐	堂姐	N.	cousin (daughter of father's brother) (older than the speaker)	6s
tángjiěfu	堂姐夫	堂姐夫	N.	cousin (husband of 堂姐)	6s
tángmèi	堂妹	堂妹	N.	cousin (daughter of father's brother) (younger than the speaker)	6s
tángmèifu	堂妹夫	堂妹夫	N.	cousin (husband of 堂妹)	6s
tángsǎo	堂嫂	堂嫂	N.	cousin (wife of 堂哥)	6s
tàng	燙	烫	Adj.	burning hot	11s

táozi	桃子	桃子	N.	peach	11s
tè dà	特大	特大	Adj.	extra large	13s
tè xiǎo	特小	特小	Adj.	extra small	13s
tiānqì	天氣	天气	N.	weather	17s
tiānqiáo	天橋	天桥	N.	overhead bridge	18s
tián	甜	甜	Adj.	sweet	11s
tiándiǎn	甜點	甜点	N.	dessert	11s
tiáo	條	条	M.W.	(measure word for skirt/pants)	13
tīxùshān (tīxù)	T-恤衫 (T-恤)	T-恤衫 (T-恤)	N.	T-shirt	13s
tǐwēn	體溫	体温	N.	body temperature	19s
tǐyùguǎn	體育館	体育馆	N.	gymnasium	16
tīngshuō	聽說	听说	V.	to be told; hear of; it is said	18
tíng	停	停	V.	to park	12
tíngchēchǎng	停車場	停车场	N.	parking lot	12
tōng	通	通	M.W.	(measure word for telephone conversation)	9s
tóngshì	同事	同事	N.	colleague	22
tóngxué	同學	同学	N.	classmate, student	2
tóuténg	頭疼	头疼	V.	to have a headache	19
túshūguǎn	圖書館	图书馆	N.	library	10
tuīxiāoyuán	推銷員	推销员	N.	salesman	6s
tuō	脫	脱	V.	to take off (regular clothes)	13s
tuōxià	脫下	脱下	V.C.	to take off (regular clothes)	13s
tuōxié	拖鞋	拖鞋	N.	slippers	13s

W

wàzi	襪子	袜子	N.	socks	13s
wàigōng	外公	外公	N.	maternal grandfather	6s
wàipó	外婆	外婆	N.	maternal grandmother	6s
wàisheng	外甥	外甥	N.	nephew (sister's son)	6s
wàishengnǚ	外甥女	外甥女	N.	niece (sister's daughter)	6s
wàitào	外套	外套	N.	coat	13s
wàizǔfù	外祖父	外祖父	N.	maternal grandfather	6s
wàizǔmǔ	外祖母	外祖母	N.	maternal grandmother	6s
wán	玩	玩	V.	to play, have fun	12
wǎn	晚	晚	Adj.	late	10s
	碗	碗	M.W.	bowl	11
wǎnfàn	晚飯	晚饭	N.	dinner	8s
wǎnshàng	晚上	晚上	N.	evening, night	9
wǎngbā (wǎngkā)	網吧 (網咖)	网吧 (网咖)	N.	Internet café	9s
wǎngluò (wǎnglù)	網絡 (網路)	网络 (网路)	N.	Internet	9s

wǎngqiú	網球	网球	N.	tennis	16s
wǎngyè	網頁	网页	N.	Web page	9s
wǎngzhàn	網站	网站	N.	Web site	9s
wàngjì	旺季	旺季	N.	busy season	18s
wéijīn	圍巾	围巾	N.	scarf	13s
wèi	位	位	M.W.	(polite form, measure word for people)	9
	為	为	Prep.	(indicates the object of one's act of service)	14
(wéi)	喂	喂	Int.	hello; hey (used in greeting or to attract attention)	9
wénxué	文學	文学	N.	literature	4
wèn	問	问	V.	to ask	2
wèntí	問題	问题	N.	problem, question	12
wǒ	我	我	Pron.	I, me	1
wǒjiùshì	我就是	我就是		this is he/she speaking (on the phone)	9
wǒmen	我們	我们	Pron.	we, us	4
wòshì	臥室	卧室	N.	bedroom	15
wǔ	五/伍	五/伍	Num.	five	7
wǔfàn (zhōngfàn)	午飯 (中飯)	午饭 (中饭)	N.	lunch	8s
wǔhuì	舞會	舞会	N.	dance party	14

X

xībù	西部	西部	N.	west	18
Xībānyá	西班牙	西班牙	N.	Spain	3s
Xībānyárén	西班牙人	西班牙人	N.	Spanish (person)	3s
Xībānyáyǔ (Xibānyáwén)	西班牙語 (西班牙文)	西班牙语 (西班牙文)	N.	Spanish (language)	3s
xīguā	西瓜	西瓜	N.	watermelon	11s
xīyān	吸煙	吸烟	V.O.	to smoke	20
xīzhuāng	西裝	西装	N.	suit	13s
xǐhuān	喜歡	喜欢	V.	to like	10
xǐliǎn	洗臉	洗脸	V.O.	to wash face	10s
xǐzǎo	洗澡	洗澡	V.O.	to take a bath	10s
xǐzǎojiān	洗澡間	洗澡间	N.	bathroom, restroom	15
xì	系	系	N.	department	4s
xiā	蝦	虾	N.	shrimp	11s
xià	夏	夏	N.	summer	17
				next time	8
xiàcì	下次	下次			
xiàjiàng	下降	下降	V.C.	to decrease	17s
xiàkè	下課	下课	V.O.	to end class	8
xiàwǔ	下午	下午	N.	afternoon	10

xiàyǔ	下雨	下雨	*V.O.*	to rain	17
xiān	先	先	*Adv.*	first	11, 18
xiānsheng	先生	先生	*N.*	mister	11
xián	鹹	咸	*Adj.*	salty	11s
xiànzài	現在	现在	*Adv.*	now	16
xiāngjiāo	香蕉	香蕉	*N.*	banana	11s
xiǎng	想	想	*V.*	to want	8
xiàngliàn	項鏈	项链	*N.*	necklace	13s
xiāoyè	宵夜	宵夜	*N.*	midnight snack	8s
xiǎo	小	小	*Adj.*	small	7, 13s
xiǎofèi	小費	小费	*N.*	tip	11s
xiǎojiě	小姐	小姐	*N.*	miss	11
xiǎolóngbāo	小籠包	小笼包	*N.*	little steamed buns with stuffing	22
xiǎoshí	小時	小时	*N.*	hour	10s
xiǎoshuō	小說	小说	*N.*	novel	9s
xiàonèi	校內	校内	*N.*	on campus	7s
xiàowài	校外	校外	*N.*	off campus	7
xiézi	鞋子	鞋子	*N.*	shoes	13s
xiě	寫	写	*V.*	to write	10
xièxie	謝謝	谢谢		thank you, thanks	9
xīn	新	新	*Adj.*	new	22
Xīntáibì	新台幣	新台币	*N.*	currency of Taiwan	13s
xīnxiǎngshìchéng	心想事成	心想事成		Every wish comes true.	22s
xìn	信	信	*N.*	letter	10
xīngqī	星期	星期	*N.*	week	14
xíng	行	行	*V.*	to be all right, okay	8
xìng	姓	姓	*N.*	surname, family	2
			V.	to be surnamed	2
xiōngdìjiěmèi	兄弟姐妹	兄弟姐妹	*N.*	siblings	6s
xiūxi	休息	休息	*V.*	to rest	8s, 9s, 19
xuēzi	靴子	靴子	*N.*	boots	13s
xué	學	学	*V.*	to study, learn	1
xuédào	學到	学到	*V.C.*	to learn and master	22
xuéqī	學期	学期	*N.*	semester	10
xuésheng	學生	学生	*N.*	student	1
xuéshì	學士	学士	*N.*	bachelor's degree	21s
xuéwèi	學位	学位	*N.*	degree	21s
xuéxiào	學校	学校	*N.*	school	18
xuě	雪	雪	*N.*	snow	17

Y

yánjiūshēng	研究生	研究生	*N.*	graduate students	21s
yánjiūshēngyuàn	研究生院	研究生院	*N.*	graduate school	21
yánsè	顏色	颜色	*N.*	color	13s

yánzhòng	嚴重	严重	*Adj.*	severe	19s
yǎnjìng	眼鏡	眼镜	*N.*	glasses	13s
yào	要	要	*V.*	to want, desire	9
yéye	爺爺	爷爷	*N.*	grandfather	6s
yě	也	也	*Adv.*	also, too	1
yī	一/壹	一/壹	*Num.*	one	6
yīchú	衣櫥	衣橱	*N.*	wardrobe	15s
yīfu	衣服	衣服	*N.*	clothes	13s
yīshēng	醫生	医生	*N.*	doctor	6s, 19
yīwùshì (yīhùshì)	醫務室 (醫護室)	医务室 (医护室)	*N.*	clinic	19s
yīyuàn	醫院	医院	*N.*	hospital	19s
yídìng	一定	一定	*Aux.*	certainly, surely	14
yífù	姨父	姨父	*N.*	uncle (husband of mother's sister)	6s
yígòng	一共	一共	*Adv.*	altogether; in all	18
yílùpíng'ān	一路平安	一路平安		Have a pleasant journey.	21
yímā	姨媽	姨妈	*N.*	aunt (mother's sister)	6s
yímiàn	一面	一面	*Adv.*	at the same time	21
yíxià	一下	一下		(used after a verb to indicate a brief action)	5
yízhàng	姨丈	姨丈	*N.*	uncle (husband of mother's sister)	6s
yǐhòu	以後	以后	*N.*	after; afterwards; later	8
yǐjīng	已經	已经	*Adv.*	already	22
yǐnliào	飲料	饮料	*N.*	drink	11s
yǐqián	以前	以前	*N.*	before; previously	20
yǐzi	椅子	椅子	*N.*	chair	15s
yìdiǎr	一點兒	一点儿		a little	3
yìqǐ	一起	一起	*Adv.*	together	8
yìxiē	一些	一些	*Adj.*	some	22
yīnwèi	因為	因为	*Conj.*	because	22
yínhuīsè	銀灰色	银灰色	*Adj.*	silver	13s
yīnggāi	應該	应该	*Aux.*	should	12
Yīngguó	英國	英国	*N.*	Britain	3
Yīngwén	英文	英文	*N.*	English (language)	2
Yīngyǔ	英語	英语	*N.*	English (language)	2s
yìngjiàn (yìngtǐ)	硬件 (硬體)	硬件 (硬体)	*N.*	hardware	9s
yòng	用	用	*V.*	to use	12
yóudìyuán (yóuchāi)	郵遞員 (郵差)	邮递员 (邮差)	*N.*	mailman	6s
yóuyǒng	游泳	游泳	*V.O.*	to swim	16
			N.	swimming	16s
yóuyǒngchí	游泳池	游泳池	*N.*	swimming pool	16

yǒu	有	有	V.	to have	5
yǒudiǎr	有點兒	有点儿	Adv.	a little	4s
yǒukòng	有空	有空	V.O.	to have free time	14
yǒushíhou	有時候	有时候	Adv.	sometimes	17
yǒuyìsi	有意思	有意思	Adj.	interesting, enjoyable	21
yòubiān	右邊	右边	N.	on the right	15s
yú	魚	鱼	N.	fish	11s
yúkuài	愉快	愉快	Adj.	happy	21
yǔmáoqiú	羽毛球	羽毛球	N.	badminton	16s
yùfángzhēn	預防針	预防针	N.	immunization shot	19s
yuán	元	元	N.	dollar	13s
yuǎn	遠	远	Adj.	far	18
yuǎnzú	遠足	远足	N.	hiking	16s
yuè	月	月	N.	month	10
yuèyěchē	越野車	越野车	N.	off-road vehicle	18s
yùndòng	運動	运动	N.	sports	16s

Z

zázhì	雜誌	杂志	N.	magazine	15s
zài	在	在	V.	to be at, be in	6
			Prep.	at, in	
zài	再	再	Adv.	again	8
zàijiàn	再見	再见		see you again; goodbye	8
zàixiàn yóuxì (xiànshàng yóuxì)	在線遊戲 (線上遊戲)	在线游戏 (线上游戏)	N.	on-line game	9s
zāng	髒	脏	Adj.	dirty	15s
zǎo	早	早	Adj.	early	10s
zǎofàn	早飯	早饭	N.	breakfast	8s
zěnmeyàng	怎麼樣	怎么样	Pron.	how (used as a predicative or complement)	8
zhāi	摘	摘	V.	to take off (accessories)	13s
zhāixià	摘下	摘下	V.C.	to take off (accessories)	13s
zhànxiàn	佔線	占线	V.O.	to occupy a (phone) line, the line is busy	9s
zhāng	張	张	M.W.	(measure word for piece of paper)	13
zhǎo	找	找	V.	to seek for, look for	21
zhè	這	这	Pron.	this	4
zhècì	這次	这次	Pron.	this time	12
zhèyàng	這樣	这样	Pron.	thus; in this way	12
zhēn	真	真	Adv.	really	15
zhěnsuǒ	診所	诊所	N.	clinic	19s
zhěnglǐ	整理	整理	V.	to arrange, put in order	15s

zhěngqí	整齊	整齐	*Adj.*	tidy	15s
zhèngzài	正在	正在	*Adv.*	in the process of; in the course of (to indicate an action in progress)	9
zhī	隻	只	*M.W.*	(measure word for certain animals, boats, or containers; or for one of a pair)	6
zhīdào	知道	知道	*V.*	to know; be aware of; realize	9
zhínǚ	姪女	侄女	*N.*	niece (brother's daughter)	6s
zhíyè	職業	职业	*N.*	occupation	6s
zhíyuán	職員	职员	*N.*	staff	6s
zhízi	姪子	侄子	*N.*	nephew (brother's son)	6s
zhǐyào	只要	只要	*Adv.*	only	18
zhōng	中	中	*Adj.*	medium	13s
zhōngjiān	中間	中间	*N.*	middle	15
zhōngtóu	鐘頭	钟头	*N.*	hour	10s
Zhōngguó	中國	中国	*N.*	China	3
Zhōngwén	中文	中文	*N.*	Chinese (language)	2
zhūròu	豬肉	猪肉	*N.*	pork	11s
zhù	住	住	*V.*	to live	7
	祝	祝	*V.*	to wish	10
Zhù nǐ shēngrì kuàilè.	祝你生日快樂	祝你生日快乐		Happy birthday to you.	14s
zhuānyè (zhǔxiū)	專業 (主修)	专业 (主修)	*N.*	major	4s
zhuōzi	桌子	桌子	*N.*	table	15
zhǔnbèi	準備	准备	*V.*	to prepare	19
zǐsè	紫色	紫色	*Adj.*	purple	13s
zìdòngpáidǎng (zìpái)	自動排擋 (自排)	自动排挡 (自排)	*Adj.*	automatic transmission	12s
zìjǐ	自己	自己	*N.*	oneself	6s
zìwǒjièshào	自我介紹	自我介绍	*N.*	self-introduction	6s
			V.	to introduce oneself	
zìxíngchē	自行車	自行车	*N.*	bicycle	18
zōngsè (kāfēisè)	棕色 (咖啡色)	棕色 (咖啡色)	*Adj.*	brown	13s
zǒu	走	走	*V.*	to walk	15
zǒulù	走路	走路	*V.O.*	to walk	18
zū	租	租	*V.*	to rent, hire, lease	18
zūwū	租屋	租屋	*V.O.*	to rent a house	20s
zúqiú	足球	足球	*N.*	soccer	16s
zǔfù	祖父	祖父	*N.*	grandfather	6s
zǔmǔ	祖母	祖母	*N.*	grandmother	6s
zuì	最	最	*Adv.*	most, the highest degree (indicates the superlative degree)	17, 22

zuǒbiān	左邊	左边	N.	on the left	15s
zuò	坐	坐	V.	to sit	11
	做	做	V.	to do, to make	9, 14
zuótiān	昨天	昨天	N.	yesterday	16
zuòfàn	做飯	做饭	V.O.	to cook	20
zuòyè	作業	作业	N.	homework; assignment	4s, 16

Each entry lists English meaning, traditional character, simplified character, Pinyin, part of speech, and lesson number.

Note: The letter "s" means that the entry occurs in the supplementary vocabulary to that lesson.

Units of Measurement

10 jiao = 1 yuan	角	角	jiǎo	N.	13s
10 mao = 1 kuai	毛	毛	máo	N.	13s
100 fen = 10 jiao/10 mao = 1 yuan/1 kuai	分	分	fēn	N.	13s

Measure Words (Classifiers) for

books	本	本	běn	M.W.	4
certain animals, boats, or containers, or for one of a pair	隻	只	zhī	M.W.	6
clothes	件	件	jiàn	M.W.	13
company, enterprises, store, etc.	家	家	jiā	M.W.	21
cups, buildings, characters	個	个	gè	M.W.	5
people (polite form)	位	位	wèi	M.W.	9
a piece of paper	張	张	zhāng	M.W.	13
school courses	門	门	mén	M.W.	10
skirt/pants	條	条	tiáo	M.W.	13
telephone conversation	通	通	tōng	M.W.	9s
vehicles	輛	辆	liàng	M.W.	6

A

above, over, on top of	上邊	上边	shàngbiān	N.	15
accessory	飾品	饰品	shìpǐn	N.	13s
accountant	會計師	会计师	kuàijìshī	N.	6s
action	動作	动作	dòngzuò	N.	13s
activity	活動	活动	huódòng	N.	22
address	地址	地址	dìzhǐ	N.	10
after, afterwards, later	以後	以后	yǐhòu	N.	8
afternoon	下午	下午	xiàwǔ	N.	10
again	再	再	zài	Adv.	8
age, years old	歲	岁	suì	N.	14
agent	經紀人	经纪人	jīngjìrén	N.	6s
airplane	飛機	飞机	fēijī	N.	12

airport	機場	机场	jīchǎng	N.	12
all, everybody	大家	大家	dàjiā	Pron.	6
all, both	都	都	dōu	Adv.	5
already	已經	已经	yǐjīng	Adv.	22
already, as early as	就	就	jiù	Adv.	10
also, too	也	也	yě	Adv.	1
altogether, in all	一共	一共	yígòng	Adv.	18
among (whom, which)	其中	其中	qízhōng		17
and	和	和	hé	Conj.	3
apartment	公寓	公寓	gōngyù	N.	7s
apple	蘋果	苹果	píngguǒ	N.	11s
to apply	申請	申请	shēnqǐng	V.	21
architect	建築師	建筑师	jiànzhùshī	N.	6s
to arrange, put in order	整理	整理	zhěnglǐ	V.	15s
to arrive	到	到	dào	V.	12
to ask	問	问	wèn	V.	2
at, in	在	在	zài	Prep.	6
at the same time	同時	同时	tóngshí	Adv.	21
to attend classes, begin class	上課	上课	shàngkè	V.O.	8
aunt (father's sister)	姑媽	姑妈	gūmā	N.	6s
	姑姑	姑姑	gūgu	N.	6s
(mother's sister)	姨媽	姨妈	yímā	N.	6s
	阿姨	阿姨	āyí	N.	6s
(wife of father's elder brother)	伯母	伯母	bómǔ	N.	6s
(wife of father's younger brother)	嬸嬸	婶婶	shěnshen	N.	6s
(wife of mother's brother)	舅媽	舅妈	jiùmā	N.	6s
automatic transmission	自動排擋 (自排)	自动排挡 (自排)	zìdòngpáidǎng (zìpái)	Adj.	12s
autumn	秋	秋	qiū	N.	17

B

bachelor's degree	學士	学士	xuéshì	N.	21s
badminton	羽毛球	羽毛球	yǔmáoqiú	N.	16s
ball game, match	球賽	球赛	qiúsài	N.	16
banana	香蕉	香蕉	xiāngjiāo	N.	11s
baseball	棒球	棒球	bàngqiú	N.	16s
basketball	籃球	篮球	lánqiú	N.	16, 16s
to bathe, take a bath	洗澡	洗澡	xǐzǎo	V.O.	10s
bathroom, restroom	洗澡間	洗澡间	xǐzǎojiān	N.	15
to be all right, okay	行	行	xíng	V.	8
to be at, be in,	在	在	zài	V.	6
to be like, seem	好像	好像	hǎoxiàng	V.	19

to be off, away, from	離	离	lí	*V.*	18
to be online	上網	上网	shàngwǎng	*V.O.*	9
to be surnamed	姓	姓	xìng	*V.*	2
to be told, hear of, It is said . . .	聽說	听说	tīngshuō	*V.*	18
to be, yes (affirmative answer)	是	是	shì	*V.*	1
to be without, not have	沒有	没有	méiyǒu	*V.*	5s, 6
bean curd	豆腐	豆腐	dòufu	*N.*	11s
beautiful	美麗	美丽	měilì	*Adj.*	22
because	因為	因为	yīnwèi	*Conj.*	22
bed	床	床	chuáng	*N.*	15s
bedroom	臥室	卧室	wòshì	*N.*	15
beef	牛肉	牛肉	niúròu	*N.*	11s
beer	啤酒	啤酒	píjiǔ	*N.*	11
before, previously	以前	以前	yǐqián	*N.*	20
behind, at the back	後邊	后边	hòubiān	*N.*	15
bicycle	自行車 單車 (腳踏車)	自行车 单车 (脚踏车)	zìxíngchē dānchē (jiǎotàchē)	*N.*	18, 18s
big	大	大	dà	*Adj.*	7
birthday	生日	生日	shēngrì	*N.*	14
bitter	苦	苦	kǔ	*Adj.*	11s
black	黑 黑色	黑 黑色	hēi hēisè	*Adj.* *Adj.*	13 13s
to blow (wind)	刮風	刮风	guāfēng	*V.O.*	17
blue	藍色	蓝色	lánsè	*Adj.*	13s
body temperature	體溫	体温	tǐwēn	*N.*	19s
book	書	书	shū	*N.*	4
boots	靴子	靴子	xuēzi	*N.*	13s
to borrow	借	借	jiè	*V.*	12
boss	老闆	老板	lǎobǎn	*N.*	6s, 22
bottle	瓶	瓶	píng	*M.W.*	11
bowl	碗	碗	wǎn	*M.W.*	11
boyfriend	男朋友	男朋友	nánpéngyou	*N.*	5s, 6
bracelet	手鐲	手镯	shǒuzhuó	*N.*	13s
bread	麵包	面包	miànbāo	*N.*	11s
breakfast	早飯	早饭	zǎofàn	*N.*	8s
to bring over	帶來	带来	dàilái	*V.C.*	20
Britain	英國	英国	Yīngguó	*N.*	3
brown	棕色 (咖啡色)	棕色 (咖啡色)	zōngsè (kāfēisè)	*Adj.*	13s
to brush one's teeth	刷牙	刷牙	shuāyá	*V.O.*	10s
to burn the midnight oil	熬夜	熬夜	áoyè	*V.O.*	10s
burning hot	燙	烫	tàng	*Adj.*	11s

bus	公共汽車	公共汽车	gōnggòngqìchē	N.	18
	公車	公车	gōngchē	N.	18s
	(巴士)	(巴士)	(bāshì)		
businessman	商人	商人	shāngrén	N.	6s
busy	忙	忙	máng	Adj.	4s, 9
busy season	旺季	旺季	wàngjì	N.	18s
but	但是	但是	dànshì	Conj.	20
but, however	不過	不过	búguò	Conj.	22
but, yet, however	可是	可是	kěshì	Conj.	4
to buy	買	买	mǎi	V.	13
by the way (a phrase used to start a new topic)	對了	对了	duìle	Conj.	3

C

cake	蛋糕	蛋糕	dàngāo	N.	11s, 14
California State	加州	加州	Jiāzhōu	N.	21
to call	叫	叫	jiào	V.	2
calligraphy	書法	书法	shūfǎ	N.	22
can	能	能	néng	Aux.	12
can, be able to	會	会	huì	Aux.	3
can, may	可以	可以	kěyǐ	Aux.	12
Canada	加拿大	加拿大	Jiānádà	N.	3s
Canadian (people)	加拿大人	加拿大人	Jiānádàrén	N.	3s
candle	蠟燭	蜡烛	làzhú	N.	14s
car	車	车	chē	N.	6
	汽車	汽车	qìchē	N.	18s
cat	貓	猫	māo	N.	6s
to celebrate a birthday	慶生	庆生	qìngshēng	V.O.	14s
cell phone	手機	手机	shǒujī	N.	7
Centigrade	攝氏	摄氏	shèshì	N.	17s
certainly, surely	一定	一定	yídìng	Aux.	14
chair	椅子	椅子	yǐzi	N.	15s
chat room	聊天室	聊天室	liáotiānshì	N.	9s
chicken	雞肉	鸡肉	jīròu	N.	11s
child	孩子	孩子	háizi	N.	6s
China	中國	中国	Zhōngguó	N.	3
Chinese (language)	中文	中文	Zhōngwén	N.	2
	漢語	汉语	Hànyǔ	N.	2s
chopstick	筷子	筷子	kuàizi	N.	11
city	城市	城市	chéngshì	N.	22
class	班	班	bān	N.	21
classmate, student	同學	同学	tóngxué	N.	2
classroom	教室	教室	jiàoshì	N.	15s

clean	乾淨	干净	gānjìng	*Adj.*	15s
climate	氣候	气候	qìhòu	N.	17
to climb a mountain	爬山	爬山	páshān	V.O.	16s
clinic	醫務室	医务室	yīwùshì	N.	19s
	(醫護室)	(医护室)	(yīhùshì)		
	診所	诊所	zhěnsuǒ	N.	19s
clothes	衣服	衣服	yīfu	N.	13s
clothing (for upper body)	上衣	上衣	shàngyī	N.	13s
club	俱樂部	俱乐部	jùlèbù	N.	16s
coach, trainer	教練	教练	jiàoliàn	N.	16
coat	外套	外套	wàitào	N.	13s
coffee	咖啡	咖啡	kāfēi	N.	11s
cola	可樂	可乐	kělè	N.	11
cold	冷	冷	lěng	*Adj.*	17
cold, flu	感冒	感冒	gǎnmào	N.	19
colleague	同事	同事	tóngshì	N.	22
college, university	大學	大学	dàxué	N.	10
college student(s)	大學生	大学生	dàxuéshēng	N.	6s, 21s
color	色	色	sè	N.	12
	顏色	颜色	yánsè	N.	13s
to come over	過來	过来	guòlái	V.C.	20
to come (used before a verb to indicate that one is about to do something)	來	来	lái	V.	5
comfortable	舒服	舒服	shūfu	*Adj.*	19
common	常見	常见	chángjiàn	*Adj.*	11s
company	公司	公司	gōngsī	N.	21
computer	計算機	计算机	jìsuànjī	N.	4s
	(電腦)	(电脑)	(diànnǎo)	N.	21
computer game	電腦遊戲	电脑游戏	diànnǎo yóuxì	N.	9s
computer programmer	程序員	程序员	chéngxùyuán	N.	6s
	(程式設計師)	(程式设计师)	(chéngshì shèjìshī)		
conscientious, serious	認真	认真	rènzhēn	*Adj.*	22
consultant	顧問	顾问	gùwèn	N.	6s
to cook	做飯	做饭	zuòfàn	V.O.	20
cool	涼	凉	liáng	*Adj.*	11s
correct, right	對	对	duì	*Adj.*	9
to cough	咳嗽	咳嗽	késòu	V.	19
country	國	国	guó	N.	3
cousin (daughter of father's brother)	堂姐	堂姐	tángjiě	N.	6s
	堂妹	堂妹	tángmèi	N.	6s
(daughter of parents' sister or mother's brother)	表姐	表姐	biǎojiě	N.	6s
	表妹	表妹	biǎomèi	N.	6s
(husband of 表姐)	表姐夫	表姐夫	biǎojiěfu	N.	6s

(husband of 表妹)	表妹夫	表妹夫	biǎomèifu	N.	6s
(husband of 堂姐)	堂姐夫	堂姐夫	tángjiěfu	N.	6s
(husband of 堂妹)	堂妹夫	堂妹夫	tángmèifu	N.	6s
(son of father's brother)	堂哥	堂哥	tánggē	N.	6s
	堂弟	堂弟	tángdì	N.	6s
(son of parents' sister or mother's brother)	表哥	表哥	biǎogē	N.	6s
	表弟	表弟	biǎodì	N.	6s
(wife of 表弟)	表弟妹	表弟妹	biǎodìmèi	N.	6s
(wife of 表哥)	表嫂	表嫂	biǎosǎo	N.	6s
(wife of 堂弟)	堂弟妹	堂弟妹	tángdìmèi	N.	6s
(wife of 堂哥)	堂嫂	堂嫂	tángsǎo	N.	6s
cracker	餅乾	饼干	bǐnggān	N.	11s
cup	杯	杯	bēi	M.W.	11
currency	貨幣	货币	huòbì	N.	13s
currency of Hong Kong	港幣	港币	Gǎngbì	N.	13s
currency of the People's Republic of China	人民幣	人民币	Rénmínbì	N.	13s
currency of Taiwan	新台幣	新台币	Xīntáibì	N.	13s
to cycle, to ride a bike	騎自行車	骑自行车	qí zìxíngchē	V.O.	16s

D

dance party	舞會	舞会	wǔhuì	N.	14
dark	深色	深色	shēnsè	Adj.	13s
dark blue	深藍色	深蓝色	shēnlánsè	Adj.	13s
day	日	日	rì	N.	10
to decide	決定	决定	juédìng	V.	21
to decrease	下降	下降	xiàjiàng	V.C.	17s
degree	度	度	dù	N.	17
	學位	学位	xuéwèi	N.	21s
department	系	系	xì	N.	4s
desk	書桌	书桌	shūzhuō	N.	15s
dessert	甜點	甜点	tiándiǎn	N.	11s
to dial a wrong number	打錯了	打错了	dǎcuòle		9s
difficult	難	难	nán	Adj.	4
dining room	餐廳	餐厅	cāntīng	N.	15
dinner	晚飯	晚饭	wǎnfàn	N.	8s
dirty	髒	脏	zāng	Adj.	15s
dish	菜	菜	cài	N.	8
to dive	潛水	潜水	qiánshuǐ	V.O.	16s
to do	做	做	zuò	V.	9
doctor	醫生	医生	yīshēng	N.	6s, 19
doctoral degree	博士	博士	bóshì	N.	21s
doctoral students	博士生	博士生	bóshìshēng	N.	21s
dog	狗	狗	gǒu	N.	6

dollar	塊	块	kuài	N.	13, 13s
	元	元	yuán	N.	13s
dollar (U.S.)	美金	美金	Měijīn	N.	13s
door	門	门	mén	N.	15s
dorm(itory)	宿舍	宿舍	sùshè	N.	7
drink	飲料	饮料	yǐnliào	N.	11s
to drink	喝	喝	hē	V.	11
to drive	開	开	kāi	V.	12
driver	司機	司机	sījī	N.	18s
dumpling (crescent-shaped)	餃子	饺子	jiǎozi	N.	11

E

early	早	早	zǎo	Adj.	10s
earrings	耳環	耳环	ěrhuán	N.	13s
east	東	东	dōng	N.	18s
easy	容易	容易	róngyì	Adj.	4s
to eat	吃	吃	chī	V.	8
to eat, have a meal	吃飯	吃饭	chīfàn	V.O.	8
economist	經濟師	经济师	jīngjìshī	N.	6s
educator	教育工作者	教育工作者	jiàoyù gōngzuòzhě	N.	6s
eight	八/捌	八/捌	bā	Num.	7
elder brother	哥哥	哥哥	gēge	N.	6s
elder sister	姐姐	姐姐	jiějie	N.	6
e-mail	電子郵件	电子邮件	diànzǐ yóujiàn	N.	10
to end class	下課	下课	xiàkè	V.O.	8
engineer	工程師	工程师	gōngchéngshī	N.	6, 6s
engineering	工程	工程	gōngchéng	N.	4
English (language)	英文	英文	Yīngwén	N.	2
	英語	英语	Yīngyǔ	N.	2s
to enter	進	进	jìn	V.	20
Euro	歐元	欧元	Ōuyuán	N.	13s
evening, night	晚上	晚上	wǎnshàng	N.	9
every day	每天	每天	měitiān	N.	10
Every wish comes true.	心想事成	心想事成	xīnxiǎngshìchéng		22s
everywhere	到處	到处	dàochù	Adv.	22
exam	考試	考试	kǎoshì	N.	4s, 19
Excuse me, I'm sorry.	對不起	对不起	duìbuqǐ		22
to exercise	鍛煉	锻炼	duànliàn	V.	16
expensive	貴	贵	guì	Adj.	13s
extra large	特大	特大	tè dà	Adj.	13s
extra small	特小	特小	tè xiǎo	Adj.	13s
extremely	極	极	jí	Adv.	17

F

Fahrenheit	華氏	华氏	huáshì	*N.*	17
to fall ill	生病	生病	shēngbìng	*V.O.*	19
far	遠	远	yuǎn	*Adj.*	18
fast	快	快	kuài	*Adj.*	16
father	爸爸	爸爸	bàba	*N.*	6
female	女	女	nǚ	*N.*	6s
fen (RMB unit)	分	分	fēn	*N.*	13s
few, little	少	少	shǎo	*Adj.*	4
first	先	先	xiān	*Adv.*	11, 18
first day	第一天	第一天	dìyītiān	*N.*	20
fish	魚	鱼	yú	*N.*	11s
to fish	釣魚	钓鱼	diàoyú	*V.O.*	16s
five	五/伍	五/伍	wǔ	*Num.*	7
flu	流感 (流行性感冒)	流感 (流行性感冒)	liúgǎn (liúxíngxìng gǎnmào)	*N.*	19s
flu shot	流感疫苗	流感疫苗	liúgǎn yìmiáo	*N.*	19s
food	食品	食品	shípǐn	*N.*	11s
football	橄欖球	橄榄球	gǎnlǎnqiú	*N.*	16s
for a long time	久	久	jiǔ	*Adj.*	17
for example	比如	比如	bǐrú	*Conj.*	22
for public use, communal	公用	公用	gōngyòng	*Adj.*	15
for, to	給	给	gěi	*Prep.*	
form of address	稱謂	称谓	chēngwèi	*N.*	6s
four	四/肆	四/肆	sì	*Num.*	6
four seasons	四季	四季	sìjì	*N.*	17s
four-wheel drive	四輪驅動 (四輪傳動)	四轮驱动 (四轮传动)	sìlúnqūdòng (sìlúnchuándòng)	*N.*	18s
France	法國	法国	Fǎguó	*N.*	3
French (language)	法文	法文	Fǎwén	*N.*	3
friend	朋友	朋友	péngyou	*N.*	5
from	從	从	cóng	*Prep.*	6

G

German (language)	德語 (德文)	德语 (德文)	Déyǔ (Déwén)	*N.*	3s
(people)	德國人	德国人	Déguórén	*N.*	3s
Germany	德國	德国	Déguó	*N.*	3s
to get up	起床	起床	qǐchuáng	*V.O.*	10
gift	禮物	礼物	lǐwù	*N.*	14s
girlfriend	女朋友	女朋友	nǚpéngyou	*N.*	5s, 6s, 20

to give (as a present)	送(禮)	送(礼)	sòng(lǐ)	*V.*	14
give or receive an injection	打針	打针	dǎzhēn	*V.O.*	19s
glasses	眼鏡	眼镜	yǎnjìng	*N.*	13s
gloves	手套	手套	shǒutào	*N.*	13s
to go	去	去	qù	*V.*	8
to go to bed, sleep	睡覺	睡觉	shuìjiào	*V.O.*	9s, 10
to go out	出去	出去	chūqù	*V.C.*	20
gold	金黃色	金黄色	jīnhuángsè	*Adj.*	13s
golf	高爾夫球	高尔夫球	gāo'ěrfūqiú	*N.*	16s
good-looking	好看	好看	hǎokàn	*Adj.*	13
Good luck.	好運	好运	hǎoyùn		21
good, well	好	好	hǎo	*Adj.*	1
goodbye, see you again	再見	再見	zàijiàn		8
government official	官員	官员	guānyuán	*N.*	6s
to graduate	畢業	毕业	bìyè	*V.*	21
graduate school	研究生院	研究生院	yánjiūshēngyuàn	*N.*	21
graduate student	研究生	研究生	yánjiūshēng	*N.*	21s
grandfather	爺爺	爷爷	yéye	*N.*	6s
	祖父	祖父	zǔfù	*N.*	6s
grandmother	奶奶	奶奶	nǎinai	*N.*	6s
	祖母	祖母	zǔmǔ	*N.*	6s
grape	葡萄	葡萄	pútao	*N.*	11s
gray	灰色	灰色	huīsè	*Adj.*	13s
green	綠	绿	lǜ	*Adj.*	11
	綠色	绿色	lǜsè	*Adj.*	13s
gym	健身房	健身房	jiànshēnfáng	*N.*	16
gymnasium	體育館	体育馆	tǐyùguǎn	*N.*	16

H

half	半	半	bàn	*Adj.*	10
handkerchief	手絹	手绢	shǒujuàn	*N.*	13s
happy	愉快	愉快	yúkuài	*Adj.*	21
	高興	高兴	gāoxìng	*Adj.*	22
	開心	开心	kāixīn	*Adj.*	22
Happy birthday to you.	祝你生日快樂	祝你生日快乐	Zhù nǐ shēngrì kuàilè.		14s
hardware	硬件(硬體)	硬件(硬体)	yìngjiàn (yìngtǐ)	*N.*	9s
hat	帽子	帽子	màozi	*N.*	13s
to have	有	有	yǒu	*V.*	5
to have a fever	發燒	发烧	fāshāo	*V.O.*	19
to have a headache	頭疼	头疼	tóuténg	*V.*	19
Have a pleasant journey.	一路平安	一路平安	yílùpíng'ān		21
to have a try, taste	嚐嚐	尝尝	chángchang	*V.*	22

to have a try, taste	嚐嚐	尝尝	chángchang	V.	22
to have free time	有空	有空	yǒukòng	V.O.	14
to have or start (a vacation)	放假	放假	fàngjià	V.O.	17
he, him	他	他	tā	Pron.	1
healthy	健康	健康	jiànkāng	Adj.	22s
hello, hey (used in greetings or to attract attention)	喂	喂	wèi (wéi)	Int.	9
to help	幫	帮	bāng	V.	13
hiking	遠足	远足	yuǎnzú	N.	16s
home, family	家	家	jiā	N.	6
homework	作業	作业	zuòyè	N.	16
homework, assignment	作業	作业	zuòyè	N.	4s
	功課	功课	gōngkè	N.	4
hospital	醫院	医院	yīyuàn	N.	19s
hot	熱	热	rè	Adj.	17
hour	點鐘	点钟	diǎnzhōng	N.	10s
	鐘頭	钟头	zhōngtóu	M.W.	10s
	小時	小时	xiǎoshí	N.	10s
house, room	房子	房子	fángzi	N.	7s
housewife	家庭主婦	家庭主妇	jiātíng zhǔfù	N.	6s
how (used as a predicative or complement)	怎麼樣	怎么样	zěnmeyàng	Pron.	8
how many	幾	几	jǐ		5
how many, how much	多少	多少	duōshǎo	Pron.	7
how old	多大	多大	duōdà		14
hundred	百	百	bǎi	Num.	17
hungry	餓	饿	è	Adj.	19

I

I, me	我	我	wǒ	Pron.	1
ice	冰	冰	bīng	N.	11
ice hockey	冰球	冰球	bīngqiú	N.	16s
immediately	馬上	马上	mǎshàng	Adv.	20
immunization shot	預防針	预防针	yùfángzhēn	N.	19s
to improve	進步	进步	jìnbù	V.	12
in front of	前邊	前边	qiánbiān	N.	15
in the process of, in the course of (to indicate an action in progress)	正在	正在	zhèngzài	Adv.	9
to increase	上升	上升	shàngshēng	V.C.	17s
(indicates assumption)	了	了	le	Part.	9
(indicates one's act of service)	為	为	wèi	Prep.	14
(indicates the superlative degree)	最	最	zuì	Adv.	17

inexpensive	便宜	便宜	piányi	*Adj.*	13s
inside	裡邊	里边	lǐbiān	N.	15
interesting, enjoyable	有意思	有意思	yǒuyìsi	*Adj.*	21
international students	留學生	留学生	liúxuéshēng	N.	6s
Internet	網絡 (網路)	网络 (网路)	wǎngluò (wǎnglù)	N.	9s
Internet café	網吧 (網咖)	网吧 (网咖)	wǎngbā (wǎngkā)	N.	9s
internship	實習	实习	shíxí	N.	21
to introduce	介紹	介绍	jièshào	V.	5
to introduce oneself; self-introduction	自我介紹	自我介绍	zìwǒjièshào	*V./N.*	6s
(introduces the object of a verb)	把	把	bǎ	*Prep.*	20
introduction	介紹	介绍	jièshào	N.	5
it seems	看來	看来	kànlái		22

J

jacket	夾克衫 (夾克)	夾克衫 (夹克)	jiákèshān (jiákè)	N.	13s
Japan	日本	日本	Rìběn	N.	3s, 8
Japanese (language)	日語 (日文)	日语 (日文)	Rìyǔ (Rìwén)	N.	3s
(people)	日本人	日本人	Rìběnrén	N.	3s
jeans	牛仔褲	牛仔裤	niúzǎikù	N.	13s
jeep	吉普車	吉普车	jípǔchē	N.	18s
jiao (RMB unit of 10 cents) 10 fen	角	角	jiǎo	N.	13s
job, to work	工作	工作	gōngzuò	*N./V.*	6
juice	果汁	果汁	guǒzhī	N.	11s

K

kitchen	廚房	厨房	chúfáng	N.	15
to know	認識	认识	rènshi	V.	5s
to know, recognize	認識	认识	rènshi	V.	8
to know, be aware of, realize	知道	知道	zhīdào	V.	9
Korea	韓國	韩国	Hánguó	N.	3s, 8
Korean (language)	韓語 (韓文)	韩语 (韩文)	Hányǔ (Hánwén)	N.	3s
(people)	韓國人	韩国人	Hánguórén	N.	3s

L

to lack	差	差	chà	V.	10s
landlord	房東	房东	fángdōng	N.	20s
large	大	大	dà	Adj.	13s
late	晚	晚	wǎn	Adj.	10s
lawyer	律師	律师	lǜshī	N.	6s
to learn, to master	學到	学到	xuédào	V.C.	22
leather shoes	皮鞋	皮鞋	píxié	N.	13s
to leave a message	留言	留言	liúyán	V.O.	9
	(留話)	(留话)	(liúhuà)		
to let, allow	讓	让	ràng	V.	13
letter	信	信	xìn	N.	10
library	圖書館	图书馆	túshūguǎn	N.	10
life	生活	生活	shēnghuó	N.	10
to lift weights	舉重	举重	jǔzhòng	V.O.	16s
light	淺色	浅色	qiǎnsè	Adj.	13s
light green	淺綠色	浅绿色	qiǎnlǜsè	Adj.	13s
to like	喜歡	喜欢	xǐhuān	V.	10
literature	文學	文学	wénxué	N.	4
little, a	一點兒	一点儿	yìdiǎr		3
	有點兒	有点儿	yǒudiǎr	Adv.	4s
little steamed buns with stuffing	小籠包	小笼包	xiǎolóngbāo	N.	22
to live	住	住	zhù	V.	7
living room	客廳	客厅	kètīng	N.	15
to look at, see, watch	看	看	kàn	V.	9
long	長	长	cháng	Adj.	17s
long pants	長褲	长裤	chángkù	N.	13s
to love	愛	爱	ài	V.	6
lunch	午飯	午饭	wǔfàn	N.	8s
	(中飯)	(中饭)	(zhōngfàn)		

M

magazine	雜誌	杂志	zázhì	N.	15s
magnetic railway	磁浮鐵路	磁浮铁路	cífú tiělù	N.	18s
mailman	郵遞員	邮递员	yóudìyuán	N.	6s
	(郵差)	(邮差)	(yóuchāi)		
major	專業	专业	zhuānyè	N.	4s
	(主修)	(主修)	(zhǔxiū)		
to make a phone call	打電話	打电话	dǎ diànhuà	V.O.	9
to make, do	做	做	zuò	V.	14
male	男	男	nán	N.	6
manager	經理	经理	jīnglǐ	N.	6s

manual transmission	手排擋 (手排)	手排挡 (手排)	shǒupáidǎng (shǒupái)	N.	12
many, much	多	多	duō	Adj.	4
mao (the RMB unit of 　　10 cents) 1/10 of yuan	毛	毛	máo	N.	13s
map	地圖	地图	dìtú	N.	14
master's degree	碩士	硕士	shuòshì	N.	21s
maternal grandfather	外公	外公	wàigōng	N.	6s
	外祖父	外祖父	wàizǔfù	N.	6s
	老爺	姥爷	lǎoye	N.	6s
maternal grandmother	外婆	外婆	wàipó	N.	6s
	外祖母	外祖母	wàizǔmǔ	N.	6s
	姥姥	姥姥	lǎolao	N.	6s
mathematics	數學	数学	shùxué	N.	4s
matter, thing, business	事兒	事儿	shèr	N.	8
may I ask	請問	请问	qǐng wèn		2
medium	中	中	zhōng	Adj.	13s
to meet each other	見面	见面	jiànmiàn	V.O.	17
menu	菜單	菜单	càidān	N.	11s
messy	亂	乱	luàn	Adj.	15s
middle	中間	中间	zhōngjiān	N.	15
midnight snack	宵夜	宵夜	xiāoyè	N.	8s
minibus, van	麵包車 (包型車)	面包车 (包型车)	miànbāochē (bāoxíngchē)	N.	18s
miniskirt	迷你裙	迷你裙	mínǐqún	N.	13s
minor	輔修	辅修	fǔxiū	N.	4s
minute	分	分	fēn	N.	10
	分鐘	分钟	fēnzhōng	N.	10s, 18
miss	小姐	小姐	xiǎojiě	N.	11
mister	先生	先生	xiānsheng	N.	11
money	錢	钱	qián	N.	13
month	月	月	yuè	N.	10
most, the superlative degree	最	最	zuì	Adv.	22
mother	媽媽	妈妈	māma	N.	6
to move	搬	搬	bān	V.	20
movie	電影	电影	diànyǐng	N.	9s, 13
MRT (Mass Rapid 　　Transportation) in 　　Taiwan	捷運	捷运	jiéyùn	N.	18s
multicolor	彩色	彩色	cǎisè	Adj.	13s
must	必須	必须	bìxū	Aux.	20
must, have to	得	得	děi	Aux.	12

N

name	名字	名字	míngzi	*N.*	2
name card	名片	名片	míngpiàn	*N.*	8s
near	近	近	jìn	*Adj.*	18
nearby	旁邊	旁边	pángbiān	*N.*	15
necklace	項鏈	项链	xiàngliàn	*N.*	13s
necktie	領帶	领带	lǐngdài	*N.*	13s
nephew (brother's son)	姪子	侄子	zhízi	*N.*	6s
(sister's son)	外甥	外甥	wàisheng	*N.*	6s
new	新	新	xīn	*Adj.*	22
New York	紐約	纽约	Niǔyuē	*N.*	6
next time	下次	下次	xiàcì		8
niece (brother's daughter)	姪女	侄女	zhínǚ	*N.*	6s
(sister's daughter)	外甥女	外甥女	wàishengnǚ	*N.*	6s
nine	九/玖	九/玖	jiǔ	*Num.*	7
No problem	沒關係	没关系	méiguānxi		20
noble, honored; expensive	貴	贵	guì	*Adj.*	2
noodle	麵	面	miàn	*N.*	11
north	北	北	běi	*N.*	18s
not bad, okay	還好	还好	hái hǎo		4s
not bad, pretty good	不錯	不错	búcuò		13
not, no (used to form negation)	不	不	bù	*Adv.*	1
notes	筆記	笔记	bǐjì	*N.*	19
novel	小說	小说	xiǎoshuō	*N.*	9s
now	現在	现在	xiànzài	*Adv.*	16
number	號	号	hào	*N.*	7
	號碼	号码	hàomǎ	*N.*	7
nurse	護士	护士	hùshi	*N.*	6s, 19s

O

occupation	職業	职业	zhíyè	*N.*	6s
to occupy a (phone) line, the line is busy	佔線	占线	zhànxiàn	*V.O.*	9s
o'clock	點	点	diǎn	*M.W.*	10
off campus	校外	校外	xiàowài	*N.*	7
off-road vehicle, jeep	越野車	越野车	yuèyěchē	*N.*	18s
off-season	淡季	淡季	dànjì	*N.*	18s
often, frequently	常	常	cháng	*Adv.*	5
on campus	校內	校内	xiàonèi	*N.*	7s
on the left	左邊	左边	zuǒbiān	*N.*	15s
on the right	右邊	右边	yòubiān	*N.*	15s
one	一/壹	一/壹	yī	*Num.*	6

oneself	自己	自己	zìjǐ	N.	6s
on-line games	在線遊戲 (線上遊戲)	在线游戏 (线上游戏)	zàixiàn yóuxì (xiànshàng yóuxì)	N.	9s
only	只要	只要	zhǐyào	Adv.	18
opportunity	機會	机会	jīhuì	N.	22
opposite	對面	对面	duìmiàn	N.	15
or	還是	还是	háishì	Conj.	11
or, either . . . or . . .	或者	或者	huòzhě	Conj.	13
orange	橙色 (橘色)	橙色 (橘色)	chéngsè (júsè)	Adj.	13s
orange juice	橙汁	橙汁	chéngzhī	N.	11s
to order food	點菜	点菜	diǎncài	V.O.	11s
organization	社團	社团	shètuán	N.	16s
out, to be	出	出	chū	V.	20
overcoat	大衣	大衣	dàyī	N.	13s
overhead bridge	天橋	天桥	tiānqiáo	N.	18s
overseas, abroad	國外	国外	guówài	N.	21

P

pair	雙	双	shuāng	M.W.	11
pants	褲子	裤子	kùzi	N.	13
to park	停	停	tíng	V.	12
park	公園	公园	gōngyuán	N.	15
parking lot	停車場	停车场	tíngchēchǎng	N.	12
to participate, join	參加	参加	cānjiā	V.	14
to pass	過	过	guò	V.	10s, 17
to pay	付	付	fù	V.	20
to pay the bills	買單	买单	mǎidān	V.O.	11s
peach	桃子	桃子	táozi	N.	11s
pear	梨子	梨子	lízi	N.	11s
Peking Opera	京劇	京剧	jīngjù	N.	22
person	人	人	rén	N.	3
pet	寵物	宠物	chǒngwù	N.	6s
phone	電話	电话	diànhuà	N.	7
to pick up	接	接	jiē	V.	12
pilot	飛行員	飞行员	fēixíngyuán	N.	6s
pink	粉紅色	粉红色	fěnhóngsè	Adj.	13s
place	地方	地方	dìfang	N.	22
plain	清淡	清淡	qīngdàn	Adj.	11s
plate	盤	盘	pán	M.W.	11
to play basketball/badminton/ tennis/table tennis	打球	打球	dǎqiú	V.O.	10
to play, have fun	玩	玩	wán	V.	12

please (polite)	請	请	qǐng		2
pork	豬肉	猪肉	zhūròu	N.	11s
to practice	練習	练习	liànxí	V.	12
to prepare	準備	准备	zhǔnbèi	V.	19
problem, question	問題	问题	wèntí	N.	12
professor	教授	教授	jiàoshòu	N.	6s
purple	紫色	紫色	zǐsè	Adj.	13s
to put on (accessories)	戴上	戴上	dàishàng	V.C.	13s
(clothes)	穿上	穿上	chuānshàng	V.C.	13s

Q

| quarter (of an hour) | 刻 | 刻 | kè | M.W. | 10 |

R

to rain	下雨	下雨	xiàyǔ	V.O.	17
real estate agent	房地產顧問	房地产顾问	fángdìchǎn gùwèn	N.	6s
really	真	真	zhēn	Adv.	15
to receive	收到	收到	shōudào	V.C.	22
red	紅	红	hóng	Adj.	11
	紅色	红色	hóngsè	Adj.	13s
relatively	比較	比较	bǐjiào	Adv.	13
relatives	親屬	亲属	qīnshǔ	N.	6s
rent	房租	房租	fángzū	N.	20
to rent a house	租屋	租屋	zū wū	V.O.	20s
to rent, hire, lease	租	租	zū	V.	18
to rest	休息	休息	xiūxi	V.	8s, 9s, 19
restaurant	飯館	饭馆	fànguǎn	N.	11s
	餐廳	餐厅	cāntīng	N.	11s
	餐館	餐馆	cānguǎn	N.	11s
	飯店	饭店	fàndiàn	N.	11s
resume	簡歷 (履歷表)	简历 (履历表)	jiǎnlì (lǚlìbiǎo)	N.	21s
(retroflex ending)	兒	儿	ér		3
to return	回	回	huí	V.	8
	回來	回来	huílai	V.C.	9
to review	復習	复习	fùxí	V.	19
rice, meal	飯	饭	fàn	N.	8
to ride	騎	骑	qí	V.	18
ring	戒指	戒指	jièzhi	N.	13s
road, street	馬路	马路	mǎlù	N.	18s
room	房間	房间	fángjiān	N.	7
roommate	室友	室友	shìyǒu	N.	5

| to row a boat | 划船 | 划船 | huáchuán | V.O. | 16s |
| to run | 跑步 | 跑步 | pǎobù | V.O. | 16s |

S

salad	沙拉	沙拉	shālā	N.	11s
salesman	推銷員	推销员	tuīxiāoyuán	N.	6s
salesman, saleswoman	店員	店员	diànyuán	N.	13
salty	鹹	咸	xián	Adj.	11s
sandals	涼鞋	凉鞋	liángxié	N.	13s
scarf	圍巾	围巾	wéijīn	N.	13s
scenery	風景	风景	fēngjǐng	N.	18
scenery, view	景色	景色	jǐngsè	N.	18
school	學校	学校	xuéxiào	N.	18
scooter, motorcycle	摩托車 (機車)	摩托车 (机车)	mótuōchē (jīchē)	N.	18s
seafood	海鮮	海鲜	hǎixiān	N.	11s
seashore	海灘	海滩	hǎitān	N.	18s
seaside	海邊	海边	hǎibiān	N.	18
season (of sports)	球季	球季	qiújì	N.	16s
second	秒	秒	miǎo	N.	10s
secretary	祕書	秘书	mìshū	N.	6s
to see	見	见	jiàn	V.	8
to seek for, to look for	找	找	zhǎo	V.	21
to sell	賣	卖	mài	V.	13s
to send a short (cell phone) message	發短信 (送簡訊)	发短信 (送简讯)	fā duǎnxìn (sòng jiǎnxùn)	V.O.	9s
semester	學期	学期	xuéqī	N.	10
to settle the account	結賬 (結帳)	结账 (结帐)	jiézhàng (jiézhàng)	V.O.	11s
seven	七/柒	七/柒	qī	Num.	7
severe	嚴重	严重	yánzhòng	Adj.	19s
severely, very much	厲害	厉害	lìhài	Adj.	19s
she, her	她	她	tā	Pron.	2
ship	船	船	chuán	N.	18
shirt	襯衫	衬衫	chènshān	N.	13
shoes	鞋子	鞋子	xiézi	N.	13s
short	短	短	duǎn	Adj.	17
short pants	短褲	短裤	duǎnkù	N.	13s
should	應該	应该	yīnggāi	Aux.	12
shrimp	蝦	虾	xiā	N.	11s
siblings	兄弟姐妹	兄弟姐妹	xiōngdìjiěmèi	N.	6s
to sign a contract	簽約	签约	qiānyuē	V.O.	20s

silver	銀灰色	银灰色	yínhuīsè	*Adj.* 13s
to sit	坐	坐	zuò	*V.* 11
six	六/陸	六/陆	liù	*Num.* 7
size	號	号	hào	*N.* 13s
to skate	滑冰	滑冰	huábīng	*V.O.* 16s
skirt	裙子	裙子	qúnzi	*N.* 13
to sleep	睡覺	睡觉	shuìjiào	*V.O.* 9s
slippers	拖鞋	拖鞋	tuōxié	*N.* 13s
slow	慢	慢	màn	*Adj.* 16
small	小	小	xiǎo	*Adj.* 7, 13s
to smoke	吸煙	吸烟	xīyān	*V.O.* 20
smooth	順利	顺利	shùnlì	*Adj.* 22s
sneakers	球鞋	球鞋	qiúxié	*N.* 13s
snow	雪	雪	xuě	*N.* 17
to snow ski	滑雪	滑雪	huáxuě	*V.O.* 16s
soccer	足球	足球	zúqiú	*N.* 16s
socks	襪子	袜子	wàzi	*N.* 13s
software	軟件 (軟體)	软件 (软体)	ruǎnjiàn (ruǎntǐ)	*N.* 9s
some	一些	一些	yìxiē	*Adj.* 22
sometimes	有時候	有时候	yǒushíhou	*Adv.* 17
sorry	對不起	对不起	duìbuqǐ	9
soup	湯	汤	tāng	*N.* 11
sour	酸	酸	suān	*Adj.* 11s
south	南部	南部	nánbù	*N.* 18
Spain	西班牙	西班牙	Xībānyá	*N.* 3s
Spanish (language)	西班牙語 (西班牙文)	西班牙语 (西班牙文)	Xībānyáyǔ (Xibānyáwén)	*N.* 3s
(people)	西班牙人	西班牙人	Xībānyárén	*N.* 3s
to speak	說	说	shuō	*V.* 3
Speaking (phone)	我就是	我就是	Wǒjiùshì	9
to spend (time), celebrate (e.g., birthday), live	過	过	guò	*V.* 14
spicy	辣	辣	là	*Adj.* 11s
sports	運動	运动	yùndòng	*N.* 16s
sports car	跑車	跑车	pǎochē	*N.* 18s
spring	春天	春天	chūntiān	*N.* 17
spring break	春假	春假	chūnjià	*N.* 17
spring roll	春捲	春卷	chūnjuǎn	*N.* 11s
staff	職員	职员	zhíyuán	*N.* 6s
to start, begin	開始	开始	kāishǐ	*V.* 22
to starve	餓	饿	è	*V.* 19
steamed rice	白飯	白饭	báifàn	*N.* 11s
to stir fry	炒	炒	chǎo	*V.* 11

English	Traditional	Simplified	Pinyin	Type	Lesson
stop, station	車站	车站	chēzhàn	N.	18s
strawberry	草莓	草莓	cǎoméi	N.	11s
(structural particle)	的	的	de	Part.	2
student	學生	学生	xuésheng	N.	1
to study abroad	留學	留学	liúxué	V.O.	21
to study, to learn	學	学	xué	V.	1
subway	地鐵	地铁	dìtiě	N.	18s
suit	西裝	西装	xīzhuāng	N.	13s
summer	夏	夏	xià	N.	17
	暑期	暑期	shǔqī	N.	21
summer vacation	暑假	暑假	shǔjià	N.	17s, 21
surname, family name	姓	姓	xìng	N.	2
sweater	毛衣	毛衣	máoyī	N.	13s
sweet	甜	甜	tián	Adj.	11s
to swim; swimming	游泳	游泳	yóuyǒng	V.O./N.	16
swimming pool	游泳池	游泳池	yóuyǒngchí	N.	16

T

English	Traditional	Simplified	Pinyin	Type	Lesson
table	桌子	桌子	zhuōzi	N.	15
to take medicine	吃藥	吃药	chīyào	V.O.	19
Take care	保重	保重	bǎozhòng		22s
to take off (accessories)	摘	摘	zhāi	V.	13s
	摘下	摘下	zhāixià	V.C.	13s
(clothes)	脫	脱	tuō	V.	13s
	脫下	脱下	tuōxià	V.C.	13s
tall building	大樓	大楼	dàlóu	N.	22
tangerine juice	柳橙汁 (柳丁汁)	柳橙汁 (柳丁汁)	liǔchéngzhī (liǔdīngzhī)	N.	11s
taxi	出租汽車 (計程車)	出租汽车 (计程车)	chūzūqìchē (jìchéngchē)	N.	18s
tea	茶	茶	chá	N.	11
to teach, coach	教	教	jiāo	V.	16
teacher	老師	老师	lǎoshī	N.	1, 6s
T-shirt	T-恤衫 (T-恤)	T-恤衫 (T-恤)	tīxùshān (tīxù)	N.	13s
television	電視	电视	diànshì	N.	9
temperature	氣溫	气温	qìwēn	N.	17s
ten	十/拾	十/拾	shí	Num.	7s, 11
tenant	房客	房客	fángkè	N.	20s
tennis	網球	网球	wǎngqiú	N.	16s
Thai (language)	泰語 (泰文)	泰语 (泰文)	Tàiyǔ (Tàiwén)	N.	3s
(people)	泰國人	泰国人	Tàiguórén	N.	3s

Thailand	泰國	泰国	Tàiguó	N.	3s
to thank, be grateful for	感謝	感谢	gǎnxiè	V.	19
Thank you, Thanks.	謝謝	谢谢	xièxie		9
that	那	那	nà	Pron.	4
then, after that, afterwards	然後	然后	ránhòu	Adv.	10
therefore	就	就	jiù	Adv.	12
therefore, consequently	所以	所以	suǒyǐ	Conj.	19
they, them	他們	他们	tāmen	Pron.	5
thing	東西	东西	dōngxi	N.	22
to think, feel	覺得	觉得	juéde	V.	13
this	這	这	zhè	Pron.	4
this time	這次	这次	zhècì	Pron.	12
three	三/叁	三/叁	sān	Num.	7
thus, in this way	這樣	这样	zhèyàng	Pron.	12
ticket	票	票	piào	N.	13
tidy	整齊	整齐	zhěngqí	Adj.	15s
time	時間	时间	shíjiān	N.	17
(duration of point in)	時候	时候	shíhou	N.	9
tip	小費	小费	xiǎofèi	N.	11s
tired	累	累	lèi	Adj.	4s
today	今天	今天	jīntiān	N.	8
together	一起	一起	yìqǐ	Adv.	8
tomorrow	明天	明天	míngtiān	N.	12
too	太	太	tài	Adv.	4
tourist guide	導遊	导游	dǎoyóu	N.	6s
train	火車	火车	huǒchē	N.	18, 18s
to travel	旅行	旅行	lǚxíng	V.	18
truck	大貨車	大货车	dàhuòchē	N.	18s
to try	試試	试试	shìshi	V.	13
tunnel	隧道	隧道	suìdào	N.	18s
two	兩	两	liǎng	Num.	5
	二/貳	二/贰	èr	Num.	7
two people (colloquial)	倆	俩	liǎ		16

U

uncle (father's elder brother)	伯伯	伯伯	bóbo	N.	6s
(father's younger brother)	叔叔	叔叔	shūshu	N.	6s
(husband of father's sister)	姑父	姑父	gūfù	N.	6s
	姑丈	姑丈	gūzhàng	N.	6s
(husband of mother's sister)	姨丈	姨丈	yízhàng	N.	6s
	姨父	姨父	yífù	N.	6s
(mother's brother)	舅舅	舅舅	jiùjiu	N.	6s

underground passage	地下道	地下道	dìxiàdào	*N.*	18s
underpants	內褲	内裤	nèikù	*N.*	13s
underwear	內衣	内衣	nèiyī	*N.*	13s
United States of America, the	美國	美国	Měiguó	*N.*	3
upstairs	樓上	楼上	lóushàng	*N.*	20
to use	用	用	yòng	*V.*	12
(used after a personal pronoun or noun to show plural number)	們	们	men		4
(used after a verb to indicate a brief action)	一下	一下	yíxià		5
(used at the end of a sentence to indicate surprise)	啊	啊	a	*Int.*	20
(used at the end of a sentence to transform it into a question)	嗎	吗	ma	*Part.*	1
(used at the end of an interrogative sentence)	呢	呢	ne	*Part.*	1
(to indicate an assumption or a suggestion)	吧	吧	ba	*Part.*	9
(used before a verb to indicate that something is rather late)	才	才	cái	*Adv.*	10
(used between a verb or an adjective and its complement to indicate result, possibility or degree)	得	得	de	*Part.*	16

V

vacation	假期	假期	jiàqī	*N.*	17s
vegetable	青菜	青菜	qīngcài	*N.*	11s
very	非常	非常	fēicháng	*Adv.*	16
very, quite	很	很	hěn	*Adv.*	3
vest	背心	背心	bèixīn	*N.*	13s
virus	病毒	病毒	bìngdú	*N.*	9s
to visit	參觀	参观	cānguān	*V.*	15
volleyball	排球	排球	páiqiú	*N.*	16s

W

to wait	等	等	děng	V.	9
to wait for a moment	等一下兒	等一下儿	děng yíxiàr		9
waiter/waitress	服務員	服务员	fúwùyuán	N.	11
to walk	走	走	zǒu	V.	15
	走路	走路	zǒulù	V.O.	18
to want	想	想	xiǎng	V.	8
to want, desire	要	要	yào	V.	9
wardrobe	衣櫥	衣橱	yīchú	N.	15s
warm	暖和	暖和	nuǎnhuo	Adj.	17
warmhearted	熱心	热心	rèxīn	Adj.	22
to wash one's face	洗臉	洗脸	xǐliǎn	V.O.	10s
watch	手錶	手表	shǒubiǎo	N.	13s
watermelon	西瓜	西瓜	xīguā	N.	11s
we, us	我們	我们	wǒmen	Pron.	4
wear, put on (accessories)	戴	戴	dài	V.	13s
(clothes)	穿	穿	chuān	V.	13s
to wear	穿	穿	chuān	V.	13
weather	天氣	天气	tiānqì	N.	17s
Web page	網頁	网页	wǎngyè	N.	9s
Web site	網站	网站	wǎngzhàn	N.	9s
week	星期	星期	xīngqī	N.	14
to welcome	歡迎	欢迎	huānyíng	V.	15
west	西部	西部	xībù	N.	18
wharf, dock, pier	碼頭	码头	mǎtóu	N.	18s
what	什麼	什么	shénme	Pron.	2
where	哪兒	哪儿	nǎr	Pron.	7
which	哪	哪	nǎ	Pron.	3
what size	幾號	几号	jǐ hào		13s
white	白	白	bái	Adj.	12
	白色	白色	báisè	Adj.	13s
who, whom	誰	谁	shéi	Pron.	2
window	窗戶	窗户	chuānghu	N.	15s
winter	冬	冬	dōng	N.	17
winter vacation	寒假	寒假	hánjià	N.	17s
to wish	祝	祝	zhù	V.	10
with	跟	跟	gēn	Prep.	5
wonderful	棒	棒	bàng	Adj.	14
wonton	餛飩	馄饨	húntun	N.	11s
to work for others	打工	打工	dǎgōng	V.O.	21
to wrap	包	包	bāo	V.	16
to write	寫	写	xiě	V.	10
to write a letter	來信	来信	láixìn	V.O.	22
(to the speaker)					

Y

year	年	年	nián	N.	10
yellow	黃	黃	huáng	*Adj.*	13
	黃色	黃色	huángsè	*Adj.*	13s
yesterday	昨天	昨天	zuótiān	N.	16
you	你	你	nǐ	*Pron.*	1
you (polite)	您	您	nín	*Pron.*	2
You're welcome.	不客氣	不客气	Búkèqi		9s, 14
(in reply to thank you)	不謝	不谢	Búxiè		9s
younger brother	弟弟	弟弟	dìdi	N.	6s
younger sister	妹妹	妹妹	mèimei	N.	6s, 12

Z

zero	〇/零	〇/零	líng	*Num.*	7s

The following list shows the 432 characters that appear in the Character Book, grouped by the lesson in which they are first introduced. Students are required to memorize how to read and write these key characters to build up their literacy skills. The number of new characters introduced in each lesson is carefully controlled, and is provided in the list.

(1) 第一課　你好! (13 characters)
你 好 是 學 生 嗎 我 呢 也 他 不 老 師

(2) 第二課　您貴姓? (17 characters)
您 貴 姓 請 問 的 英 文 名 字 中 叫 什 麼 她 誰 同

(3) 第三課　你是哪國人? (14 characters)
哪 國 人 很 對 了 法 美 說 會 一 點 兒 和

(4) 第四課　你學什麼? (14 characters)
那 書 這 本 工 程 難 太 可 功 課 多 們 少

(5) 第五課　這是我朋友 (14 characters)
朋 友 來 介 紹 下 室 有 幾 兩 個 都 常 跟

(6) 第六課　我的家 (16 characters)
家 大 從 在 四 爸 媽 姐 作 男 沒 輛 車 隻 狗 愛

(7) 第七課　你住哪兒? (21 characters)
住 宿 舍 號 房 間 電 話 小 碼 二 三 五 六 七 八 九 手 機 校 外

(8) 第八課　你認識不認識他? (21 characters)
認 識 去 上 以 後 事 想 回 起 吃 飯 菜 今 天 次 怎 樣 行 再 見

(9) 第九課　他正在打電話 (22 characters)
打 喂 等 知 道 謝 吧 忙 正 看 視 做 網 就 位 留 言 時 候 晚 要 給

(10) 第十課　我每天七點半起床 (29 characters)
活 期 門 每 床 睡 覺 半 才 刻 分 然 圖 館 午 喜 歡 球 寫 信 子 郵 件 地 址 祝 年 月 日

(11) 第十一課　你要紅茶還是綠茶? (25 characters)
紅 茶 還 綠 服 務 員 坐 先 喝 杯 冰 樂 瓶 啤 酒 麵 餃 盤 炒 十 碗 湯 雙 筷

(12) 第十二課　我可以借你的車嗎? (25 characters)

借 明 用 得 場 接 妹 飛 玩 到 排 擋 開 應 該 題 白 色 停 到 習 練 能 進 步

(13) 第十三課　我想買一件襯衫 (23 characters)

買 襯 衫 店 條 裙 或 者 褲 黃 錯 比 較 穿 黑 試 幫 讓 錢 塊 張 影 票

(14) 第十四課　我今年二十歲 (15 characters)

歲 空 星 過 為 舞 參 加 定 蛋 糕 送 棒 客 氣

(15) 第十五課　圖書館在宿舍前邊 (18 characters)

前 邊 迎 觀 裡 廚 公 旁 走 廳 面 餐 洗 澡 臥 桌 園 真

(16) 第十六課　她打籃球打得很好 (20 characters)

籃 倆 教 游 泳 非 快 體 育 池 健 身 鍛 煉 現 昨 賽 業 包 慢

(17) 第十七課　春天就要來了 (22 characters)

春 久 放 假 夏 秋 冬 其 最 暖 短 熱 華 氏 百 度 極 刮 風 雨 冷 雪

(18) 第十八課　我們要坐火車去旅行 (20 characters)

火 旅 離 遠 只 鐘 騎 自 共 汽 路 近 西 部 景 船 南 聽 海 租

(19) 第十九課　我感冒了 (23 characters)

感 冒 餓 像 舒 頭 疼 發 燒 咳 嗽 病 考 復 所 醫 藥 休 息 準 備 筆 記

(20) 第二十課　我把小謝帶來了 ... (17 characters)

把 帶 啊 搬 出 吸 煙 關 係 但 女 必 須 第 付 樓 馬

(21) 第二十一課　暑假你要做什麼? (18 characters)

暑 畢 決 申 研 究 院 找 司 實 腦 班 意 思 愉 平 安 運

(22) 第二十二課　我到上海了 (25 characters)

因 已 經 麗 城 市 處 新 些 方 動 如 京 劇 東 籠 噹 始 高 興 收 心 闖 保 重